Data and Decision Analytics for Business Operations

Michelle L. F. Cheong • Ma Nang Laik

Data and Decision Analytics for Business Operations

Principles, Problems, and Practice

Springer

Michelle L. F. Cheong
School of Computing and Information Systems (SCIS)
Singapore Management University (SMU)
Singapore, Singapore

Ma Nang Laik
School of Business
Singapore University of Social Sciences (SUSS)
Singapore, Singapore

ISBN 978-3-031-72254-7 ISBN 978-3-031-72255-4 (eBook)
https://doi.org/10.1007/978-3-031-72255-4

This Springer imprint is published by the registered company Springer Nature Switzerland AG
The registered company address is: Gewerbestrasse 11, 6330 Cham, Switzerland

With the support from past and present colleagues from Singapore Management University, we are able to prepare and publish this book to fulfil our commitment to sharing our knowledge in this area to learners around the world.

We would like to dedicate this book to our colleagues, our community, our families and friends.

Preface

Every business is faced with operations-related problems including demand forecasting, inventory management, distribution management, capacity planning, resource allocation, workforce scheduling and service system management. Very often, the business owner knows that problems exist but has no idea what caused the problems and therefore does not know what to do to solve the problems.

There are many books written and published by esteemed authors on operations management topics. Each topic will have the theories and concepts covered and business problems to solve. One key missing ingredient is the identification of the root cause to these business problems. Not clearly identifying the root cause may lead to solving the wrong problem, wasting time, effort and valuable resources, and may even lead to greater harm to the business.

So, what's so different in this book? In this book, the readers will be exposed to the *data and decision analytics framework*, which helps the analyst to first identify the root cause of business problems by collecting, preparing and exploring data to gain business insights before proposing what objectives and solutions can and should be developed to solve the problems. Such a framework combines the identification of the root causes by data analytics and developing solutions supported by decision analytics. This framework is an expansion of a typical operations management solution methodology to include data analytics to exploit the linkages across data, operations, analytics and technology to offer businesses with the right solutions to their operations problems.

The goals of this book are for the readers to:

- Develop a strong understanding of the theories, concepts and techniques of operations management from a practice viewpoint
- Analyse data collected to identify the root cause of the problems and develop business insights
- Apply the knowledge acquired in the field of operations management to develop operational solutions for business improvements

The target audience for this book include:

- Senior-year undergraduate or graduate-level students studying industrial engineering degree, business management degree with focus on operations, or data science degree.
- Instructors who teach these students and need good teaching cases with a description of the data used, solution methodologies and suggested hands-on exercises. More details on the cases and their associated data can be provided to course instructors by contacting the first author directly.

Singapore

Michelle L. F. Cheong
Ma Nang Laik

About This Book

The content in this book was derived from materials in a module called *Operations Analytics and Applications* in a master's degree programme taught since 2011. The Master of IT in Business (MITB) programme has specialization tracks, which includes the Analytics track, which has been highly ranked in the QS Business Masters Ranking: Business Analytics for many consecutive years since 2019.

To guide the readers through the learning and application of the *data and decision analytics framework*, several cases are included in the book to illustrate the typical operations management problems faced by businesses. The cases were prepared and modified from the authors' work experiences in a few business domains, including retail, healthcare, transportation and logistics operations, and banking. For each case, a complete mapping of the case into the *data and decision analytics framework* was done to explain how this framework was applied to derive insights from data analytics, to define the business objectives, make the necessary assumptions and then develop the solution to the business problem. For details on the case studies, readers can search for the published papers listed in the references section at the end of each chapter.

Readers should expect some mathematical formulations in each operations management topic. However, it is not the intention of this book to go deep into the mathematical derivations, but rather to focus on explaining the theories and concepts in the context of real-world applications.

This book will focus on six operations management areas, including demand forecasting, inventory management, distribution management, capacity planning and resource allocation, workforce planning and scheduling, and service system management. For each area, one or more chapters will be dedicated to cover the theories and concepts, worked examples and case studies. The chapters are listed below:

- Chapter 1—Introduction
- Chapter 2—Demand Forecasting
- Chapter 3—Inventory Management
- Chapter 4—Distribution Management

- Chapter 5—Capacity Planning
- Chapter 6—Optimization Theory
- Chapter 7—Special Optimization Problems
- Chapter 8—Workforce Planning and Scheduling
- Chapter 9—Heuristic Algorithms
- Chapter 10—Queuing Theory
- Chapter 11—Simulation

It is recommended for the reader to start with Chap. 1, which explains the *data and decision analytics framework* using an example of long waiting time in a queue system, which is a typical business problem. After gaining an initial understanding of how the framework can be applied, readers are encouraged to read the subsequent chapters according to the flowchart in Fig. 1.2 provided in Chap. 1 for a better flow to gain the most from this book.

In some chapters, worked examples will be used to explain how the theories and concepts are applied, followed by case studies. The Excel workbooks for the worked examples and two case studies can be provided to the readers by emailing the first author directly. Readers are encouraged to work on the Excel workbooks on their own to gain hands-on experience. At the end of each chapter, there will be questions to supplement further practice that the readers may wish to continue to apply what they have learned.

We hope that this book will give the readers a new perspective towards looking at business operations problems from a combined data and decision analytics angle and learn important insights from the case studies.

Contents

About the Authors

Michelle L. F. Cheong Michelle L. F. Cheong is Professor of Information Systems (Education) and Associate Dean of Postgraduate Professional Education at the Singapore Management University (SMU) School of Computing and Information Systems (SCIS), where she is in charge of the Master of IT in Business (MITB) and the Doctor of Engineering (EngD) programmes. She had 8 years of industry experience leading teams to develop complex enterprise-wide IT systems covering business functions from sales to engineering, inventory management, planning, production and distribution. Upon obtaining her PhD in Operations Management from the Singapore-MIT Alliance (SMA) at Nanyang Technological University (NTU), she joined SMU in 2005, where she teaches courses in business modeling, data analytics and decision analytics. Michelle has conducted executive and professional trainings in data and decision analytics topics for many public and private organizations, as well as individuals from open enrolment courses. She has won many teaching awards at SMU. She also bagged the inaugural Teradata University Network Teaching Innovation Award 2013, which recognizes excellence in the teaching of Business Intelligence and Business Analytics. Michelle is the co-author of the textbook *Business Modeling with Spreadsheets: Problems, Principles and Practice*, and she has also published extensively in conferences and journals in operations management, data and decision analytics areas. She also published articles related to technology-enhanced learning including AI in education, with applications in learning operations management topics.

Ma Nang Laik Ma Nang Laik is an Associate Professor at the School of Business at the Singapore University of Social Sciences (SUSS). She teaches courses on data analytics, logistics and supply chains, quantitative methods, business skills and management, and business analytics applications, and she also supervises students' final-year projects. Prior to joining SUSS, she worked as the Director of the Master of IT in Business (Analytics) programme at the School of Computing and Information Systems at Singapore Management University (SMU) for 3 years. She holds a

PhD from Imperial College, London. Her research expertise lies in the simulation and modeling of large-scale real-world problems and the development of computationally efficient algorithms to enable sound and intelligent decision-making in the organization. Nang Laik also served as a consultant for one of the best airports, Changi Airport Group, to use data and decision analytics to generate insights, make better decisions and improve business efficiency. She had a few years of industry experience and worked in one of the largest container ports, PSA, to develop and implement a multi-million-dollar decision support system to aid in its yard planning process. Nang Laik also worked at the IT Department in the Development Bank of Singapore (DBS) and was involved in developing the Remittance System and integrating with other banking systems.

Chapter 1
Introduction

In this chapter, the *data and decision analytics framework* will be explained using a typical business problem, long waiting time in a queue, beginning with asking the right questions to data collection and analysis, to defining the problem objective(s), to making the right assumptions and then using decision analytics methods to obtain solution to the problem. The chapter ends with explaining how the six operations management areas are linked and the chapters covering them to depict the flow of topics covered in this book.

Learning Outcomes
By the end of this chapter, readers will achieve the following learning outcomes:

- Explain the *data and decision analytics framework.*
- Appraise how the framework is applied to a typical business problem.
- Identify how the six operations management areas are linked and the flow of the topics covered in this book.
- Describe the 15 case studies included in this book.

1.1 Data and Decision Analytics Framework

The *data and decision analytics framework* was proposed by the first author in a winning submission to the inaugural Teradata University Network Teaching Innovation Award 2013. In this framework, the problem solution process is split into two main segments—data analytics and decision analytics, as shown in Fig. 1.1.

When a business operations management problem exists, symptoms will surface, such as customer complaints of long waiting time in a queue, or insufficient stock to meet demand or late deliveries. With such symptoms, the analyst assigned to solve the problem has to ask the right questions, a critical starting point in problem-solving.

M. L. F. Cheong, Ma Nang Laik, *Data and Decision Analytics for Business Operations*, https://doi.org/10.1007/978-3-031-72255-4_1

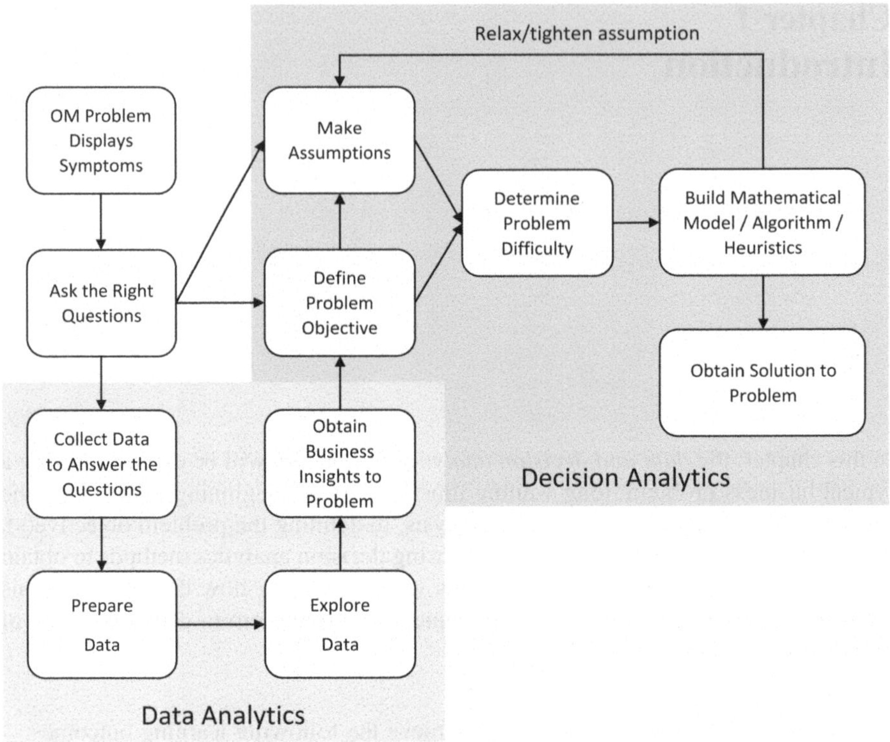

Fig. 1.1 Data and decision analytics framework

To illustrate the application of the *data and decision analytics framework*, let us look at a typical customer complaints problem due to long waiting time in a single stage system. A single-stage system is described as one where there is one single queue line with customers joining at the end of the queue and the server serves the next customer at the front of the queue. After the customer gets served, he/she leaves the queue system.

Asking the relevant questions is so important, and we recommend asking them by following the five Ws and one H (Who, What, When, Where, Why and How), and keep in mind that these questions must be as specific as possible. In the case of the long-waiting-time-in-a-queue problem, the relevant questions using the five Ws and one H can include:

- Who are these customers who complained?
- What services are they requesting at the server?
- When do they face the long-waiting-time problem?
- Where did the long-waiting-time problem occur?
- Why is the waiting time long?
- How do we provide the service to the customers?

Among these questions, some are easier to answer than others, some are more important to answer than others, while some can create immediate and direct positive impact than others when answered. It is thus crucial for the analyst to decide which questions to focus on. Of these questions, the more crucial ones can be:

- When do they face the long-waiting-time problem?
- Why is the waiting time long?
- How do we provide the service to the customers?

Once the critical questions are decided, the *data analytics* segment will begin. The analyst will collect the relevant data needed to answer the questions, and the data can include:

- Day of the week
- Start and end time which long-waiting-time problem exists
- Arrival times of customers to the queue
- Service start time of each customer
- Service end time of each customer
- Number of servers available to serve the customers

With the data collected, some data preparation will be needed to explore the data to better understand the problem. Data preparation work can include computing the average inter-arrival time (t_a) of the customers to the queue and average service times (t_s) of customers at the server, during the period when the problem exists. Using t_a and t_s, one can quickly assess the severity of the longwaiting time experienced by the customers. If $t_s > t_a$, this means that on average, customers are spending a longer time at the server than new customers arriving to the queue. This will inevitably lead to a queue which will grow in length rather quickly.

From the insights obtained in this case, the analyst will need to resolve the long-waiting-time problem. At this stage, the *decision analytics* segment will begin. There could be a couple of possible problem objectives:

- Determine the optimal number of servers to reduce the waiting time to satisfy a certain acceptable service level.
- Reduce the average service time (t_s) of the existing servers by using automation or improving business process, so that $t_s < t_a$, thereby resolving the long-waiting-time problem.

Once the problem objective is defined, there could be some assumptions that need to be made, for example:

- Customers arrive at the queue one at a time.
- There is no balking situation, which means that customers who want the service will join the queue regardless of the length of the queue.
- There is no reneging situation, which means that customers who joined the queue will not leave the queue pre-maturely without completing the service.

At this stage, the problem definition is fixed, and depending on the problem difficulty, different types of solution method can be applied, which can include building a mathematical model, algorithm or heuristic to compute the mathematical solution to the problem. In this case, a Monte Carlo simulation model can be built to simulate the queue system to determine the optimal number of servers or the target average service time to reduce the waiting time satisfying a certain acceptable service level.

Going further, one may relax some of the earlier assumptions made. For example, instead of no balking, we can look at the situation where customers will balk if the queue length exceeds a certain number (e.g. 10) and improve the solution method to obtain a new solution.

1.2 Focused Operations Management Areas

This book will focus on the six operations management areas labelled as 1 to 6 in rectangular boxes and linked in a flowchart as depicted in Fig. 1.2. These six operations management areas' problems and scenarios will be solved using concepts and techniques covered from Chaps. 2 to 11. Many of the concepts and techniques are referenced from classic textbooks including Hillier and Lieberman (2001) and Hopp and Spearman (2011).

1. Demand forecasting problems will be handled using forecasting models covered in Chap. 2.
2. Inventory management problems will be handled using four inventory models and policies covered in Chap. 3.
3. Distribution management problems will be handled using routing and vehicle scheduling techniques covered in Chap. 4.
4. Capacity planning problems will be handled using concepts introduced in Chap. 5.
5. Resource allocation problems will be handled using optimization concepts and models covered in Chaps. 6 and 7, and heuristic algorithms introduced in Chap. 9.
6. Workforce planning and scheduling problems will be introduced in Chap. 8 and solved using optimization concepts and models introduced in Chaps. 6 and 7, and heuristic algorithms introduced in Chap. 9.
7. Service system problems will be handled with queuing theory concepts and models covered in Chap. 10 and simulation models covered in Chap. 11.

1.3 Fifteen Case Studies Included in This Book

This book contains 15 case studies which are derived from the authors' real-world experience in solving business problems. A brief description of each case study is given below:

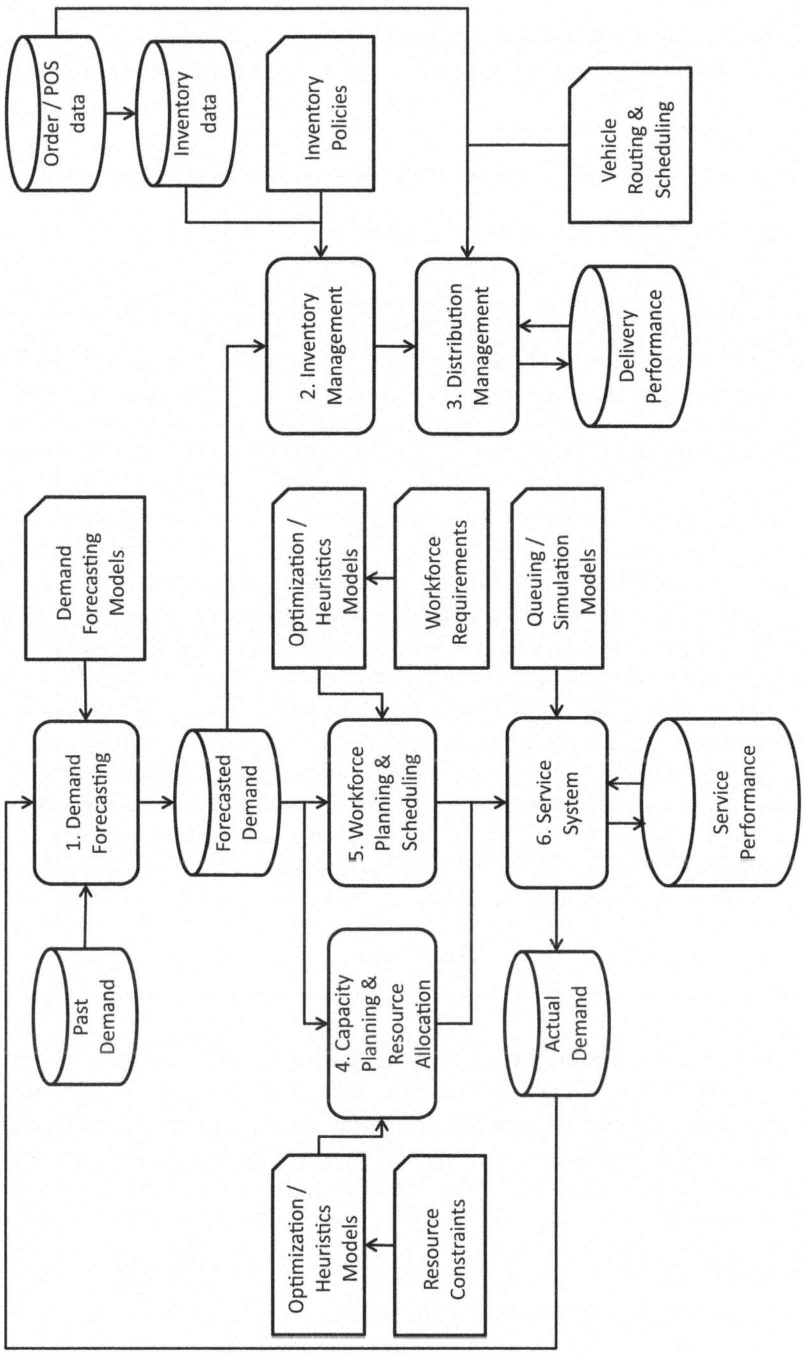

Fig. 1.2 Focused operations management areas

1. Chapter 2—Case 2A: Travel Retailer Inventory Imbalance

   This case study describes the inventory imbalance problem faced by a travel retailer for the luxury watches sold at its nine sales divisions. The problem was solved by applying the best forecasting method to perform aggregate-disaggregate forecasting, taking advantage of risk pooling and executing the delivery via a central GDC, to reduce demand variability.

2. Chapter 2—Case 2B: Forecasting of ATM Ad hoc Failures

   This case study describes how a bank tackled the allocation of field engineers to attend to ad hoc failures of ATM machines in four different zones in Singapore. The problem was solved by applying the best forecasting method to perform aggregate-disaggregate forecasting to forecast the number of ad hoc failures in each zone and determine the appropriate number of service engineers to deploy for the next 14 days.

3. Chapter 3—Case 3: Inventory Management of Fast-Moving Consumer Goods (FMCG)

   This case study describes the inventory management problem faced by an integrated distribution and logistics services provider. The fluctuating order quantities from the retailers made it harder to manage inventory and deliveries. The main challenge stemmed from the lack of point-of-sales (POS) data from the retail stores as the retail store owners were not keen to share them. The problem was solved by determining the number of orders placed by the retailers on each day of the week and assuming that retailers will only place one order per week on their top order day. With the mean and standard deviation of order quantities for all the retailers, the expected demand and safety stock can be determined to better manage inventory.

4. Chapter 4—Case 4: Distribution Management of Fast-Moving Consumer Goods (FMCG)

   This is a continuation from Case 3. After determining the inventory levels to meet the fluctuating demands on different days of the week, there is a need to ensure that distribution of the orders will also be on time. To manage the number of trucks needed for delivery, the logistics provider needs to know the ordering behaviour of the retailers. By using statistical inference method, the retailers were identified to be adopting periodic review (PR) or continuous review (CR) inventory policy. PR retailers were identified to be causing fluctuation in the number of orders across different days of the week, and thus by smoothing out the number of PR retailer orders, the number of trucks needed can be reduced. With the PR retailers' geographical location, Cluster First, Route Second approach can be applied to plan the delivery route.

5. Chapter 5—Case 5: Hospital Beds Capacity Planning

   In this case study, we looked at planning which year to increase the number of hospital beds in existing hospitals and the year to add a new hospital to cater for the growing needs of healthcare. The problem is solved by projecting the population growth, forecasting the percentage of people who needs to be served by the hospital and forecasting the expected length of stay in the hospital. With these figures forecasted for the next 7 years, we can determine the number of beds required against the number of beds available, to decide when and how many beds to add to meet a target utilization rate.

6. Chapter 6—Case 6A: Container Optimization for Carbon Footprint Reduction

   This case study describes the shipping container optimization problem faced by a consumer goods manufacturer. It is quite common to ship containers Less-than-Container Load (LCL), which will result in higher shipping cost and increased carbon footprint. The problem is solved by building a Container Size Optimization (CSO) model to minimize the total carbon emission by determining the optimal container mix (number of containers of different sizes) that will satisfy the total shipment volume required.

7. Chapter 6—Case 6B: Container Consolidation and Optimization for Carbon Footprint Reduction

   This is a continuation from Case 6A. After determining the optimal container mix, the manufacturer wishes to increase the container fill rates by consolidating several shipments bound for the same destination to further reduce carbon footprint. The problem is solved by building a new optimization model, called the Consolidation of Shipment within Country (CSC) model, to combine shipments from different ports of origin to a single consolidation port before shipping.

8. Chapter 7—Case 7: Load Balancing at the Airport Terminals

   This case study describes the problem faced by an Asian international airport. Due to imbalanced load at the three terminals caused by inefficient assignment of airlines to the terminals, problems such as long waiting time at check-in counters at busier terminals have caused dissatisfaction among passengers. The problem was modeled as an assignment problem in the form of a Binary Integer Non-Linear Programming (BINLP) model. Due to the complexity of the model, the SAS/OR software tool was used to obtain a solution which distributed the flight and passenger loads more evenly among the three terminals.

9. Chapter 8—Case 8A: Ambulance Drivers Planning and Scheduling

   In this case study, we will plan and schedule ambulance drivers for 7 days with AM and PM shifts. With the forecasted number of calls for ambulance received in each shift for each day, the number of full-time and part-time ambulance drivers was determined to minimize total cost. With fixed shift schedule, the actual number of full-time ambulance drivers was further minimized. After that, using the preference score provided by each named full-time driver, we can schedule the work schedule for each named driver by maximizing the total preference score.

10. Chapter 8—Case 8B: Faculty Members' Teaching Schedule

    In this case study, we will plan and schedule faculty members to teach two courses in a business school. Based on the number of class sections required, the number of full-time and part-time faculty members available, their teaching loads, the number of time slots per week and the number of classrooms available, we can optimize the allocation of faculty members to teach the two courses and plan their teaching schedule.

11. Chapter 9—Case 9A: Nurse Scheduling for 14 Days and 15 Nurses

    In this case study, we explored the scheduling of a 14-day nurse schedule for a hospital ward of 15 nurses. There are three shifts in a day, AM, PM and midnight shifts, as well as rest days. We developed and applied the Greedy Double Swap Heuristic (GDSH) algorithm to determine a good and feasible schedule considering both hard and soft constraints.

12. Chapter 9—Case 9B: Beer Distribution

    In this case study, the objective was to allocate 81 retail outlet zones to a maximum of eight warehouses to distribute different pack types of beer from the warehouses to the retail outlet zones, minimizing the total logistics cost. Due to practical business considerations which are difficult to model completely, we developed and applied a heuristic algorithm using candidate choice approach to effectively allocate the retail outlet zones to the warehouses while minimizing total logistics cost.

13. Chapter 10—Case 10: Queue Buster at a Grocery Store

    In this case study, we determined the effectiveness of a queue buster tool to better manage the queue performance for a grocery store. By using queuing theory concepts and formulas, we computed the queue performance for different system length, to determine the best system length to trigger queue busting.

14. Chapter 11—Case 11A: Simulation to Optimize Number of Check-in Counters at an Airport

    In this case study, we looked at the congestion problem at the check-in counters at a large Asian international airport. Using discrete-event simulation model, we determined the optimal number of check-in counters to open, based on the predicted number of passengers, to ensure that 90% of the passengers do not need to wait more than 10 minutes at the check-in counters to meet the service-level agreement (SLA).

15. Chapter 11—Case 11B: Simulation of Container Flows at a Container Terminal

    In this case study, we used discrete-event simulation to validate the goodness of two different yard deployment policies using the optimal number of yard cranes (YC) required. The simulation model was run to compare the performance of the two policies, namely, "No sharing of YC" and "Sharing of YC". The performance results were used to support decision-making in policy implementation.

1.4 Summary

This chapter explains the *data and decision analytics framework* in detail using a long-wait time in a queue system example to bring the readers through the stages in the framework. It also explains how the six operations management areas covered in this book are linked using a flowchart and lists the chapters covering each area. All the 15 case studies are also briefly described to provide the readers with an initial idea of what application cases are included in each chapter. In the next chapter, we will cover our first operations management area, demand forecasting, by first exploring the three basic laws of forecasting, and then learn several forecasting models and how to select the best forecasting model. We will be looking at two case studies on forecasting, where the first case will touch on forecasting the demand of luxury watches and the second case on forecasting ATM ad hoc failures.

References

Hillier, F. S., & Lieberman, G. J. (2001). *Introduction to operations research* (7th ed.). McGraw-Hill.

Hopp, W., & Spearman, M. (2011). *Factory physics* (3rd ed.). McGraw-Hill.

Chapter 2
Demand Forecasting

All businesses need to perform demand forecasting to respond better to future demand. No businesses want to be caught in situations where there are insufficient resources to meet demand or too many unused resources when demand turns out to be lower than expected. However, the sad truth is that not many companies perform proper demand forecasting and would rather rely on gut feel and experience to estimate what the future demand would be.

Since proper demand forecasting is so crucial, should one expect that the forecast result be absolutely correct? The answer is a resounding no. One may argue that since forecasting is not always right, why bother to forecast? Ashton and Ashton (1985) concluded that "even simple quantitative forecasting technique will outperform unstructured intuitive assessment of experts in many cases". A business performs proper forecasting to have a mathematical and a more reliable forecast results to rely on for future planning, including planning the inventory of raw materials, equipment and manpower resources, in response to future demand. Therefore, acquiring knowledge and skills in forecasting will benefit any business in a big way.

In this chapter, we will first explore the three basic laws of forecasting to manage our expectations of forecasting and then learn about several forecasting models, before we learn how to select the best forecasting model using quantitative measures. After that, we will look at ARIMA and Seasonal ARIMA (SARIMA) forecasting models in detail. For each forecasting model, an example will be used to illustrate its application. Finally, we will look at two case studies, luxury-watch inventory imbalance in a travel retailer case and ATM ad hoc failure case, to understand how each case study applied aggregate and disaggregate forecasting to solve their respective problems.

Learning Outcomes

By the end of this chapter, readers will achieve the following learning outcomes:

- Explain the three basic laws of forecasting.
- Calculate coefficient of variations (CV) of aggregated demand and the reduction in CV due to risk pooling or variability pooling.

M. L. F. Cheong, Ma Nang Laik, *Data and Decision Analytics for Business Operations*, https://doi.org/10.1007/978-3-031-72255-4_2

- Compare rolling-window versus non-rolling window forecasting.
- Explain the difference between qualitative and quantitative forecasting.
- Explain time series and the components of a time series.
- Distinguish between additive and multiplicative forms for time series with strong seasonality component.
- Explore the different forms of Moving Average forecasting models.
- Explore and assess the different forms of Exponential Smoothing forecasting models.
- Apply the different forms of Exponential Smoothing forecasting models.
- Suggest and demonstrate how to select the best forecasting model.
- Explore ARIMA and SARIMA models.
- Explain autocorrelation and partial autocorrelation.
- Apply the three main steps in identifying the ARIMA model.
- Apply the three main steps in identifying the SARIMA model.
- Explain the pros and cons of ARIMA and SARIMA models.
- Explore Stepwise Autoregression forecasting model.
- Discuss how forecasting concepts and models are applied in two real-world scenarios to manage demand of luxury watches and attending to ATM ad hoc failures, using the *data and decision analytics framework.*

2.1 Three Basic Laws of Forecasting

Before we delve further into the concepts and models of forecasting, let us understand the three basic laws of forecasting to manage our expectations of the results of forecasting.

2.1.1 Law 1 of Forecasting

The first law of forecasting states that "Forecasting is always wrong". This is to imply that *perfect* forecasting is impossible as no one will ever know what will happen in the future. In general, any simple quantitative forecasting technique will outperform intuition and gut feel (Ashton & Ashton, 1985).

2.1.2 Law 2 of Forecasting

The second law of forecasting states that "Aggregate forecast is always better than detailed forecast". We can aggregate past demand data of the same product across

Table 2.1 Aggregated demand has lower coefficient of variation (CV)

	Mean (μ)	Standard deviation (σ)	$CV = \frac{\sigma}{\mu}$	% Reduction in CV
Location X	39.29	10.10	0.26	(0.26 − 0.13)/0.26 = 47.6%
Location Y	44.31	7.06	0.16	(0.16 − 0.13)/0.16 = 15.5%
Aggregated T	83.60	11.26	0.13	

multiple locations if this product is sold over many locations, or we can aggregate past demand data of the same product into higher level time bucket, that is, aggregate daily data into weekly, weekly data into monthly, monthly data into yearly and so on. After successful aggregate forecasting, the forecast results will then be disaggregated back to a specific location or time bucket for detailed planning purposes.

A high demand variability will lead to higher risk and higher forecasting error. By performing aggregation, a process known as *variability pooling* or *risk pooling*, we will reduce the variability in the demand data, which will lead to better forecast results. For example, in Table 2.1, Product A is sold at two different locations X and Y following mean μ_X and μ_Y with standard deviations σ_X and σ_Y, respectively. The aggregated demand of both locations will have mean μ_T and standard deviation σ_T computed as given below.

$$\mu_T = \mu_X + \mu_Y$$

$$\sigma_T = \sqrt{\sigma_X^2 + \sigma_Y^2 + 2COV_{XY}}$$

where $COV_{XY} = \frac{1}{M}\sum_{M}[D_{X,t} - \mu_X][D_{Y,t} - \mu_Y]$ for $t = 1$ to M, is the covariance between X and Y computed using the demand data of Product A at locations X and Y over M periods.

Using the mean and standard deviation, we can compute the coefficient of variations (CV) of the aggregated demand and that of the individual locations X and Y using $CV = \sigma/\mu$. We can see that the CV of aggregated demand is reduced by 47.6% and 15.5% as compared to the CV of the individual locations X and Y, respectively. A reduction in CV would imply that the variability of the data has been reduced as compared to the mean, since $CV = \sigma/\mu$.

With reduced variability, the forecast results will become more stable and accurate. Thus, aggregate forecast is always better than detailed forecast. Due to risk pooling, high demand at one location can be offset by the low demand at another location, thus reducing overall demand variability, leading to lower inventory holding, a concept which we will cover in the next chapter.

Table 2.2 Non-rolling window and rolling window forecasts

	Non-rolling window forecast		Rolling window forecast	
Period	Actual demand	Forecasted demand	Actual demand	Forecasted demand
1	10		10	
2	12		12	
3 = Today	11		11	
4		11	12	11
5		11.33		11.67

2.1.3 *Law 3 of Forecasting*

The third law states that "The further one forecasts into the future, the less reliable the forecast result will be". This should not be surprising as we know that the future has a higher potential to change. Therefore, if a company were to forecast 12 months into the future, it should expect that the forecast for month 12 will be the least accurate as compared to that of month 1. So, how do companies handle such uncertainties?

Instead of using a non-rolling window forecast, a rolling window forecast is used to reduce uncertainty. Look at the example in Table 2.2, where period 3 is today and the company will use the past demand data to forecast the future demand for periods 4 and 5.

- In the non-rolling window forecast, period 4 is forecasted using the average values of the actual demand in periods 1, 2 and 3. That is, (10 + 12 + 11)/3 = 11. Period 5 is forecasted using the average values of the actual demand in periods 2 and 3 and the forecasted demand in period 4. That is, (12 + 11 + 11)/3 = 11.33.
- In the rolling window forecast, period 4 is forecasted the same way as in the non-rolling window forecast. However, for period 5, the forecast is updated only when the actual demand in period 4 is known. Assuming that the actual demand in period 4 turns out to be 12, then the forecast for period 5 will be (12 + 11 + 12)/3 = 11.67.

Therefore, in the rolling window forecast, future forecast is being constantly updated when new actual demand data is known, to reduce the uncertainty.

Now that we are familiar with the three basic laws of forecasting, let us move on to understand time series forecasting.

2.2 Time Series Forecasting

There are two main types of forecasting, qualitative and quantitative. Qualitative forecasting relies mainly on the expertise of people who use factors to predict the future, and the factors are mostly not quantitative themselves. Imagine the fashion world where colour forecasting is used to determine the upcoming colour trends. The Pantone Color Institute (www.patone.com) decides the next colour of the year based on research by their colour forecasters on factors related to arts, sports, entertainment, travel, technology and fashion, and even the mood of people at that specific moment in time. One good example would be the year 2020 where classic blue was chosen to be the colour of the year due to the global pandemic caused by COVID-19 and the consequent economic and social distress experienced by many countries.

Quantitative forecasting, on the other hand, relies on mathematical models such as causal model and time series model, to predict the future using observations collected in the past. Causal model uses a function to link the causality of input factors to the output of interest. Such a function can be a multiple regression model to predict the new output value when the new values of the input factors are known. For example, a salesman would like to predict the amount his new customer would spend. He could use a multiple regression model to predict the spending amount based on input factors such as the age and income level of the customer.

Our focus in this chapter is time series model demand forecasting where the future demand is predicted as a function of the past demand values, assuming that past demand values have impact on the future demand. A time series is a collection of observations over regularly spaced time intervals, which are usually hourly, daily, weekly, monthly, quarterly or yearly. There could be situations where some observations are not collected at certain pockets of time intervals due to various reasons. Such a collection with missing observations will not be considered as time series in a strict sense, but approximation methods such as linear interpolation can be used to fill in any missing observations, if the number of missing observations is not too excessive.

A time series is made up of one or more of the following components: trend, seasonality, cycle and error. To forecast into the future, we will project each component individually into the future and then combine them back to get the future forecast. The explanation of each component is as follows:

- *Trend* component describes the overall upward or downward movement of the data over time, and it is the component we are most interested in. Trend can be constant, linear or quadratic, which represents the overall shape of the time series curve.
- *Seasonality* component describes the repeat pattern of demand fluctuations above or below the trend line. The pattern can be repeated once every week, every month, every quarter or every year. A good example will be the repeat pattern of travelers at different months of the year, where months during the summer will usually have the most travelers.
- *Cycle* is meant to describe a repeat pattern which occurs once every several years. Such a cycle is usually tied to a certain phenomenon like a business cycle or a financial cycle. As businesses usually do not forecast so long into the future, therefore, the cycle component is often ignored.

- *Error*, also known as irregularity or residual, are small random up-and-down fluctuations which are neither systematic nor predictable. Since error is not predictable, no forecasting method will predict error. Instead, the error component will usually be added into the forecasting equation as an error term ε_t if needed.

In this chapter, we will be looking at time series forecasting using several models including Moving Average, Single Exponential Smoothing, Double Exponential Smoothing, Triple Exponential Smoothing, ARIMA, SARIMA and Stepwise Autoregression. The following notations will be used consistently across all the forecasting models:

- A(i) = Actual data observation at time i where i = 1, 2, . . ., t and t is the most recent observation. We will forecast from t+1 onwards.
- F(t+τ) = Forecasted data τ periods into the future.
- L(t) = Smoothed estimate which is the estimate of the current level at time t.
- T(t) = Smoothed trend which is the estimate of the current trend at time t.
- S(t) = Seasonality at time t.
- E(t) = Random error at time t, which is assumed to follow a normal distribution with a constant mean and variance, also denoted as ε_t.

Time series data can be expressed in terms of its components as

$$A(t) = f(T(t), S(t), E(t))$$

When the time series is an additive form, then

$$A(t) = T(t) + S(t) + E(t)$$

When the time series is a multiplicative form, then

$$A(t) = T(t).S(t).E(t)$$

It is important to distinguish between additive and multiplicative forms when the time series has strong seasonality component.

- For additive form (Fig. 2.1), the magnitude of the seasonality does not vary with the magnitude of the data. Even when the data increases/decreases in magnitude, the exact same pattern is repeated in every cycle.
- For multiplicative form (Fig. 2.2), the seasonality pattern repeats in every cycle, and the magnitude of the seasonality increases/decreases when the data increases/decreases, due to multiplicative effect.

When we perform forecasting for such time series, we need to first de-seasonalize the time series before we perform forecasting, and then after forecasting, we will add the seasonality back.

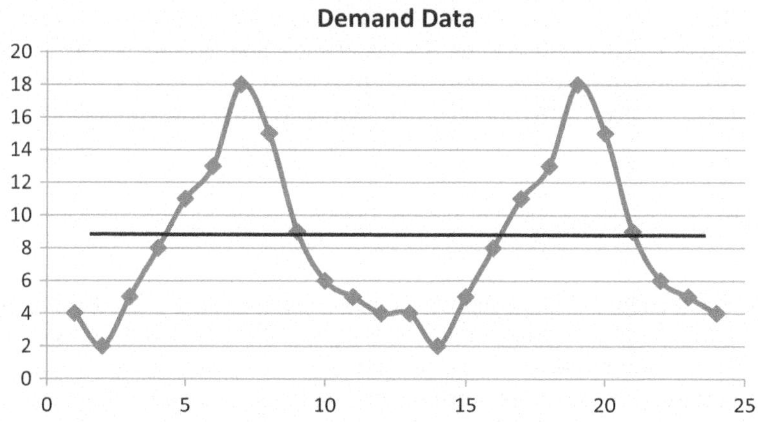

Fig. 2.1 Additive form

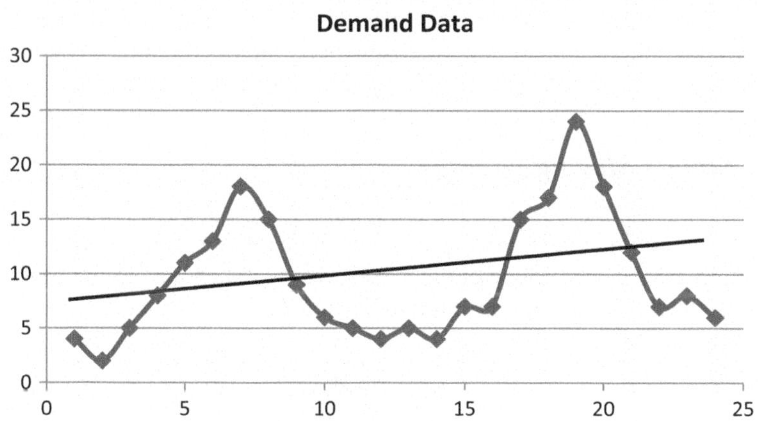

Fig. 2.2 Multiplicative form

- For the additive form, to remove the seasonality factor, we deduct the seasonality factor S(t) from A(t).

$$A(t) - S(t) = T(t) + E(t)$$

- For the multiplicative form, to remove the seasonality factor, we divide A(t) by the seasonality factor S(t).

$$A(t)/S(t) = T(t).E(t)$$

From the two de-seasonalized equations, we can deduce that forecasting mainly aims to determine the future trend T(t), and then add S(t) for additive form, or multiply S(t) for multiplicative form, on top of the forecast results. This methodology will be explained clearly in Sect. 2.6, "Triple Exponential Smoothing".

2.3 Moving Average

The moving average model computes the next forecast value by taking the average of several sequential data points in the recent past. There are many types of moving average forecasting models, and they differ in the way the average value is computed. The basic concept adopted here is that demand observations that are close to each other are likely to be similar.

Such an average value represents the smoothed estimate value L(t). Therefore, moving average is a suitable forecast model when there is no strong trend T(t) and seasonality S(t) displayed in the past data. There are other advanced models of moving average that can take care of seasonality which will not be covered here.

2.3.1 Simple Moving Average

The most common is simple moving average where the next forecast value F(t+1) is calculated by taking the average of the most recent m data points from t to (t−m+1). This implies that equal weight is given to each of the m data points.

$$F(t+1) = L(t) = \frac{\sum_{i=t-m+1}^{t} A(i)}{m}$$

Moving average thus creates a new average value each time a new actual demand becomes available by dropping the oldest demand data, making the selection of sequential data points a moving selection.

The choice of m will depend on the availability of past data and the application. Usually, for short-term applications, a smaller m will be used to take into account only the recent past. Conversely, for long-term applications, a larger m will be used to take into account data points over a longer period and to smooth out all the effects occurring over the long period.

To observe the effects of small m versus large m, build a small Excel model according to Table 2.3. Given ten past data points A(t), use m = 3 and m = 5 to forecast by applying the formula accordingly.

Table 2.3 Simple moving average

t	A(t)	F(t), m = 3	F(t), m = 5
1	10		
2	12		
3	12		
4	11	11.33	
5	15	11.67	
6	14	12.67	12.00
7	18	13.33	12.80
8	22	15.67	14.00
9	18	18.00	16.00
10	28	19.33	17.40
11		22.67	20.00

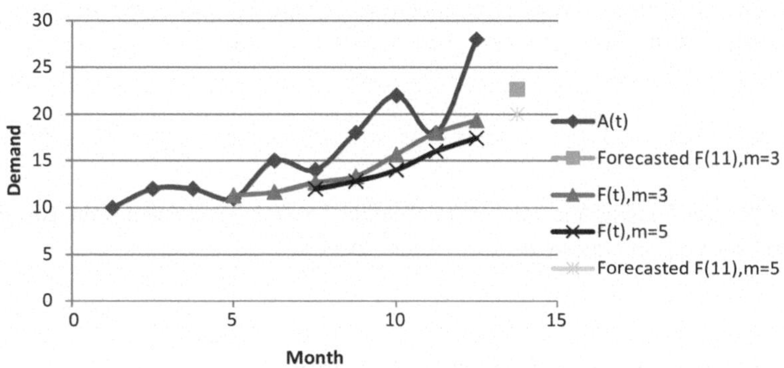

Fig. 2.3 Simple moving average

$$\text{For m} = 3, \mathrm{F}(4) - \mathrm{L}(3) - \frac{10 + 12 + 12}{3} = 11.33$$

$$\text{For m} = 5, \mathrm{F}(6) = \mathrm{L}(5) = \frac{10 + 12 + 12 + 11 + 15}{5} = 12.00$$

Using the Excel equations for F(4) and F(6), repeat the same calculations using Excel fill function until period 11.

Figure 2.3 shows the results of the forecast values. We can observe that when m is small, the forecast value will be more responsive to changes in the data. On the other hand, a large m will be more stable and less responsive. Overall, moving average tends to underestimate when there is an increasing trend in the data and overestimate when there is a decreasing trend. Therefore, moving average is suitable to predict only one period into the future and tends to lose accuracy after two or more periods prediction.

This loss in accuracy can be inferred from the formula itself, which requires m most recent demand data to be used. To forecast for two or more periods, forecast value has to be used in the formula, decreasing the forecast accuracy. For example, to forecast F(t+2) using m = 3, then F(t+2) = [A(t−1) + A(t) + F(t+1)] / 3. To reduce this uncertainty, the rolling window forecast method can be used, as explained in Sect. 2.1.3.

2.3.2 Geometric Moving Average

Geometric moving average is usually applied in financial applications as it takes into account compounding effect, like in compounding interest. Thus, financial investors tend to rely more on geometric mean than arithmetic mean as given in the simple moving average.

Geometric moving average computes the average by taking the mth root of the multiplication of the m most recent data points, from t to (t−m+1).

$$\mathrm{F(t+1)} = \sqrt[m]{\prod\nolimits_{i=t-m+1}^{t} \mathrm{A(i)}} = \sqrt[m]{A(t-m+1).A(t-m+2)\ldots A(t)}$$

Try it yourself. Using the same data given in Table 2.3, perform forecasting using geometric moving average with m = 3 and m = 5.

2.3.3 Linear Weighted Moving Average

So far, both simple moving average and geometric moving average apply equal weight to each of the m data points. Linear weighted moving average applies different weights, which are linearly decreasing from m to 1, for the m most recent data points. Such a model is suitable for applications where the most recent data point will have the most influence on the next forecast, and the influence decreases linearly towards the last data point.

$$\mathrm{F(t+1)} = \frac{\mathrm{mA(t) + (m-1)A(t-1) + \ldots + A(t-m+1)}}{\mathrm{m(m+1)/2}}$$

Try it yourself. Using the same data given in Table 2.3, perform forecasting using linear weighted moving average with m = 3 and m = 5.

2.3.4 *Exponential Moving Average*

Similar to linear weighted moving average, exponential moving average applies different weights, which are exponentially decreasing. However, all past data points until the very first data point A(1) will be used in the formula, instead of just the m most recent ones.

$$F(t+1) = \alpha A(t) + \alpha(1-\alpha)A(t-1) + \alpha(1-\alpha)^2 A(t-2) + \ldots \\ + \alpha(1-\alpha)^{t-1}A(1) + (1-\alpha)^t F(1)$$

As α is usually < 1, the weight will decrease exponentially from α for A(t) to $\alpha(1 - \alpha)^{t-1}$ for A(1). A careful inspection of the formula will reveal that the very last term with weight $(1 - \alpha)^t$ is F(1), which is the forecast of the first actual demand value. This implies that one needs to use an estimated value of F(1) to perform forecasting, and F(1) is usually assumed to be A(1) for convenience. One final point to note is that exponential moving average is in fact the same as the single exponential smoothing model, which we will be discussing in the next section.

Try it yourself. Using the same data given in Table 2.3, perform forecasting using exponential moving average.

2.4 Single Exponential Smoothing

Single exponential smoothing is very much a moving average model with exponentially decreasing weights applied, as explained in the earlier section. This means that it cannot take care of trend and seasonality components in the data. The next forecast is computed as the weighted sum of the actual and forecast values of the previous period.

$$F(t+1) = \alpha A(t) + (1-\alpha)F(t)$$

If we re-arrange the terms, we can obtain the next formula, which means that the next forecast is equal to the previous forecast adjusted by the forecast error of the previous period. For either formula, we need an estimated value of F(t).

$$F(t+1) = F(t) + \alpha(A(t) - F(t))$$

What is the implication of α value? When $\alpha = 1$, this means that the next forecast is sensitive to the previous forecast error. Conversely when $\alpha = 0$, this means that the next forecast is exactly the same as previous forecast. To observe the effects of different α values, build a small Excel model according to Table 2.4. Given ten past

Table 2.4 Single exponential smoothing

t	A(t)	F(t), α = 0.2	F(t), α = 0.6
1	10	10.00	10.00
2	12	10.00	10.00
3	12	10.40	11.20
4	11	10.72	11.68
5	15	10.78	11.27
6	14	11.62	13.51
7	18	12.10	13.80
8	22	13.28	16.32
9	18	15.02	19.73
10	28	15.62	18.69
11		18.09	24.28

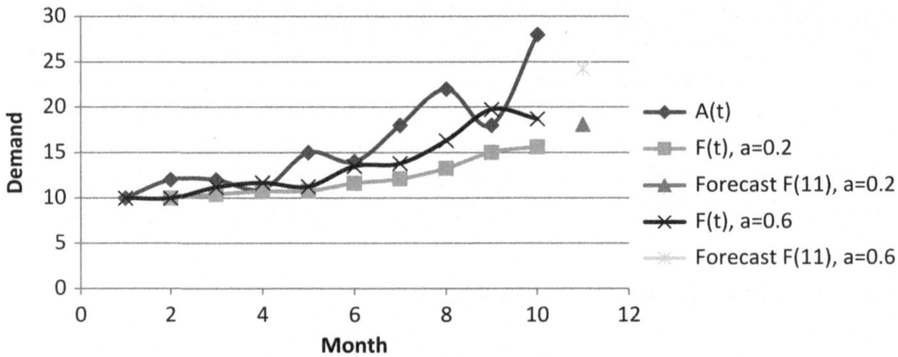

Fig. 2.4 Single exponential smoothing before optimization

data points A(t), use α = 0.2 and α = 0.6 to forecast by applying the formula accordingly. We will assume F(1) = A(1).

For α = 0.2

$$F(2) = \alpha A(1) + (1 - \alpha)F(1) = 0.2 * 10 + 0.8 * 10 = 10.00$$
$$F(3) = \alpha A(2) + (1 - \alpha)F(2) = 0.2 * 12 + 0.8 * 10 = 10.40$$

For α = 0.6

$$F(2) = \alpha A(1) + (1 - \alpha)F(1) = 0.6 * 10 + 0.4 * 10 = 10.00$$
$$F(3) = \alpha A(2) + (1 - \alpha)F(2) = 0.6 * 12 + 0.4 * 10 = 11.2$$

Using the Excel equations for F(2) and F(3), repeat the same calculations using Excel fill function until period 11.

Table 2.5 Single exponential smoothing forecast error before optimization

t	A(t)	F(t), $\alpha = 0.2$	A(t) – F(t)
1	10	10.00	0
2	12	10.00	2.00
3	12	10.40	1.60
4	11	10.72	0.28
5	15	10.78	4.22
6	14	11.62	2.38
7	18	12.10	5.90
8	22	13.28	8.72
9	18	15.02	2.98
10	28	15.62	12.38
11		18.09	

Figure 2.4 shows the results of the forecast values. We can observe that when α is small, the forecast value will be more stable but less responsive to changes in the data. On the other hand, a large α will be less stable and more responsive. Overall, single exponential smoothing tends to underestimate when there is an increasing trend in the data and overestimate when there is a decreasing trend. This behaviour is similar to that of moving average.

What will be the best α value to set? The best α is the one that will minimize the sum of squared error (SSE) between the forecast F(t) and actual A(t). Let us use the forecast F(t) for $\alpha = 0.2$ to compute the forecast error A(t) – F(t) in the last column of Table 2.5. Using Excel, we can set the α value of 0.2 into a specific cell location (say, cell C3) and compute the SSE in another cell location (say, E3), and its value is 303.27. Using Solver Add-in in Excel, we can set the objective cell to be the SSE and minimize it by changing the α value. To ensure that the α value does not fall outside the permitted range, we can add constraints to set $0 \leq \alpha \leq 1$. The optimal α is 0.725 with the minimized SSE at 154.30. Using the optimal α, one can use it to forecast F (11) more accurately as 25.44. Try to do this yourself.

2.5 Double Exponential Smoothing

If there is a strong upward or downward trend in the past data, we can use the double exponential smoothing method, also known as the Holt-Winter's two-parameter model. The two parameters refer to the smoothed estimate L(t) and the trend estimate T(t).

$$L(t) = \alpha A(t) + (1 - \alpha)[L(t - 1) + T(t - 1)]$$

$$T(t) = \beta[L(t) - L(t - 1)] + (1 - \beta)T(t - 1)$$

Table 2.6 Double exponential smoothing forecast before optimization

t	A(t)	L(t)	T(t)	F(t)	A(t) − F(t)
1	10	10.00	0		
2	12	10.40	0.08	10.00	2.00
3	12	10.78	0.14	10.48	1.52
4	11	10.94	0.14	10.92	0.08
5	15	11.87	0.30	11.08	3.92
6	14	12.53	0.37	12.17	1.83
7	18	13.93	0.58	12.91	5.09
8	22	16.00	0.88	14.50	7.50
9	18	17.10	0.92	16.88	1.12
10	28	20.02	1.32	18.03	9.97
11				21.43	

From the formulas, we can interpret them as follows:

- The current smoothed estimate L(t) is computed as the weighted sum of current actual A(t), and the sum of the previous period's smoothed estimate L(t − 1) and trend T(t − 1), weighted by α and $(1 - \alpha)$ respectively. Thus, α plays the role of modifying the smoothed estimate value.
- The current trend T(t) is computed as the weighted sum of the difference between the smoothed estimate of current and previous periods, and previous period's trend T(t − 1), weighted by β and $(1 - \beta)$ respectively. Thus, β plays the role of modifying the trend estimate value.

To compute L(t) and T(t) using the formulas, initial estimates of L(t − 1) and T(t − 1) are needed. After L(t) and T(t) are computed, the forecast value at τ periods into the future is given as

$$F(t + \tau) = L(t) + T(t)\tau$$

The interpretation for $F(t + \tau)$ is that the future forecast is simply an extension of L(t) along a constant slope T(t), τ periods into the future. This implies that one can forecast one or more periods into the future by setting τ as 1, 2, 3 and so on.

Let us build a small Excel model according to Table 2.6. Given ten past data points A(t), use $\alpha = 0.2$ and $\beta = 0.2$ to forecast by applying the formulas accordingly. We will assume L(1) = A(1) = 10 and T(1) = 0, which means that F(2) = L(1) + T(1) = 10. Alternatively, you can assume L(1) and T(1) to be the intercept and slope of the best fit linear line of the past demand data.

$$L(2) = \alpha A(2) + (1 - \alpha)[L(1) + T(1)] = 0.2 * 12 + 0.8(10 + 0) = 10.4$$

$$T(2) = \beta[L(2) - L(1)] + (1 - \beta)T(1) = 0.2 * (10.4 - 10) + 0.8 * 0 = 0.08$$

$$F(3) = L(2) + T(2) = 10.4 + 0.08 = 10.48$$

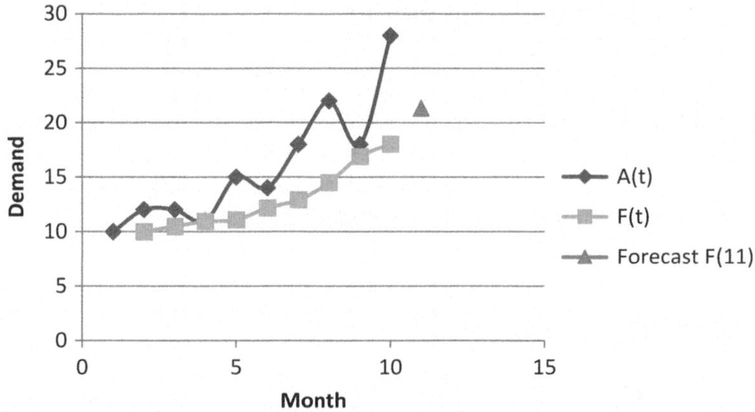

Fig. 2.5 Double exponential smoothing before optimization

Using the Excel equations for L(2), T(2) and F(3), repeat the same calculations using Excel fill function until period 11.

Figure 2.5 shows the results of the forecast values. We can observe that when α is small, the smoothed estimate L(t) will be more influenced by the previous smoothed estimate L(t − 1) and previous trend T(t − 1), which is why the model will be more stable and less responsive to changes and vice versa. When β is small, the trend estimate T(t) will be more influenced by the previous trend T(t − 1), which is why the trend is followed more religiously and vice versa. Overall, the model tends to underestimate when there is an increasing trend in the data and overestimate when there is a decreasing trend. This behaviour is similar to that of moving average and single exponential smoothing.

We can determine the best values for α and β by minimizing the sum of squared error (SSE) between the forecast F(t) and actual A(t) for periods 1 to 10. The forecast error A(t) − F(t) is computed in the last column of Table 2.6. Using Excel, we can set the α and β values as 0.2 into two specific cell locations (say, cells A1 and A2) and compute the SSE in another cell location (say, B2), and its value is 207.87. Using Solver Add-in in Excel, we can set the objective cell to be the SSE and minimize it by changing the α and β values. To ensure that the α and β values do not fall outside the permitted range, we can add constraints to set $0 \leq \alpha \leq 1$ and $0 \leq \beta \leq 1$. The optimal α and β values are 0.264 and 1.0 respectively, with the minimized SSE at 80.08.

Using the optimal α and β values, one can forecast F(11) more accurately as 27.46. Try to do this yourself and forecast period 11 and beyond using the optimal α and β values and setting τ as 1, 2, 3, 4 and so on. You will observe that the forecast follows a linear extension line from L(10) with step increments of T(10).

2.6 Triple Exponential Smoothing

If there is strong seasonality component, we can use the triple exponential smoothing method, also known as the Holt-Winter's three-parameter model. The three parameters refer to the smoothed estimate L(t), the trend estimate T(t) and the seasonality S (t). Depending on whether the seasonality is additive or multiplicative, the appropriate additive or multiplicative model should be used.

2.6.1 *Holt-Winters (Additive)*

For the additive form, the three parameters are given as

$$L(t) = \alpha[A(t) - S(t-s)] + (1-\alpha)[L(t-1) + T(t-1)]$$

$$T(t) = \beta[L(t) - L(t-1)] + (1-\beta)T(t-1)$$

$$S(t) = \gamma[A(t) - L(t)] + (1-\gamma)S(t-s)$$

$$F(t+\tau) = L(t) + T(t)\tau + S(t-s+\tau)$$

From the formulas, we can interpret them as follows:

- The current smoothed estimate L(t) is computed as the weighted sum of the difference between the current actual A(t) and previous cycle's seasonality factor S(t − s), and the sum of the previous period's smoothed estimate L(t − 1) and trend T(t − 1), weighted by α and (1 − α) respectively. This is similar to double exponential smoothing, except the seasonality factor S(t − s) is deducted from A(t) as a form of de-seasonalization, as discussed in Sect. 2.2.
- The current trend T(t) is computed as the weighted sum of the difference between the smoothed estimate of current and previous periods, and previous period's trend T(t − 1), weighted by β and (1 − β) respectively. This is similar to double exponential smoothing.
- The current seasonality factor S(t) is computed as the weighed sum of the difference between current actual A(t) and current smoothed estimate L(t), and previous cycle's seasonality factor S(t − s), weighted by γ and (1 − γ) respectively.
- The forecast F(t + τ) is simply an extension of L(t) along a constant slope T(t), τ periods into the future, topped up with the previous cycle's seasonality factor. As discussed in Sect. 2.2, forecasting mainly aims to determine the future trend, and then seasonality factor is added back for the additive form.

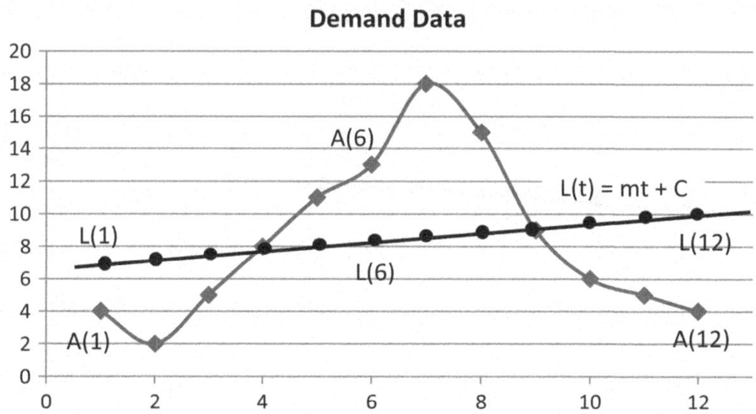

Fig. 2.6 Best fitted linear line to determine seasonality factor for monthly data

To apply the formulas, the previous cycle's seasonality factor S(t − s) must be computed first, where the small s refers to the number of periods for the seasonality. If the seasonality is repeated every year for monthly data, then s = 12. We will need 12 months of data to determine the seasonality S(1) to S(12). First, we will compute L(12), which represents the smoothed estimate of the 12 months of data given as

$$L(12) = \frac{\sum_{t=1}^{12} A(t)}{12}$$

Then, S(t) = A(t) − L(12) for t = 1 to 12, to determine S(1) to S(12). Thus, it is easy to understand that S(t) is in fact the amount of demand above (if positive) or below (if negative) the smoothed estimate.

Alternatively, a best fit linear line can be fitted across the 12 months' data to obtain the equation L(t) = mt + C as shown in Fig. 2.6 with L(1), L(6) and L (12) labeled for illustration. Then, seasonality factor can be computed using S(t) = A (t) − L(t) for t = 1 to 12.

If the seasonality is repeated every year for quarterly data, then s = 4. We will need at least four quarters of data, while eight quarters will be preferred, to determine seasonality S(1) to S(4), where 1 to 4 refer to quarter 1 to quarter 4, respectively. Figure 2.7 shows the best fit linear line L(t) = mt + C over eight quarters of data. Then the seasonality factor will be computed as

$$S(t) = \text{Average}[A(t) - L(t), A(t+4) - L(t+4)]$$

For Quarter 1, we have L(1) and L(5). For Quarter 2, we have L(2) and L(6) and so on. Therefore

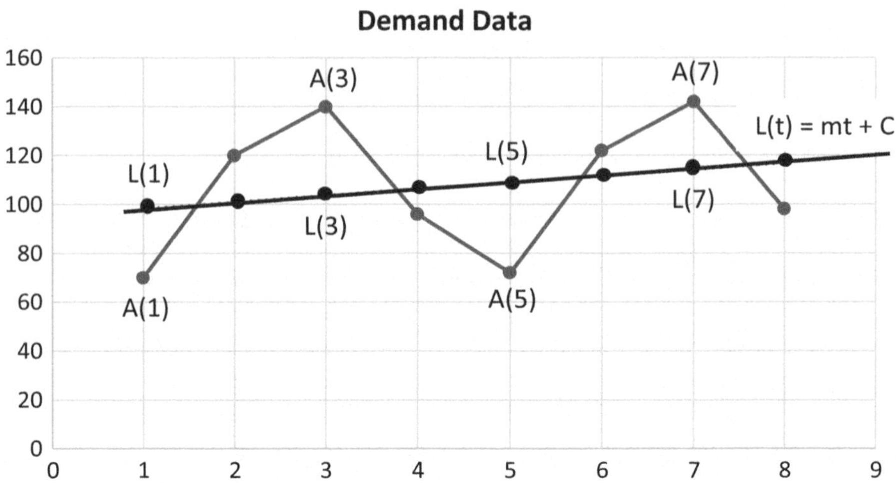

Fig. 2.7 Best fitted linear line to determine seasonality factor for quarterly data

$$S(1) = \text{Average}[A(1) - L(1), A(5) - L(5)]$$

$$S(2) = \text{Average}[A(2) - L(2), A(6) - L(6)]$$

$$S(3) = \text{Average}[A(3) - L(3), A(7) - L(7)]$$

$$S(4) = \text{Average}[A(4) - L(4), A(8) - L(8)]$$

Let us build a small Excel model according to Table 2.7. Given 24 months (two cycles) of past data A(t), use $\alpha = 0.1$, $\beta = 0.1$ and $\gamma = 0.1$ to forecast by applying the formulas accordingly. We will compute L(12) using the average of first 12 months of past data and assume T(12) = 0.

$$L(12) = \frac{\sum_{t=1}^{12} A(t)}{12} = 8.33$$

Next, we will compute S(1) to S(12) using S(t) = A(t) – L(12) for t = 1 to 12. For example, S(1) = 4 – 8.33 = –4.33.

After the seasonality factors S(1) to S(12) have been computed, we will move on to the second cycle to compute L(t), T(t), S(t) and $F(t + \tau)$, for t = 13 to t = 24.

Table 2.7 Triple exponential smoothing (additive) forecast before optimization

t	A(t)	L(t)	T(t)	S(t)	F(t)
1	4			−4.33	
2	2			−6.33	
3	5			−3.33	
4	8			−0.33	
5	11			2.67	
6	13			4.67	
7	18			9.67	
8	15			6.67	
9	9			0.67	
10	6			−2.33	
11	5			−3.33	
12	4	8.33	0.00	−4.33	
13	4	8.33	0.00	−4.33	4.00
14	3	8.43	0.01	−6.24	2.00
15	6	8.53	0.02	−3.25	5.11
16	8	8.53	0.02	−0.35	8.22
17	12	8.62	0.02	2.74	11.21
18	13	8.62	0.02	4.64	13.32
19	18	8.61	0.02	9.64	18.31
20	14	8.50	0.01	6.55	15.29
21	9	8.49	0.00	0.65	9.17
22	7	8.57	0.01	−2.26	6.16
23	4	8.46	0.00	−3.45	5.25
24	4	8.45	0.00	−4.34	4.13

$$L(13) = \alpha[A(13) - S(1)] + (1 - \alpha)[L(12) + T(12)] = 0.1 * (4 + 4.33) + 0.9 * (8.33 + 0) = 8.33$$

$$T(13) = \beta[L(13) - L(12)] + (1 - \beta)T(12) = 0.1 * (8.33 - 8.33) + 0.9 * 0 = 0$$

$$S(13) = \gamma[A(13) - L(13)] + (1 - \gamma)S(1) = 0.1 * (4 - 8.33) + 0.9 * -4.33 = -4.33$$

$$F(13) = L(12) + T(12) * 1 + S(12 - 12 + 1) = 8.33 + 0 * 1 - 4.33 = 4.00$$

Using the Excel equations for L(13), T(13), S(13) and F(13), repeat the same calculations using Excel fill function until period 24. One may notice that the forecast $F(t + \tau)$ for t = 13 to t = 24 are all using $\tau = 1$ and the seasonality factor applied are S(1) to S(12). Once we have the values F(13) to F(24), we can optimize the values of α, β and γ by minimizing the SSE of the forecast error A(t) − F(t) for

Table 2.8 Triple exponential smoothing (additive) forecast for third cycle after optimization

t	F(t)
25	4.00
26	2.10
27	5.10
28	8.00
29	11.10
30	13.00
31	18.00
32	14.90
33	9.00
34	6.10
35	4.90
36	4.00

t = 13 to t = 24. The optimal values are $\alpha = 0$, $\beta = 0.0398$ and $\gamma = 0.1$ with the minimized SSE at 6.0. Try to do this yourself.

You may notice that γ remains unchanged at 0.1. This is because γ is only used in computing the next cycle's seasonality factors. The forecast values F(13) to F(24) applied only the seasonality factors of the previous cycle, S(1) to S(12). Thus, the optimization process does not affect γ.

With the optimal values of α, β and γ, we will then forecast for F(25) to F(36) where S(13) to S(24) are applied and by setting $\tau = 1, 2, 3$ and so on.

$$F(25) = L(24) + T(24) * 1 + S(24 - 12 + 1) \text{ for } \tau = 1$$

$$F(26) = L(24) + T(24) * 2 + S(24 - 12 + 2) \text{ for } \tau = 2$$

and so on until F(36) where $\tau = 12$, as given in Table 2.8.

Figure 2.8 shows three curves, A(t) for the original two cycles, F(t) for second cycle overlapping A(t), and forecasted value for the third cycle, based on the optimal values of α, β and γ. In general, triple exponential smoothing gives reasonable performance if the shape of the seasonality does not vary too much from cycle to cycle.

2.6.2 *Holt-Winters (Multiplicative)*

When the magnitude of the seasonality increases/decreases when the data increases/decreases, due to multiplicative effect, then we have to use the multiplicative form. The three parameters are given as

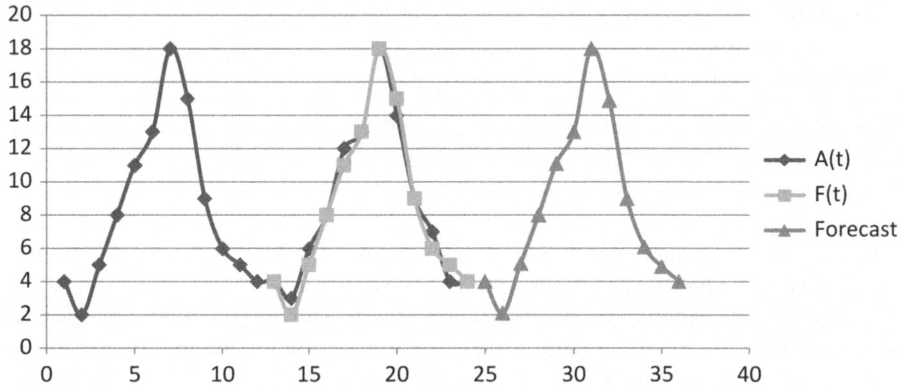

Fig. 2.8 Triple exponential smoothing (additive) after optimization

$$L(t) = \alpha \frac{A(t)}{S(t-s)} + (1-\alpha)[L(t-1) + T(t-1)$$

$$T(t) = \beta[L(t) - L(t-1)] + (1-\beta)T(t-1)$$

$$S(t) = \gamma \frac{A(t)}{L(t)} + (1-\gamma)S(t-s)$$

$$F(t+\tau) = [L(t) + T(t)\tau]S(t-s+\tau)$$

From the formulas, we can interpret them as follows:

- The current smoothed estimate L(t) is computed as the weighted sum of the current actual A(t) scaled by the previous cycle's seasonality factor S(t – s) by division, and the sum of the previous period's smoothed estimate L(t – 1) and trend T(t – 1), weighted by α and (1 – α), respectively. The scaling of A(t) using previous cycle's seasonality factor S(t – s) is de-seasonalization, as discussed in Sect. 2.2.
- The current trend T(t) is computed as the weighted sum of the difference between the smoothed estimate of current and previous periods, and previous period's trend T(t – 1), weighted by β and (1 – β), respectively. This is similar to double exponential smoothing.
- The current seasonality factor S(t) is computed as the weighed sum of the ratio of the current actual A(t) and current smoothed estimate L(t), and previous cycle's seasonality factor S(t – s), weighted by γ and (1 – γ), respectively.
- The forecast F(t + τ) is simply an extension of L(t) along a constant slope T(t), τ periods into the future, scaled with the previous cycle's seasonality factor by

multiplication. As discussed in Sect. 2.2, forecasting mainly aims to determine the future trend, and then seasonality factor is multiplied back for the multiplicative form.

A quick inspection of the formulas will reveal that the formulas look very similar to the additive form. The main difference comes from the treatment of de-seasonalization using S(t − s), which is now divided instead of subtracted in the L(t) formula and multiplied instead of added in the F(t + τ) formula. The computation of seasonality S(t) also differs in terms of taking the ratio of A(t) and L(t) instead of deducting L(t) from A(t).

To apply the formulas, the previous cycle's seasonality factor S(t − s) must be computed first. If the seasonality is repeated every year for monthly data, then s = 12, and we can compute L(12) as the smoothed estimate of past 12 monthly data.

$$L(12) = \frac{\sum_{t=1}^{12} A(t)}{12}$$

Then, S(t) = A(t)/L(12) for t = 1 to 12, to determine S(1) to S(12). Here, it is easy to understand that S(t) is in fact the ratio of demand and smoothed estimate, and it will be > 1 if the demand is above, or < 1 if the demand is below the smoothed estimate.

Similarly, a best fit linear line can be fitted across the 12 months' data to obtain the equation L(t) = mt + C as shown in Fig. 2.6. Then, seasonality factor can be computed using S(t) = A(t)/L(t) for t = 1 to 12.

If the seasonality is repeated every year for quarterly data, then s = 4. Following Fig. 2.7, we can fit a best fit linear line L(t) = mt + C over eight quarters of data. Then the seasonality factor will be computed as

$$S(t) = \text{Average}[A(t)/L(t), A(t+4)/L(t+4)]$$

For Quarter 1, we have L(1) and L(5). For Quarter 2, we have L(2) and L(6), and so on. Therefore

$$S(1) = \text{Average}[A(1)/L(1), A(5)/L(5)]$$

$$S(2) = \text{Average}[A(2)/L(2), A(6)/L(6)]$$

$$S(3) = \text{Average}[A(3)/L(3), A(7)/L(7)]$$

$$S(4) = \text{Average}[A(4)/L(4), A(8)/L(8)]$$

Let us build a small Excel model according to Table 2.9. Given 24 months (two cycles) of past data A(t), use $\alpha = 0.1$, $\beta = 0.1$ and $\gamma = 0.1$ to forecast by applying the

Table 2.9 Triple exponential smoothing (multiplicative) forecast before optimization

t	A(t)	L(t)	T(t)	S(t)	F(t)
1	4			0.48	
2	2			0.24	
3	5			0.60	
4	8			0.96	
5	11			1.32	
6	13			1.56	
7	18			2.16	
8	15			1.80	
9	9			1.08	
10	6			0.72	
11	5			0.60	
12	4	8.33	0	0.48	
13	5	8.54	0.02	0.49	4.00
14	4	9.37	0.10	0.26	2.06
15	7	9.69	0.12	0.61	5.68
16	7	9.57	0.10	0.94	9.43
17	15	9.83	0.12	1.34	12.76
18	17	10.04	0.13	1.57	15.52
19	24	10.26	0.13	2.18	21.97
20	18	10.36	0.13	1.79	1872
21	12	10.55	0.14	1.09	11.33
22	7	10.59	0.13	0.71	7.69
23	8	10.98	0.15	0.61	6.43
24	6	11.27	0.17	0.49	5.34

formulas accordingly. We will compute L(12) using the average of first 12 months of past data and assume T(12) = 0.

$$L(12) = \frac{\sum_{t=1}^{12} A(t)}{12} = 8.33$$

Next, we will compute S(1) to S(12) using S(t) = A(t)/L(12) for t = 1 to 12. For example, S(1) = 4/8.33 = 0.48, a ratio < 1, which means that the demand is below the smoothed estimate at period 1.

After the seasonality factors S(1) to S(12) have been computed, we will move on to the second cycle to compute L(t), T(t), S(t) and F(t + τ), for t = 13 to t = 24.

$$L(13) = \alpha[A(13)/S(1)] + (1-\alpha)[L(12) + T(12)] = 0.1 * (5/0.48) + 0.9 * (8.33 + 0) = 8.54$$

$$T(13) = \beta[L(13) - L(12)] + (1-\beta)T(12) = 0.1 * (8.54 - 8.33) + 0.9 * 0 = 0.02$$

Table 2.10 Triple exponential smoothing (multiplicative) forecast for third cycle after optimization

t	F(t)
25	5.99
26	3.23
27	7.79
28	12.17
29	17.73
30	21.22
31	29.93
32	25.12
33	15.48
34	10.38
35	9.06
36	7.30

$$S(13) = \gamma[A(13)/L(13)] + (1-\gamma)S(1) = 0.1 * (5/8.54) + 0.9 * 0.48 = 0.49$$

$$F(13) = (L(12) + T(12) * 1) * S(12 - 12 + 1) = (8.33 + 0) * 0.48 = 4.00$$

Using the Excel equations for L(13), T(13), S(13) and F(13), repeat the same calculations using Excel fill function until period 24. Once we have the values F(13) to F(24), we can optimize the values of α, β and γ by minimizing the SSE of the forecast error A(t) − F(t) for t = 13 to t = 24. The optimal values are $\alpha = 0.09$, $\beta = 0.25$ and $\gamma = 0.1$ with the minimized SSE at 24.10. Try to do this yourself.

With the optimal values of α, β and γ, we will then forecast for F(25) to F(36) where S(13) to S(24) are applied and τ set as 1, 2, 3 and so on.

$$F(25) = (L(24) + T(24) * 1) * S(24 - 12 + 1) \text{ for } \tau = 1$$

$$F(26) = (L(24) + T(24) * 2) * S(24 - 12 + 2) \text{ for } \tau = 2$$

and so on until F(36) where $\tau = 12$, as given in Table 2.10.

Figure 2.9 shows three curves, A(t) for the original two cycles, F(t) for second cycle overlapping A(t), and forecasted values for the third cycle, based on the optimal values of α, β and γ. One can observe that the seasonality repeat pattern grows bigger in size due to the multiplicative effect.

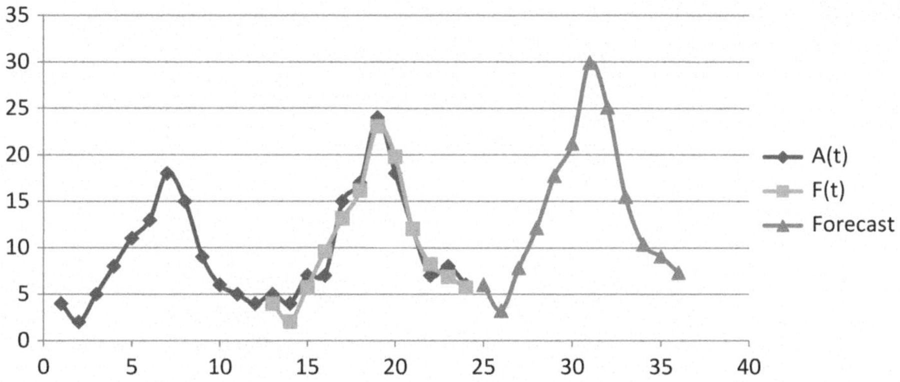

Fig. 2.9 Triple exponential smoothing (multiplicative) after optimization

2.7 Selecting the Best Forecasting Model

After having learned several forecasting models, one might ask, "So, which forecasting model is the best?" We need a systematic way to assess the forecasting model to ensure that the most accurate model is selected. To do so, a quantitative measure of forecasting accuracy will be needed. There are several possible measures.

- Mean Error (ME) takes the average of the sum of all the errors. As each error can either be positive or negative, this will lead to cancelation of errors, and thus ME is not such a good indicator of accuracy.

$$\mathrm{ME} = \frac{1}{\mathrm{M}}\sum_{\mathrm{t}-1}^{\mathrm{M}} (\mathrm{A(t)} - \mathrm{F(t)})$$

- Mean Absolute Deviation (MAD) takes the average of the sum of the absolute value of all errors. It can take care of the canceling effort of ME and is thus a stronger indicator of accuracy.

$$\mathrm{MAD} = \frac{1}{\mathrm{M}}\sum_{\mathrm{t}=1}^{\mathrm{M}} |\mathrm{A(t)} - \mathrm{F(t)}|$$

- Mean Squared Error (MSE) is the average of the sum of the square of all errors. It can take care of the canceling effect of ME. In addition, it penalizes large errors more than small errors due to the squaring and thus gives a tighter measure. Thus, MSE is usually used as the indicator of accuracy.

$$\mathrm{MSE} = \frac{1}{\mathrm{M}}\sum_{\mathrm{t}=1}^{\mathrm{M}} [\mathrm{A(t)} - \mathrm{F(t)}]^2$$

Fig. 2.10 In-sample and out-of-sample methodology

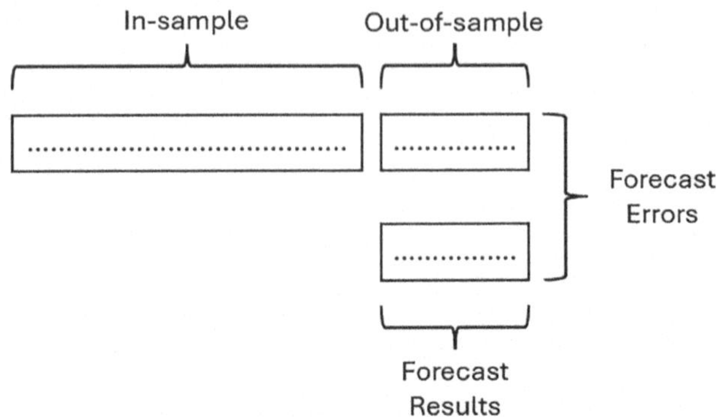

After we have decided to use MSE as the measure of assessment, we will adopt the steps in the *In-Sample and Out-of-Sample* methodology to perform the assessment and selection as shown in Fig. 2.10.

1. Divide the dataset into in-sample set and out-of-sample set.
2. Use the in-sample set to create forecast results using a selected forecast model.
3. Compute the forecast errors MSE by comparing the forecast results with the out-of-sample set.
4. Select another forecast model and repeat steps 2 and 3.
5. Among all the forecast models, select the one with the lowest MSE, and use this final model to forecast into the future using the entire dataset.

One key thing to note is that the assessment and selection were done by using the in-sample set to forecast; however, the final forecast into the future uses the entire dataset. Such a methodology did not consider the impact of the out-of-sample set during the assessment stage. When forecasting into the future using the selected model and the entire dataset, the impact of the out-of-sample set will be included, which may conflict with how the final model was selected in the first place.

2.8 Autoregressive Integrated Moving Average

Autoregressive integrated moving average or ARIMA model was popularized by Box and Jenkins in the 1970s (Box & Jenkins, 1970). A good set of online materials on ARIMA is provided by Professor Robert Nau from Duke University, which is available on the university's Web site (Duke, n.d.-a). The objective of ARIMA is to obtain a forecasting model that contains explanatory variables from the original past data, by using autocorrelations and partial autocorrelations among the data.

Autocorrelation refers to the correlation of a time series with its own past and future values, that is, the correlation between members of a series of numbers arranged in time. A positive autocorrelation means that there is a tendency for the time series to remain in the same state. Therefore, by identifying which member in the time series has strong positive autocorrelation or partial autocorrelation, we can use this member to predict the future.

ARIMA model is classified as ARIMA(p, d, q), where:

- p = number of autoregressive term (AR term) or lags of differences.
- d = number of non-seasonal differences (I).
- q = number of moving average term (MA term) or lags of forecast error.

There are three main steps in identifying the ARIMA model:

- Step 1: Identification
  - Step 1A—Identify order of differencing.
  - Step 1B—Identify AR and/or MA terms.
- Step 2: Estimation
- Step 3: Diagnostic checking

2.8.1 *Step 1: Identification*

In Step 1, there are two sub-steps:

- Step 1A: First is to identify the order of differencing needed to achieve a stationary time series. Stationary time series refers to time series where its statistical properties such as mean and standard deviation do not change over time. If the time series is not stationary, we must transform it by differencing.
- Step 1B: Second is to identify the AR and/or MA terms to be added into the model to further correct any autocorrelation that remains using the Autocorrelation Function (ACF) plot and Partial Autocorrelation Function (PACF) plot.

2.8.1.1 Identify Order of Differencing

How do we know if a time series is stationary or not? There are a few ways to do so. First is to create a run sequence plot, which is essentially a plot with the value of interest along the y-axis and time or sequence along the x-axis. If the plot displays trend and/or seasonality pattern, then it is not stationary. The second method is to run stationary tests such as random walk with drift test. The third would be to observe the ACF plot. If the ACF plot does not die down quickly, then the time series is not stationary. We will discuss ACF plot in Sect. 2.8.1.2.

There are two main types of differencing, regular differencing and seasonal differencing. Seasonal differencing will be applied only when the time series has seasonality pattern and will be discussed in Sect. 2.9. For quick reference, the notation D for seasonal differencing is equivalent to notation d for regular differencing, to indicate the order of differencing.

- First-order regular differencing (d = 1)

$$Z(t) = A(t) - A(t - 1)$$

where A(t) = actual data at time t and Z(t) is the transformed data at time t.

- Second-order regular differencing (d = 2)

$$Z(t) = [A(t) - A(t - 1)] - [A(t - 1) - A(t - 2)] = A(t) - 2A(t - 1) + A(t - 2)$$

- First-order seasonal differencing (D = 1)

$$Z(t) = A(t) - A(t - L)$$

where L = 4 for quarterly data, L = 12 for monthly data and so on.

- First-order regular and first-order seasonal differencing (d = 1 and D = 1)

$$Z(t) = [A(t) - A(t - 1)] - [A(t - L) - A(t - L - 1)]$$

How do we know how many orders of differencing will be needed? By looking at the run sequence plot, if there is an obvious upward or downward linear trend, then a first-order regular differencing will be needed. If there is a quadratic trend, then a second-order regular differencing will be needed. For quadratic trend accompanied by increasing variance, there may be a need to first remove the variance using logarithm, square root or quartic root before performing differencing. Note that it is very rare that one needs to go beyond second-order regular differencing. Figure 2.11 shows a run sequence plot with a quadratic trend generated using SAS tool. Readers can refer to Ngo (2013) for more information on ARIMA modeling using SAS.

The rule of thumb is this—Do not use more than a *total* of two differencing, regular and seasonal combined, which means that there should be at most one regular differencing and one seasonal differencing or at most a second-order regular differencing. This implies that the four types of differencing described above will suffice for all models. Over-differencing will result in adding unnecessary MA terms into the model just to correct the over-differencing, which we will discuss later.

First-order regular differencing is akin to removing the trend component in the data. Figure 2.12 illustrates how a first-order regular differencing transforms a

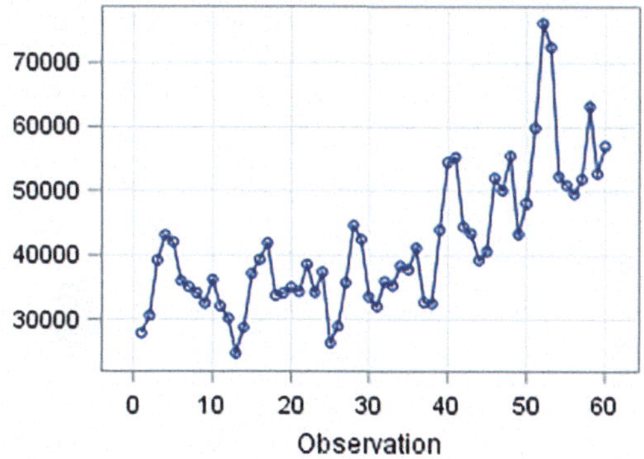

Fig. 2.11 Run sequence plot of a time series with 60 observations

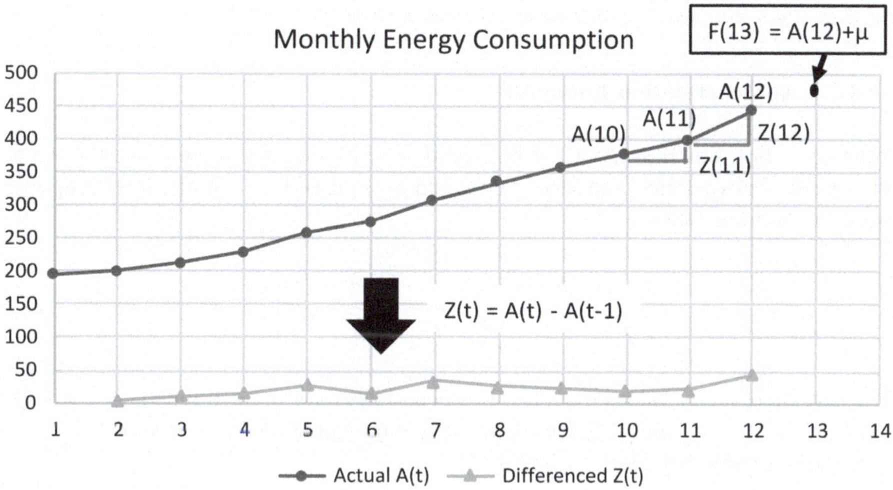

Fig. 2.12 First-order regular differencing

non-stationary time series to a stationary one. The ARIMA model identified up to this point will be F(t + 1) = A(t) + μ, where μ = average of all Z(t) or the average of period-to-period change, representing the trend factor. F(13) will then be A(12) + μ.

Similarly, first-order seasonal differencing will follow the same way to difference the actual data using Z(t) = A(t) − A(t − L) where L is the seasonality. Figure 2.13 illustrates the transformation of quarterly data (L = 4). The ARIMA model identified up to this point will be F(t + 1) = A(t − 3) + μ, where μ = average of all Z(t) or the average of year-to-year change representing the annual trend factor. F(17) will then be A(13) + μ.

After we have understood differencing, we will look at autocorrelation and partial autocorrelation, which can help us identify whether the time series is stationary or not, and also if any AR and/or MA terms need to be added to the model.

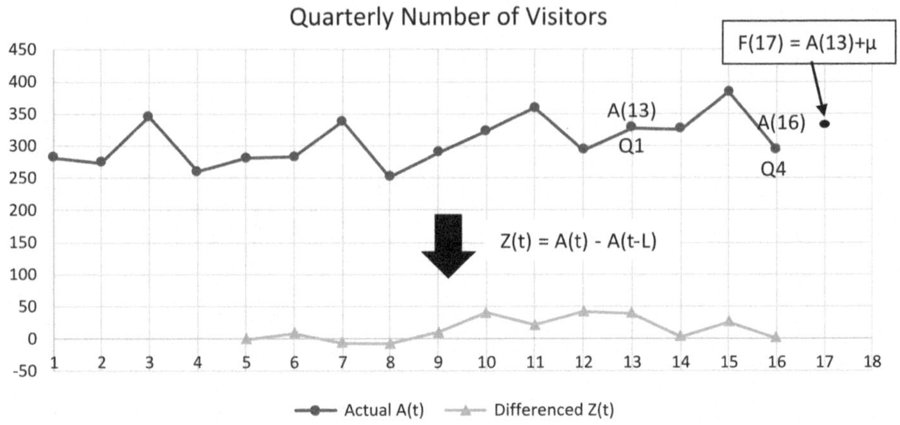

Fig. 2.13 First-order seasonal differencing of quarterly data

2.8.1.2 Autocorrelation Function

Autocorrelation function (ACF) at lag k is denoted by r_k, and it measures the linear relationship between the time series separated by a lag of k time units. It is computed using the formula below.

$$r_k = \frac{\sum_{t=1}^{N-k} (Z_{t-k} - \overline{Z})(Z_t - \overline{Z})}{\sum_{t=1}^{N} (Z_t - \overline{Z})^2}$$

where there are N values from $t = 1$ to N and Z_t is the value at time t, Z_{t-k} is the value at time $(t - k)$ and $\overline{Z}$ is the mean or average value of the time series.

r_k takes a value between -1 and $+1$:

- $r_k > 0$ would mean that the time series is positively correlated to values at k lag.
- $r_k < 0$ would mean that the time series is negatively correlated to values at k lag.

If r_k does not diminish rapidly towards zero, then the time series is not stationary, and further differencing is needed. Figure 2.14 illustrates an ACF plot which does not diminish rapidly, signalling that differencing is needed. The centre line represents $r_k = 0$, and the shaded region represents the 95% confidence interval. Any bars that go beyond the shaded region are said to be significant, and they are known as spikes. Note that the first bar or spike is at lag 0, which represents the autocorrelation of a member with itself. So, it should rightly be at the height of 1.0.

Differencing will introduce negative correlations, pushing the bars down. When the order of differencing increases, the positive correlation will start to go towards the negative direction. When autocorrelation is -0.5 or more, then it will be considered over-differenced, and the order of differencing should be reduced.

After appropriate differencing is performed, the value of r_k should diminish or die down rapidly towards zero from the top (from positive value) or from the bottom

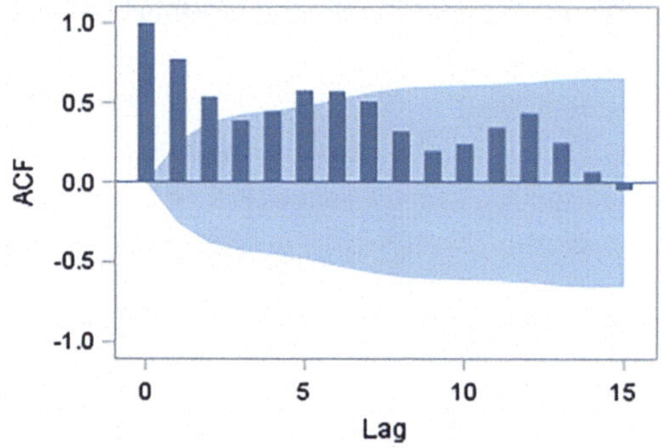

Fig. 2.14 ACF plot with r_k diminishing slowly towards zero

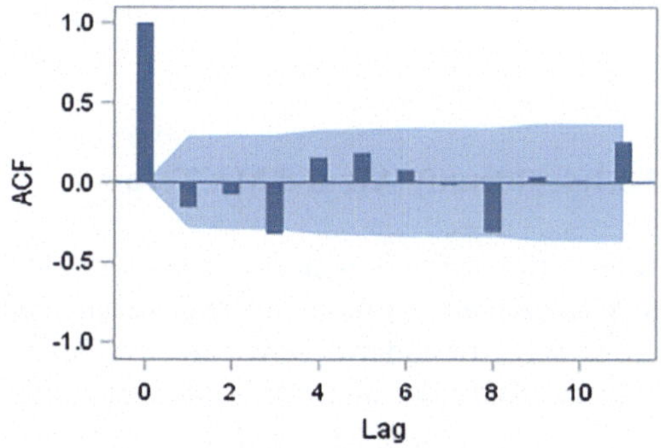

Fig. 2.15 ACF plot with r_k diminishing rapidly towards zero

(from negative value) as k increases, and this means that the time series is stationary. Figure 2.15 illustrates an ACF plot which dies down to zero in a somewhat oscillatory manner. As long as the die down is quick, it can take many forms including exponential, damned exponential and sine wave.

2.8.1.3 Partial Autocorrelation Function

Partial autocorrelation function (PACF) at lag k is denoted by r_{kk}, and it is similar to autocorrelation, except that the intervening effects due to the linear dependence between adjacent data points are eliminated. Calculation of r_{kk} is rather complex using the two sets of formulas below.

$$r_{kk} = \frac{r_k - \sum_{j=1}^{k-1} r_{k-1,j} r_{k-j}}{1 - \sum_{j=1}^{k-1} r_{k-1,j} r_j}$$

$$r_{kj} = r_{k-1,j} - r_{kk} r_{k-1,k-j}$$

To understand the formulas better, let us unpack r_{11}, r_{22}, r_{21} and r_{33}.

$$r_{11} = r_1$$

$$r_{22} = \frac{r_2 - \sum_{j=1}^{1} r_{11} r_1}{1 - \sum_{j=1}^{1} r_{11} r_1} = \frac{r_2 - r_1 r_1}{1 - r_1 r_1}$$

$$r_{21} = r_{11} - r_{22} r_{11}$$

$$r_{33} = \frac{r_3 - r_{21} r_2 - r_{22} r_1}{1 - r_{21} r_1 - r_{22} r_2}$$

2.8.1.4 Identify AR and MA Terms

After differencing is done, we need to identify if there is a need to add AR and/or MA terms into the model to remove any remaining autocorrelations due to over-differencing or under-differencing. To identify AR and MA terms, we only need to read the ACF plot and PACF plot. Such interpretation should only be done after differencing is completed and the time series is stationary.

- AR term is given as $\varnothing[A(t) - A(t-1)]$.

This means that adding an AR term will add $\varnothing$ more differencing into the model. This is suitable when we are in an under-differenced situation. Since $\varnothing$ is usually < 1, this implies that you are adding an additional small amount of differencing into the model. However, if $\varnothing = 1$ or the sum of all AR coefficients ($\varnothing_1 + \varnothing_2 + \ldots$) is close to 1, then it implies that you should remove the AR terms and increase the order of differencing by one.

When the PACF plot displays sharp cutoff after lag p (which means that there are p spikes) while the ACF plot decays, then it will be AR of order (p).

- MA term is given as $\theta[A(t) - F(t)]$.

This means that adding an MA term will add θ more error correction into the model. This is suitable when we are in the over-differenced situation, to undo a small amount of over-differencing since θ is usually < 1. However, if $\theta = 1$ or the sum of all MA coefficients ($\theta_1 + \theta_2 + \ldots$) is close to 1, then it implies that you should remove the MA terms and decrease the order of differencing by one.

When the ACF plot displays sharp cutoff after lag q (which means that there are q spikes) while the PACF plot decays, then it will be MA of order (q).

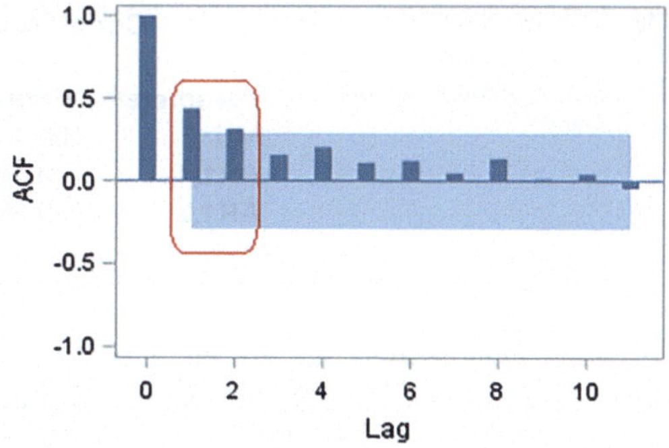

Fig. 2.16 ACF plot with spikes at lag 1 and lag 2

Table 2.11 AR and MA terms identification

ACF	PACF	Model
Has spikes at lags up to q and cuts off after lag q	Dies down	MA of order (q)
Dies down	Has spikes at lags up to p and cuts off after lag p	AR of order (p)
Has spikes at lags up to q and cuts off after lag q	Has spikes at lags up to p and cuts off after lag p	Follow the one that cuts off earlier, and use MA(q) if $q < p$, or AR(p) if $p < q$. If $p = q$, then test all models AR(p), MA(q) and ARMA(p, q) using diagnostic test

What is a cutoff? Cutoff refers to a sudden drop in the autocorrelation or partial autocorrelation value, from a significant level (spike) to a non-significant level (non spike). Figure 2.16 shows an ACF plot with two spikes at lag 1 and lag 2.

In summary, we can apply the principles provided in Table 2.11 to identify the AR and MA terms. There are some additional considerations to take note:

- Ensure that $p \leq 3$, $q \leq 3$, and they are usually 1 or 2.
- For mixed model, $p + q \leq 3$.
- Do not pay attention to isolated spikes beyond lag 3 for non-seasonal data.

2.8.2 *Step 2: Estimation*

2.8.2.1 Estimating Parameters

In Step 2, we need to estimate the parameters of the constant, and ∅ and θ for the AR term and MA term, respectively. Such estimations are performed using the conditional least squares method and are automatically performed by the forecasting

Fig. 2.17 An example illustrating p-values to determine if parameters are significant

Conditional Least Squares Estimation					
Parameter	Estimate	Standard Error	t Value	Approx Pr > |t|	Lag
MU	158.42831	330.71465	0.48	0.6343	0
AR1,1	-0.18754	0.13902	-1.35	0.1842	1
AR1,2	-0.38864	0.14824	-2.62	0.0120	3

software. Diagnostic tests will be carried out to test the significance of the estimations. For testing $\varnothing$ and θ, the t-values will be computed as

$$t = \frac{\varnothing}{s_{\varnothing}} \ or \ \frac{\theta}{s_{\theta}}$$

where $s_{\varnothing}$ and s_{θ} are the respective standard errors.

Using the t value, the p value will be computed. Statistically, the p-value is equal to 2 × area under the t-distribution curve with degree of freedom (n – n') to the right of |t|, where n = number of data points and n' is the number of parameters. Using the p-value, hypothesis testing with a Type 1 error equal to α (usually 0.05) will be used to determine if the null hypothesis H0 can be rejected or not.

The null and alternate hypothesis are defined as:

- H0: parameter = 0.
- H1: parameter ≠ 0.

If the p value < α, then we will reject the null hypothesis H0 in favour of the alternative hypothesis H1, which means that the parameter is significant. Figure 2.17 shows an example where both the MU and coefficient at lag 1 ($\varnothing_1$) have p-values > 0.05; thus, we cannot reject H0, meaning they are not significant. Only the coefficient at lag 3 ($\varnothing_3$) is significant because its p-value is < 0.05, and we can reject H0.

The MU estimate needs to be interpreted differently for AR versus MA models. MU estimate refers to the mean of the differenced time series. For MA models, the MU estimate is equal to the μ in the forecast equation representing the constant drift or growth for a first-order differencing. However, for AR models, the internal calculation for the estimation of MU will involve converting the slope intercept of the model to an equivalent format as deviation from MU. Thus, the μ in the forecast equation will be equal to MU * (1 – SUM of AR Coefficients) for AR models.

2.8.2.2 Common ARIMA Models

Let us look at some of the common ARIMA models in Table 2.12. μ in the forecast equation represents the constant drift or growth. The value of μ will be the MU for MA models and MU * (1 – SUM of AR Coefficients) for AR models.

Among all the models, a mixed model will be least preferred as it includes a combination of AR and MA terms. As discussed, AR terms are meant for correcting

Table 2.12 Common ARIMA models

	ARIMA(p, d, q) model	Forecast equation
1	ARIMA(0, 1, 0) without constant/drift (random walk)	$F(t+1) = A(t)$
2	ARIMA(0, 1, 0) with constant/drift (random walk with growth)	$F(t+1) = A(t) + \mu$
3	ARIMA(1, 1, 0) without constant/drift (differenced first order AR model)/AR(1)	$F(t+1) = A(t) + \varnothing[A(t) - A(t-1)]$
4	ARIMA(1, 1, 0) with constant/drift (differenced first order AR model with growth)/ AR(1) with growth	$F(t+1) = A(t) + \mu + \varnothing[A(t) - A(t-1)]$
5	ARIMA(0, 1, 1) without constant/drift (Single Exponential Smoothing)/MA(1)	$F(t+1) = A(t) - \theta[A(t) - F(t)]$
6	ARIMA(0, 1, 1) with constant/drift (Single Exponential Smoothing with growth)/MA (1) with growth	$F(t+1) = A(t) + \mu - \theta[A(t) - F(t)]$
7	ARIMA(0, 2, 1) or ARIMA(0, 2, 2) without constant/drift (Double Exponential Smoothing)	$F(t+1) = 2A(t) - A(t-1)$ $-\theta_1[A(t) - F(t)]$ $-\theta_2[A(t-1) - F(t-1)]$
8	ARIMA(1, 1, 1) with constant/drift (mixed model)	$F(t+1) = A(t) + \mu + \varnothing[A(t) - A(t-1)] -$ $\theta[A(t) - F(t)]$

under-differenced situations, while MA terms are meant for correcting over-differenced situations. Having both AR and MA terms would imply that their effects will cancel each other out and thus would not be meaningful at all. Therefore, pure AR and pure MA models are preferred to mixed models.

2.8.2.3 Other Representations of ARIMA Models

This section is a detour from the chapter flow, but it is necessary to highlight other representations of ARIMA models which one may come across. We will be looking at two other representations just to make sure that any future references which apply these representations can be understood easily.

In some materials, AR terms $[A(t) - A(t-1)]$ are represented as Z_t , while MA terms $[A(t) - F(t)]$ are represented as e_t.

Thus, a general AR model of order p given as

$$F(t+1) = A(t) + \mu + \varnothing_1(A(t) - A(t-1)) + \ldots + \varnothing_p(A(t-p+1) - A(t-p))$$

will be represented as

$$Z_{t+1} = \mu + \varnothing_1 Z_t + \ldots + \varnothing_p Z_{t-p+1}$$

Let us see how the models 1 to 4 in Table 2.12 will be represented using this representation in Table 2.13.

Table 2.13 New representation of common AR models

	ARIMA(p, d, q) model	Forecast equation
1	ARIMA(0, 1, 0) without constant/drift (random walk)	This model has $\mu = 0$ and $\varnothing = 0$; then $F(t + 1) = A(t)$ will be represented as $Z_{t+1} = 0$
2	ARIMA(0, 1, 0) with constant/drift (random walk with growth)	This model has $\mu > 0$ and $\varnothing = 0$; then $F(t + 1) = A(t) + \mu$ will be represented as $Z_{t+1} = \mu$
3	ARIMA(1, 1, 0) without constant/drift (differenced first order AR model)/AR(1)	This model has $\mu = 0$ and $\varnothing > 0$; then $F(t + 1) = A(t) + \varnothing[A(t) - A(t - 1)]$ will be represented as $Z_{t+1} = \varnothing Z_t$
4	ARIMA(1, 1, 0) with constant/drift (differenced first-order AR model with growth)/AR(1) with growth	This model has $\mu > 0$ and $\varnothing > 0$; then $F(t + 1) = A(t) + \mu + \varnothing[A(t) - A(t - 1)]$ will be represented as $Z_{t+1} = \mu + \varnothing Z_t$

Table 2.14 New representation of common MA models

	ARIMA(p, d, q) model	Forecast equation
5	ARIMA(0, 1, 1) without constant/drift (Single Exponential Smoothing)/MA(1)	This model has $\mu = 0$ and $\theta > 0$; then $F(t + 1) = A(t) - \theta[A(t) - F(t)]$ will be represented as $Z_{t+1} = \theta e_t$
6	ARIMA(0, 1, 1) with constant/drift (Single Exponential Smoothing with growth)/MA (1) with growth	This model has $\mu > 0$ and $\theta > 0$; then $F(t + 1) = A(t) + \mu - \theta[A(t) - F(t)]$ will be represented as $Z_{t+1} = \mu + \theta e_t$

Similarly, a general MA model of order q given as

$$F(t+1) = A(t) + \mu - \theta_1(A(t) = F(t)) + \ldots + \theta_q(A(t-q+1) - F(t-q+1)) + e_{t+1}$$

will be represented as

$$Z_{t+1} = \mu + \theta_1 e_t + \ldots + \theta_q e_{t-q+1} + e_{t+1}$$

Let us see how models 5 and 6 in Table 2.12 will be represented using this representation in Table 2.14.

The ARIMA models can also be represented using the backshift operator B. Using the B notation before Z_t means to move the element back one time period. Therefore, $BZ_t = Z_{t-1}$, $B^2Z_t = Z_{t-2}$ and so on.

So, for a general AR model of order p given as

$$Z_{t+1} = \mu + \varnothing_1 Z_t + \ldots + \varnothing_p Z_{t-p+1}$$

Without loss of generality, we move the equation one time period.

$$Z_t = \mu + \varnothing_1 Z_{t-1} + \ldots + \varnothing_p Z_{t-p}$$

Applying the backshift operator B

$$Z_t = \mu + \varnothing_1 B Z_t + \ldots + \varnothing_p B^p Z_t$$

$$\left(1 - \varnothing_1 B - \ldots - \varnothing_p B^p\right) Z_t = \mu$$

$$\boldsymbol{\varnothing}(\mathbf{B}) Z_t = \mu$$

where

$$\boldsymbol{\varnothing}(\mathbf{B}) = \left(1 - \varnothing_1 B - \ldots - \varnothing_p B^p\right)$$

Similarly, for a general MA model of order q given as

$$Z_{t+1} = \mu + \theta_1 e_t + \ldots + \theta_q e_{t-q+1} + e_{t+1}$$

Without loss of generality, we move the equation one time period.

$$Z_t = \mu + \theta_1 e_{t-1} + \ldots + \theta_q e_{t-q} + e_t$$

Applying the backshift operator B

$$Z_t = \mu + \theta_1 B e_t + \ldots + \theta_q B^q e_t + e_t$$

$$Z_t = \mu + \left(1 + \theta_1 B + \ldots + \theta_q B^q\right) e_t$$

$$Z_t = \mu + \boldsymbol{\theta}(\mathbf{B}) e_t$$

where

$$\boldsymbol{\theta}(\mathbf{B}) = \left(1 + \theta_1 B + \ldots + \theta_q B^q\right)$$

2.8.3 *Step 3: Diagnostic Checking*

After we have completed Step 2 to obtain a suitable ARIMA forecast model, we can apply the Ljung-Box test to test the adequacy of the model. The null and alternate hypothesis are defined as:

- H0: the model is adequate.
- H1: the model is inadequate.

Note that this test is applied to the residuals of the ARIMA model. This means that if the model is adequate, then the model will not have any autocorrelation left.

This test computes the Ljung-box statistics Q given by

$$Q = n'(n' + 2)\sum_{i=1}^{K} \frac{\widehat{r_i^2}}{(n' - i)}$$

where

$$n' = n - d$$

d = degree of regular order differencing.
K = number of lags in the model to be tested.
$\widehat{r_i^2}$ = square of the autocorrelation at lag i for sample size n'.

If the p value > α or equivalently Q < chi-square distribution with (K − p − q) degree of freedom, we cannot reject the null hypothesis H0 and conclude that the model is adequate. In the SAS software, ACF and PACF plots for the residual correlation diagnostic test will be given. If all the bars lie within the 95% confidence interval, then this model is adequate. However, if there are spikes that exceed two standard errors, then this model is inadequate.

2.8.4 Forecasting Using ARIMA Model

Quite often, we could end up with more than one suitable ARIMA model. The general rule is to choose the model with the lower order of differencing or the simplest model with the fewest number of parameters. However, some real-world situations may encourage you to choose a higher-order model. For example, if a time varying trend in the future is expected, then a second-order differencing model could be preferred to a first-order differencing model, or if a quantitative measure is needed in the decision process, choose the model with the lowest white noise standard deviation, AIC or standard error.

2.8.5 Worked Example for ARIMA Model

Let us run through the entire process steps for a worked example. We have the monthly sales data of a certain product for 36 months, from January 2010 to

Name of Variable = Sales	
Mean of Working Series	2939.639
Standard Deviation	498.8589
Number of Observations	36

Autocorrelation Check for White Noise									
To Lag	Chi-Square	DF	Pr > ChiSq	Autocorrelations					
6	83.35	6	<.0001	0.699	0.617	0.611	0.564	0.506	0.433

Random Walk with Drift Tests			
Type	Lags	Tau	Pr < Tau
Drift	0	0.65	0.5176
	1	1.31	0.1989
	2	1.84	0.0748

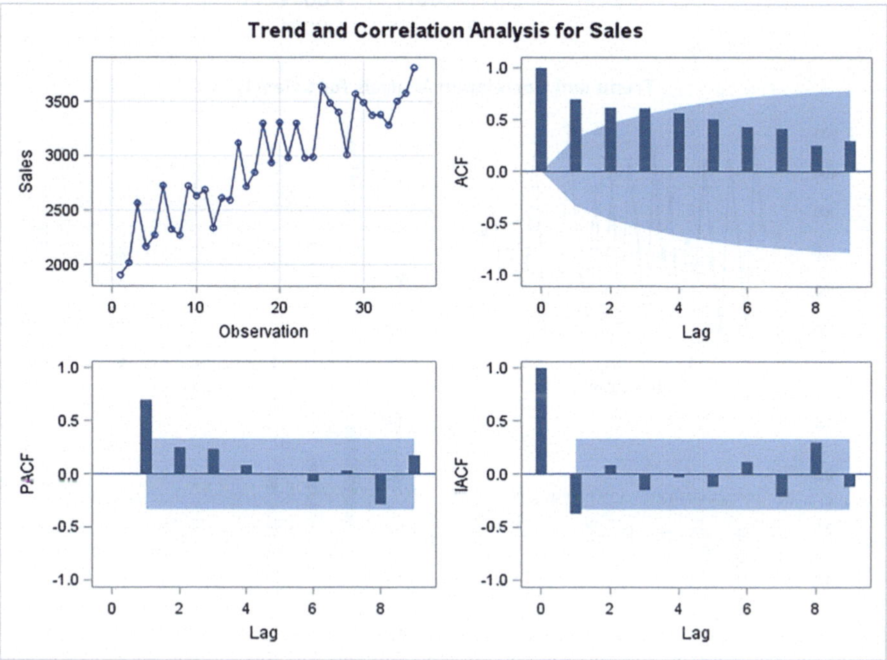

Fig. 2.18 Random walk with drift test, run sequence plot, ACF and PACF plots before differencing

December 2012. Figure 2.18 shows the results of running the data using SAS software, displaying the random walk with drift test results, the run sequence plot and the ACF and PACF plots. The random walk test shows that all the Pr < Tau results are greater than 0.05, which means that the time series is not stationary. A visual inspection shows that there is a strong upward trend in the data, but no strong seasonality, which also concludes that the time series is not stationary. In addition, the ACF plot does not die down quickly, another result to confirm that the time series is not stationary. Note that the standard deviation before differencing is 498.8589.

Name of Variable = Sales	
Period(s) of Differencing	1
Mean of Working Series	54.51429
Standard Deviation	314.0976
Number of Observations	35
Observation(s) eliminated by differencing	1

Autocorrelation Check for White Noise									
To Lag	Chi-Square	DF	Pr > ChiSq	Autocorrelations					
6	15.13	6	0.0192	-0.499	-0.032	0.021	0.018	0.159	-0.317

Random Walk with Drift Tests			
Type	Lags	Tau	Pr < Tau
Drift	0	-9.46	<.0001
	1	-7.11	<.0001
	2	-5.00	<.0001

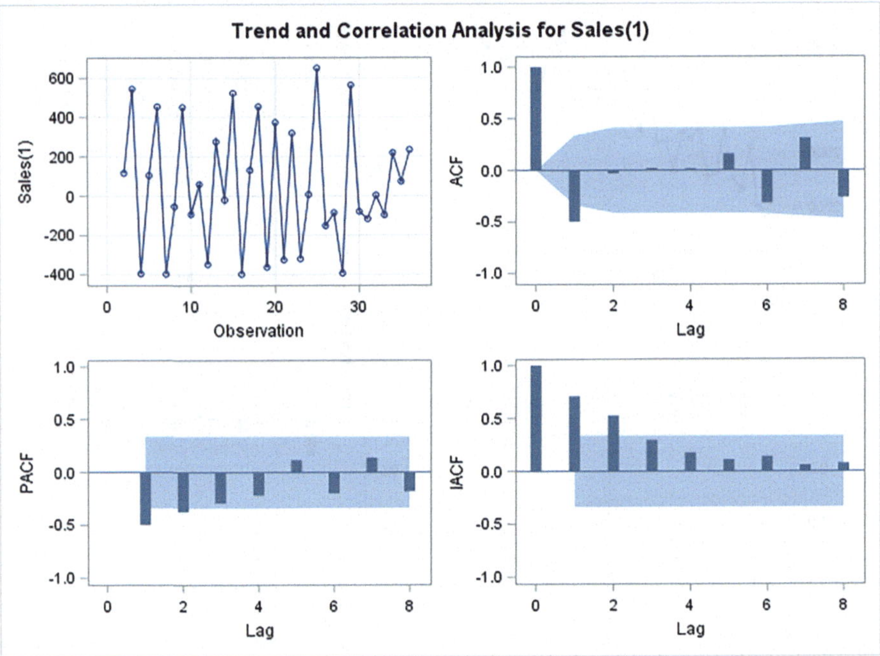

Fig. 2.19 Random walk with drift test, run sequence plot, ACF and PACF plots after first-order regular differencing

In Step 1A, we will need to add a first-order regular differencing to this time series, and the results obtained are given in Fig. 2.19. The random walk test shows that all the Pr < Tau results are smaller than 0.05, which means that the time series is stationary. A visual inspection shows that the trend has been removed and the time series is stationary. In addition, the ACF plot has died down quickly with only one spike at lag 1, another result to confirm that the time series is stationary. Note that the standard deviation is reduced to 314.0976 after differencing.

Fig. 2.20 Parameters estimation, AIC and standard error for MA (1) model

Conditional Least Squares Estimation					
Parameter	Estimate	Standard Error	t Value	Approx Pr > |t|	Lag
MU	47.61094	8.34457	5.71	<.0001	0
MA1,1	0.82663	0.10468	7.90	<.0001	1

Constant Estimate	47.61094
Variance Estimate	58445.12
Std Error Estimate	241.7543
AIC	485.4208
SBC	488.5315
Number of Residuals	35

Fig. 2.21 Parameters estimation, AIC and standard error for AR (1) model

Conditional Least Squares Estimation					
Parameter	Estimate	Standard Error	t Value	Approx Pr > |t|	Lag
MU	52.37025	31.70760	1.65	0.1081	0
AR1,1	-0.50399	0.15133	-3.33	0.0021	1

Constant Estimate	78.76435
Variance Estimate	78315.75
Std Error Estimate	279.8495
AIC	495.6639
SBC	498.7746
Number of Residuals	35

In Step 1B, we will identify if any AR and/or MA terms need to be added to the model to remove any autocorrelations that are still left behind. As both the ACF and PACF plots have a single spike at lag 1, we will test all three possible models ARIMA(1,1,0) or AR(1), ARIMA(0,1,1) or MA(1) and ARIMA(1,1,1) or ARMA (1,1), taking note of the AIC and standard errors for each case. A quick evaluation will suggest that a MA(1) model will be more suitable as the ACF plot's single spike at lag 1 is approaching -0.5, which represents slight over-differencing and may need some error correction.

In Step 2, we will estimate the parameters for each model. The MA(1) model results are given in Fig. 2.20. Both the MU and θ are significant.

The AR(1) model results are given in Fig. 2.21. Only $\varnothing$ is significant.

The ARMA(1,1) model results are given in Fig. 2.22. Only MU and θ are significant, which suggests that the AR term is not important. By comparing the AIC and standard error for all three models, the MA(1) model has the lowest values, and therefore, the MA(1) model is the most suitable.

Fig. 2.22 Parameters estimation, AIC and standard error for ARMA (1,1) model

Conditional Least Squares Estimation

Parameter	Estimate	Standard Error	t Value	Approx Pr > |t|	Lag
MU	47.27620	8.88701	5.32	<.0001	0
MA1,1	0.79187	0.13944	5.68	<.0001	1
AR1,1	-0.10730	0.22090	-0.49	0.6304	1

Constant Estimate	52.34917
Variance Estimate	59811.51
Std Error Estimate	244.5639
AIC	487.1526
SBC	491.8187
Number of Residuals	35

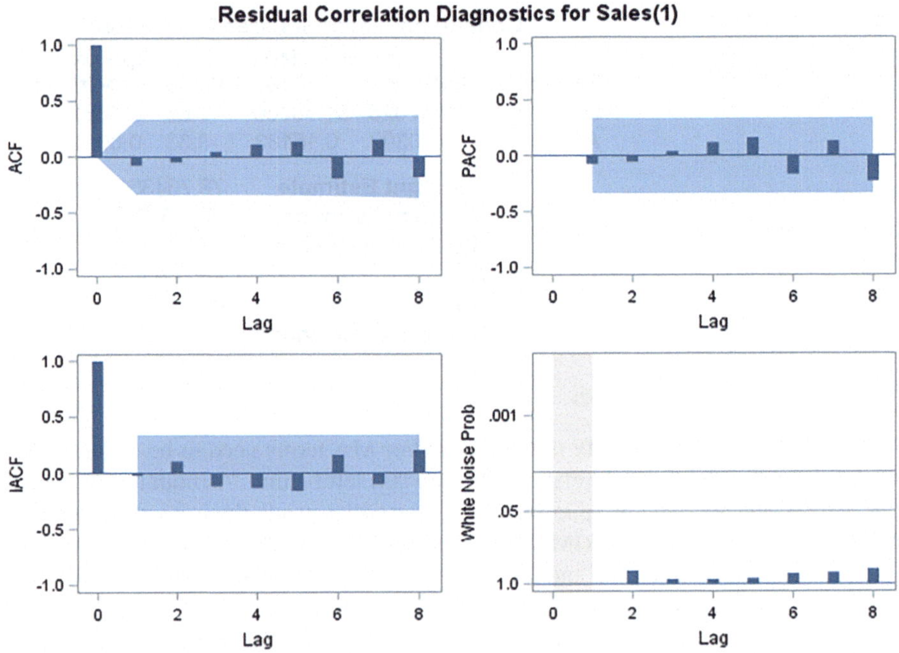

Fig. 2.23 Residual correlation diagnostics for MA(1) model

In Step 3, the diagnostic check results provided are given in Fig. 2.23 for the MA(1) model. Both the ACF and PACF plots have all the bars within the 95% confidence interval, which shows that the MA(1) model is adequate.

And finally, the forecast for the next 12 months using the MA(1) model is given in Fig. 2.24. As this is a MA(1) model, the forecast is essentially a linear line.

Model for variable Sales	
Estimated Mean	47.61094
Period(s) of Differencing	1

Moving Average Factors	
Factor 1:	1 - 0.82663 B**(1)

Forecasts for variable Sales				
Obs	Forecast	Std Error	95% Confidence Limits	
37	3730.6033	241.7543	3256.7737	4204.4330
38	3778.2143	245.3604	3297.3166	4259.1119
39	3825.8252	248.9144	3337.9620	4313.6884
40	3873.4362	252.4183	3378.7054	4368.1669
41	3921.0471	255.8742	3419.5429	4422.5513
42	3968.6580	259.2841	3460.4706	4476.8454
43	4016.2690	262.6497	3501.4851	4531.0528
44	4063.8799	265.9727	3542.5831	4585.1768
45	4111.4909	269.2547	3583.7614	4639.2203
46	4159.1018	272.4972	3625.0172	4693.1864
47	4206.7128	275.7015	3666.3477	4747.0778
48	4254.3237	278.8690	3707.7504	4800.8970

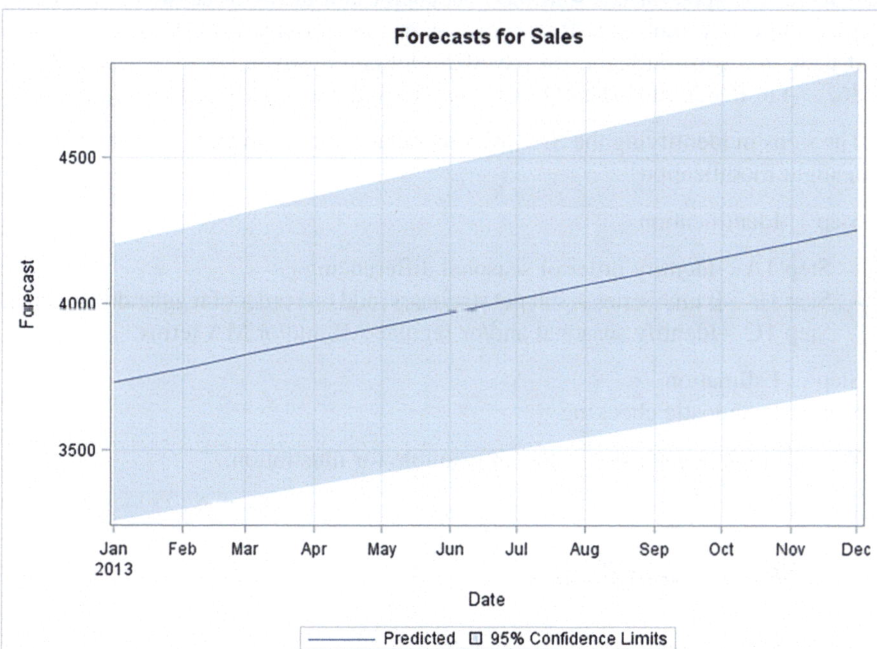

Fig. 2.24 Next 12 months forecast using the MA(1) model

2.9 ARIMA with Seasonality

Seasonal ARIMA or SARIMA takes care of time series with seasonality. A good set of online materials on SARIMA is provided by Professor Robert Nau from Duke University, which is available on the university's Web site (Duke, n.d.-b). SARIMA model is classified as ARIMA(p, d, q)×$(P,D,Q)_m$ where:

- P = number of autoregressive term (AR term) or lags of differences for seasonal lags only
- D = number of seasonal differences (I)
- Q = number of moving average term (MA term) or lags of forecast error for seasonal lags only
- m = number of observations per year (e.g. monthly = 12, quarterly = 4)

What are seasonal lags? Seasonal lags are lags that align with the seasonality. For example, if m = 4, then seasonal lags will occur at lags 4, 8, 12 and so on. Similarly, if m = 12, then seasonal lags will occur at lags 12, 24, 36 and so on. When we identify P and Q at the seasonal lags, we will classify as follows:

- If there is a spike at lag 4 in the PACF plot and decay at seasonal lags (4, 8, 12, ...) in ACF plot, then P = 1, m = 4 and we classify as $(1,0,0)_4$.
- If there is a spike at lag 12 in the ACF plot and decay at seasonal lags (12, 24, 36, ...) in PACF plot, then Q = 1, m = 12 and we classify as $(0,0,1)_{12}$.

The steps in identifying the SARIMA model are similar to that of ARIMA model with slight modification.

- Step 1: Identification
  - Step 1A—Identify order of seasonal differencing.
  - Step 1B—If time series is still not stationary, add one order of regular differencing.
  - Step 1C—Identify seasonal and/or regular AR and/or MA terms.
- Step 2: Estimation
- Step 3: Diagnostic checking

We will look at each step using an example for illustration.

2.9.1 *Step 1: Identification*

When the time series run sequence plot displays strong seasonality, or the ACF and PACF plot display spikes at the seasonal lags, then a seasonal differencing will be needed. We are using a set of 168 data points of the average number of visitors per month to the Singapore Night Safari from January 2005 to December 2008. Figure 2.25 shows the results of running the data using SAS software, displaying the random walk with drift test results, the run sequence plot and the ACF and PACF plots. The random walk test shows that all the Pr < Tau results are greater than 0.05, which means that the time series is not stationary. A visual inspection shows that

Name of Variable = Night_Safari	
Mean of Working Series	95.81369
Standard Deviation	17.61727
Number of Observations	168

Autocorrelation Check for White Noise									
To Lag	Chi-Square	DF	Pr > ChiSq	Autocorrelations					
6	22.80	6	0.0009	0.132	0.186	-0.115	-0.119	0.225	-0.039
12	136.33	12	<.0001	0.206	-0.131	-0.098	0.138	0.073	0.727
18	155.11	18	<.0001	0.056	0.106	-0.200	-0.168	0.093	-0.093
24	238.46	24	<.0001	0.198	-0.183	-0.124	0.030	0.034	0.577

Random Walk with Drift Tests			
Type	Lags	Tau	Pr < Tau
Drift	0	-1.42	0.1568
	1	-0.68	0.4980
	2	-0.64	0.5243

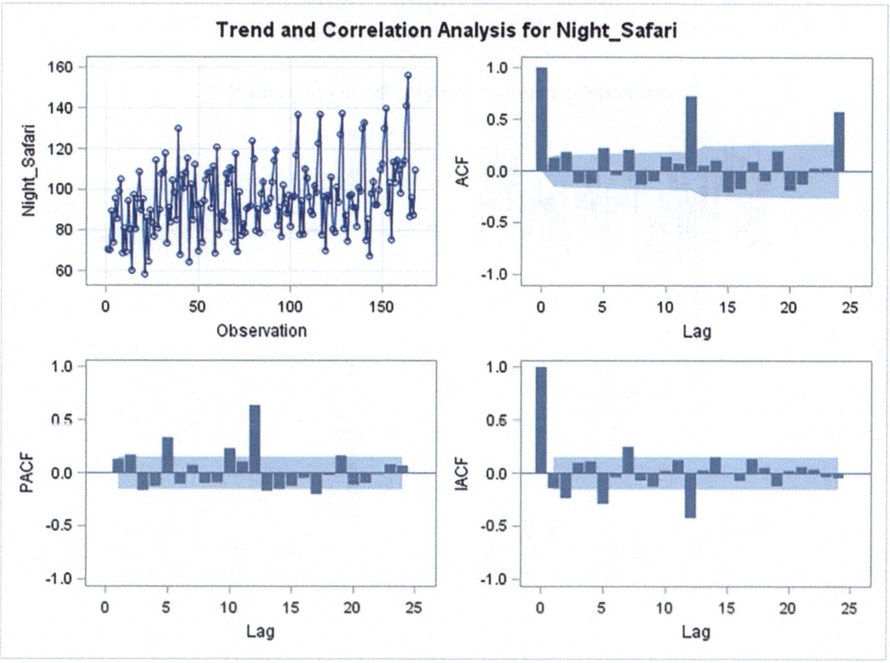

Fig. 2.25 Random walk with drift test, run sequence plot, ACF and PACF plots before seasonal differencing

there is an upward trend and seasonality of 12 months in the data, which also concludes that the time series is not stationary. In addition, the ACF plot did not die down quickly, and there are spikes at lag 12 and 24. Note that the standard deviation is 17.61727 before differencing.

In Step 1A, we will identify the seasonal differencing at 12 (D = 1) for this time series, and the results obtained are given in Fig. 2.26. The random walk test shows

Name of Variable = Night_Safari	
Period(s) of Differencing	12
Mean of Working Series	2.094231
Standard Deviation	10.39278
Number of Observations	156
Observation(s) eliminated by differencing	12

Autocorrelation Check for White Noise									
To Lag	Chi-Square	DF	Pr > ChiSq	Autocorrelations					
6	17.10	6	0.0089	0.065	0.174	0.080	0.073	0.228	0.088
12	34.41	12	0.0006	-0.095	0.040	0.107	0.039	-0.011	-0.279
18	45.49	18	0.0004	-0.069	-0.057	-0.175	-0.027	-0.119	-0.098
24	63.66	24	<.0001	0.119	-0.105	0.158	-0.013	0.210	-0.070

Random Walk with Drift Tests			
Type	Lags	Tau	Pr < Tau
Drift	0	-11.24	<.0001
	1	-6.74	<.0001
	2	-5.42	<.0001

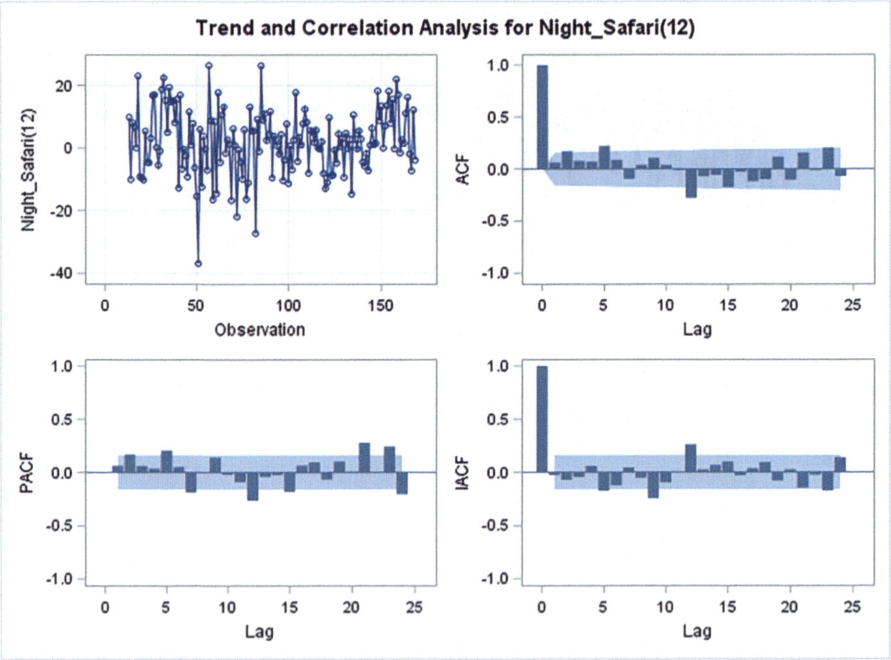

Fig. 2.26 Random walk with drift test, run sequence plot, ACF and PACF plots after seasonal differencing

that all the Pr < Tau results are smaller than 0.05, which means that the time series is stationary. At this point, the model is ARIMA(0,0,0)×$(0,1,0)_{12}$. Note that the standard deviation is reduced to 10.39278.

In Step 1B, if the time series is not stationary, we can consider adding a first-order regular differencing. Do not use more than a total of two differencing, seasonal and

Fig. 2.27 Parameters estimation, AIC and standard error for ARIMA $(0,0,0)\times(0,1,1)_{12}$

Conditional Least Squares Estimation					
Parameter	Estimate	Standard Error	t Value	Approx Pr > |t|	Lag
MU	1.72840	0.37213	4.64	<.0001	0
MA1,1	0.56215	0.06939	8.10	<.0001	12

Constant Estimate	1.728397
Variance Estimate	93.53568
Std Error Estimate	9.671385
AIC	1152.677
SBC	1158.777
Number of Residuals	156

non-seasonal combined. That is, there should only be at most one seasonal differencing and one regular differencing. Since the time series is stationary, we do not need to add any regular differencing.

In Step 1C, we will add seasonal and non-seasonal AR and/or MA terms to the model to remove any autocorrelations that are still left behind. For seasonal AR and/or MA terms, they occur only at the seasonal lags. The ACF plot has died down quickly with only one spike at lag 12, while the PACF plot decays at seasonal lags 12 and 24. This represents $Q = 1$ at lag 12, which is a seasonal MA(1) model. There are no non-seasonal AR or MA terms needed. At this point, the model is ARIMA $(0,0,0)\times(0,1,1)_{12}$.

2.9.2 Step 2: Estimation

In Step 2, we will estimate the parameters for the seasonal MA(1) model, and the results are given in Fig. 2.27. Both the MU and θ are significant.

2.9.3 Step 3: Diagnostic Checking

In Step 3, the diagnostic check results provided are given in Fig. 2.28 for the MA(1) model at lag 12. Both the ACF and PACF plots of the residual have all the bars within the 95% confidence interval, except for lags 5 and 15, which are spikes. Since these spikes do not exceed two standard errors, then this model is adequate.

2.9.4 Alternate SARIMA Model

So far, the seasonal MA(1) model only takes care of the seasonality in the time series. What if we want to take care of the upward trend? Let us go back to Step 1B to

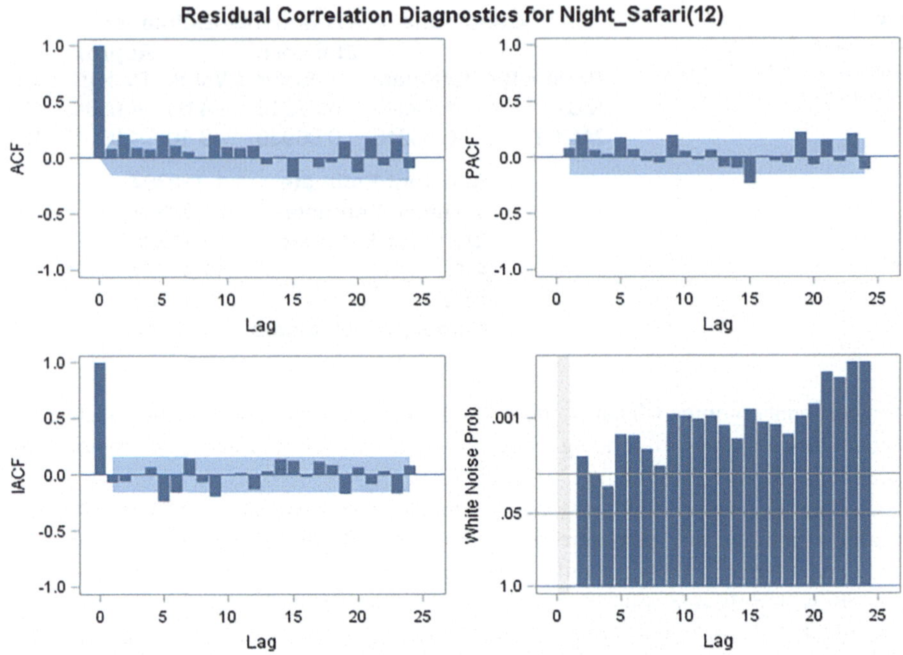

Fig. 2.28 Residual correlation diagnostics for ARIMA$(0,0,0)\times(0,1,1)_{12}$

add a first-order regular differencing (d = 1) in addition to the seasonal differencing (D = 1). The results obtained are given in Fig. 2.29. The random walk test shows that all the Pr < Tau results are smaller than 0.05, which means that the time series is stationary. At this point, the model is ARIMA$(0,1,0)\times(0,1,0)_{12}$. Note that the standard deviation is reduced to 14.23767 as compared to 17.61727 before differencing.

In Step 1C, we will identify if any seasonal and non-seasonal AR and/or MA terms need to be added to the model to remove any autocorrelations that are still left behind. For seasonal AR and/or MA terms, they occur only at the seasonal lags. The ACF plot has died down quickly with only one spike at lag 1, while the PACF plot has gradual die-down or late cutoff after lag 4. This represents that we need to add an MA term at lag 1 (q = 1). At this point, the model is ARIMA$(0,1,1)\times(0,1,0)_{12}$.

In Step 2, we will estimate the parameters for ARIMA$(0,1,1)\times(0,1,0)_{12}$, and the results are given in Fig. 2.30. Only θ is significant. We can compare the AIC and standard error with that of the ARIMA$(0,0,0)\times(0,1,1)_{12}$ obtained earlier. ARIMA $(0,0,0)\times(0,1,1)_{12}$ has lower values and thus is a better model.

To satisfy our curiosity, we can perform forecasting using both models, and the plots are given in Fig. 2.31. ARIMA$(0,1,1)\times(0,1,0)_{12}$ (grey dotted line graph) displays an upward trend in the forecast, while ARIMA$(0,0,0)\times(0,1,1)_{12}$ (grey solid line graph) does not as it does not have a first-order regular differencing. If

Name of Variable = Night_Safari	
Period(s) of Differencing	1,12
Mean of Working Series	-0.08839
Standard Deviation	14.23767
Number of Observations	155
Observation(s) eliminated by differencing	13

Autocorrelation Check for White Noise									
To Lag	Chi-Square	DF	Pr > ChiSq	Autocorrelations					
6	54.99	6	<.0001	-0.552	0.100	-0.045	-0.082	0.151	0.029
12	74.05	12	<.0001	-0.170	0.036	0.072	-0.006	0.112	-0.255
18	85.69	18	<.0001	0.101	0.072	-0.139	0.128	-0.062	-0.108
24	146.27	24	<.0001	0.234	-0.257	0.231	-0.215	0.272	-0.195

Random Walk with Drift Tests			
Type	Lags	Tau	Pr < Tau
Drift	0	-23.25	<.0001
	1	-14.64	<.0001
	2	-11.59	<.0001

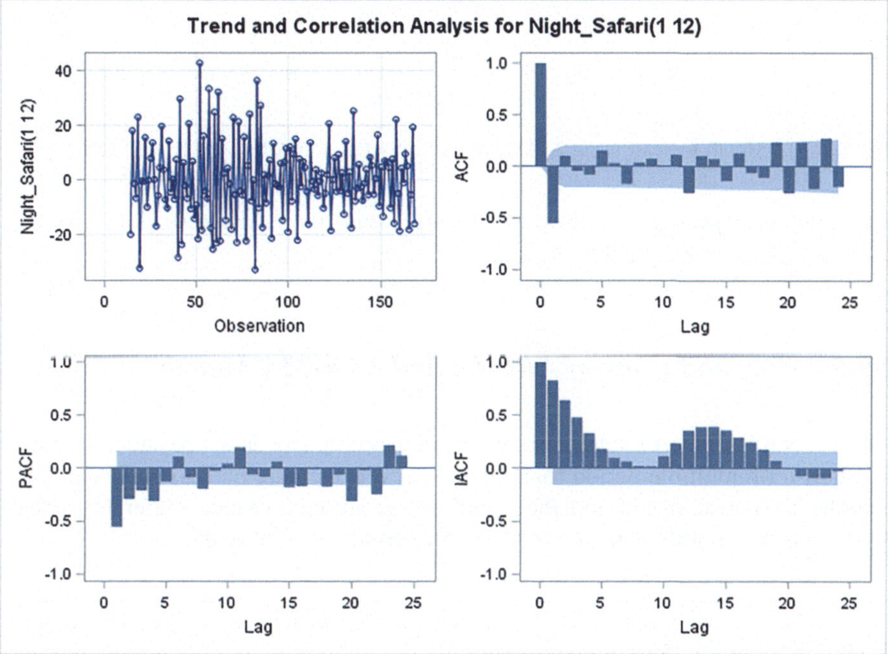

Fig. 2.29 Random walk with drift test, run sequence plot, ACF and PACF plots after first-order regular differencing and seasonal differencing

Fig. 2.30 Parameters estimation, AIC and standard error for ARIMA $(0,1,1)\times(0,1,0)_{12}$

Conditional Least Squares Estimation					
Parameter	Estimate	Standard Error	t Value	Approx Pr > |t|	Lag
MU	-0.0075698	0.09285	-0.08	0.9351	0
MA1,1	0.89552	0.03576	25.04	<.0001	1

Constant Estimate	-0.00757
Variance Estimate	112.5829
Std Error Estimate	10.61051
AIC	1174.03
SBC	1180.117
Number of Residuals	155

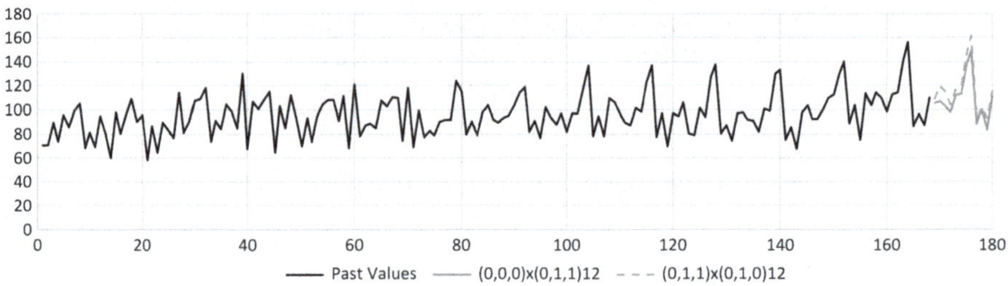

Fig. 2.31 12-Month forecast using ARIMA$(0,0,0)\times(0,1,1)_{12}$ and ARIMA$(0,1,1)\times(0,1,0)_{12}$

the future is expected to follow an upward trend, then ARIMA$(0,1,1)\times(0,1,0)_{12}$ could well be a more suitable model.

2.9.5 Pros and Cons of ARIMA and SARIMA Models

ARIMA and SARIMA models are capable of handling any data type and are suitable for short-term multiple-period forecasts. However, they are hard to understand and complicated to use. In addition, they require large amounts of data, preferably at least 36 periods of monthly data and at least 156 periods of weekly data.

2.10 Stepwise Autoregression

The stepwise autoregression method will combine a time trend regression model with an autoregressive model u_t made up of AR terms.

$$x_t = b_0 + b_1 t + b_2 t^2 + u_t$$

The time trend regression model contains the first three terms

$$x_t = b_0 + b_1 t + b_2 t^2$$

where:

- b_0 represents a constant
- $b_0 + b_1 t$ represents a linear trend
- $b_0 + b_1 t + b_2 t^2$ represents a quadratic trend

The autoregressive model u_t is expressed as

$$u_t = \varnothing_1 u_{t-1} + \ldots + \varnothing_p u_{t-p} + \varepsilon_t$$

Let us remind ourselves the forecasting equation for AR model provided in Sect. 2.8.2.3.

$$Z_{t+1} = \mu + \varnothing_1 Z_t + \ldots + \varnothing_p Z_{t-p+1}$$

Without loss of generality and shift by one time period, we will get

$$Z_t = \mu + \varnothing_1 Z_{t-1} + \ldots + \varnothing_p Z_{t-p}$$

One may observe that the u_t expression looks similar to the Z_t expression, except that the μ in the Z_t expression has been replaced by the time trend regression model.

The AR terms are added or deleted into the autoregressive model u_t via an automatic procedure by performing f-test or t-test to determine if the AR term is significant or not, similar to the process described in Sect. 2.8.2.1. The procedure can take one of the three formats described below:

- Forward selection—involves starting with no variables in the model, testing the variables one by one and including them only if they are statistically significant
- Backward elimination—involves starting will all candidate variables in the model, testing the variables one by one and deleting them if they are statistically not significant
- Complete testing—involves testing which can either add or delete variables

2.11 Case 2A: Travel Retailer Inventory Imbalance

DG is one of the world's leading travel retailer of internationally recognized luxury brands in fashion, liquor, beauty, watches and fine jewellery. By 1999, decisions relating to planning and merchandizing were centrally made to improve overall visibility.

Mr M, the Group Planner for luxury watches, received his Open-To-Buy budget on an annual basis to make decisions on the quantity of watches to buy. He performed the function as the central decision maker for the purchase of watches for nine divisions, resulting in nine different purchase orders, each written into the nine warehouses around the world.

After the orders were placed, the Director of Distribution would ensure that all the watch vendors located in Switzerland deliver the watches to the nine warehouse locations directly. Importing luxury watches requires the proper documentation for customs clearance, including the location of the manufacturer, and indicating the type of leather and precious stones on the watches.

In early 2004, several division managers highlighted inadequate in-stock rate of watches at their retail stores. This had resulted in some potential lost sales. Inspecting the inventory reports from the nine divisions, it was realized that some of the watches requested were actually sitting idle at the other warehouse locations. Expedited transfer between divisions could be a quick-fix solution but would definitely drive the cost sky-high.

To solve the problem, DG decided to turn to aggregated demand forecasting method to reduce variability in the demand and to change the delivery from the watch vendors in Switzerland directly to the Global Distribution Center (GDC) located in Hongkong. Apart from its cost advantage and tax incentives, Hongkong was selected because of its warehouse infrastructure, which was the most equipped to handle the value-added services such as kitting, picking and packing, plus handling the regulatory requirements. Vendors would ship the watches to the Hongkong GDC, which would in turn transfer the watches on a just-in-time arrangement to the division warehouses.

With the GDC concept, Mr M no longer made purchases for the nine divisions separately. Instead, a single purchase order was made with the overall quantity of watches sufficient to supply to all the nine divisions. The overall quantity was determined by performing aggregated demand forecasting. Such a demand risk pooling method handles demand fluctuations among the nine divisions and would reduce overall inventory holding.

Mr M recounted his demand forecasting tasks as follows:

1. 72 months (equivalent to 6 years) of monthly demand data captured in the IT system was retrieved for all the nine divisions.
2. Using the data, perform aggregate demand forecasting for 12 months, using different forecasting models and select the best model.
3. Using the best forecast model, perform aggregate demand forecasting 12 months into the future.
4. After the aggregate demand forecast results were obtained, disaggregate the forecast results back to the nine divisions based on past proportions, to support just-in-time delivery decisions.

GDC implementation together with aggregate demand forecasting were proven to be a great success for DG. Sales rose tremendously because the watches were supplied to the stores that need them and not sit idling at stores which did not. The

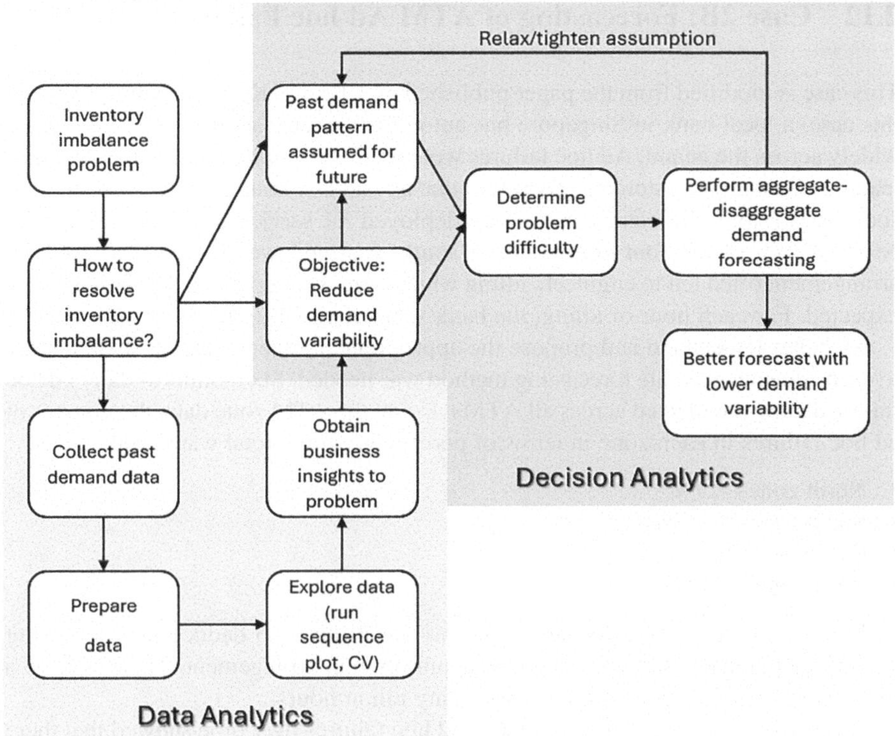

Fig. 2.32 Data and decision analytics framework map for Case 2A

outstanding sales performance led to a global shortage of luxury and fine watches in DG that the Open-To-Buy budget had to be raised.

Let us map the problem and solution method for this case study against *the data and decision analytics framework* proposed in Chap. 1. As shown in Fig. 2.32, in this case study, the problem faced was inventory imbalance despite implementing central planning and merchandizing. Therefore, the right question to ask was "How can DG resolve the inventory imbalance situation?" Next was to collect the relevant data which will be needed to answer the question. With the demand data collected, the analyst can explore the data by plotting the run sequence plot for each division to visualize the high and low demands met by different divisions in different months and compute the coefficient of variation (CV) for each division. From the insights obtained, the problem objective would be to reduce the CV so that demand variation can be reduced. The solution method proposed was to perform aggregate demand forecasting to take advantage of risk pooling and to execute the delivery via a central GDC, based on the assumption that past demand data will provide a good basis for forecasting future demand. The result obtained was a better forecast with lower demand variability.

2.12 Case 2B: Forecasting of ATM Ad hoc Failures

This case is modified from the paper published by Cheong, Koo and Babu (2015). In this case, a local bank in Singapore has automated teller machines (ATMs) located widely across the island. Ad hoc failures were reported despite regular maintenance, leading to unhappy customers. To ensure that any ad hoc failures were attended to as soon as possible, the bank consistently deployed 14 service engineers on a daily basis to each of the four zones (north, south, east and west). However, such an arrangement often led to engineers idling when there were fewer ad hoc failures than expected. For each hour of idling, the bank will suffer a $20 in manpower cost.

To better understand and propose the appropriate number of engineers to deploy to each zone, an accurate forecasting method was needed. Six months of daily ad hoc failure data was collected across all ATMs. Using the ATM zone data, the number of ad hoc failures in each zone in terms of percentage of the total was computed as:

- North zone—27%
- South zone—17.5%
- East zone—30%
- West zone—25.5%

From the percentage information, it was not difficult to deduce that deploying 14 service engineers to each zone was a sub-optimal arrangement. There will be a high chance for the south zone to have many idling hours.

A run sequence plot of the number of ad hoc failures over time showed that there was a slight increasing trend but no strong seasonality. Thus, the best forecasting model would be needed to perform aggregate forecasting of the number of ad hoc failures for the next 14 days and then disaggregate according to the percentage of total for each zone. Once the forecasted number of failures were obtained for the next 14 days, the bank would be able to deploy the appropriate number of engineers needed to meet the service requirement for each zone, at the lowest manpower cost.

Let us map this case study against the *data and decision analytics framework* proposed in Chap. 1. As shown in Fig. 2.33, in this case study, the problem faced was high manpower cost due to inappropriate number of service engineers deployed. Therefore, the right question to ask was "How many engineers to deploy to each zone?". Next was to collect the relevant data which will be needed to answer the question. With the number of past ad hoc failure data collected, the analyst can explore the data by computing and visualizing the percentage of failures in each zone and use the run sequence plot to visualize the time series. From the insights obtained, the problem objective would be to determine the appropriate number of service engineers to deploy for the next 14 days based on the forecasted number of failures in each zone. The solution method proposed was to perform aggregate forecasting and then disaggregate according to percentage, based on the assumption that past data will provide a good basis for future forecasting. The result obtained was the appropriate number of service engineers to deploy in each zone.

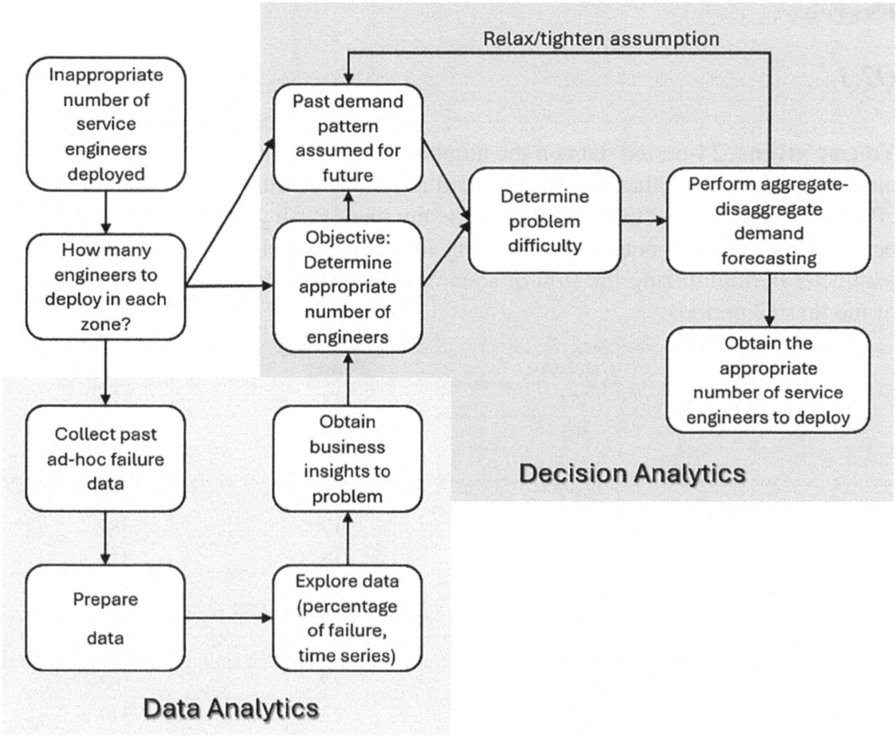

Fig. 2.33 Data and decision analytics framework map for Case 2B

2.13 Summary

This chapter covered the three basic laws of forecasting, as well as several forecasting models, from the simplest Moving Average models to the complex ARIMA and SARIMA models. Two case studies were included to provide realism to actual forecasting challenges faced by businesses. After reliable forecast results are obtained, businesses can use them to plan many downstream business operations, including inventory management, capacity planning and workforce planning. In the next chapter, we will look at inventory management to explore several inventory ordering policies and inventory monitoring or review policies that can take care of deterministic and stochastic demand for both single period and multiple periods problems.

Exercises

Q2.1

You are given a 24-period data on the number of fish caught, and when the data was plotted, you observed that there is no trend or seasonal pattern. You want to use an effective forecasting method to forecast the number of fish you can catch in the next period. Using the Exponential Smoothing forecasting model, determine the best α parameter by minimizing the sum of squared error (SSE). For F(1), use the average of the first 12 periods.

Period	Catch A(t)	Period	Catch A(t)
1	362	13	276
2	381	14	334
3	317	15	394
4	297	16	334
5	399	17	384
6	402	18	314
7	375	19	344
8	349	20	337
9	386	21	345
10	328	22	362
11	389	23	314
12	343	24	365

Q2.2

You are given 52 weeks of weekly sales data. There is an upward trend in the later weeks; however, there is no seasonal pattern observed. Use the Double Exponential Smoothing method to determine the best α and β parameters that minimize the sum of squared error (SSE). Let L(1) = A(1) and T(1) = 0. Forecast for period 53.

Week	Sales A(t)	Week	Sales A(t)	Week	Sales A(t)	Week	Sales A(t)
1	206	14	189	27	172	40	255
2	245	15	244	28	210	41	303
3	185	16	209	29	205	42	282
4	169	17	207	30	244	43	291
5	162	18	211	31	218	44	280
6	177	19	210	32	182	45	255
7	207	20	173	33	206	46	312
8	216	21	194	34	211	47	296

(continued)

Week	Sales A(t)	Week	Sales A(t)	Week	Sales A(t)	Week	Sales A(t)
9	193	22	234	35	273	48	307
10	230	23	156	36	248	49	281
11	212	24	206	37	262	50	308
12	192	25	188	38	258	51	280
13	162	26	162	39	233	52	345

Q2.3

Consider the quarterly sales of bicycles for a bicycle shop over 4 years (i.e. 16 quarters). The time series plot shows that the sales display a linear demand and constant additive seasonal variation. Apply the Holt-Winters Additive Method to determine the best α, β and γ parameters which minimize the sum of squared error (SSE). Forecast for quarter 17. You can estimate L(8) and T(8) using the best fit line of the first eight quarters of data.

Quarter	Sales A(t)	Quarter	Sales A(t)
1	10	9	14
2	31	10	36
3	43	11	50
4	16	12	21
5	11	13	19
6	33	14	41
7	45	15	55
8	17	16	25

Q2.4

The quarterly sales of beer for the last 8 years (i.e. 32 quarters) are given in the table below. The time series plot indicates that there is a linear increase in sales over the 8-year period and the seasonal pattern is increasing as the level of the time series increases. Apply the Holt-Winters Multiplicative Method to determine the best α, β and γ parameters which minimize the sum of squared error (SSE). Forecast for quarter 33. You can estimate L(16) and T(16) using the best fit line of the first 16 quarters of data.

Quarter	Sales A(t)	Quarter	Sales A(t)
1	72	17	94
2	116	18	147
3	136	19	177
4	96	20	128
5	77	21	102
6	123	22	162
7	146	23	191
8	101	24	134
9	81	25	106
10	131	26	170
11	158	27	200
12	109	28	142
13	87	29	115
14	140	30	177
15	167	31	218
16	120	32	149

References

Ashton, A. H., & Ashton, R. H. (1985). Aggregating subjective forecasts. *Management Science, 31*(12), 1499–1508.

Box, G., & Jenkins, G. (1970). *Time series analysis: Forecasting and control*. Holden-Day.

Cheong, M. L. F., Koo, P. S., & Babu, B. C. (2015). *Ad-hoc automated teller machine failure forecast and field service optimization* (pp. 1427–1433). 11th IEEE International Conference on Automation Science and Engineering (CASE), August 24-28, Gothenburg, Sweden: Proceedings. IEEE. https://doi.org/10.1109/CoASE.2015.7294298

Duke. (n.d.-a). Introduction to ARIMA: Nonseasonal models. https://people.duke.edu/~rnau/411arim.htm

Duke. (n.d.-b). General Seasonal ARIMA Models: (0,1,1)x(0,1,1). https://people.duke.edu/~rnau/seasarim.htm

Ngo, T. H. D. (2013). *The Box-Jenkins methodology for time series models*. SAS Global Forum 2013.

Chapter 3
Inventory Management

Ever wonder how successful companies like Amazon, TMall and Lazada manage their inventory of tons of different types of products? How do companies know what is the right order quantity, what is the right safety stock level and when to place order?

Inventory is the stock of products and services, which can be perishable or non-perishable, held to satisfy future demand. Perishable items can be fresh foods like fish as a product and hotel rooms as a service, while non-perishable items can be bolts and nuts as a product and music license as a service.

All inventory consumes cash flow and increases opportunity cost since the money tied inside the inventory could be used to earn more money in alternative investments. If this is so, why hold inventory? Companies need to hold inventory due to the need to satisfy demand, which can be random. Even when demand is deterministic, there could be a lead time due to production or delivery before the new inventory can arrive in time. The other reason can be economies of scale where it makes economic sense to buy a higher quantity due to quantity discounts. Another reason can be due to seasonality as the product or service could be available or in demand only during a certain period, thus buying and holding the inventory in advance to take advantage of seasonal supply or to meet a seasonal demand. With so many different reasons to hold inventory, businesses only want to hold the *right* amount of inventory, which is the amount that will incur the least total cost for the entire inventory management. For a good reference on inventory management, readers can refer to Herron (1967).

In this chapter, we will be looking at several inventory ordering policies and inventory monitoring or review policies. For inventory ordering policies, we will determine when to order and how much to order for a single period or multiple periods problem, deterministic or stochastic demand, while incurring the minimum cost. Four policies will be covered including the economic order quantity (EOQ) model, Wagner-Whitin Procedure (WWP), newsvendor or newsboy model and the Order-up-to-Q* model as shown in Fig. 3.1.

M. L. F. Cheong, Ma Nang Laik, *Data and Decision Analytics for Business Operations*, https://doi.org/10.1007/978-3-031-72255-4_3

		Demand Type	
		Deterministic	Stochastic
Number of Periods	Single Period	EOQ Model	Newsvendor Model
	Multiple Periods	Wagner-Whitin Procedure	Order-up-to-Q* Model

Fig. 3.1 Four inventory ordering policies for different conditions

In inventory review policies, the review of the inventory can be either continuous or periodic due to the stochastic nature of the demand (which means demand is random) and a positive lead time, which magnifies the randomness. Therefore, in such a situation, we need to track inventory position, which includes both actual inventory on hand and inventory in-transit, to better manage the inventory. We will be looking at continuous review policy or the (R, Q) policy and the periodic review policy or (S, T) policy.

Finally, we will look at one case study to apply inventory management theory and concept to determine the expected demand and safety stock on different days of the week for a fast-moving consumer good (FMCG) company.

Learning Outcomes

By the end of this chapter, readers will achieve the following learning outcomes:

- Distinguish between deterministic versus stochastic demand.
- Explain the EOQ model and its three key insights.
- Apply the EOQ model.
- Explain the Wagner-Whitin Procedure and the Wagner-Whitin Property.
- Apply the Wagner-Whitin Procedure to solve problems.
- Explain the Newsvendor model and the derivation of $G(Q^*)$ and Q^* equations.
- Assess the impact of overage and underage costs on Q^* for the Newsvendor model.
- Assess the impact of demand variability on Q^* for the Newsvendor model.
- Apply the Newsvendor model.
- Explain the Order-up-to-Q^* model.
- Discuss how to take care of unsatisfied demand for the Order-up-to-Q^* model.
- Apply the Order-up-to-Q^* model.
- Explain the continuous review policy or (R, Q) policy.
- Compute R and Q^* for (R, Q) policy.
- Apply the (R, Q) policy.
- Explain the periodic review policy or (S, T) policy.
- Compute S and T for (S, T) policy.
- Apply the (S, T) policy.

- Discuss how inventory management concepts and models are applied in a real-world scenario to manage the inventory of fast-moving consumer goods (FMCG) using the *data and decision analytics framework.*

3.1 Economic Order Quantity

The economic order quantity (EOQ) model is one of the most robust models which many businesses know about and like to apply it. The basic concept behind is to trade off between the cost in placing the order and the cost in holding the inventory. When you order a small quantity, you will incur a lower inventory holding cost, but you will need to order more frequently, thus incurring a higher ordering cost. On the other hand, when you order a large quantity, you will incur a higher inventory holding cost, but you will need to order less frequently, thus incurring a lower ordering cost.

To understand how we can determine the best order quantity, let us look at Fig. 3.2. In Fig. 3.2, we assume that demand is deterministic at a constant rate, and thus whatever inventory on hand will be consumed at a constant rate along a straight line towards zero. Once the inventory on hand reaches zero, we will place an order of quantity equals to the EOQ. Assuming zero lead time, the inventory on hand

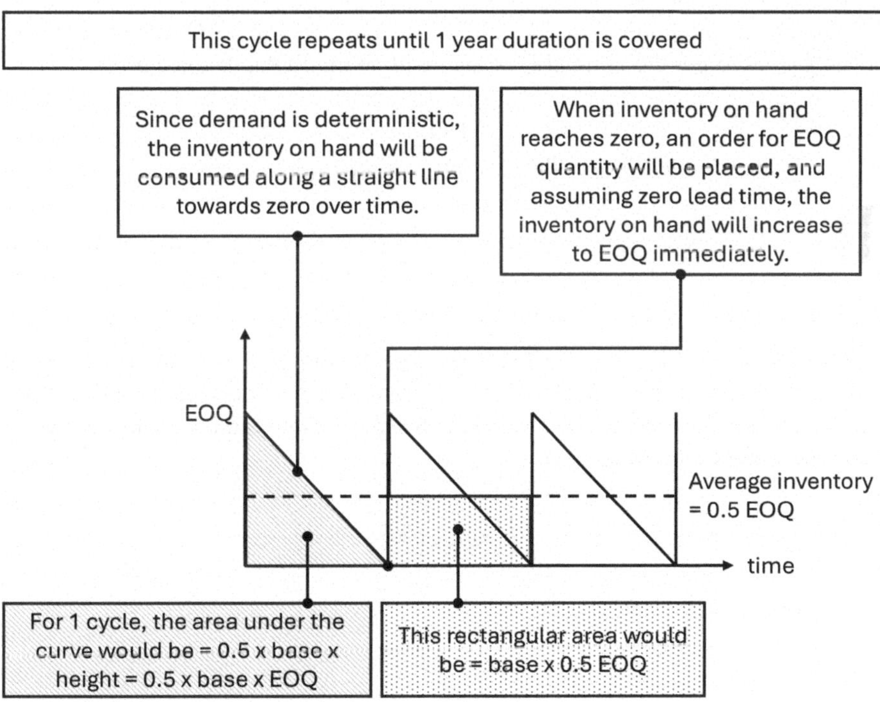

Fig. 3.2 EOQ model illustration

will increase to the EOQ level immediately. This cycle will repeat itself until a 1-year duration is covered. Note that the EOQ model can be easily extended to positive lead time.

Revisiting our basic geometry knowledge, we can see that the area of the triangle will be computed as 0.5 × base × height, where the height is the EOQ level. Similarly, the area of the rectangle will be 0.5 × EOQ × base. In fact, both areas are exactly the same. Thus, by replacing all the triangles with rectangles, the average inventory will be 0.5 × EOQ throughout the entire year, as represented by the dotted line.

With this understanding, we can compute the total yearly cost incurred as the number of orders per year × ordering cost + average inventory × inventory holding cost per unit per year. Mathematically, it will be

$$C = \left(\frac{D}{Q}\right)O + \left(\frac{Q}{2}\right)h$$

where:

D = deterministic and constant annual demand (units)
Q = order quantity (units)
O = ordering cost per order ($)
h = inventory holding cost per unit per year ($)

To obtain the minimum cost solution, we need to differentiate C with respect to Q and set $\frac{dC}{dQ} = 0$ to get the optimal Q, which will be the EOQ, denoted as Q^*.

$$\frac{dC}{dQ} = -\frac{DO}{Q^2} + \frac{h}{2} = 0$$

.

$$Q^* = \sqrt{\frac{2DO}{h}}$$

This powerful expression for EOQ can also be obtained by equating the total ordering cost with the total inventory holding cost, since the basic concept of EOQ is to trade off between these two costs. Let us equate them, and we will be able to obtain the same EOQ expression.

$$\left(\frac{D}{Q}\right)O = \left(\frac{Q}{2}\right)h$$

$$Q^* = \sqrt{\frac{2DO}{h}}$$

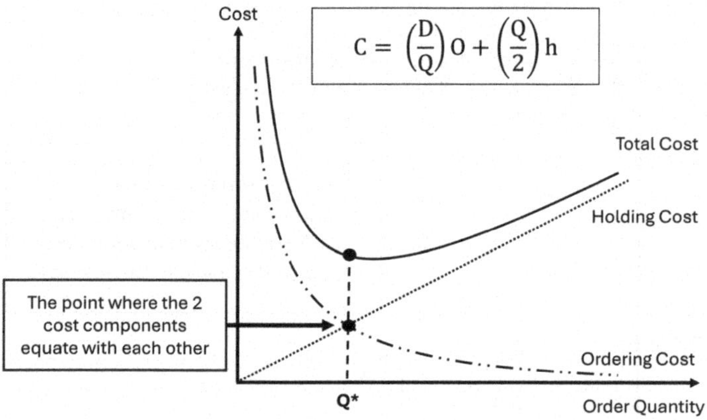

Fig. 3.3 EOQ cost curves

Figure 3.3 illustrates how the total cost, ordering cost and inventory holding cost vary with different order quantity Q. The inventory holding cost is a linearly increasing line with slope h/2 as Q increases. The ordering cost is an exponential curve that decreases as Q increases. The total cost will be the sum of the two cost items. The optimal quantity Q^* will occur at the minimum total cost, which is also the point where the two cost component curves intersect and equate with each other.

The EOQ model is a very robust model as it can handle variation in the order quantity different from the actual EOQ and the variation in the order time interval to fit real-world situation without significant increase in total cost. Let us explore the three key insights from the EOQ model in the following sections.

3.1.1 Key Insight 1

The EOQ equation states that the value of EOQ is dependent on the annual demand D and the ratio of O/h. If we assume that D is kept as a constant, then the ratio of O/h will determine the size of EOQ. When O/h is large, then EOQ will be large and vice versa. This simple insight provides for easy interpretation and application.

As shown in Fig. 3.4, there are two different products A and B with the same D. If the ratio of O/h for A is three times that of B, then the EOQ for A will be three times that of B. So, to satisfy the same annual demand D, we will need to order B three times for every one order of A.

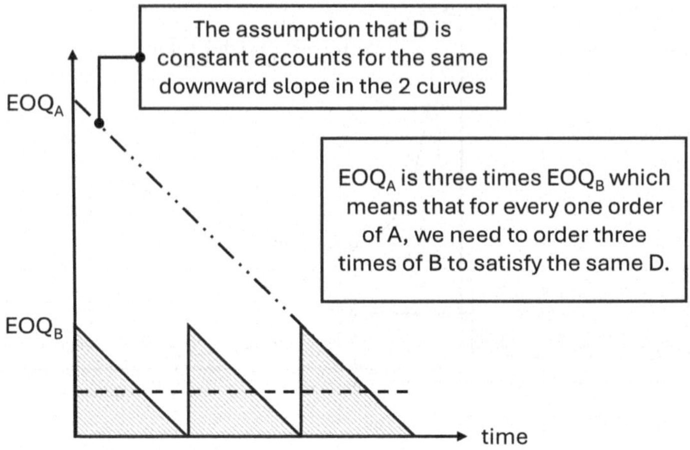

Fig. 3.4 EOQ key insight 1

3.1.2 Key Insight 2

The second key insight will help businesses understand the additional cost incurred if they were to order quantity different from EOQ. The EOQ model states that the change in total cost is fairly insensitive to the change in order quantity. Let us perform the sensitivity analysis to assess this. A similar assessment derivation can be found in Hopp and Spearman (2011).

When $Q = Q^*$, we know that the total cost will be the minimum at C^*.

$$C^* = \left(\frac{D}{Q^*}\right)O + \left(\frac{Q^*}{2}\right)h$$

Replacing Q^* with the EOQ equation

$$C^* = \frac{DO}{\sqrt{2DO/h}} + \frac{h\sqrt{2DO/h}}{2}$$

$$= \sqrt{\frac{D^2O^2h}{2DO}} + \frac{\sqrt{2DOh}}{2}$$

$$= \sqrt{DOh/2} + \sqrt{DOh/2}$$

$$= \sqrt{2DOh}$$

If the business places an order quantity $Q^{'}$ which is different from Q^*, then the total cost will be

$$C' = \left(\frac{D}{Q'}\right)O + \left(\frac{Q'}{2}\right)h$$

The ratio of the total cost $C^{'}/C^*$ will be given as

$$\frac{C'}{C^*} = \frac{\frac{DO}{Q'} + \frac{hQ'}{2}}{\sqrt{2DOh}}$$

$$= \frac{1}{Q'}\sqrt{\frac{D^2O^2}{2DOh}} + \frac{Q'}{2}\sqrt{\frac{h^2}{2DOh}}$$

$$= \frac{1}{2Q'}\sqrt{2DO/h} + \frac{Q'}{2}\sqrt{h/2DO}$$

Since $Q^* = \sqrt{2DO/h}$, then

$$\frac{C'}{C^*} = \frac{Q^*}{2Q'} + \frac{Q'}{2Q^*} = \frac{1}{2}\left(\frac{Q^*}{Q'} + \frac{Q'}{Q^*}\right)$$

How do we interpret this formula? For example, if the business makes a 100% error and places an order quantity $Q^{'} = 2Q^*$ or $Q^{'} = 0.5Q^*$, the ratio $C^{'}/C^* = 1.25$. In plain English, even if a 100% error was made on the order quantity, the additional cost incurred will increase by only 25%, a fourfold difference. Thus, the total cost is fairly insensitive to the order quantity.

3.1.3 Key Insight 3

The third key insight will help businesses understand the additional cost incurred if they were to place orders at power-of-two order time intervals, different from the recommended time interval T^* given by the EOQ model. The EOQ model states that the change in total cost is very insensitive to the change in order time interval. Let us perform the sensitivity analysis to assess this. A similar assessment derivation can be found in Hopp and Spearman (2011).

Table 3.1 Power-of-two order time interval

Order interval	Power-of-two representation with 2^m
1 week	2^0
2 weeks	2^1
4 weeks (1 month)	2^2
8 weeks (2 months)	2^3

For any order quantity Q, the time interval to place the next order will be $T = Q/D$ since D is the constant demand rate. If Q^* is placed, then the corresponding $T^* = Q^*/D$. Similarly, if Q' is placed, then the corresponding $T' = Q'/D$.

From the cost ratio formula obtained earlier, we will replace Q' and Q^* in the formula

$$\frac{C'}{C^*} = \frac{1}{2}\left(\frac{Q^*}{Q'} + \frac{Q'}{Q^*}\right)$$

and will become

$$\frac{C'}{C^*} = \frac{1}{2}\left(\frac{T^*}{T'} + \frac{T'}{T^*}\right)$$

How do we interpret this new formula? We know that order intervals practiced in the real world are usually in terms of weekly, bi-weekly, monthly, bi-monthly and so on, for easy management. If we express these order intervals as power-of-two, we will get Table 3.1.

Suppose now the recommended order interval from the EOQ model is T*, and T* lies between two consecutive power-of-two order intervals $T_1' = 2^m$ and $T_2' = 2^{m+1}$. In the worst case, T* lies exactly right in the middle of T_1' and T_2', which means that it makes no difference if the business decides to change the order time interval from T^* to either T_1' or T_2'. T^* will be given as

$$T^* = 2^{m+0.5} = 2^m\sqrt{2}$$

The ratio of T_1'/T^* will be

$$\frac{T_1'}{T^*} = \frac{2^m}{2^m\sqrt{2}} = \frac{1}{\sqrt{2}}$$

And similarly, the ratio of T_2'/T^* will be

$$\frac{T_2'}{T^*} = \frac{2^{m+1}}{2^m\sqrt{2}} = \sqrt{2}$$

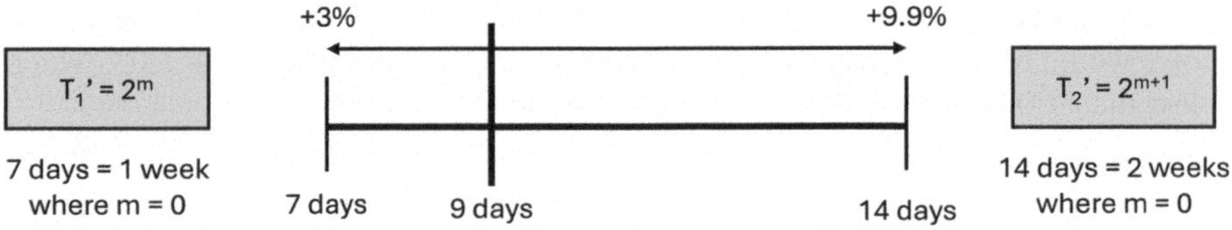

Fig. 3.5 Power-of-two order interval example

Putting the ratio of T_1'/T^* into the cost ratio formula,

$$\frac{C_1'}{C^*} = \frac{1}{2}\left(\frac{T^*}{T_1'} + \frac{T_1'}{T^*}\right) = \frac{1}{2}\left(\frac{\sqrt{2}}{1} + \frac{1}{\sqrt{2}}\right) = 1.06$$

Similarly, putting the ratio of T_2'/T^* into the cost ratio formula,

$$\frac{C_2'}{C^*} = \frac{1}{2}\left(\frac{T^*}{T_2'} + \frac{T_2'}{T^*}\right) = \frac{1}{2}\left(\frac{1}{\sqrt{2}} + \frac{\sqrt{2}}{1}\right) = 1.06$$

Since C' represents the cost incurred due to the worst-case scenario where T^* is right in the middle of T_1' and T_2', then C' must be the largest cost that can be incurred if the business decides to change the order time interval from T^* to either T_1' or T_2'. Therefore,

$$\frac{C'}{C^*} \leq 1.06$$

This means that in all other scenarios where T^* is not right in the middle, the additional cost incurred will be less than 6%. Thus, when businesses place orders at power-of-two order time intervals different from the recommended T*, the total cost is guaranteed to increase not more than 6%, illustrating that the total cost is very insensitive to order time interval. To understand this better, let us use an example shown in Fig. 3.5 where the recommended order interval from the EOQ model is 9 days (T^*). T^* lies between two consecutive power-of-two order time intervals, 7 days ($T_1' = 2^0$) and 14 days ($T_2' = 2^1$). Let us compute the cost ratios.

For $\frac{T_1'}{T^*} = \frac{7}{9}$,

$$\frac{C_1'}{C^*} = \frac{1}{2}\left(\frac{9}{7} + \frac{7}{9}\right) = 1.03$$

For $\frac{T_2'}{T^*} = \frac{14}{9}$,

$$\frac{C_2'}{C^*} = \frac{1}{2}\left(\frac{9}{14} + \frac{14}{9}\right) = 1.099$$

With two possible power-of-two order time intervals to choose from, the logical choice would be to choose the one that incurs the lower additional cost at 1.03, which is less than 1.06.

3.1.4 Worked Example for EOQ Model

Pencils at the campus bookstore are sold at a steady rate of 60 per week. Each pencil costs 30 cents each to the bookstore and is sold at 80 cents each. It costs the bookstore \$12 to initiate an order, and holding costs are based on an annual interest rate of 25%.

(a) Determine the optimal order quantity, ordering interval, the average yearly holding and the total yearly cost in placing the order and holding the inventory for this item.

Annual demand rate, D = 60 per week × 52 weeks = 3120.

Holding cost per unit per year, h = 25 % × \$0.30 = \$0.075.

Optimal order quantity, $Q^* = (2dO/h)^{0.5}$
$=(2 \times 3120 \times 12/0.075)^{0.5} = 999.2$ units (approx. to 1000 units).

Ordering interval, $T^* = Q^*/d = 1000/3120$
=0.3205 years = 16.667 weeks = 116.67 days (approx. to 117 days).

Average yearly holding cost = $h \times 0.5 \times Q^*$
= \$0.075 × 0.5 × 1000 = \$37.50.

Total yearly cost
C^* = number of orders × ordering cost + average yearly holding cost
= (52/16.667) × \$12 + \$37.50 = \$74.94 (approx. to \$75).

(b) Using the power-of-two order interval, determine the percentage increase in total yearly cost if the order interval is changed to 16 weeks.

Let $T' = 16$ weeks and $T^* = 16.667$ weeks.

$$\frac{C'}{C^*} = 0.5\left(\frac{T'}{T^*} + \frac{T^*}{T'}\right)$$

= 0.5 * (16/16.667 + 16.667/16) = 1.0008

The percentage increase in total yearly cost is 0.08%.

(c) Using the new order interval of 16 weeks (T' and not T*), determine the new order quantity and the resulting percentage error in Q and the percentage increase in total yearly cost.

Let Q' = 16 × 60 = 960, which represents an error of (1000 − 960)/1000 = 4%.

$$\frac{C'}{C^*} = 0.5\left(\frac{Q'}{Q^*} + \frac{Q^*}{Q'}\right)$$

$$= 0.5(960/1000 + 1000/960) = 1.0008$$

The percentage increase in total yearly cost is 0.08%. This is the same as that computed in part b, which it rightly should be.

3.2 Wagner-Whitin Procedure

We have covered the EOQ model, which is a single-period, deterministic demand model. What if we need to plan the inventory for a multiple-period model? We will look at the Wagner-Whitin Procedure (WWP), which is a multiple-period, deterministic but time-varying demand model (Wagner & Whitin, 1958).

The WWP was designed to determine the optimal order quantity in each period to minimize the overall total cost across all the periods. The solution is found by a forward recursive algorithm where it first breaks down an N period problem into N single-period sub-problems. Then, it will solve each sub-problem sequentially until the overall N-period problem is solved. This algorithm assumes that there will be no backorders, which means that any unsatisfied demand will be permanently lost.

To appreciate how an N-period problem with deterministic time-varying demand can be solved using the WWP, let us look at a five-period example given in Table 3.2. Assuming we have a unit ordering cost O of \$100 and holding cost per unit per period h of \$1, let us compute the total cost by ordering in each period the same quantity as the demand quantity. Since the order quantity is the same as the demand quantity, there will be zero inventory to carry over to the next period. The

Table 3.2 Wagner-Whitin Procedure example solution 1

Period	1	2	3	4	5	
Demand	30	40	10	60	40	
Order quantity	30	40	10	60	40	
Excess inventory	0	0	0	0	0	
Ordering cost	\$100	\$100	\$100	\$100	\$100	
Holding cost	\$0	\$0	\$0	\$0	\$0	Total
Total cost	\$100	\$100	\$100	\$100	\$100	\$500

Table 3.3 Wagner-Whitin Procedure example solution 2

Period	1	2	3	4	5	
Demand	30	40	10	60	40	
Order quantity	70	0	90	0	20	
Excess inventory	40	0	80	20	0	
Ordering cost	\$100	\$0	\$100	\$0	\$100	
Holding cost	\$40	\$0	\$80	\$20	\$0	Total
Total cost	\$140	\$0	\$180	\$20	\$100	\$440

total cost will simply be 5 × \$100 = \$500. Note that we assume zero lead time and the order quantity in a specific period will be able to satisfy demand in the same period and any future periods.

Since the ordering cost is so high, perhaps we should order a larger quantity to satisfy demand for more periods. In Table 3.3, we will order in periods 1, 3 and 5. The order quantity in period 1 (70) will satisfy demand for period 1 (30) and period 2 (40), while the order quantity in period 3 (90) will satisfy demands in period 3 (10) and 4 (60) and partially satisfy demand in period 5 (20). The order quantity in period 5 (20) is to add additional order quantity to satisfy the demand in period 5. The total ordering cost is now reduced to \$440. So, is there an optimal ordering policy that will minimize the total ordering cost?

3.2.1 *Wagner-Whitin Property*

The Wagner-Whitin Property states the two properties that an optimal ordering policy should satisfy. The first property is the inventory carried over from period t to period t + 1 must be 0, and the second property is the order quantity in period t + 1 must be 0.

Let us understand the first property. When the inventory carried over from period t to period t + 1 is 0, then the order quantity in period t + 1 must include the demand in period t + 1 and even demand in subsequent periods. Expressing this in equation for k periods,

$$Q_{t+1} = D_{t+1} + D_{t+2} + \ldots + D_{t+k}$$

For the second property, when the order quantity in period t + 1 is 0, then the demand in period t + 1 must be satisfied by order in the earlier periods. Expressing this in equation,

$$Q_{t+1} = 0$$

What does this mean in plain English? The Wagner-Whitin Property states that in an optimal ordering policy, the ordering quantity Q_t at time period t must be either one of these equations (generalized by replacing t + 1 with t).

$$Q_t = D_t + D_{t+1} + \ldots + D_{t+k-1}$$

$$Q_t = 0$$

Let us examine Table 3.3 again. Order quantity in period 1 ($Q_1 = 70$) satisfies the first property since it is equal to the sum of the demand in periods 1 and 2 ($Q_1 = D_1 + D_2$). Order quantity in period 2 ($Q_2 = 0$) satisfies the second property since the demand in period 2 was satisfied by Q_1. However, order quantity in period 3 ($Q_3 = 90$) does not satisfy any of the properties since it is equal to the sum of the demand in periods 3 and 4 and only partial demand in period 5 ($Q_3 = D_3 + D_4 + 30$). Order quantity in period 4 ($Q_4 = 0$) satisfies the second property since the demand in period 4 was satisfied by Q_3. Finally, order quantity in period 5 ($Q_5 = 20$) does not satisfy any of the properties since it is equal to partial demand in period 5. Thus, we can conclude that the solution in Table 3.3 is not optimal.

3.2.2 *Define j_k*

Before we work on getting the optimal solution for the worked example, let us learn about the notation j_k. j_k denotes the period in which the order quantity is obtained to serve the demand in period k. Since there is no backorder, $j_k \leq k$, which means that the period in which the order is placed to serve the demand in period k cannot be later than period k. For example, $j_2 = 1$ would mean that the demand in period 2 is served by the order in period 1. So, j_2 can only be 1 or 2 assuming zero lead time, and j_2 cannot be ≥ 3.

3.2.3 *Optimal Solution Using WWP*

Let us go back to the example shown in Table 3.4 and use the j_k notation to denote the possible decision choices in each period.

In period 1, there is only one possible decision, and that is to order in period 1 to satisfy the demand in period 1. Since it is the only possible decision, it must be the optimal decision for this period. So, we use an asterisk (*) to denote optimal decision and compute the cost incurred as C^*.

$$j_1^* = 1 \rightarrow C_1^* = O_1 = \$100$$

Table 3.4 Wagner-Whitin Procedure example

Period	1	2	3	4	5
Demand	30	40	10	60	40

In period 2, there are two possible decisions, either order in period 1 or order in period 2 for demand in period 2, denoted as $j_2 = 1$ or $j_2 = 2$. We will compute the costs for both decision options and select the optimal decision. Note that when we compute the cost for $j_2 = 2$, the optimal decision before period 2, that is, C_1^*, will be applied.

$$j_2 = 1 \rightarrow C_2 = O_1 + h_1 D_2 = \$100 + \$1 \text{ x } 40 = \$140$$

$$j_2 = 2 \rightarrow C_2 = C_1^* + O_2 = \$100 + \$100 = \$200$$

Optimal decision is

$$j_2^* = 1 \rightarrow C_2^* = \$140$$

In period 3, there are three possible decisions, either order in period 1, order in period 2 or order in period 3 for demand in period 3, denoted as $j_3 = 1$, $j_3 = 2$ or $j_3 = 3$. We will compute the costs for three decision options and select the optimal decision.

$$j_3 = 1 \rightarrow C_3 = O_1 + h_1 D_2 + (h_1 + h_2) D_3 = \$100 + \$1 \text{ x } 40 + \$2 \text{ x } 10 = \$160$$

$$j_3 = 2 \rightarrow C_3 = C_1^* + O_2 + h_2 D_3 = \$100 + \$100 + \$1 \text{ x } 10 = \$210$$

$$j_3 = 3 \rightarrow C_3 = C_2^* + O_3 = \$140 + \$100 = \$240$$

Optimal decision is

$$j_3^* = 1 \rightarrow C_3^* = \$160$$

In period 4, there are four possible decisions, order in period 1, order in period 2, order in period 3 or order in period 4 for demand in period 4, denoted as $j_4 = 1$, $j_4 = 2$, $j_4 = 3$ or $j_4 = 4$. We will compute the costs for four decision options and select the optimal decision.

$$j_4 = 1 \rightarrow C_4 = O_1 + h_1 D_2 + (h_1 + h_2) D_3 + (h_1 + h_2 + h_3) D_4 = \$100 + \$1 \text{ x } 40 + \$2 \text{ x } 10 + \$3 \text{ x } 60 = \$340$$

$$j_4 = 2 \rightarrow C_4 = C_1^* + O_2 + h_2 D_3 + (h_2 + h_3) D_4 = \$100 + \$100 + \$1 \text{ x } 10 + \$2 \text{ x } 60 = \$330$$

$$j_4 = 3 \rightarrow C_4 = C_2^* + O_3 + h_3 D_4 = \$140 + \$100 + \$1 \text{ x } 60 = \$300$$

$$j_4 = 4 \rightarrow C_4 = C_3^* + O_4 = \$160 + \$100 = \$260$$

Optimal decision is

$$j_4^* = 4 \rightarrow C_4^* = \$260$$

When the optimal decision is $j_k^* = k$, the optimal ordering decisions for *subsequent* periods, k + 1 onwards, must be in the set $j_{k+1} = k$, $j_{k+1} = k + 1$ and so on. In this case, since $j_4^* = 4$, the optimal ordering decision for $k = 5$ must be in the set $j_5 = 4$ or $j_5 = 5$. This means that we do not need to consider $j_5 = 1$, $j_5 = 2$ and $j_5 = 3$. So, for period 5, the costs for the two decision options are

$$j_5 = 4 \rightarrow C_5 = C_3^* + O_4 + h_4 D_5 = \$160 + \$100 + \$1 \text{ x } 40 = \$300$$

$$j_5 = 5 \rightarrow C_5 = C_4^* + O_5 = \$260 + \$100 = \$360$$

Optimal decision is

$$j_5^* = 4 \rightarrow C_5^* = \$300$$

After we have completed all the calculations, we can tabulate all the decision options in each period and their associated optimal decision as given in Table 3.5. The total cost incurred for this five-period problem is $300 by ordering in period 1 for demand in periods 1, 2 and 3, and order in period 4 for demand in periods 4 and 5.

Note that the cost computed in each period is cumulative, taking into account the cost incurred from the optimal decision in the earlier period. The assumptions made in this procedure include zero lead time, constant O and h, and constant item cost

Table 3.5 Wagner-Whitin Procedure example with optimal solution

Period	1	2	3	4	5
Demand	30	40	10	60	40
Order in period 1	$100	$140	$160	$340	
Order in period 2		$200	$210	$330	
Order in period 3			$240	$300	
Order in period 4				$260	$300
Order in period 5					$360
C_k^*	$100	$140	$160	$260	$300
j_k^*	1	1	1	4	4

(which is ignored in the calculation). We can extend the procedure with positive lead time, varying O and h, and varying item cost for different periods.

3.3 Newsvendor Model

Both the EOQ and WWP assume deterministic demand. When the demand is stochastic, we can look at the newsvendor model (aka newsboy model) for a single-period problem. The objective is to determine the optimal order quantity, which will minimize the *expected* total cost. This model is suitable for products and services which will perish after one period, and any leftover units cannot be carried over to the next period. Products and services such as newspaper, weekly magazines, fresh foods, air tickets and hotel rooms fall under this category.

We define the following parameters in Table 3.6, which will be used in our cost computations.

3.3.1 Derive G(Q)*

When facing stochastic demand X, there are only two possible outcomes. We either order too much or too little. When we order too much, there will be leftover units = Q – X, where Q is the order quantity. Conversely, when we order too little, there will be shortage = X – Q. To determine the optimal order quantity Q^*, we will first derive $G(Q^*)$. A similar derivation can be found in Hopp and Spearman (2011).

Since X is stochastic, we will compute the expected units over or expected units short. The expected value is computed as the probability of X multiplied by the value of X. This computation for a continuous random variable X must be in the form of an integration function. The expected units over will be given by

$$\mathrm{E[Units\ over]} = \int_0^{\infty} \max(Q - x, 0) g(x) dx$$

Table 3.6 Parameters definition for newsvendor model

Parameter	Description
X	Random demand (unit)
$G(x) = P(X \leq x)$	Cumulative distribution function of demand
$g(x) = dG(x)/dx$	Probability density function of demand
μ	Mean demand (unit)
σ	Standard deviation of demand (unit)
Co	Cost per unit leftover (overage cost)
Cs	Cost per unit of shortage (underage cost)

Note that we use the MAX function to ensure that we only consider the positive units over. If the units over are negative, that would mean that $Q < X$, which implies the shortage situation and will be taken care of by the units short expression. So, when units over are negative, we will set it to zero. Let us simplify the expression further. Since we are integrating from 0 to ∞, and for units over, x can only be between 0 and Q. As such, we can replace the upper limit ∞ with Q and remove the MAX function to get the expression below.

$$E[\text{Units over}] = \int_0^Q (Q - x)g(x)dx$$

Similarly, units short will be given by the expression below and simplified to remove the MAX function. Also, since for units short, x can only be between Q and ∞, we will replace the lower limit 0 with Q.

$$E[\text{Units short}] = \int_0^\infty \max(x - Q, 0)g(x)dx$$

$$= \int_Q^\infty (x - Q)g(x)dx$$

The total expected cost incurred will be computed as

$$Y(Q) = C_o \int_0^Q (Q - x)g(x)dx + C_s \int_Q^\infty (x - Q)g(x)dx$$

To minimize the total expected cost, we need to take the first derivative and set it to zero. Let us represent the first derivative to take the following form:

$$\frac{dY(Q)}{dQ} = C_o \frac{dA}{dQ} + C_s \frac{dB}{dQ}$$

Consider the first term $\frac{dA}{dQ}$ and using Leibnitz' rule,

$$\frac{dA}{dQ} = \frac{d}{dQ} \int_0^Q (Q - x)g(x)dx$$

$$\frac{dA}{dQ} = \int_0^Q \frac{\partial (Q - x)}{\partial Q} g(x)dx + (Q - Q)g(Q)\frac{dQ}{dQ} - (Q - 0)g(0)\frac{d0}{dQ}$$

The second and third terms will go to zero since (Q − Q) = 0 and $\frac{d0}{dQ} = 0$. Thus,

$$\frac{dA}{dQ} = \int_0^Q \frac{\partial(Q-x)}{\partial Q} g(x)dx$$

$$\frac{dA}{dQ} = \int_0^Q 1.g(x)dx = G(Q)$$

Now, consider the second term $\frac{dB}{dQ}$ and using Leibnitz' rule,

$$\frac{dB}{dQ} = \frac{d}{dQ} \int_Q^\infty (x-Q)g(x)dx$$

$$\frac{dB}{dQ} = \int_Q^\infty \frac{\partial(x-Q)}{\partial Q} g(x)dx + (\infty - Q)g(\infty)\frac{d\infty}{dQ} - (Q-Q)g(Q)\frac{dQ}{dQ}$$

Again, the second and third terms will go to zero since $\frac{d\infty}{dQ} = 0$ and (Q − Q) = 0. Thus,

$$\frac{dB}{dQ} = \int_Q^\infty \frac{\partial(x-Q)}{\partial Q} g(x)dx$$

$$\frac{dB}{dQ} = \int_Q^\infty -1.g(x)dx = -[1 - G(Q)]$$

Putting $\frac{dA}{dQ}$ and $\frac{dB}{dQ}$ back into the $\frac{dY(Q)}{dQ}$ equation and setting it to zero, we get the cumulative distribution function of demand $G(Q^*)$ expressed in terms of the overage cost C_o and underage cost C_s.

$$\frac{dY(Q)}{dQ} = C_o G(Q) - C_s[1 - G(Q)] = 0$$

$$G(Q^*) = \frac{C_s}{C_o + C_s}$$

3.3.2 Optimal Order Quantity Q*

The G(Q*) expression can be applied to any demand distribution function. If the demand follows a normal distribution with mean μ and standard deviation σ, then we get

$$G(Q^*) = \Phi\left(\frac{Q^* - \mu}{\sigma}\right) = \frac{C_s}{C_o + C_s}$$

For a normal distribution, $\Phi\left(\frac{Q^* - \mu}{\sigma}\right)$ refers to $\Phi(z')$ of the normal distribution curve where z' is the horizontal axis value that gives the area under the curve to the left of z' to be equal to $\frac{C_s}{C_o + C_s}$. Let us see this in Fig. 3.6.

With known C_o and C_s values, we can compute the critical ratio $\frac{C_s}{C_o + C_s}$ and read the value of z' from the standard normal table to get the Q^* equation by replacing z' with z for simplification.

$$\Phi(z') = \frac{C_s}{C_o + C_s} \rightarrow \frac{Q^* - \mu}{\sigma} = z'$$

$$Q^* = \mu + z\sigma$$

The Q^* equation states that the optimal order quantity for a stochastic demand following the normal distribution for a single-period problem is simply the mean of the distribution plus z multiply by the standard deviation of the distribution. The value of z is determined by the critical ratio $\frac{C_s}{C_o + C_s}$.

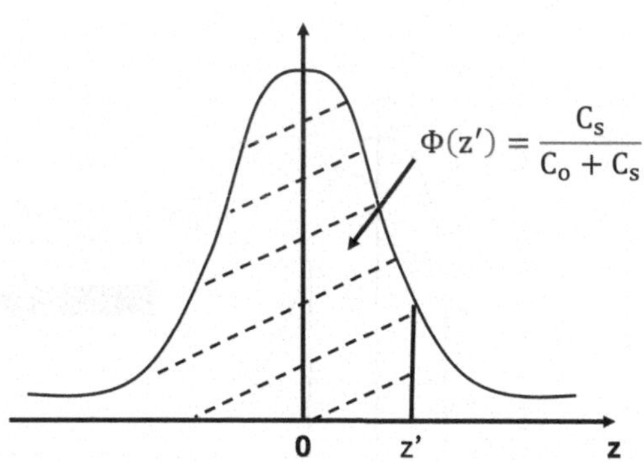

Fig. 3.6 Cumulative normal distribution at z'

3.3.3 *Impact of Co and Cs on Q**

With this understanding, businesses may be keen to know how C_o and C_s will affect the optimal order quantity. From the $G(Q^*)$ equation, we note that $G(Q^*)$ represents the cumulative probability that demand is $\leq Q^*$.

$$G(Q^*) = \frac{C_s}{C_o + C_s}$$

Since $G(Q^*)$ is a monotonically increasing function, increasing the right-hand side of the equation will increase the probability that demand is $\leq Q^*$, which means that Q^* must become larger as well. Thus, intuitively, increasing C_s will increase Q^*, while increasing C_o will decrease Q^*.

Practically what this means is when the shortage cost is high, we do not want to experience shortage, so we should order more. Conversely, when the overage cost is high, we do not want to have too much leftover, so we should order less.

3.3.4 *Impact of Demand Variability on Q**

How would the variability of the demand affect Q^*? Looking at the Q^* equation, we note that increasing σ will affect Q^*, but it will depend on whether the z value is positive or negative.

$$Q^* = \mu + z\sigma$$

Refer to Fig. 3.7. When the critical ratio $\frac{C_s}{C_o + C_s} > 0.5$, then z value will be positive given as Z_1'. Increasing σ will flatten the curve pushing Z_1' more to the right side, making it more positive. Therefore, Q^* will increase.

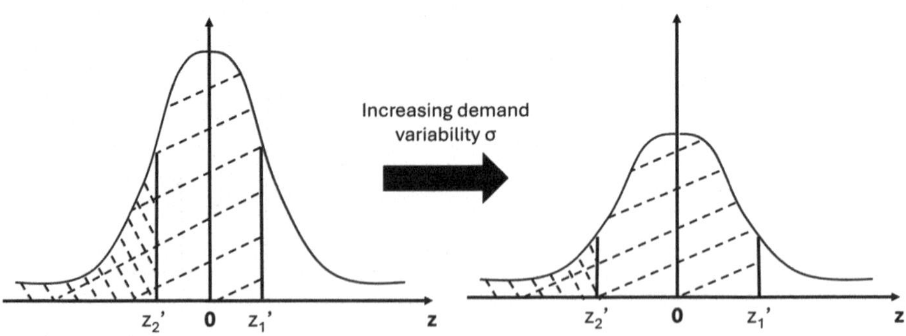

Fig. 3.7 Increasing demand variability

Conversely, when the critical ratio $\frac{C_s}{C_o + C_s} < 0.5$, then z value will be negative, given as Z_2'. Increasing σ will flatten the curve, pushing Z_2' more to the left side, making it more negative. Therefore, Q^* will decrease.

This finding is counter intuitive as most people would think that as σ increases, demand will become more variable and less predictable; therefore, the optimal order quantity Q^* should increase to handle higher variability. However, Q^* increases or decreases depending on critical ratio $\frac{C_s}{C_o + C_s}$ which affects whether the z value is positive or negative.

3.3.5 *Worked Example for Newsvendor Model*

From experience, it was observed that the weekly demand for a weekly magazine at a newsstand is approximately normally distributed with mean 11.73 and standard deviation of 4.74. The newsstand purchases the magazine at \$1.20 and sells it at \$2.50. Any unsold copies are salvaged at \$0.50 per copy. Determine the optimal order quantity for the weekly magazine.

Let us identify the key parameters in this example.

- Overage cost, $C_o = \$1.20 - \$0.50 = \$0.70$.
- Underage cost, $C_s = \$2.50 - \$1.20 = \$1.30$.
- Critical ratio $\frac{C_s}{C_o + C_s} = \frac{1.3}{(0.7 + 1.3)} = 0.65$.
- We can use the Excel function NORMSINV(probability) to compute the z value.

$$z = \text{NORMSINV}(0.65) = 0.38532$$

$$Q^* = \mu + z\sigma = 11.73 + 0.38532 \times 4.74 = 13.556$$

- Alternatively, we can use the Excel function NORMINV(probability, mean, SD) to compute Q^* directly.

$$Q^* = \text{NORMINV}(0.65, 11.73, 4.74) = 13.556$$

Hence, the newsstand should order 14 copies of the weekly magazine.

3.4 Order-up-to-Q* Model

The newsvendor model can be easily extended to the Order-up-to-Q^* model for a multiple-period stochastic demand problem where any excess inventory can be carried to the next period. We assume that the demand in each period is independent and all demand follows the same distribution function G(x). This assumption is also known as independent and identically distributed (i.i.d.).

In addition, we can consider two possible situations where (1) unsatisfied demand in this period will be satisfied in the next period, and (2) unsatisfied demand will be lost permanently. We will look at how to handle each situation.

3.4.1 Unsatisfied Demand Satisfied in Next Period

In the Order-up-to-Q^* model, Q^* is interpreted as the order-up-to level or the maximum level. The definitions for C_o and C_s are modified as:

- C_o = cost to hold one unit of excess inventory to the next period, usually the inventory holding cost.
- C_s = cost of fulfilling an unsatisfied demand in the next period, which can be discounts given to entice customers to wait for one period or transportation cost incurred to deliver the products to customers in the next period.

With the modified definitions of C_o and C_s, we can compute the critical ratio $\frac{C_s}{C_o + C_s}$ and obtain the z value to be substituted into the Q^* equation to compute Q^*.

$$Q^* = \mu + z\sigma$$

Referring to Fig. 3.8, after period 1, there are some leftover inventory to be carried over to period 2, making the order quantity $Q_1 < Q^*$. After period 2, the unsatisfied demand will be satisfied in period 3, making $Q_2 > Q^*$. Similarly, due to low demand, a large quantity of excess inventory will be carried over from period 3 to period 4, making $Q_3 < Q^*$. The basic concept is that the order quantity is affected by the inventory carried over or unsatisfied demand from the previous period. Thus, the order quantity can either be $< Q^*$ or $> Q^*$ to bring the inventory on hand up to Q^* level at the start of the next period, assuming zero lead time.

3.4.2 Unsatisfied Demand Permanently Lost

In the case where unsatisfied order is permanently lost, we need to only modify the definition of C_s to represent lost profit, and the Order-Up-To-Q^* model can still be applied. The corresponding Fig. 3.9 will explain the change. After period 2, the

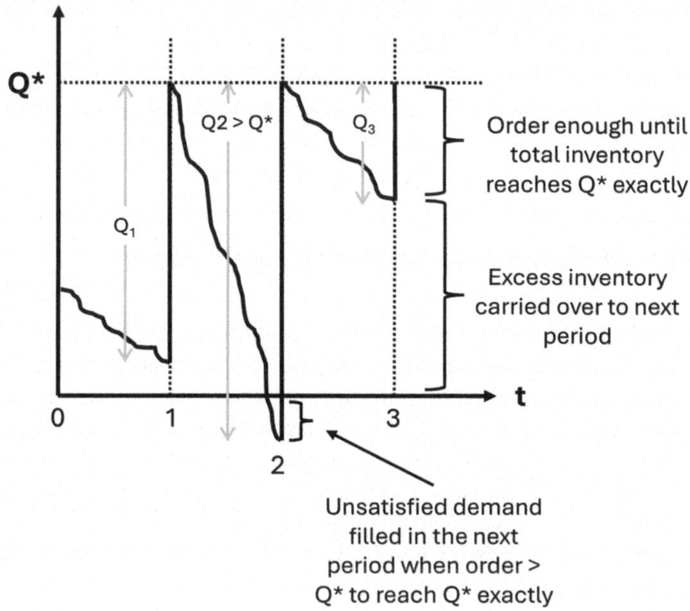

Fig. 3.8 Order-up-to-Q* model with unsatisfied demand satisfied in the next period

Fig. 3.9 Order-up-to-Q* model with unsatisfied demand permanently lost

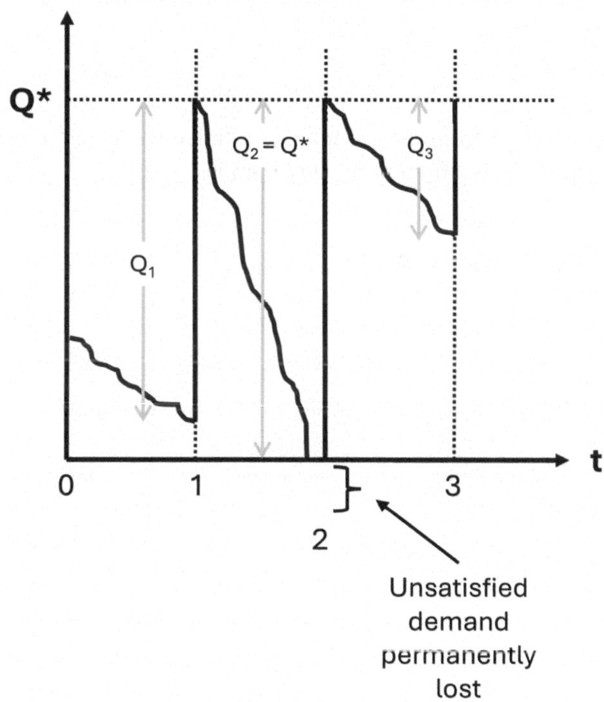

unsatisfied demand will be permanently lost, making $Q_2 = Q^*$. The basic concept is that the order quantity is affected by the inventory carried over from the previous period only. Thus, the order quantity can only be $\leq Q^*$ to bring the inventory on hand up to Q^* level at the start of the next period, assuming zero lead time.

3.4.3 Worked Example for Order-up-to-Q* Model

A bookshop sells a specific assessment book which is ordered monthly. Copies of the assessment book that are unsold at the end of the month will be kept on the shelves for future sales. Assume that the customers who want to buy the assessment books when the bookshop runs out of stock are willing to wait until the following month. The bookshop buys the assessment books for \$11.50 each and sells it for \$14.70. The bookshop estimates that there is cost incurred in maintaining an unsatisfied order to be around \$0.50. The holding cost per unit per month is estimated to be 2% of the cost of goods. The past monthly sales records are given in Table 3.7. Determine Q^*.

Since we do not have the distribution for assessment book demand, we can build the cumulative relative frequency table using the 12-month records, given in Table 3.8.

Let us identify the key parameters in this example.

- Overage cost, C_o = holding cost per unit per month $= 2\% \times \$11.50 = \$0.23$.
- Underage cost, $C_s = \$0.50$.
- Critical ratio $\frac{C_s}{C_o + C_s} = \frac{0.5}{(0.5 + 0.23)} = 0.685$.

Reading from the cumulative relative frequency table, Q^* will be six copies, as 0.685 is in between 0.667 and 0.833.

Table 3.7 Monthly sales data for worked example

Month	1	2	3	4	5	6	7	8	9	10	11	12
Sales	4	6	5	3	3	4	5	5	8	7	6	4

Table 3.8 Cumulative probability table for worked example

Sales quantity	Frequency of occurrence	Probability	Cumulative probability
3	2	2/12	2/12 = 0.167
4	3	3/12	5/12 = 0.417
5	3	3/12	8/12 = 0.667
6	2	2/12	10/12 = 0.833
7	1	1/12	11/12 = 0.917
8	1	1/12	12/12 = 1.0

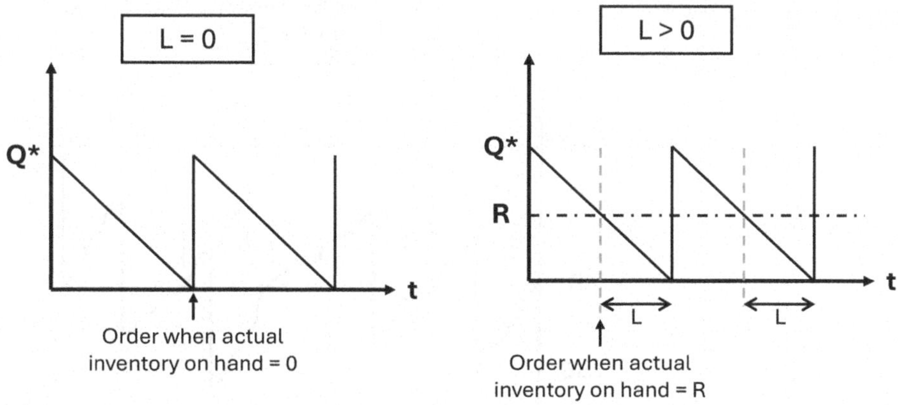

Fig. 3.10 Monitoring actual inventory on hand for deterministic demand

3.5 Actual Inventory On-Hand vs Inventory Position

When demand is deterministic, managing inventory is simple and straightforward as we only need to monitor the actual inventory on hand. As shown in Fig. 3.10, when the lead time is zero ($L = 0$), we will track the actual inventory and order Q^* when the actual inventory reaches zero. However, if the lead time $L > 0$, then we will order Q^* when the actual inventory reaches the reorder point R. The reorder point $R = D \times L$, where D is the deterministic demand rate per period and L is the lead time. The concept is that the amount of inventory R is sufficient to satisfy the demand during lead time L.

When demand is stochastic and delivery lead time is positive ($L > 0$), then we will need to monitor inventory position instead. Inventory position refers to the inventory level that includes both the actual inventory on hand and inventory in transit where the order has been placed but has not arrived. This monitoring or review of inventory position can adopt one of the two review policies, continuous review policy and periodic review policy, which we will cover in the next two sections.

3.6 Continuous Review Policy or (R, Q) Policy

Continuous review policy or (R, Q) policy is suitable for managing expensive items as the monitoring is conducted on a continuous basis. The objective is to order Q^* when the inventory position reaches R, the reorder point. As demand is stochastic, the time period where the inventory position will reach R varies. Thus, the order interval T_j varies for every order j.

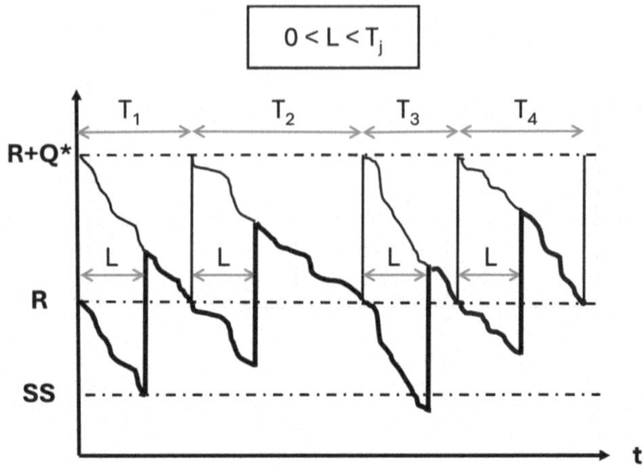

Fig. 3.11 (R, Q) policy for $L < T_j$

Let us look at the first situation where the lead time $L <$ the order interval T_j. In Fig. 3.11, there are three horizontal lines, safety stock level (SS), reorder point (R) and maximum inventory position ($R + Q^*$). There are two sets of curvy lines, where the thicker line represents the actual inventory on hand, while the thinner line represents the inventory position.

At the start, the actual inventory is at R and the inventory position at ($R + Q^*$), assuming that an order of Q^* has been placed but has not arrived. When the inventory gets consumed, both curves will decrease in the same fashion. After lead time L, the ordered quantity Q^* arrives, bringing the actual inventory curve up to meet with the inventory position curve. When inventory position and actual inventory reach R again at time interval T_1, a new order Q^* is placed, and the inventory position rises up to ($R + Q^*$). The cycle repeats itself.

Next, we will look at the situation where the lead time $L >$ the order interval T_j. In Fig. 3.12, we begin with the actual inventory at R and the inventory position at ($R + Q^*$), assuming that an order of Q^* has been placed but has not arrived. When the inventory gets consumed, both curves will decrease in the same fashion. As $L > T_1$, the inventory position reaches R again at time interval T_1, a new order Q^* is placed even before the first order arrives and the inventory position rises up to ($R + Q^*$). However, since L is long, the first ordered quantity has not arrived, the inventory continues to get consumed and both curves will decrease in the same fashion. After lead time L, the first ordered quantity Q^* arrives, bringing the actual inventory curve up. The cycle repeats itself. In this case, it is observed that the actual inventory on hand curve and the inventory position curve do not meet.

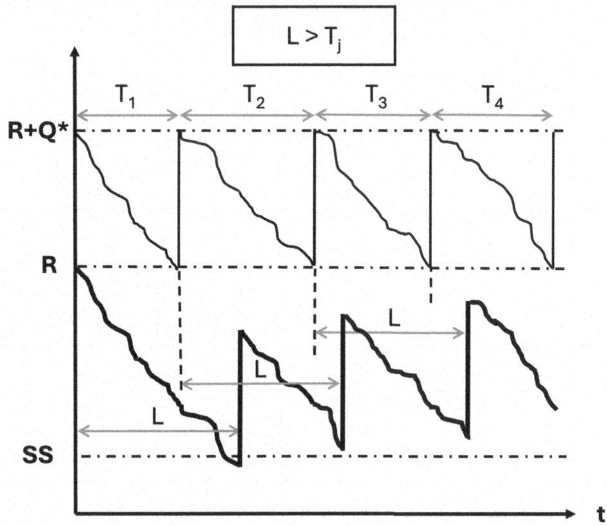

Fig. 3.12 (R, Q) policy for $L > T_j$

3.6.1 *Compute Q* and R*

Now that we have seen how the actual inventory and inventory position change over time, we need to determine Q^* and R. Let us define D_i as the demand at time period i assumed to be independent and identically distributed (i.i.d.) with mean E[D] and standard deviation $\sigma[D]$. Q^* will be computed following the newsvendor model as

$$Q^* = \mu + z\sigma$$

$$Q^* = E[D] + z\sigma[D]$$

To compute R, let us define demand during lead time as DDLT, where the expected demand during lead time $E[DDLT] = L.E[D]$ and the variance for demand during lead time $\sigma^2[DDLT] = L.\ \sigma^2[D]$.

$$DDLT = D_1 + D_2 + \ldots + D_L$$

Since L is positive, R must be sufficient to meet the demand during the lead time. As such, the probability that $DDLT \leq R$ must be equal to the area under the curve given by the critical ratio $\frac{C_s}{C_o + C_s}$. The definitions of C_o and C_s will follow that of the extended newsvendor model for multiple periods.

$$P(\text{DDLT} \leq R) = \frac{C_s}{C_o + C_s}$$

$$P\left(\frac{\text{DDLT} - L.E[D]}{\sqrt{L}.\sigma[D]} \leq \frac{R - L.E[D]}{\sqrt{L}.\sigma[D]}\right) = \frac{C_s}{C_o + C_s}$$

$$P\left(Z \leq \frac{R - L.E[D]}{\sqrt{L}.\sigma[D]}\right) = \frac{C_s}{C_o + C_s}$$

$$\Phi\left(\frac{R - L.E[D]}{\sqrt{L}.\sigma[D]}\right) = \frac{C_s}{C_o + C_s}$$

With the cumulative probability given by the critical ratio as the area under the curve, we can read the value of z from the standard normal table.

$$\Phi(z) = \frac{C_s}{C_o + C_s} \rightarrow \frac{R - L.E[D]}{\sqrt{L}.\sigma[D]} = z$$

Thus,

$$R = L.E[D] + z\sqrt{L}.\sigma[D]$$

$$R = \text{cycle stock} + \text{safety stock}$$

The R formula has two terms where the first term represents the cycle stock and the second term represents the safety stock. In Fig. 3.13, we can see that the safety stock SS is meant for taking care of demand variability indicated by the $\sigma[D]$ term, while the cycle stock is the vertical distance between SS and R, or simply R − SS or L.E[D], meant for taking care of positive lead time L.

3.6.2 *Worked Example for (R, Q) Policy*

RQ Engineering Company keeps stocks for the engineering parts in its workshop to perform repairs and parts replacements for its customers. One of the parts, model X, is a part which has a long ordering lead time of 6 months. RQ does not wish to lose out to competitors because of its own inability to manage the inventory of its parts,

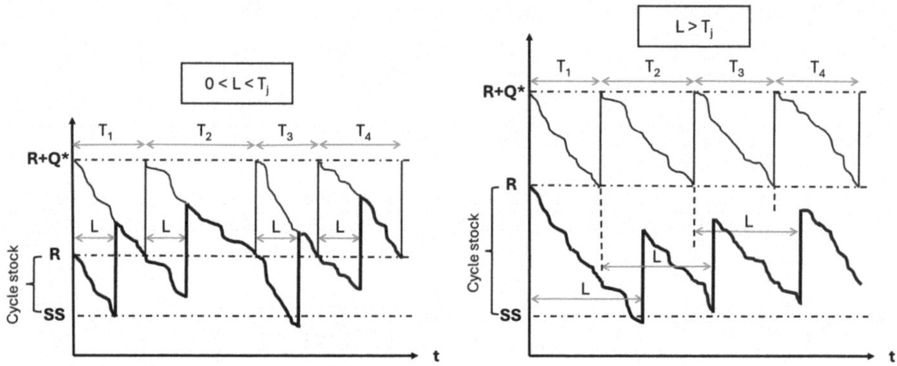

Fig. 3.13 Safety stock and cycle stock for (R, Q) policy

especially for model X. RQ buys the part model X for \$1000 per piece and estimates that the holding cost is about 24% annual interest rate. When it runs out of stock for model X, the customer will go to the competitors, causing a loss of potential profit of \$250. RQ estimates that the ordering cost for model X is about \$50. On average, the number of model X needed per month is 100, and the standard deviation is 25. How should RQ manage the inventory of model X?

Let us identify the key parameters in this example.

- Holding cost per unit per month = 24%/12 × \$1000 = \$16.667.
- Ordering cost = \$50.
- Critical ratio $\frac{C_s}{C_o + C_s} = \frac{250}{(16.667 + 250)} = 0.937$.

Assume that demand is normally distributed, and using Excel function NORMSINV (0.937), we get z = 1.534.

Thus, the optimal order quantity $Q^* = E[D] + z \times \sigma[D] = 100 + 1.534 \times 25 = 138.35$ (approximated to 139).

The reorder point $R = L.E[D] + z\sqrt{L}.\sigma[D] = 6 \times 100 + 1.534 \times (6)^{0.5} \times 25 = 693.9$ (approximated to 694).

3.7 Periodic Review Policy or (S, T) Policy

Periodic review policy or (S, T) policy is suitable for managing lower-value items as the monitoring is conducted on a periodic basis. The objective is to order the quantity needed to bring the inventory position up to the order-up-to-level S, at every fixed reorder time interval T. As demand is stochastic, the amount of inventory leftover after reorder time interval T always changes. Thus, the order quantity Q_j varies for every order j.

Table 3.9 Comparison between (S, T) policy and order-up-to-Q* policy

	(S, T) Policy	Order-up-to-Q* policy
Lead time	Positive lead time	Zero lead time
Safety stock	Variation in demand taken care by safety stock	Does not consider safety stock
Ordering policy	Order at every T interval so that inventory position goes up to S	Order at every period so that actual inventory on hand goes up to Q*

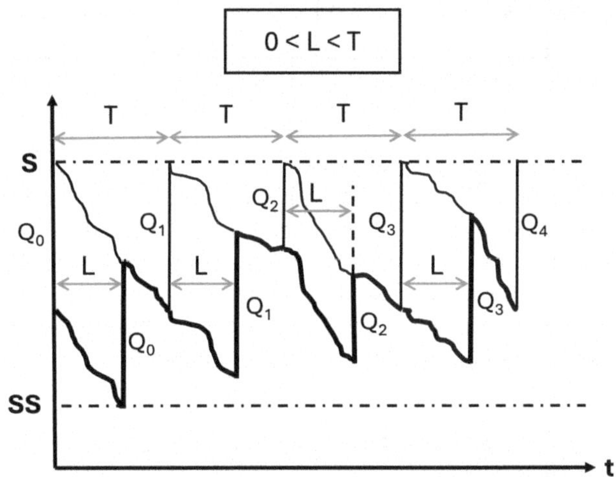

Fig. 3.14 (S, T) policy for L < T

(S, T) policy is quite similar to the Order-up-to-Q* policy. However, there are some differences between them, as given in Table 3.9.

Let us look at the first situation where the lead time L < the reorder interval T. In Fig. 3.14, there are two horizontal lines, safety stock level (SS) and order-up-to-level (S). Similarly, there are two sets of curvy lines, where the thicker line represents the actual inventory on hand, while the thinner line represents the inventory position.

At the start, we begin with the inventory position at S, and an order quantity Q_0 has been placed but has not arrived. When the inventory gets consumed, both curves will decrease in the same fashion. After lead time L, the ordered quantity Q_0 arrives, bringing the actual inventory curve up to meet with the inventory position curve. When the reorder time interval T is reached, a new order Q_1 is placed, and the inventory position rises up to S. The cycle repeats itself.

Next, we will look at the situation where the lead time L > the order interval T. In Fig. 3.15, we begin with the inventory position at S, and an order quantity Q_0 has been placed but has not arrived. When the inventory gets consumed, both curves will decrease in the same fashion. As L > T, the reorder time interval is reached again, a new order Q_1 is placed even before the first order Q_0 arrives and the inventory position rises up to S. However, since L is long, the first ordered quantity Q_0 has not arrived, the inventory continues to get consumed and both curves will decrease in the

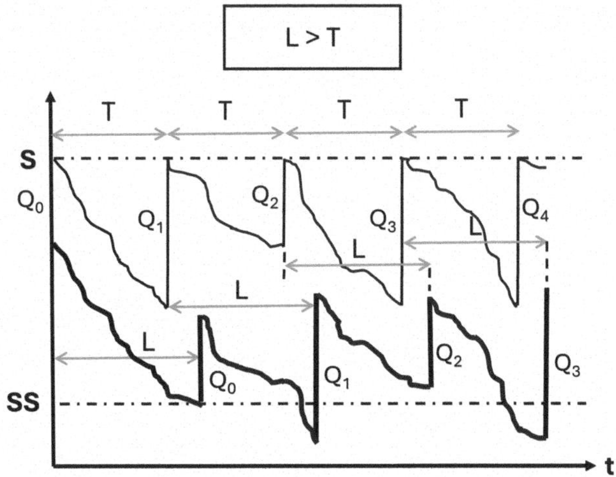

Fig. 3.15 (S, T) policy for L > T

same fashion. After lead time L, the first ordered quantity Q_0 arrives, bringing the actual inventory curve up. The cycle repeats itself. In this case, it is observed that the actual inventory on-hand curve and the inventory position curve do not meet.

3.7.1 *Compute S and T*

Now that we have seen how the actual inventory and inventory position change over time, we need to determine S and T. As previously defined, D_i is the demand at time period i with mean E[D] and standard deviation σ[D].

To compute T, we need to compute Q^* first, which will be computed following the newsvendor model as before. Then,

$$T = \frac{Q^*}{E[D]}$$

To compute S, let us define demand during lead time and reorder time interval as DDLTR, where the expected demand E[DDLTR] = Lr.E[D] and the variance σ^2[DDLTR] = Lr. σ^2[D].

$$DDLTR = D_1 + D_2 + \ldots + D_{Lr}$$

where Lr = L + T.

Since Lr is positive, S must be sufficient to meet the demand during the lead time and reorder time interval. As such, the probability that DDLTR ≤ S must be equal to the area under the curve given by the critical ratio $\frac{C_s}{C_o + C_s}$. Similarly, definitions of C_o and C_s will follow that of the extended newsvendor model for multiple periods.

$$P(\mathrm{DDLTR} \leq S) = \frac{C_s}{C_o + C_s}$$

$$P\left(\frac{\mathrm{DDLTR} - \mathrm{Lr.E[D]}}{\sqrt{\mathrm{Lr}}.\sigma[\mathrm{D}]} \leq \frac{S - \mathrm{Lr.E[D]}}{\sqrt{\mathrm{Lr}}.\sigma[\mathrm{D}]}\right) = \frac{C_s}{C_o + C_s}$$

$$P\left(Z \leq \frac{S - \mathrm{Lr.E[D]}}{\sqrt{\mathrm{Lr}}.\sigma[\mathrm{D}]}\right) = \frac{C_s}{C_o + C_s}$$

$$\Phi\left(\frac{S - \mathrm{Lr.E[D]}}{\sqrt{\mathrm{Lr}}.\sigma[\mathrm{D}]}\right) = \frac{C_s}{C_o + C_s}$$

With the cumulative probability given by the critical ratio as the area under the curve, we can read the value of z from the standard normal table.

$$\Phi(z) = \frac{C_s}{C_o + C_s} \rightarrow \frac{S - \mathrm{Lr.E[D]}}{\sqrt{\mathrm{Lr}}.\sigma[\mathrm{D}]} = z$$

Thus,

$$S = \mathrm{Lr.E[D]} + z\sqrt{\mathrm{Lr}}.\sigma[\mathrm{D}]$$

$$S = \text{cycle stock} + \text{safety stock}$$

We can observe that the S formula is very similar to the R formula, except L is replaced with Lr. Similar to the R formula, the S formula has two terms where the first term represents the cycle stock and the second term represents the safety stock. In Fig. 3.16, we can see that the safety stock SS is meant for taking care of demand variability indicated by the σ[D] term, while the cycle stock is the vertical distance between SS and S, or simply S − SS or Lr.E[D], meant for taking care of positive lead time and reorder time interval.

3.7.2 Worked Example for (S, T) Policy

ST Hardware Shop sells handyman tools, which include hand drills, hammers, nails, screws, drill bits, etc. The screws are inexpensive and come in bags of ten units. As these items are inexpensive, the shop owner intends to monitor their inventory on a

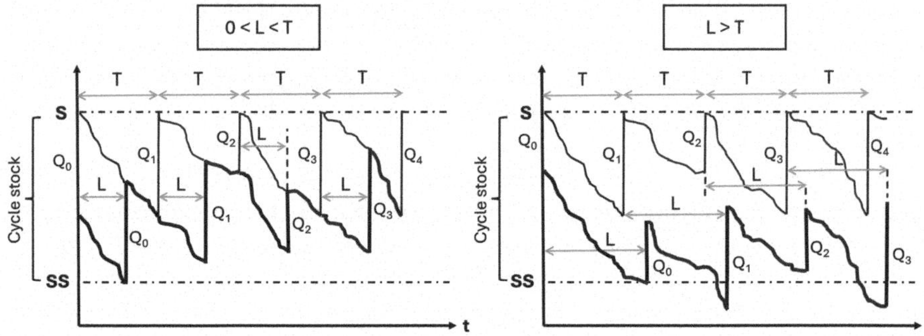

Fig. 3.16 Safety stock and cycle stock for (S, T) policy

monthly basis rather than continuously monitoring them. The demand for screws is about 60 bags per month and has a standard deviation of 5. The cost of each bag is $2, and the shop sells it for $2.50. If the screws run out of stock, customers will just buy from another neighbouring shop. The delivery lead time for screws is 1 week, and the ordering cost is $10 per order. The estimated holding cost per bag per month is 15% annual interest rate. How often should the shop place orders for the screws, and what is the order-up-to-level?

Let us identify the key parameters in this example.

- Holding cost per unit per month = 15%÷12 × $2 = $0.025.
- Ordering cost = $10.
- Critical ratio $\frac{C_s}{C_o + C_s} = \frac{0.50}{(0.025 + 0.50)} = 0.952.$

Assume that demand is normally distributed, and using Excel function NORMSINV(0.952), we get z = 1.668.

Thus, the optimal order quantity $Q^* = E[D] + z \times \sigma[D] = 60 + 1.668 \times 5 = 68.34$. With Q^*, we can compute the reorder time interval $T = Q^*/E[D] = 68.34/60 = 1.14$ months.

We need to determine $Lr = L + T = ¼ + 1.14 = 1.39$ months.

Thus, $S = Lr.E[D] + z\sqrt{Lr}.\sigma[D] = 1.39 \times 60 + 1.668 \times (1.39)^{0.5} \times 5 = 93.17$ (approximated to 94).

3.8 Case 3: Inventory Management of Fast-Moving Consumer Goods

This case is modified from the paper published by Cheong and Choy (2015). In this case, Company IM is an integrated distribution and logistics services provider covering logistics, distribution, manufacturing and international transportation. The logistics and distribution division plays the middleman role to manage the inventory and distribution of fast-moving consumer goods (FMCG) for their brand owners to the retail stores. The FMCG include food items and health and beauty products. The division was often faced with fluctuating orders but still had to try its best to manage the inventory well and deliver the goods on time to maintain contracted service level.

The main challenge stemmed from the lack of point-of-sales (POS) data from the retail stores as the retail store owners were not keen to share them. Some stores placed orders more frequently than others, and the order quantities fluctuated, making it harder to manage inventory and deliveries. To better understand the problem, IM collected 1 year of historical data of the orders from their 148 retailers, which included order date and order quantity. It was found that all the retailers placed orders in a random fashion and did not practise ordering only on a fixed day of the week. Some of them ordered several times a week, while others ordered once a week, once every 2 weeks or once a month.

To ensure that there will be sufficient inventory to meet the demand of all the retailers on different days of the week, IM needed an approximate and yet reliable methodology to anticipate the number of orders that will be placed on each day to compute the expected demand for that specific day of week. The following parameters were defined for the problem:

- i = index for retailer where $i = 1$ to 148.
- j = index for day of week where $j = 1$ to 7.
- N_i = total number of orders by retailer i.
- M_{ij} = total number of orders by retailer i on day j.
- $X_{ij} = M_{ij}/N_i$ = percentage of orders by retailer i that falls on day j.
- k = index of order number. For retailer i, $k = 1$ to N_i.
- Q_{ik} = order quantity for order k by retailer i.
- q_i = average order quantity per week by retailer $i = \frac{7}{365}\sum_{k=1}^{N_i} Q_{ik}$.
- D_i = top order day for retailer i, that is, D_i occurs on day j' where $X_{ij'} = MAX_j(X_{ij})$.
- Z_j = number of retailers with top order day on day j.
- y = index for retailer with top order day on day j, where $y = 1$ to Z_j.
- $\mu_j = \sum_{y=1}^{Z_j} q_y$ = average order quantity per week on top order day j.
- σ_j = standard deviation of average order quantity per week of all retailers with top order day on day j.

Figure 3.17 shows the number of retailers for each day of week based on their top order day. The assumption is that retailer i will only place one order on its top order day per week; thus, the expected total demand for a specific day of week will be the sum of the mean for all the retailers for that day of the week given by μ_j, and the standard deviation is given by σ_j. With σ_j , IM can compute the safety stock to maintain for day j.

Let us map the problem and solution method for this case study against the *data and decision analytics framework* proposed in Chap. 1. As shown in Fig. 3.18, in this case study, the problem faced was fluctuating order quantities by the retailers on different days of the week. Therefore, the right question to ask was "How much

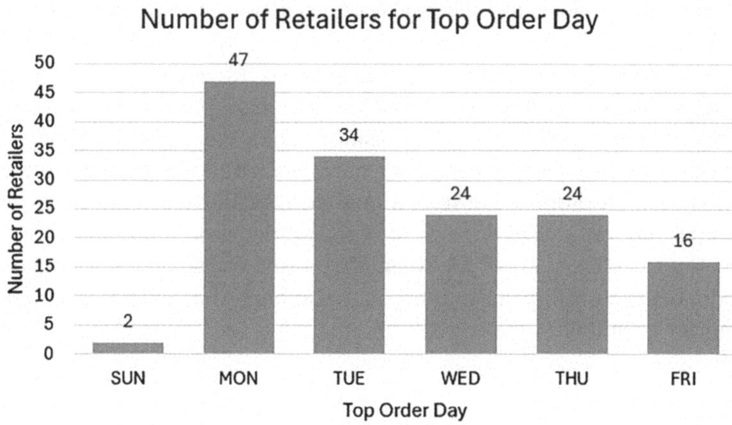

Fig. 3.17 Number of retailers for each top order day

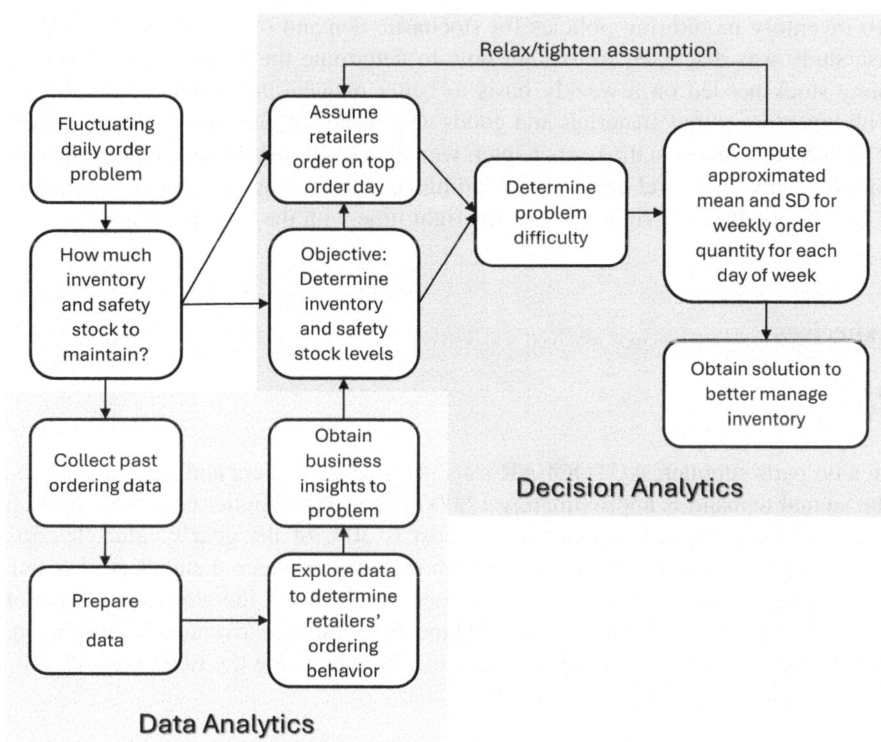

Fig. 3.18 Data and decision analytics framework map for Case 3

inventory and safety stock to maintain for each day of the week?". Next was to collect the relevant data needed to answer the question. With the historical order data collected, the analyst can perform initial analysis to determine if the retailers practised fixed ordering behaviour. From the insights obtained, it was found that retailers placed their orders in a random fashion. Thus, the problem objective would be to determine the expected demand and safety stock on different days of the week. The solution method proposed assumed that each retailer will only place order on their top order day on a weekly basis to compute the expected demand and safety stock to maintain for each day of the week. The result was an inventory management strategy with better visibility and control on the amount of inventory and safety stock to maintain for each day of the week.

3.9 Summary

This chapter covered four inventory ordering policies to take care of deterministic and stochastic demand, for both single-period and multiple-period problems, and two inventory monitoring policies for stochastic demand over multiple periods. A case study was discussed to explain how to determine the average inventory and safety stock needed on a weekly basis to better manage the inventory of FMCG. With inventory of raw materials and goods well managed, the next challenge would be to distribute them. In the next chapter, we will look at distribution management to explore operational level decisions including vehicle routing and vehicle scheduling to deliver goods to the right place at the right time with the right quantities.

Exercises

Q3.1

An auto parts supplier, AUTOGEAR sells gears to car dealers and auto mechanics. The annual demand is approximately 12,000 gears. The supplier pays $25 for each gear, and the estimated annual holding cost is 30% of the gear's value. It costs approximately $50 to place an order (which includes managerial and clerical costs). The supplier currently orders 1000 gears per month. Now, the general manager of AUTOGEAR has decided to use the EOQ model to improve inventory management. How much money can the company save in a year by using the EOQ model?

Q3.2

After some years of development, AUTOGEAR has gained a good reputation in the industry. Now, a famous car dealer, FASTCAR, intends to cooperate with

AUTOGEAR for a long period. Both companies would partner each other in a contract for the next five years. FASTCAR estimates the demand for gears for the next 5 years as given below:

Year	1	2	3	4	5
Demand	200	500	100	500	500

Assume that AUTOGEAR holds zero inventory at the beginning of the contract. AUTOGEAR knows that it can get quantity discounts from its manufacturer according to the discount table below.

Quantity purchased	Discount percentage
1–200	0%
201–500	5%
501–800	10%
801–1000	15%
More than 1000	20%

Other parameters include the holding cost of $2 per unit per period, the ordering cost of $50 and the delivery lead time of one period. That is, for example, if you order in period 1, the inventory will arrive in period 2 in time to satisfy period 2 demand.

Using the Wagner-Whitin procedure, determine the optimal ordering policy for AUTOGEAR, which minimizes the overall costs to satisfy FASTCAR's demand for the next 5 years.

Q3.3

A game arcade has 60 game machines, and gamers insert $1 coins into the machines to play the games. On average, gamers spend about $10 per game machine within 1 hour. Every game machine needs to be switched on, and each machine consumes electricity power at $2 per hour, regardless of whether it is used or idling.

The arcade owner provided the following data for the past year, assuming that they follow a normal distribution.

Month	Total number of hours the 60 machines are generating revenue
1	12,531
2	12,650
3	12,570
4	12,502
5	12,447
6	12,596
7	12,031

(continued)

Month	Total number of hours the 60 machines are generating revenue
8	11,796
9	12,475
10	12,030
11	12,485
12	12,705

(a) Determine the optimal total number of hours the arcade must provide per month for 60 machines to satisfy the demand from the gamers.
(b) Each game machine is switched on for 360 hours per month, ready to be used. However, the arcade owner realized that not all the machines are busy all the time. There will be times when some machines are idling and not generating revenue. He wonders if he can remove some machines from the arcade and free up the space to run a small café. Based on the answer you have obtained for part (a), determine the optimal number of game machines the arcade should have and how many machines can be removed.

Q3.4

An electrical appliance shop specializes in selling only refrigerators and rice cookers. The sales data for the last 12 months is given below.

Month	Refrigerator	Rice cooker
1	5	19
2	4	29
3	2	49
4	1	44
5	1	48
6	1	26
7	1	21
8	3	26
9	2	33
10	2	45
11	2	13
12	5	27

Due to stochastic demand, inventory management was challenging for the shop owner. The owner requested you to assist him to design the best inventory management policy, either (R, Q) or (S, T), he should adopt.

The owner will sell the refrigerators at 20% above the cost price and rice cookers at 10% above the cost price. The average cost of a refrigerator is $1000, while the average cost of a rice cooker is $100. He also charges $50 and $8, respectively, for the delivery of the refrigerator and rice cooker to the customer. We assume that at any one time, one customer will purchase only one refrigerator or one rice cooker, but not both. We also assume that delivery to customers takes zero time.

Due to unpredictable demand, sometimes, he has too many products in his shop, causing his cash to be locked up in his inventory, resulting in losing potential bank interest of 30% per month. At other times, demand is too high, and he runs out of inventory to sell to his customers. He often mitigates such situations by offering free delivery to his customer, if the customer is willing to wait 1 month for the product, since the lead time from his suppliers is 1 month. However, only half of such customers are willing to wait. Determine the optimal ordering policy for each product which minimizes total costs.

References

Cheong, M. L. F., & Choy, J. (2015). Data analysis of retailer orders to improve order distribution. In L. S. Iyer & D. J. Power (Eds.), *Reshaping society through analytics, collaboration, and decision support: Role of business intelligence and social media* (pp. 211–238). Springer. https://doi.org/10.1007/978-3-319-11575-7_15

Herron, D. P. (1967). Inventory management for minimum cost. *Management Science, 14*(4), 219–235.

Hopp, W., & Spearman, M. (2011). *Factory physics* (3rd ed.). McGraw-Hill.

Wagner, H. M., & Whitin, T. M. (1958). Dynamic version of lot size model. *Management Science, 5*(1), 89–96.

Chapter 4
Distribution Management

In a supply chain, goods must be delivered to the right place at the right time in the right quantities. To ensure this, different levels of distribution planning and execution can occur. At the strategic level, the decisions will include the number and locations of the distribution hubs to set up as well as the mode of transport to engage to distribute the goods, which can be via air, sea or land, and if there is international transportation, global transportation route needs to be determined as well. At the tactical level below the strategic level, the decisions will include which suppliers or manufacturers to engage and to coordinate the quantities to order from each of them. At the lowest level, which is the operational level, the decisions will include planning and scheduling of vehicles for last-mile delivery. Readers can refer to Larson and Odoni (1981) for more information.

In this chapter, we will be solving the traveling salesman problem (TSP) and vehicle routing problem (VRP) via two heuristic solution methodologies, namely, the nearest neighbour procedure (NNP) and the Clarke and Wright savings heuristic (C&W). We will briefly discuss vehicle scheduling problem (VSP) before we look at one case study to apply distribution management theory and concept to manage the distribution of finished goods orders on different days of the week for a fast-moving consumer good (FMCG) company.

Learning Outcomes
By the end of this chapter, readers will achieve the following learning outcomes:

- Explain vehicle routing as nodes and arcs.
- Distinguish among TSP, multiple TSP (MTSP) and VRP.
- Appraise NNP and C&W heuristics.
- Apply NNP and C&W heuristics to solve both TSP and MTSP.
- Explain VRP.
- Explore Cluster First, Route Second and Route First, Cluster Second approaches for VRP.
- Discuss vehicle scheduling problem (VSP).

M. L. F. Cheong, Ma Nang Laik, *Data and Decision Analytics for Business Operations*, https://doi.org/10.1007/978-3-031-72255-4_4

- Discuss how distribution management concepts and models are applied in a real-world scenario to distribute fast-moving consumer goods (FMCG) using the *data and decision analytics framework.*

4.1 Vehicle Routing

Vehicle routes are represented as graphical networks which are made up of nodes and arcs as shown in Fig. 4.1. The nodes are locations of pick-up and delivery points with specific information such as demand at that location, time window for delivery, and loading and unloading time needed

The arcs are route segments connecting two nodes, which the vehicle will travel along. Arcs can be directed or non-directed, where a directed arc has strict direction to follow, that is, if the arc is directed from node A to node B, then the vehicle can only travel from node A to node B, and not the other way around. Conversely, non-directed arcs do not have strict directions to follow. On the arcs, information such as time, cost and distance are included.

For vehicle routing problems, the problem size will increase exponentially as the number of nodes increases. For a small problem with 10 nodes, the number of possible routes will be $10! = 3{,}628{,}800$ possible routes. Thus, it is not difficult to appreciate that for a sizable real-world problem, it will take too long to solve. As such, many elegant heuristics were developed to produce good, if not optimal, solutions to vehicle routing problems.

Table 4.1 shows the classification of vehicle routing problems, which depends on the number of vehicles, capacity of the vehicles, with or without depot node and demand at the delivery nodes. We shall explore each type in the subsequent chapters.

Fig. 4.1 Nodes and arcs representations of vehicle routes

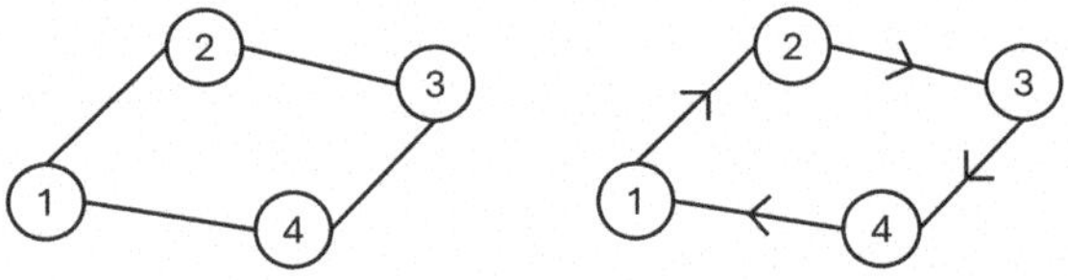

Table 4.1 Classification of vehicle routing problems

Type	Number of depots	Number of vehicles	Vehicle capacity
Traveling salesman problem (TSP)	1	1	Unlimited
Multiple traveling salesman problem (MTSP)	1	>1	Unlimited
Vehicle routing problem (VRP)	1	>1	Limited

4.2 Traveling Salesman Problem

The traveling salesman problem (TSP) is probably one of the most studied problems in management science. For a sizeable problem, most TSPs cannot be solved to optimality; thus, it is known to be an NP-hard problem in combinatorial optimization. We will explore two good heuristics, which can be used to obtain good and feasible solutions.

4.2.1 Nearest Neighbour Procedure

In the nearest neighbour procedure (NNP), the vehicle tour is built by selecting the next node based on the lowest cost or shortest distance from the last visited node. The steps are relatively simple, which generates a good and feasible solution very quickly. While the solution is not guaranteed to be optimal due to its myopic selection step, which looks at only one step ahead instead of looking at the overall picture of all the steps ahead, it can be quite close to the optimal solution. The steps are given as follows:

1. Start at the depot node.
2. Find the next node, which is the lowest cost or shortest distance from the depot node, and add it to the tour.
3. Find the next node, which is the lowest cost or shortest distance from the last node, and add it to the tour.
4. Repeat step 3 until all nodes have been added to the tour.
5. Connect the last node added to the depot node.

Table 4.2 shows a problem with six nodes, and the distance between each node is given as a symmetrical distance matrix. Assume node 1 is the depot. What would be the tour using NNP?

Using NNP, the tour would be:

- Start at Node 1 (depot node), select Node 3 (2.7).
- From Node 3, select Node 6 (3.5).
- From Node 6, select Node 2 (8.4).

Table 4.2 Six-node problem

	Node 1	Node 2	Node 3	Node 4	Node 5	Node 6
Node 1		5.3	2.7	10.4	8.1	4.0
Node 2	5.3		4.9	9.4	4.9	8.4
Node 3	2.7	4.9		7.7	5.9	3.5
Node 4	10.4	9.4	7.7		5.0	9.5
Node 5	8.1	4.9	5.9	5.0		9.1
Node 6	4.0	8.4	3.5	9.5	9.1	

- From Node 2, select Node 5 (4.9).
- From Node 5, select Node 4 (5.0).
- Since Node 4 is the last node, return to Node 1 (10.4).

The tour will be given as 1 → 3 → 6 → 2 → 5 → 4 → 1, and the total distance traveled will be 2.7 + 3.5 + 8.4 + 4.9 + 5.0 + 10.4 = 34.9. Is this tour optimal? Are we able to find a shorter tour?

Let us try to defy NNP and start with selecting Node 2 in the first step and see how the result would change.

- Start at Node 1 (depot node), select Node 2 (5.3).
- From Node 2, select Node 5 (4.9).
- From Node 5, select Node 4 (5.0).
- From Node 4, select Node 3 (7.7).
- From Node 3, select Node 6 (3.5).
- Since Node 6 is the last node, return to Node 1 (4.0).

The new tour will be given as 1 → 2 → 5 → 4 → 3 → 6 → 1, and the total distance traveled will be 5.3 + 4.9 + 5.0 + 7.7 + 3.5 + 4.0 = 30.4, which is a shorter tour! Thus, we can conclude that NNP cannot guarantee optimality, and it will be impossible to enumerate all the possible tours to find the optimal solution for a large problem.

4.2.2 Clarke and Wright Savings Heuristic

Consider a three-node network where the distances between two nodes are given in Table 4.3.

For n nodes, we will start with (n − 1) vehicles. Here, we will have two vehicles, one to travel between Node 1 and Node 2 back and forth, and the other between Node 1 and Node 3 back and forth as shown in Fig. 4.2. The total distance travelled will be = 2 × 12 + 2 × 8 = 40.

Table 4.3 Three-node problem

	Node 1	Node 2	Node 3
Node 1		12	8
Node 2	12		6
Node 3	8	6	

Fig. 4.2 Three-node network with two vehicles

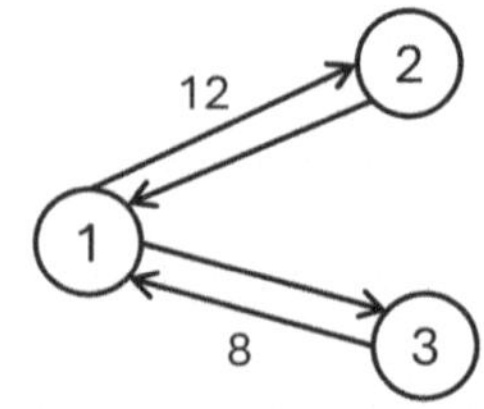

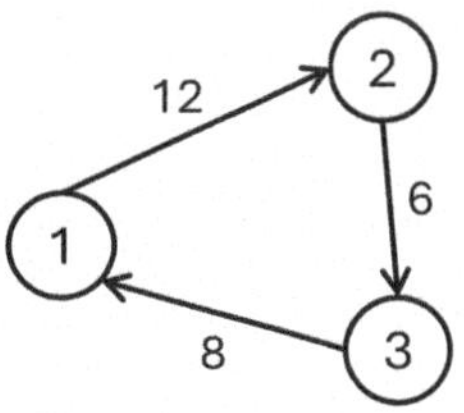

Fig. 4.3 Three-node network with one vehicle

Table 4.4 Six-node problem

	Node 1	Node 2	Node 3	Node 4	Node 5	Node 6
Node 1		5.3	2.7	10.4	8.1	4.0
Node 2	5.3		4.9	9.4	4.9	8.4
Node 3	2.7	4.9		7.7	5.9	3.5
Node 4	10.4	9.4	7.7		5.0	9.5
Node 5	8.1	4.9	5.9	5.0		9.1
Node 6	4.0	8.4	3.5	9.5	9.1	

If we link Node 2 and Node 3 in Fig. 4.3, then we can save the return trip for both vehicles and remove one vehicle. The total distance travelled will be = 12 + 6 + 8 = 26, a savings of 14. Thus, savings obtained by linking Node 2 and Node 3, denoted as $S_{23} = 12 + 8 - 6 = 14$.

The Clarke and Wright (C&W) savings heuristic computes the savings using this formula:

$$S_{ij} = C_{1i} + C_{1j} - C_{ij} \quad \forall i, j = 2, 3, \ldots, n, i \neq j$$

In the example above, we have

$$S_{23} = C_{12} + C_{13} - C_{23} \quad i = 2, j = 3$$

Therefore, the C&W heuristic builds the tour by linking pairs of nodes by removing one vehicle to achieve the most savings in terms of cost or distance, until a single vehicle is left and all nodes are linked. The steps for C&W are as follows:

1. Start at the depot node.
2. Compute the savings S_{ij} for linking node i to node j for all the nodes.
3. Rank the savings from the largest to the smallest.
4. Start from the largest savings node, and form the tour by linking appropriate nodes.
5. Repeat step 4 until a complete tour is formed.

Let us solve the same six-node problem given in Table 4.4.

1. There are six nodes, so we start with five vehicles, and Node 1 is the depot.
2. Compute the savings for all the nodes.

$$S_{23} = C_{12} + C_{13} - C_{23} = 5.3 + 2.7 - 4.9 = 3.1$$

$$S_{24} = C_{12} + C_{14} - C_{24} = 5.3 + 10.4 - 9.4 = 6.3$$

$$S_{25} = C_{12} + C_{15} - C_{25} = 5.3 + 8.1 - 4.9 = 8.5$$

$$S_{26} = C_{12} + C_{16} - C_{26} = 5.3 + 4.0 - 8.4 = 0.9$$

$$S_{34} = C_{13} + C_{14} - C_{34} = 2.7 + 10.4 - 7.7 = 5.4$$

$$S_{35} = C_{13} + C_{15} - C_{35} = 2.7 + 8.1 - 5.9 = 4.9$$

$$S_{36} = C_{13} + C_{16} - C_{36} = 2.7 + 4.0 - 3.5 = 3.2$$

$$S_{45} = C_{14} + C_{15} - C_{45} = 10.4 + 8.1 - 5.0 = 13.5$$

$$S_{46} = C_{14} + C_{16} - C_{46} = 10.4 + 4.0 - 9.5 = 4.9$$

$$S_{56} = C_{15} + C_{16} - C_{56} = 8.1 + 4.0 - 9.1 = 3.0$$

3. Rank the savings from the largest to the smallest.

$$S_{45} = C_{14} + C_{15} - C_{45} = 10.4 + 8.1 - 5.0 = 13.5$$

$$S_{25} = C_{12} + C_{15} - C_{25} = 5.3 + 8.1 - 4.9 = 8.5$$

$$S_{24} = C_{12} + C_{14} - C_{24} = 5.3 + 10.4 - 9.4 = 6.3$$

$$S_{34} = C_{13} + C_{14} - C_{34} = 2.7 + 10.4 - 7.7 = 5.4$$

$$S_{35} = C_{13} + C_{15} - C_{35} = 2.7 + 8.1 - 5.9 = 4.9$$

$$S_{46} = C_{14} + C_{16} - C_{46} = 10.4 + 4.0 - 9.5 = 4.9$$

$$S_{36} = C_{13} + C_{16} - C_{36} = 2.7 + 4.0 - 3.5 = 3.2$$

$$S_{23} = C_{12} + C_{13} - C_{23} = 5.3 + 2.7 - 4.9 = 3.1$$

$$S_{56} = C_{15} + C_{16} - C_{56} = 8.1 + 4.0 - 9.1 = 3.0$$

$$S_{26} = C_{12} + C_{16} - C_{26} = 5.3 + 4.0 - 8.4 = 0.9$$

4. Link the largest savings to the tour, and repeat until a complete tour is formed.
   - Since S_{45} is the largest, we will get 1→4→5→1.
   - Next is S_{25}; we will get 1→4→5→2→1.
   - Next is S_{24}; but both 2 and 4 are already linked, so we will ignore S_{24}.
   - Next is S_{34}; we will get 1→3→4→5→2→1.
   - Next is S_{35} or S_{46} as both of them have the same savings of 4.9. S_{35} will not be used as both 3 and 5 are already linked, so we will consider S_{46}. But to link Node 6, we will have to break up the link between Node 4 and Node 5, which will forgo a higher saving S_{45}. So, we will ignore S_{46}.

- Next is S_{36}; we will get 1→6→3→4→5→2→1, and this is the complete tour.

The total distance traveled will be 4.0 + 3.5 + 7.7 + 5.0 + 4.9 + 5.3 = 30.4, which is the same distance as the tour 1 → 2 → 5 → 4 → 3 → 6 → 1 obtained using NNP in the second attempt, except the tour direction is reversed. In general, the C&W heuristic yields a better result as compared to NNP, as C&W considers all savings when making the selection.

4.3 Multiple Traveling Salesman Problem

The multiple traveling salesman problem (MTSP) is a generalized TSP where we allow more than one vehicle. The objective is to construct tours for multiple vehicles. To do so, we will transform the MTSP into multiple TSP sub-problems, and solve each sub-problem separately, using any heuristic. So, the steps are:

1. For m vehicles, copy the depot m times to create m separate TSP sub-problems.
2. Solve each TSP using NNP or C&W.

Let us look at a larger problem with ten nodes as given in Table 4.5. We will route Vehicle 1 through Nodes 2 to 5 and route Vehicle 2 through Nodes 6 to 10, assuming Node 1 is the same depot for both vehicles. The allocation of the nodes to the two vehicles can be based on geographical location proximity.

Using NNP, we will solve the two sub-problems as follows:

- For Vehicle 1, the tour will be 1→2→4→3→5→1, and the total distance travelled = 22 + 22 + 22 + 36 + 32 = 134.
- For Vehicle 2, the tour will be 1→6→9→8→7→10→1, and the total distance travelled = 14 + 32 + 32 + 20 + 71 + 35 = 204.
- Total distance travelled for two tours = 134 + 204 = 338.

Using C&W, we will first compute the savings for all the nodes as follows:

Table 4.5 Ten-node MTSP problem

Node	1	2	3	4	5	6	7	8	9	10
1		22	22	32	32	14	45	56	51	35
2	22		32	22	54	36	67	78	67	41
3	22	32		22	36	41	42	67	70	64
4	32	22	22		56	51	71	86	83	63
5	32	54	36	56		32	10	32	45	54
6	14	36	41	51	32		40	45	32	32
7	45	67	42	71	10	40		20	42	71
8	56	78	67	86	32	45	20		32	71
9	51	67	70	83	45	32	42	32		45
10	35	41	64	63	54	32	71	71	45	

- For Vehicle 1, the savings for Nodes 2 to 5 are

$$S_{23} = C_{12} + C_{13} - C_{23} = 22 + 22 - 32 = 12$$
$$S_{24} = C_{12} + C_{14} - C_{24} = 22 + 32 - 22 = 32$$
$$S_{25} = C_{12} + C_{15} - C_{25} = 22 + 32 - 54 = 0$$
$$S_{34} = C_{13} + C_{14} - C_{34} = 22 + 32 - 22 = 32$$
$$S_{35} = C_{13} + C_{15} - C_{35} = 22 + 32 - 36 = 18$$
$$S_{45} = C_{14} + C_{15} - C_{45} = 32 + 32 - 56 = 8$$

Ranking the savings from largest to smallest, we get

$$S_{24} = C_{12} + C_{14} - C_{24} = 22 + 32 - 22 = 32$$
$$S_{34} = C_{13} + C_{14} - C_{34} = 22 + 32 - 22 = 32$$
$$S_{35} = C_{13} + C_{15} - C_{35} = 22 + 32 - 36 = 18$$
$$S_{23} = C_{12} + C_{13} - C_{23} = 22 + 22 - 32 = 12$$
$$S_{45} = C_{14} + C_{15} - C_{45} = 32 + 32 - 56 = 8$$
$$S_{25} = C_{12} + C_{15} - C_{25} = 22 + 32 - 54 = 0$$

So, the tour will be 1→2→4→3→5→1, which is the same as that given by NNP.

- For Vehicle 2, the savings for Nodes 6 to 10 are

$$S_{67} = C_{16} + C_{17} - C_{67} = 14 + 45 - 40 = 19$$
$$S_{68} = C_{16} + C_{18} - C_{68} = 14 + 56 - 45 = 25$$
$$S_{69} = C_{16} + C_{19} - C_{69} = 14 + 51 - 32 = 33$$
$$S_{610} = C_{16} + C_{110} - C_{610} = 14 + 35 - 32 = 17$$
$$S_{78} = C_{17} + C_{18} - C_{78} = 45 + 56 - 20 = 81$$
$$S_{79} = C_{17} + C_{19} - C_{79} = 45 + 51 - 42 = 54$$
$$S_{710} = C_{17} + C_{110} - C_{710} = 45 + 35 - 71 = 9$$
$$S_{89} = C_{18} + C_{19} - C_{89} = 56 + 51 - 32 = 75$$
$$S_{810} = C_{18} + C_{110} - C_{810} = 56 + 35 - 71 = 20$$
$$S_{910} = C_{19} + C_{110} - C_{910} = 51 + 35 - 45 = 41$$

Ranking the savings from largest to smallest, we get

$$S_{78} = C_{17} + C_{18} - C_{78} = 45 + 56 - 20 = 81$$
$$S_{89} = C_{18} + C_{19} - C_{89} = 56 + 51 - 32 = 75$$
$$S_{79} = C_{17} + C_{19} - C_{79} = 45 + 51 - 42 = 54$$
$$S_{910} = C_{19} + C_{110} - C_{910} = 51 + 35 - 45 = 41$$
$$S_{69} = C_{16} + C_{19} - C_{69} = 14 + 51 - 32 = 33$$
$$S_{68} = C_{16} + C_{18} - C_{68} = 14 + 56 - 45 = 25$$
$$S_{810} = C_{18} + C_{110} - C_{810} = 56 + 35 - 71 = 20$$
$$S_{67} = C_{16} + C_{17} - C_{67} = 14 + 45 - 40 = 19$$
$$S_{610} = C_{16} + C_{110} - C_{610} = 14 + 35 - 32 = 17$$
$$S_{710} = C_{17} + C_{110} - C_{710} = 45 + 35 - 71 = 9$$

So, the tour will be 1→6→7→8→9→10→1, and the total distance travelled = 14 + 40 + 20 + 32 + 45 + 35 = 186.

Combining the total distance travelled for two tours = 134 + 186 = 320, which is less than that given by NNP. Again, it is illustrated here that in general, C&W will give better results than NNP.

4.4 Vehicle Routing Problem

The vehicle routing problem (VRP) extends the MTSP to consider service requirements at each node, for example, the demand at each node, and consider the capacity limit of the vehicle. Thus, the objective is to obtain the best route that will minimize the total cost or total distance while satisfying the vehicle capacity constraint. To solve a VRP, we can consider one of the two approaches:

- Cluster First, Route Second
- Route First, Cluster Second

4.4.1 Cluster First, Route Second Approach

This approach is most suitable when there are physical barriers like rivers, mountains or simply different towns or cities, which create clear segmentation. Therefore, it will make logical sense to cluster nodes which are in the same town or city or within the same region separated from other regions due to the physical barriers. To use this approach, it is necessary to lay out the nodes on a map to assist the clustering decision.

The steps are:

1. For m vehicles, begin by forming m clusters considering the capacity constraints as much as possible.
2. Some clusters may have bad tours that end up violating the capacity constraints of their assigned vehicles.
3. For such clusters, improve the bad tours by identifying potential nodes to remove to resolve the capacity violations and inserting the identified nodes to a nearby good tour. In doing so, the total tour length may be improved. Note that the potential nodes are selected based on their proximity to the good tour.
4. Compute the insertion costs for all potential nodes using the nearest neighbour insertion (NNI) formula:

$$I_{ij} = C_{ik} + C_{jk} - C_{ij} \quad \forall i, j, i \neq j$$

Where k is the potential node to be inserted between two nodes i and j.

5. If there are a few possible insertions, choose the one with the lowest cost of insertion.
6. Insert node k into the good tour if the overall tour length can be improved without violating the capacity constraint of the good tour and yet resolving the capacity constraint of the bad tour.

Let us work on an example in Fig. 4.4 with 12 nodes and two vehicles, where Vehicle 1 has a capacity limit of 45 tons, while Vehicle 2 has a capacity limit of

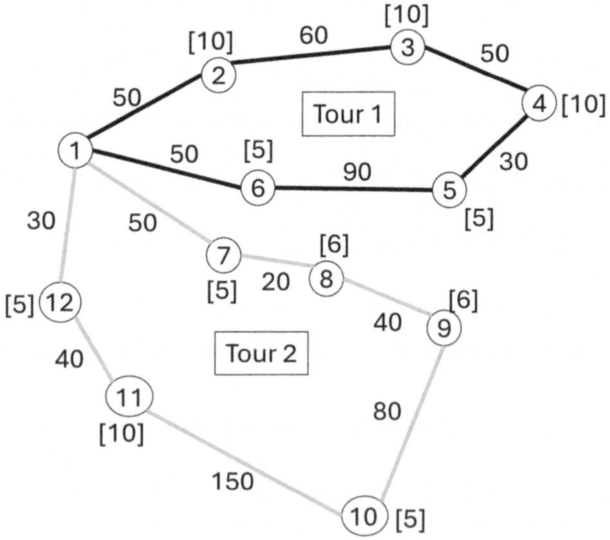

Fig. 4.4 Cluster First, Route Second example

35 tons. Laying out the 12 nodes on a map, we can form the tours using either NNP or C&W, and the tour lengths are:

- Vehicle 1 = 50 + 60 + 50 + 30 + 90 + 50 = 330.
- Vehicle 2 = 50 + 20 + 40 + 80 + 150 + 40 + 30 = 410.
- Total tour length = 330 + 410 = 740.

Next, we will compute the weight carried by each vehicle to determine if there are any capacity violations. The numbers in [ ] at each node denote the demand at each node. The weight carried by Vehicle 1 = 10 + 10 + 10 + 5 + 5 = 40 tons, which is within the capacity limit of Vehicle 1. For Vehicle 2, the weight carried = 5 + 6 + 6 + 5 + 10 + 5 = 37 tons, which exceeds the capacity limit of Vehicle 2. Therefore, we need to identify one node to remove from Tour 2 to insert into Tour 1. Based on the proximity to Tour 1, Nodes 7 and 8 are potential nodes to be considered since they are closest to Tour 1.

Assessing Nodes 7 and 8, only Node 7 can be inserted into Tour 1 as it has a demand of 5 tons, which will not violate the capacity limit of Vehicle 1 if inserted into Tour 1. Node 7 can be inserted between Nodes 1 and 6 or between Nodes 6 and 5. The distance between Node 6 and Node 7 is 30, while between Node 7 and Node 5 is 50. Let us compute the cost of inserting Node 7 into Tour 1, considering both options. In Fig. 4.5, the insertion cost to insert Node 7 ($k = 7$) between Nodes 1 and 6 ($i = 1, j = 6$) will be

$$I_{16} = C_{17} + C_{67} - C_{16} = 50 + 30 - 50 = 30$$

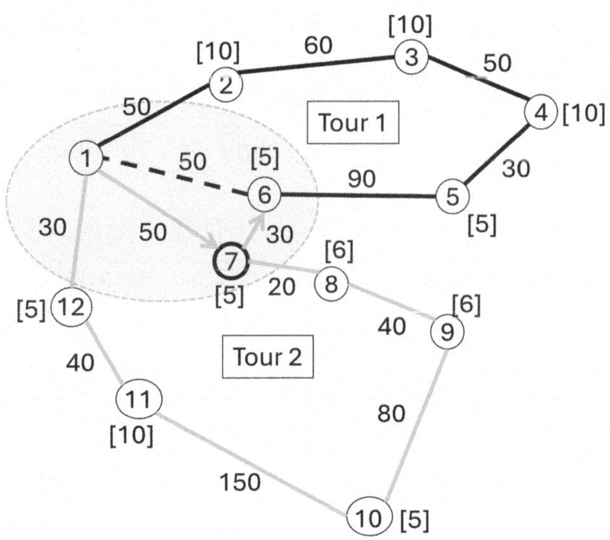

Fig. 4.5 Insert Node 7 between Node 1 and Node 6

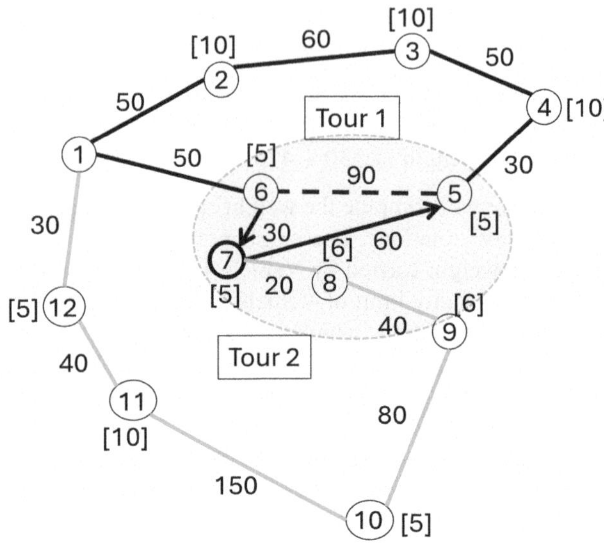

Fig. 4.6 Insert Node 7 between Node 6 and Node 5

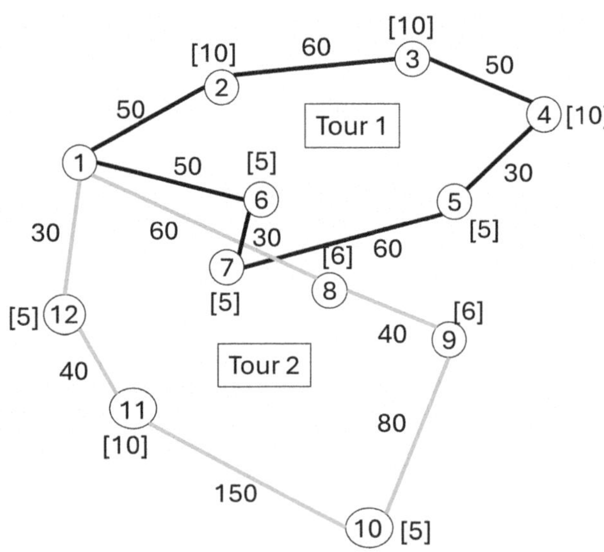

Fig. 4.7 New tours after inserting Node 7 between Node 6 and Node 5

In Fig. 4.6, the insertion cost to insert Node 7 (k = 7) between Nodes 6 and 5 (i = 6, j = 5) will be

$$I_{56} = C_{57} + C_{67} - C_{56} = 60 + 30 - 90 = 0$$

Comparing the insertion costs, inserting Node 7 between Node 6 and Node 5 will be the better option as shown in Fig. 4.7. With the distance between Node 1 and Node 8 given as 60, the new tour lengths are:

- Vehicle 1 = 50 + 60 + 50 + 30 + 60 + 30 + 50 = 330.
- Vehicle 2 = 60 + 40 + 80 + 150 + 40 + 30 = 400.
- Total tour length = 330 + 400 = 730 (a reduction of 10).

The weight carried by Vehicle 1 = 10 + 10 + 10 + 5 + 5 + 5 = 45 tons, which is within the capacity limit of Vehicle 1. For Vehicle 2, the weight carried = 6 + 6 + 5 + 10 + 5 = 32 tons, which is also within the capacity limit of Vehicle 2. Since the tour length is improved and there are no more capacity violations, we need not repeat the steps, and we can stop the procedure here.

4.4.2 Route First, Cluster Second Approach

This approach is most suitable when nodes are dispersed evenly, and there are no clear boundaries to cluster nodes together. The steps are:

1. Construct a large single tour using only one vehicle using either NNP or C&W.
2. If the vehicle capacity constraint is violated, partition the single tour into smaller feasible tours using the required number of vehicles, until all nodes are served.

For example, in Fig. 4.8, there are ten nodes, and the good and feasible single tour is just simply 1→2→3→4→5→6→7→8→9→10→1, and it violates the vehicle capacity constraint, assuming each vehicle has a capacity limit of 30 tons.

We can split this single tour by starting with adding the nodes to new tours according to the node sequence in the original tour as shown in Fig. 4.9.

- We add Nodes 1→2→3→4→1 to Vehicle 1, and the weight carried is = 10 + 10 + 10 = 30. If we were to add Node 5, the capacity constraint of Vehicle 1 would be violated, so we should stop.

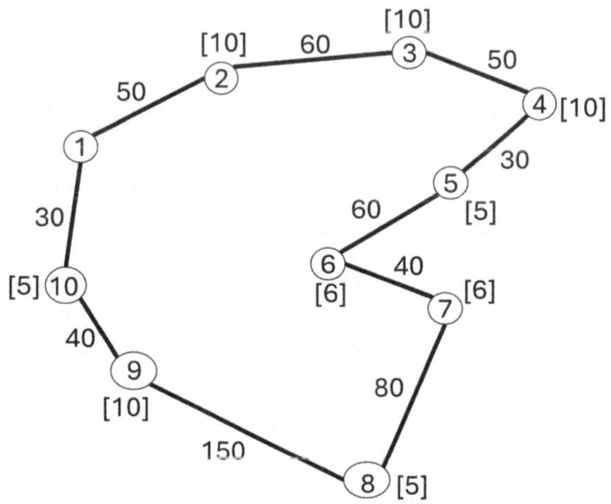

Fig. 4.8 Route First, Cluster Second approach example

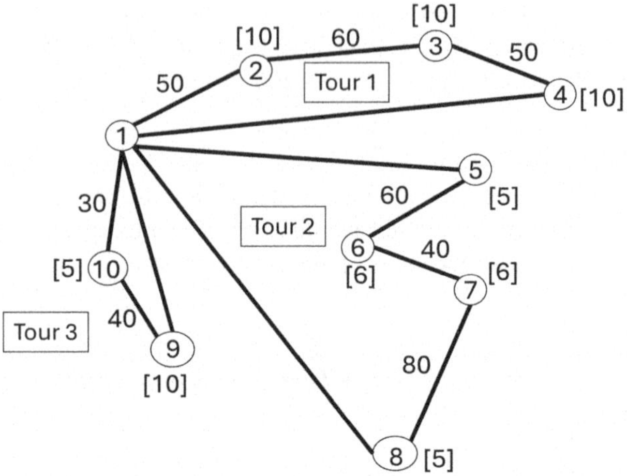

Fig. 4.9 Route First, Cluster Second approach example solution

- Then we start Vehicle 2 and add Nodes 1→5→6→7→8→1, and the weight carried is = 5 + 6 + 6 + 5 = 22. If we were to add Node 9 to Vehicle 2, the capacity constraint of Vehicle 2 would be violated, so we should stop.
- Then we start with Vehicle 3 and add Nodes 1→9→10→1, and the weight carried is = 10 + 5 = 15. Since all nodes are visited, the tours are completed.

4.5 Vehicle Scheduling

Up to this point, we have discussed how to construct tours which minimize the total cost or distance travelled by the vehicles, with and without consideration of the vehicle capacity. These problems are known as the traveling salesman problem (TSP) and the vehicle routing problem (VRP).

When there is a delivery-time restriction, we go beyond TSP and VRP and move into the vehicle scheduling problem (VSP). Time restrictions can be specified as:

- One-sided time window—e.g. no later than 9 a.m., no earlier 4 p.m.
- Two-sided time window—e.g. between 11 a.m. and 1 p.m.

To handle such time restrictions when scheduling vehicles, we need to consider additional time related data including:

- Depot opening time—to facilitate the earliest vehicle route start time
- Depot closing time—to ensure that the vehicles will return to the depot on time
- Customer's start time—to ensure that vehicle does not arrive before the start time
- Customer's end time—to ensure that vehicle does not arrive after the end time

To plan such complex schedule, heuristic algorithms are usually programmed to create a good and feasible schedule that can satisfy vehicle capacity constraint and time restrictions constraint while minimizing total cost or maximizing vehicle capacity utilization. We will discuss heuristic algorithms in Chap. 9.

4.6 Case 4: Distribution Management of Fast-Moving Consumer Goods

This is a continuation of the previous case study Case 3, which was based on the paper published by Cheong and Choy (2015). In this section, we will look at the distribution challenge of FMCG faced by IM. After determining the inventory levels to meet the fluctuating demands on different days of the week, there is a need to ensure that distribution of the orders will also be on time. While we have determined the number of retailers for each day of the week based on their top order day as given in Fig. 4.10, the challenge of distributing fluctuating orders on different days of the week remained. IM would need to maintain a fleet of trucks to meet the high number of deliveries on Monday and leave many of the trucks idle on the other days of the week.

To understand how to manage the deliveries better, IM will infer each retailer's ordering behaviour, whether they placed order based on periodic review or continuous review. The following parameters were defined for the problem:

- i = index for retailer where $i = 1$ to 148.
- j = index for weekday where $j = 1$ to 7.
- N_i = total number of orders by retailer i.
- M_{ij} = total number of orders by retailer i on day j.
- $X_{ij} = M_{ij}/N_i$ = percentage of orders by retailer i that falls on day j.

Consider ordering on a specific day j of interest as success, thus the probability of success $p = 1/7$ since there are 7 days of the week. We can determine the PMF and CDF for a binomial distribution with number of trials = 7, given in Table 4.6.

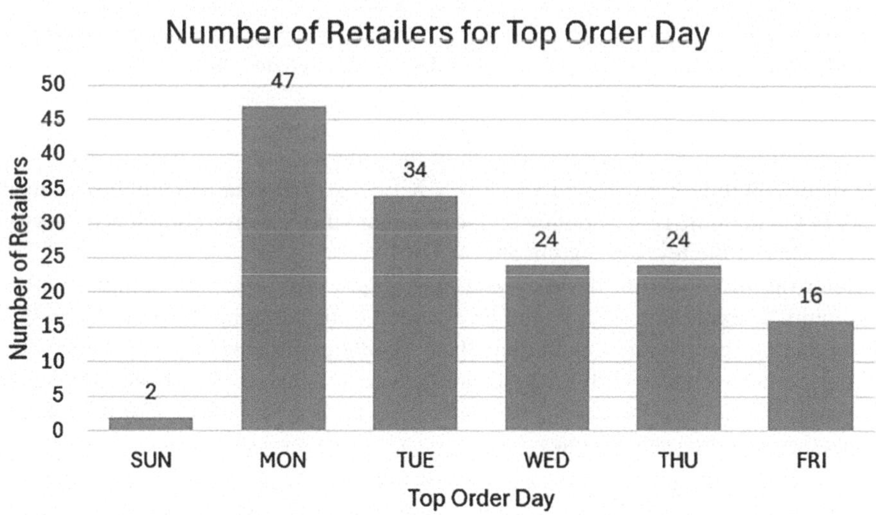

Fig. 4.10 Number of retailers for each top order day

Table 4.6 PMF and CDF for binomial distribution ~ (7, 1/7)

Number of successes	Percentage of occurrences	PMF	CDF	$\alpha\% = 1 - \text{CDF}$
0	0	0.3399	0.3399	0.6601
1	1/7 = 14.3	0.3966	0.7365	0.2635
2	2/7 = 28.6	0.1983	0.9348	0.0652
3	3/7 = 42.9	0.0551	0.9898	0.0102
4	4/7 = 57.1	0.0092	0.9990	0.0010
5	5/7 = 71.4	0.0009	0.9999	0.0001
6	6/7 = 85.7	0.0001	1.0000	0
7	7/7 = 100	0	1.0000	0

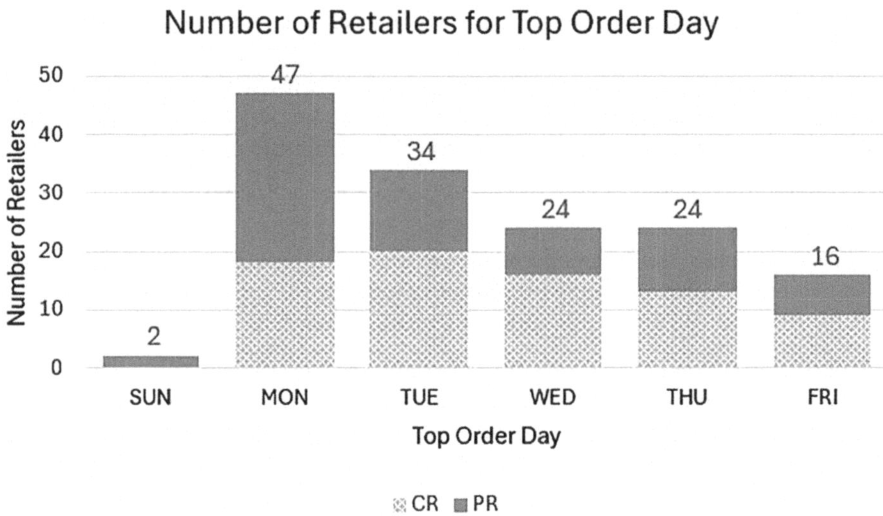

Fig. 4.11 Number of retailers for each top order day based on inferred PR and CR

A classification rule was devised to infer the ordering policy of each retailer. The rule states that if there exists a $MAX_j(X_{ij}) > X_{cut-off}$, then retailer i will be assumed to adopt the periodic review policy on the dominant day j, with a confidence interval of $(1 - \alpha)\%$ at the level of significance $\alpha\%$.

Referring to Table 4.6, if we choose $X_{cut-off} = 40\%$, then any retailer with a maximum X_{ij} exceeding 40% would be assumed to be adopting the periodic review policy on that specific day j, with more than 93.48% confidence that the observation did not occur by chance with level of significance less than 6.52%. Naturally, when the value of $X_{cut-off}$ increases, we would have higher confidence that the retailer adopts the periodic review policy.

After applying the classification rule using $X_{cut-off} = 40\%$, we obtained Fig. 4.11, which shows the number of retailers who adopted the periodic review (PR) policy versus those who adopted the continuous review (CR) policy. We could

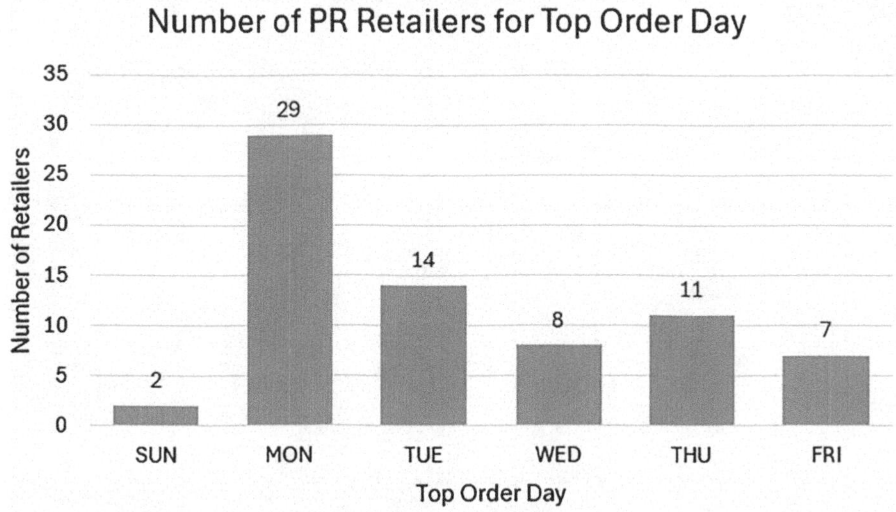

Fig. 4.12 Number of PR retailers for each top order day

see that the number of CR retailers was almost consistent from Monday to Friday, and they formed the base load of orders on these days. The number of PR retailers fluctuated wildly from 2 on Sunday to a high of 29 on Monday as shown in Fig. 4.12. This implied that it was the PR retailers who caused the fluctuations in orders. To have a more effective delivery system, there was a need to smoothen out the orders, to reduce the number of delivery trucks needed.

One suggestion would be to split the Monday PR retailers into two groups, where group 1 will receive their orders on odd week Mondays, while group two will receive their orders on even week Mondays. The split of the Monday PR retailers can be done via Cluster First, Route Second approach described in Sect. 4.4.1, and the split can be visualized in Fig. 4.13 using Google Earth.

Let us map the problem and solution method for this case study against the *data and decision analytics framework* proposed in Chap. 1. As shown in Fig. 4.14, in this case study, the problem faced was fluctuating number of orders by the retailers on different days of the week. Therefore, the right question to ask was "How to deliver on time for each day of the week with fewer trucks?". Next was to collect the relevant data, which will be needed to answer the question. With the historical order data collected, the analyst can perform initial analysis to determine if the retailers practised periodic review or continuous review ordering policy. From the insights obtained, it was found that the PR retailers caused the order fluctuations having many more orders on Monday than other days. Thus, the problem objective would be to smooth out the orders over the week so that fewer trucks are needed. The solution method proposed was to split the Monday PR retailers into two groups based on Cluster First, Route Second approach, to have a more efficient delivery system with fewer trucks.

Fig. 4.13 Split Monday PR retailers into two groups based on Cluster First Route Second approach

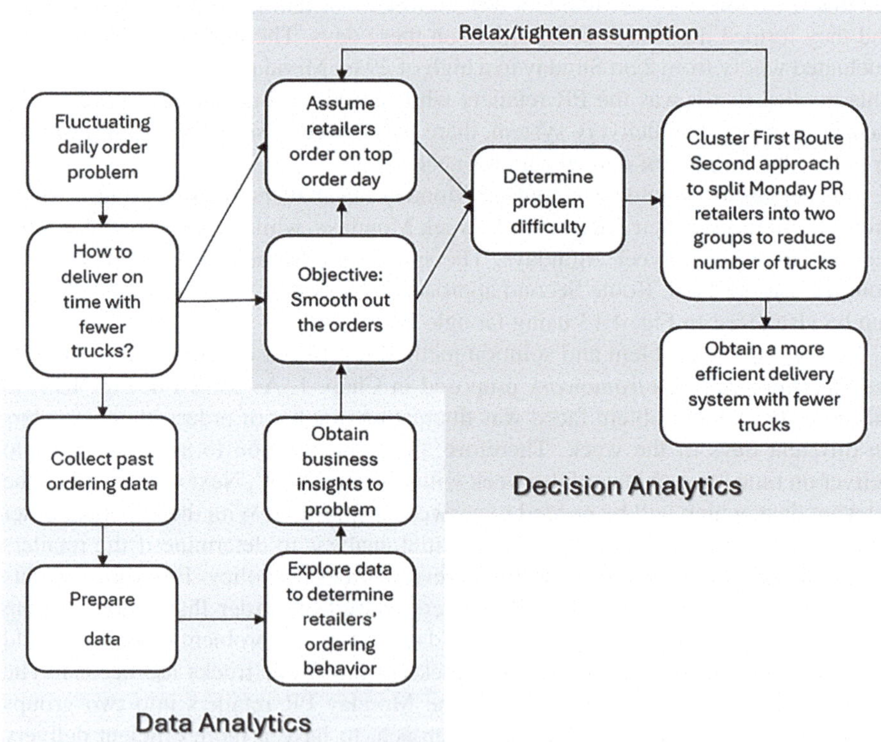

Fig. 4.14 Data and decision analytics framework map for Case 4

4.7 Summary

This chapter covered the NNP and C&W heuristics to solve TSP and MTSP problems. With the addition of vehicle capacity constraint, Cluster First, Route Second and Route First, Cluster Second approaches were introduced to handle VRP. A case study was discussed to apply distribution management concepts to better manage the distribution of FMCG with a more efficient delivery system with fewer trucks. The next topic to cover will be capacity planning to plan how much capacity to prepare to meet expected demand. Such capacity can refer to machine and human workforce. In Chap. 5, we will focus on capacity planning for machines before we move on to workforce planning and scheduling in other chapters.

Exercises

Q4.1

Starting from Node 1, determine the tour for the nodes below using:

- Nearest Neighbour Procedure
- C&W Savings Heuristic

	Node 1	Node 2	Node 3	Node 4	Node 5	Node 6
Node 1		8.2	5.3	6.4	9.1	3.3
Node 2	8.2		6.7	8.8	9.9	4.6
Node 3	5.3	6.7		7.2	8.1	5.2
Node 4	6.4	8.8	7.2		4.9	3.6
Node 5	9.1	9.9	8.1	4.9		8.7
Node 6	3.3	4.6	5.2	3.6	8.7	

Q4.2

A bus company has to pick up passengers starting from Node 1 using two buses, and Nodes 2 to 5 are assigned to bus 1, while Nodes 6 to 10 are assigned to bus 2. The table below shows the distance between the nodes, and bus 1 has capacity of 35 passengers, while bus 2 has capacity of 55 passengers.

Node	1	2	3	4	5	6	7	8	9	10
1		22	22	32	32	14	45	56	51	35
2	22		32	22	54	36	67	78	67	41
3	22	32		22	36	41	42	67	70	64

(continued)

Node	1	2	3	4	5	6	7	8	9	10
4	32	22	22		56	51	71	86	83	63
5	32	54	36	56		32	10	32	45	54
6	14	36	41	51	32		40	45	32	32
7	45	67	42	71	10	40		20	42	71
8	56	78	67	86	32	45	20		32	71
9	51	67	70	83	45	32	42	32		45
10	35	41	64	63	54	32	71	71	45	

The number of passengers to be picked up at each node is given by the table below.

Node	Number of passengers
2	10
3	10
4	5
5	5
6	5
7	5
8	20
9	10
10	5

The approximate map of nodes is shown below.

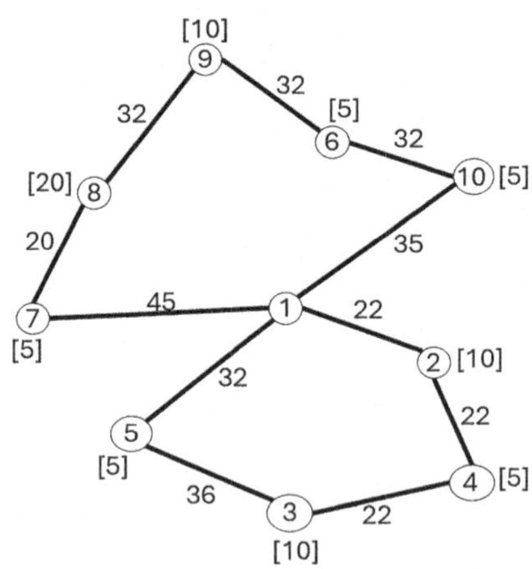

Using C&W heuristic, the two tours without considering capacity are:

- Bus 1 = 1→2→4→3→5→1 with total distance of 134.
- Bus 2 = 1→7→8→9→6→10→ with total distance of 196.
- Total distance = 134 + 196 = 330.

Improve the tour using nearest neighbour insertion (NNI) by moving passenger loads between the two buses by inserting node(s) from one tour to the other tour, without violating the capacity limits. We can consider these options:

- Option 1: Move node 6 from Tour 2 to Tour 1 to join with node 1.
- Option 2: Move node 7 from Tour 2 to Tour 1 to join with node 5.
- Option 3: Move node 5 from Tour 1 to Tour 2 to join with node 7.

Determine which option will be the best and the improved total distance travelled by both buses.

References

Cheong, M. L. F., & Choy, J. (2015). Data analysis of retailer orders to improve order distribution. In L. S. Iyer & D. J. Power (Eds.), *Reshaping society through analytics, collaboration, and decision support: Role of business intelligence and social media* (pp. 211–238). Springer. https://doi.org/10.1007/978-3-319-11575-7_15

Larson, R. C., & Odoni, A. R. (1981). *Urban operations research*. Prentice-Hall.

Chapter 5
Capacity Planning

Capacity planning refers to planning the amount of resources you will need to meet expected demand. Such resources can be machines, warehouse space, spare parts, the number of hospital beds and staffing. There are many considerations when planning capacity, including:

- What if the expected demand changes to be more or less than expected?
- Does the company have the capital to acquire the capacity needed?
- Is it cheaper to acquire the resource now or later?
- Will the machines become better and more efficient later?
- Are there alternate options as compared to acquiring the resources?
- If we increase our capacity, can our suppliers increase the supply of materials we need?
- If we increase our capacity, how will our competitors react?

Hence, capacity planning must align with the company's overall strategy in terms of its values, risk appetite and innovativeness.

In this chapter, we will be looking at the key considerations when planning capacity to decide what, where, when and how much capacity to add. We will determine how to manage short-term and long-term capacity planning and acquisition, perform capacity calculations and explore the economies and diseconomies of scale that can occur due to increasing capacity. We will look at one case study on how capacity planning concepts and models are applied in a real-world scenario to plan hospital bed capacity.

Learning Outcomes

By the end of this chapter, readers will achieve the following learning outcomes:

- Explain the key considerations when planning capacity.
- Distinguish between short-term and long-term capacity planning.
- Explain the three policies for long-term capacity acquisition and the potential impact.
- Assess how to choose the right policy for long-term capacity acquisition.

M. L. F. Cheong, Ma Nang Laik, *Data and Decision Analytics for Business Operations*, https://doi.org/10.1007/978-3-031-72255-4_5

- Distinguish among rated capacity, scheduled capacity, and actual capacity.
- Calculate machine availability and actual capacity.
- Explain short-term and long-term economies of scale.
- Explain the possible causes of diseconomies of scale.
- Discuss how capacity planning concepts and models are applied in a real-world scenario to plan hospital bed capacity using the *data and decision analytics framework.*

5.1 Capacity Planning Considerations

When we plan for capacity, we need to decide what, where and how much resources to install, and such decisions will depend on a few key considerations as described in Table 5.1.

Table 5.1 Capacity planning considerations to decide what, where and how much

Consideration	Description
Product life	How long will this new resource be used to support the production of products and services? For example, when we acquire a new machine to produce product A, for how long will we expect this machine to last before its end of life is reached or before we change to produce product B?
Vendor option	Should we produce it ourselves? Can we consider outsourcing the production to external vendors? For example, when faced with a sudden increase in demand, will it be better to spend huge investment to acquire additional resources or sub-contract the excess demand to external vendor?
Pricing	Does the potential investment return justify the price of the new resource? For example, if a new resource costs \$X, will investing \$X bring in returns more than \$X over a certain time period?
Time value of money	Should the money be spent in acquiring this new resource now or invested in alternate investment options? What is the opportunity cost? For example, compare investing \$Y in a new machine today with investing \$Y in R&D to develop a new technology
Bottleneck	Investment in a new resource should be at the bottleneck of the entire value chain to bring about the most impact. Where is the bottleneck? For example, the production of product A needs to go through three stages, and stage 2 is the slowest in terms of throughput. The entire production system can only be as fast as the slowest stage. Therefore, investing in a new resource in stage 2 will increase production output most significantly
Variability	Resources may have variable performance and thus affect the overall output. Will such variability affect your purchase decision? For example, if a newly acquired machine will be used together with the existing older machines, will the overall production output increase significantly or marginally?

5.1.1 Short-Term vs Long-Term Capacity Planning

With the above key considerations, we will explore if the decisions vary if we are planning for the short term versus the long term. When planning for the short term due to sudden increase or decrease of demand, the decisions made aim to tackle the situation temporarily until the situation returns to normal. For a sudden increase in demand, the company can request staff to work overtime, add additional work shifts or outsource the excess demand to external vendors. For a sudden decrease in demand, the decisions will be reversed, to cut down work hours or reduce work shifts.

When planning for the long term, the decisions made will be based on long-term demand forecast. As we have learned in Chap. 1, long-term demand forecasts are less reliable and more likely to change. Acquiring new resources early before the demand picks up will result in poor resource utilization in the initial periods. However, acquiring them late, the company will be less responsive to changes. A large increase in capacity may offer economies of scale during acquisition, and the company will have the capacity to cater for a large increase in demand in the future. However, it will tie down capital with huge opportunity cost and subject the company to the risk of demand lower than expected and technology getting outdated.

5.1.2 Policies for Long-Term Capacity Acquisition

So, is there a right time to acquire capacity? There are three possible policies we can refer to as given in Table 5.2, and different situations will adopt different policies.

How does a company know which policy to choose? The choice of the policy can be decided using the critical ratio given as

$$\text{Ratio} = \frac{C_s - C_o}{C_s}$$

where:

- C_s = opportunity cost per unit incurred due to shortage of capacity, which can include loss profit, manpower overtime cost, loss of goodwill, expensive outsourcing cost
- C_o = cost per unit incurred due to over capacity

Note that this critical ratio is different than that for inventory management discussed in Chap. 3.

The company will choose the right policy to adopt based on this critical ratio as given in Table 5.3; however, the actual values for C_s and C_o are hard to determine.

Table 5.2 Timing for capacity increments

Policy	Description	Why choose this policy?
A	Capacity leads demand—installs and maintains excess capacity ahead of demand 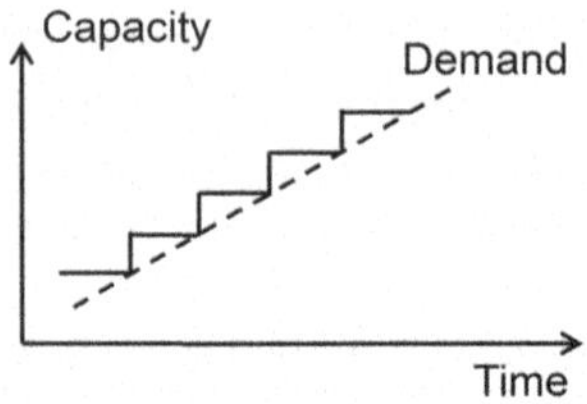	This policy is suitable when demand is highly volatile, and the market is highly competitive. The cost of not satisfying the demand is high; therefore, high responsiveness is needed However, when all competitors adopt the same policy, then very soon, there will be excessive capacity leading to a price war
B	Capacity lags demand—installs and maintains a negative capacity cushion lagging demand 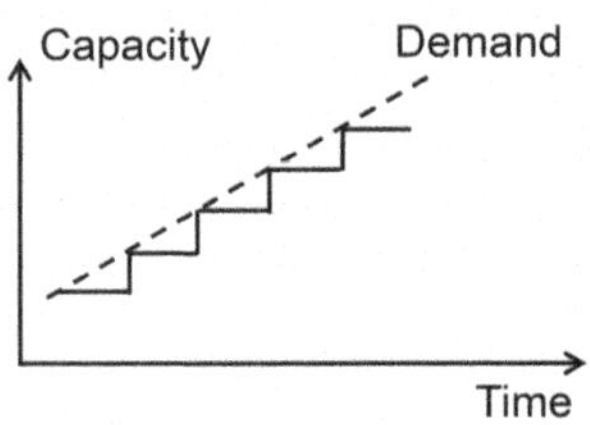	This policy is suitable when capacity is expensive and high utilization of capacity is expected. There will be a high return on investment in the resources and because the capacity is always lacking, any new addition of capacity will become fully utilized again However, a sudden increase in demand will lead to high costs due to an urgent increase in expensive resources. In addition, as capacity is always lagging demand, there is an increased risk of losing customers and market share
C	Capacity in sync with demand—installs and maintains capacity close to anticipated demand 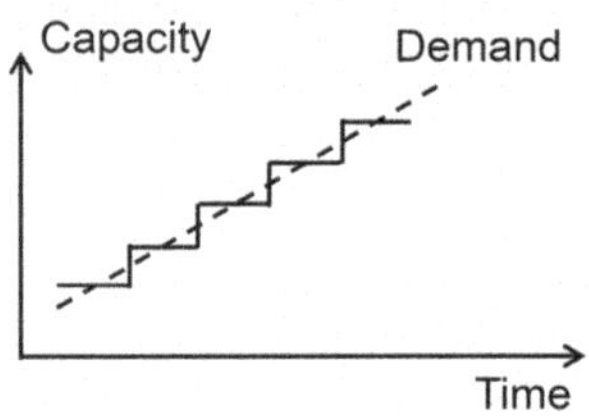	This policy seems to be the ideal one. It is suitable when adding temporary capacity and reducing excess capacity are quick, easy and not costly. This is the situation where agility and flexibility will distinguish the companies from their competitors

Table 5.3 Critical ratio to choose policy to adopt

Critical ratio	Policy
Ratio > 0.5	When ratio is > 0.5, this would mean that C_s (cost of shortage of capacity) is at least twice of C_o (cost of overcapacity). So, it is very costly to have a shortage of capacity. Thus, Policy A is chosen to ensure that capacity leads demand
Ratio < 0.5	When ratio is < 0.5, this would mean that C_s can be bigger or smaller than C_o. If C_s is bigger than C_o, it will be less than twice of C_o. If C_s is smaller than C_o, the ratio will be negative. In both cases, it is not as crucial when capacity shortage occurs. Thus, Policy B is chosen where capacity lags demand
Ratio = 0.5	When ratio = 0.5, this would mean that C_s is exactly twice of C_o. Policy C is chosen as an in-between solution, and temporary measures are needed to react to changes in demand when demand is larger or smaller than capacity

5.2 Capacity Calculations

Capacity can be defined as three different types, rated or engineering capacity, scheduled or expected capacity, and actual or effective capacity.

- Rated capacity is the amount of capacity based on the maximum the resource can perform non-stop without breaks.
- Scheduled capacity is the amount of capacity based on the planned number of hours for the operation.
- Actual capacity is the amount of scheduled capacity minus down time due to unplanned interruptions, which prevent the resource from operating as planned. The unplanned interruptions can include machine breakdown or unexpected manpower unavailability.

We can see that rated capacity > scheduled capacity > actual capacity. So, in real-world practice, businesses should plan based on actual capacity. Actual capacity is affected by resource availability. In the case of machines, machines can become unavailable due to breakdowns. Let us define the following parameters and refer to Fig. 5.1:

- m_f = mean time to failure or MTTF = average time between machine failures.
- m_r = mean time to repair or MTTR = average time taken to repair the machine.
- MTBF = mean time between failures = average time between consecutive machine failures = $m_f + m_r$.

Thus, machine availability A will be given as

$$A = \frac{m_f}{m_f + m_r}$$

With A computed, we can compute the actual capacity of machine to be the effective number of units that can be produced per day

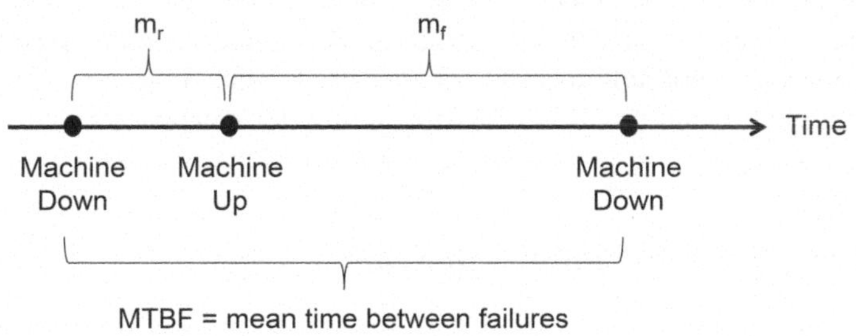

Fig. 5.1 Machine availability

$$U_e = AU_o$$

where U_o = number of units the machine can produce per day without failures

Alternatively, we can compute the actual capacity of machines to be the effective number of machines available

$$M_e = AM_o$$

where M_o = number of machine available without failures.

5.3 Economies of Scale and Diseconomies of Scale

When the decision to increase capacity has been made either for the short term or the long term, we need to consider if economies of scale or diseconomies of scale will happen.

5.3.1 *Short-Term Economies of Scale*

Short-term increase in capacity using temporary resources, such as overtime hours, adding work shift, adding temporary workers or outsourcing to external vendors, can lead to economies of scale. The cost of producing one additional unit of product will be computed as

$$\text{Cost per unit} = \text{Unit fixed cost} + \text{Unit variable cost}$$

where unit fixed cost = fixed cost/total units.

Since fixed cost is now shared by a larger number of units produced, the unit fixed cost will be smaller achieving economies of scale. The unit variable cost remains constant regardless of the number of units produced. Thus, the total cost of production will not increase linearly in the short term. However, when the fixed cost from invested capacity is not able to meet the increased production, new capacity will need to be acquired, and we will be looking at long-term capacity increase.

5.3.2 *Long-Term Economies of Scale*

Long-term capacity increase can lead to either static economies of scale or dynamic economies of scale. Static economies of scale arise from a single large increase in capacity, for example, from acquiring a large warehouse or machine, or building a

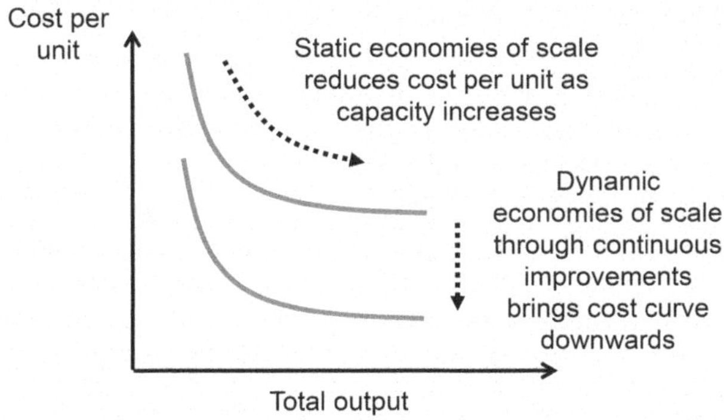

Fig. 5.2 Long-term static and dynamic economies of scale

new hospital. The cost of increase in capacity of size V is estimated using the formula below:

$$C = KV^k$$

where:

- K is a multiplier that depends on many factors
- k represents the degree of economies of scale achieved, which is between 0 and 1. When k = 1, then there will be no economies of scale. The smaller the k, the larger the economies of scale enjoyed.

However, to estimate both K and k is not easy and direct.

On the other hand, dynamic economies of scale are enjoyed due to improvements in skills and experience of the workers, using better systems and improved process flows, having better management methods and improving product designs. Such continuous improvements will accumulate over time, increasing the economies in a dynamic fashion, as shown in Fig. 5.2.

5.3.3 Diseconomies of Scale

We have learned how economies of scale can be enjoyed when increasing capacity both short term and long term. What about diseconomies scale? Will it occur and, if yes, how? We will look at possible causes such as increase in distribution cost, increase in bureaucracies and confusion, and increase in vulnerability. Businesses should be aware of such possible diseconomies of scale and have measures to overcome them.

When building a new and large facility such as a manufacturing plant or a warehouse, the location of such a large facility tends to be far away and more inaccessible. This will lead to higher distribution cost and if the distribution cost makes up a large portion of the total cost, then diseconomies of scale will occur.

Measures such as improving the packaging of goods to reduce volume, using fuel efficient transportation or even getting the customers to pick up the goods on their own will reduce the distribution cost.

As the size of the facility increases, the number of workers needed will also increase. The larger the workforce, the organization hierarchy will increase in layers, as more supervisors and managers will be needed. This will lead to an increase in management costs, a reduction in response time and an increase in misunderstanding and confusion, which can potentially lead to expensive mistakes. Establishing clear communication and workflow processes, encouraging sharing of information among employees or even displaying information on signboards or dashboards openly and clearly to reduce misunderstanding will overcome such diseconomies of scale.

Finally, with a large facility, the proportion of business allocated to this large facility will be higher. When there is a disruption in supply chain due to natural or man-made disaster, the overall negative impact will be higher as compared to a smaller facility. Sourcing from multiple suppliers, improved inventory management and flexible production capabilities are measures which can help reduce such risks.

5.4 Case 5: Hospital Bed Capacity Planning

This case is modified from the paper published by Cheong and Lim (2016). In this case, we look at how hospital bed capacity planning can be performed based on real data in Singapore.

Like many other developed countries in the world, the healthcare system in Singapore is faced with the aging population problem. The government of Singapore has planned to increase the number of hospitals and beds to cater for the growing needs. In this case, we will collect and analyse the data to plan the number of hospital beds needed in public hospitals for the next 7 years. We will approach this problem following the *data and decision analytics framework* proposed in Chap. 1, and the capacity considerations and calculations will be discussed.

Out of the six key considerations in capacity planning given in Table 5.1, we will consider only bottleneck and resource variability, as the other considerations on product life, vendor option, pricing and time value of money are not as critical for planning hospital bed capacity in this case. Bottleneck here will refer to the insufficient number of beds, while resource variability will be accounted for using an availability rate A. The chosen policy for long-term capacity acquisition will be Policy A where capacity leads demand as the cost of not satisfying the demand for hospital beds is high. As building a new hospital requires long-term planning, thus we will consider both short-term increase by adding Q number of beds in existing hospitals and long-term increase by building a new hospital with R beds, where $R \gg Q$.

The factors affecting demand for hospital beds include projected population growth, forecasted percentage of people who need to be served by the hospital and expected length of stay in the hospital. With these figures forecasted for the next 7 years, we can then determine the number of beds required against the number of beds available, to decide when and how many beds to add to meet a target utilization rate.

The following computation steps were taken:

1. Determine the current population in the country as P_0.
2. Forecast the population growth rate for the next 7 years, as G_1 to G_7.
3. Compute the future population in the country for the next 7 years as P_1 to P_7 using the formula below:

$$P_1 = P_0 G_1$$
$$P_2 = P_1 G_2$$
$$\ldots$$
$$P_7 = P_6 G_7$$

4. Forecast the percentage of people who will be served by public hospitals for the next 7 years, as H_1 to H_7.
5. Compute the number of people who will be served by public hospitals for the next 7 years, as S_1 to S_7, using the formula below:

$$S_1 = P_1 H_1$$
$$S_2 = P_2 H_2$$
$$\ldots$$
$$S_7 = P_7 H_7$$

6. Forecast the future average length of stay (LoS) per patient per year, for the next 7 years, as L_1 to L_7.
7. Compute the number of patients each hospital bed can serve per year using the average length of stay and assumed constant availability rate A, for the next 7 years, as N_1 to N_7 using the formula below:

$$N_1 = \frac{365 * A}{L_1}$$
$$N_2 = \frac{365 * A}{L_2}$$
$$\ldots$$
$$N_7 = \frac{365 * A}{L_7}$$

8. Compute the number of beds required per year, for the next 7 years, as B_1 to B_7, using the formula below:

$$B_1 = \frac{S_1}{N_1}$$

$$B_1 = \frac{S_1}{N_1}$$

$$\ldots$$

$$B_7 = \frac{S_7}{N_7}$$

9. Determine the current total number of beds available in the public hospitals as Z_0, and set the maximum utilization rate as T. Usually, public hospitals will set T to be 80% so that the remaining 20% can be used to handle unforeseen situations.
10. Set the number of additional beds that can be added in the short term as Q before a new hospital of capacity R needs to be built as the long-term decision, where $R \gg Q$.
11. Set Rflag $= 0$ and Qflag $= 0$ to initialize that the short-term and long-term decisions have not yet been made, respectively.
12. Start from year 1:

- If $\frac{B_1}{Z_0} < T$, then $Z_1 = Z_0$.
- Else:
  - If $Z_1 = Z_0 + Q$ and $\frac{B_1}{Z_1} < T$, proceed as the short-term decision, and set Qflag $= 1$.

    Else $Z_1 = Z_0 + R$, proceed as the long-term decision, and set Rflag $= 1$.

13. For year 2:

- If $\frac{B_2}{Z_1} < T$, then $Z_2 = Z_1$.
- Else:
  - If Qflag $= 0$, $Z_2 = Z_1 + Q$ and $\frac{B_1}{Z_2} < T$, proceed as the short-term decision, and set Qflag $= 2$.

    Else, if Rflag $= 0$, $Z_2 = Z_1 + R$, proceed as the long-term decision, and set Rflag $= 2$.

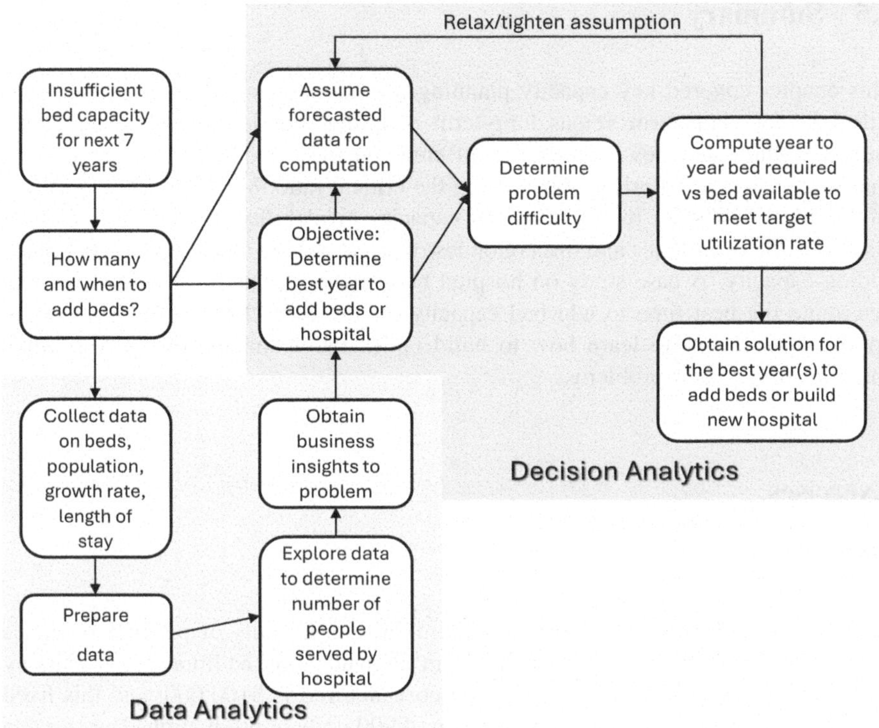

Fig. 5.3 Data and decision analytics framework map for Case 5

14. Repeat step 13 until all the decisions have been made for 7 years.
15. Decisions where Qflag > 0 and Rflag > 0 will represent the respective year to add bed capacity Q and set up a new hospital with capacity R.

Let us map the problem and solution method for this case study against the *data and decision analytics framework* proposed in Chap. 1. As shown in Fig. 5.3, in this case study, the problem faced was insufficient bed capacity for the next 7 years. Therefore, the right question to ask was "How many and when to add beds?". Next was to collect the relevant data, which will be needed to answer the question which includes the current bed capacity, the population and projected growth rate, forecasted percentage of people needing to go to the hospital and projected length of stay. With the data collected and forecasted values, the analyst can perform initial analysis to determine if the number of people served by the hospital will increase over the years. From the insights obtained, it was found that the number of beds available will not be able to meet the number of beds required. Thus, the problem objective would be to determine the best year to add beds as short-term solution or the best year to build a new hospital as long-term solution. The computation will reveal the best year(s) to add bed capacity to meet the target utilization rate.

5.5 Summary

This chapter covered key capacity planning considerations and how the decisions will vary for short-term versus long-term planning. For long-term planning, we looked at three policies to cater for different business requirements and how to choose the most appropriate policy using the critical ratio. Machine capacity calculation was covered to represent actual capacity availability. Finally, this chapter discussed the economies and diseconomies of scale and the associated impact when adding capacity. A case study on hospital bed capacity planning was discussed to determine the best time to add bed capacity. In the next chapter, we will look at optimization theory to learn how to build optimization models to obtain optimal solutions to business problems.

Exercises

Q5.1

A factory usually produces up to a maximum of 500 units of product A and is capable of handling any sudden increase in demand of an additional 400 units by increasing short-term capacity. The fixed cost incurred is \$100,000, and this fixed cost will remain the same up to a maximum of 900 units of production. The variable cost to produce one unit of product A is \$20. To better understand the short-term economies of scale, prepare a table with the following columns, and then plot the chart of total cost per unit (y-axis) versus the total quantity (x-axis) to visualize the short-term economies of scale.

- Column 1: Normal quantity = 100, 200, 300, 400, 500, 500, 500, 500, 500.
- Column 2: Additional quantity = 0, 0, 0, 0, 0, 100, 200, 300, 400.
- Column 3: Total quantity = sum of normal and additional quantities.
- Column 4: Fixed cost per unit = fixed cost/total quantity.
- Column 5: Total cost per unit = fixed cost per unit + variable cost per unit.

Q5.2

A business would like to invest in a new facility and is exploring the static long-term economies of scale it can enjoy if it has the option to decide the size of facility denoted as V. Static long-term economies of scale can be estimated using the formula

$$C = KV^k$$

where:

- K is a multiplier
- k represents the degree of economies of scale achieved, which is between 0 and 1

Using the formula, compute the cost of investment C for different values of V and k, given that K is assumed to be 1.5. Prepare a two-dimensional table with V of $100 to $500 in increment step of $100 and k from 0.6 to 1.0 in increment step of 0.1. You should have a 5 × 5 table with 25 different values of C. Plot a chart of C (y-axis) versus V (x-axis) for different k values.

Q5.3

A factory produces a product which must undergo three production stages, starting from Stage A, then Stage B and then finally Stage C. The production rate at each stage differs. With no disruptions, Stage A can produce 50 units per hour, Stage B can produce 30 units per hour and Stage C can produce 60 units per hour. In addition, the machines at different stages have varied performance due to unforeseen breakdowns. As such, Stage A machines have 80% availability, stage B machines 95% and stage C machines 90%.

(a) Determine the effective number of units that can be produced per hour.
(b) Determine the bottleneck, and compute the percentage increase in capacity at this bottleneck to maximize the production output per hour.

Reference

Cheong, M. L. F., & Lim, L. S. (2016). *Scenario-based simulation game for hospital beds capacity planning in Singapore*. 7th International Conference on Education, Training and Informatics (ICETI), Orlando, FL, March 8–11.

Chapter 6
Optimization Theory

Every business is faced with limited resources, which can be limited money, limited time, limited warehouse space or limited number of machines and manpower. To achieve the usual business objectives to maximize revenue or profit, or minimize cost or time taken, optimization models are used to determine the best outcome using these limited resources. Thus, in optimization theory, we aim to determine the optimal solution to a problem, which will maximize or minimize an objective while satisfying any constraints the problem faces.

In this chapter, we will look at three different classes of problems: linear programming (LP), integer programming (IP) and non-linear programming (NLP) problems, as shown in Fig. 6.1. Under IP, we will look at pure integer programming, mixed integer programming (MIP) and binary integer programming (BIP). Specifically, for BIP, we can learn how to use binary variables to convert intractable LP or IP problems to become tractable. Finally, we will also look at NLP to understand the characteristics of NLP solutions and conditions, which allow us to determine if the solution obtained is a global optimal solution. We will end the chapter with two case studies on how optimization concepts and models are applied in a real-world scenario to optimize the container mix for carbon footprint reduction.

Learning Outcomes

By the end of this chapter, readers will achieve the following learning outcomes:

- Explain the standard LP model.
- Interpret the LP model assumptions.
- Construct and solve LP models to obtain optimal solutions to linear problems.
- Summarize the four possible outcomes for LP problems.
- Explain binding and non-binding constraints.
- Explore reduced cost and shadow prices in terms of sensitivity analysis.
- Construct and solve IP models to obtain optimal solutions to linear integer problems.
- Explore how binary variables can be added to convert intractable IP and LP problems into tractable problems.

M. L. F. Cheong, Ma Nang Laik, *Data and Decision Analytics for Business Operations*, https://doi.org/10.1007/978-3-031-72255-4_6

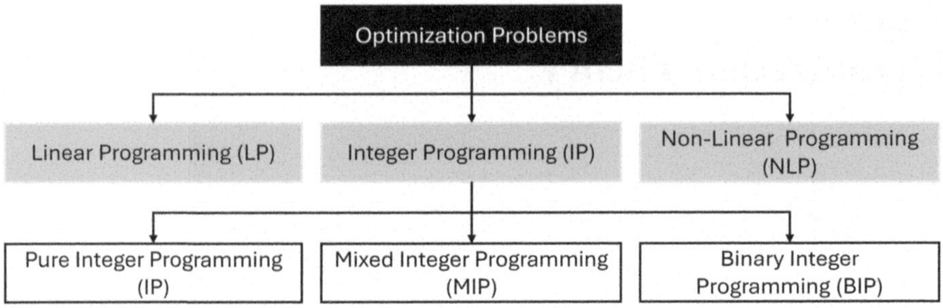

Fig. 6.1 Classes of optimization problems

- Discuss the characteristics of NLP optimal solutions.
- Summarize the conditions for NLP solution to be global optimal solution.
- Discuss how optimization concepts and models are applied in a real-world scenario to optimize the container mix for carbon footprint reduction using the *data and decision analytics framework.*

6.1 Linear Programming

Linear programming (LP) is a class of problems where the objective is to minimize a *linear* cost function subject to *linear* equality or inequality constraints. Without loss of generality, we defined as minimization of cost function, which can be easily redefined as maximization of profit function. The key thing to note is that the objective cost function and constraints must *all* be linear functions. Good references for linear programming include Dantzig (1947, 1998, 2002).

We can represent an LP problem to consist of three components:

- Decision variables, which are the inputs to the problems for the LP model to determine their best values
- Objective function, which is the output where the LP model will maximize or minimize its values by changing the values of decision variables
- Constraints, which will define the feasible region which will restrict the values of the decision variables, if constraints exist

6.1.1 Project-Manpower Example

To better understand LP problem, let us use a project-manpower example to illustrate. A company has three types of manpower, M_1, M_2 and M_3, where each manpower type performs a different role in the company. Each manpower type has limited availability with 4, 12 and 18 units, respectively. This company can

Table 6.1 Project-manpower example

	Project P_1	Project P_2	Availability
Manpower M_1	1	0	4
Manpower M_2	0	2	12
Manpower M_3	3	2	18
Revenue	\$3	\$5	

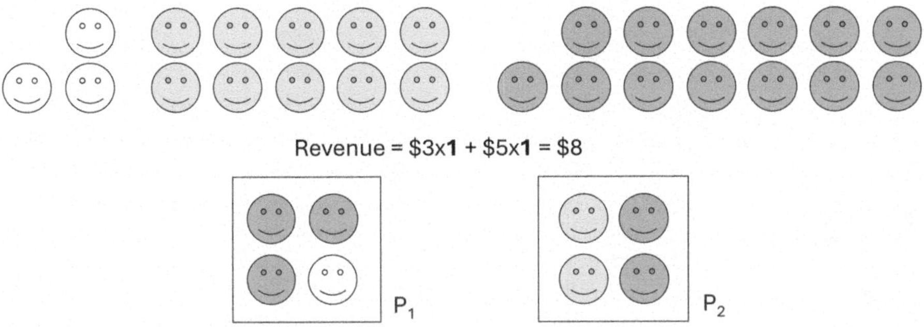

Fig. 6.2 Project-manpower example (1, 1) solution

undertake two types of projects, P_1 and P_2, and each project type will require different units of each manpower type as given in Table 6.1. Project P_1 will require 1, 0 and 3 units, while project P_2 will require 0, 2 and 2 units of manpower types M_1, M_2 and M_3, respectively. Different project types P_1 and P_2 will bring in different revenues for this company at \$3 and \$5, respectively. How many of each project type should this company undertake to maximize the revenue that it can earn?

For example, in Fig. 6.2, if the company undertakes one project P_1 and one project P_2, then it will earn only $\$3 \times 1 + \$5 \times 1 = \$8$ and will consume manpower 1, 2 and 5 units of manpower types M_1, M_2 and M_3, respectively. They will still be left with 3, 10 and 13 units of manpower types M_1, M_2 and M_3, respectively. This means that they can afford to undertake more projects.

Let us randomly allocate manpower to the projects and end up with four project P_1 and three project P_2 as shown in Fig. 6.3. This means that the company will earn $\$3 \times 4 + \$5 \times 3 = \$27$ and will consume almost all the manpower and left with 6 units of manpower M_2 only. This means that they cannot afford to undertake any more projects. Is this the best answer?

6.1.2 Standard LP Model

To determine the best answer, we need to formulate the LP model and use an optimizer to run through all possible scenarios to find the best answer. Let us define the indices and parameters for a standard LP model with n decision variables and m resource constraints:

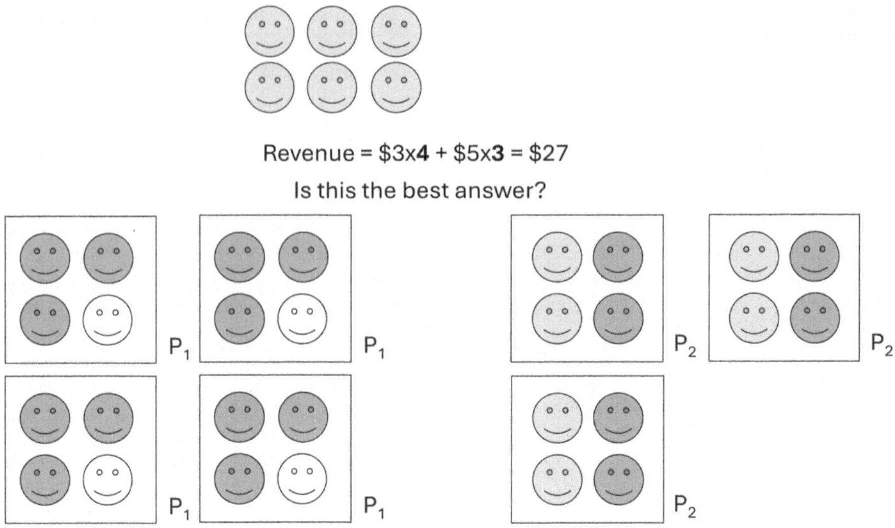

Fig. 6.3 Project-manpower example (4, 3) solution

- k = index for decision variables, k = 1 to n.
- i = index for resources, i = 1 to m.
- x_k = decision variable, k = 1 to n.
- c_k = unit cost associated with decision variable x_k, k = 1 to n.
- a_{ik} = unit consumption of resource i by decision variable x_k.
- b_i = resource availability, i = 1 to m.

A standard LP model can be represented as follows:
Objective function

$$\text{Minimize } Z = c_1x_1 + c_2x_2 + \ldots + c_nx_n$$

Constraints

$$a_{11}x_1 + a_{12}x_2 + \ldots + a_{1n}x_n \leq b_1$$

$$a_{21}x_1 + a_{22}x_2 + \ldots + a_{2n}x_n \leq b_2$$

$$\ldots$$

$$a_{m1}x_1 + a_{m2}x_2 + \ldots + a_{mn}x_n \leq b_m$$

Decision variables: $x_1, x_2, \ldots, x_n \geq 0$

The objective function is a linear function that sums up the total cost associated with decision variables x_1 to x_n, where c_1 to c_n are the respective unit costs. Each constraint is a linear function that sums up the total resource consumption by decision variable x_k (k = 1 to n) as $a_{ik}x_k$ for resource i and cannot exceed b_i (i = 1 to m). Finally, the decision variables are defined to be strictly positive. Note that there are other forms of LP model where the objective function is maximized, the constraints can have $\geq$ or $=$ signs, and the non-negativity constraints for the decision variables can be removed.

6.1.3 LP Model Assumptions

In the LP model, there are four assumptions made:

- Proportionality—this assumption states that individual activities which are associated with the decision variables x_k are considered independently and are proportional to the respective unit cost and unit consumption. This implies that there is no setup cost for different values of x_k and proportionality holds for all values of x_k.
- Additivity—this assumption states that there are no interactions between the activities, and the contributions associated with each decision variable x_k can simply be summed up.
- Divisibility—this assumption states that the decision variables x_k can be non-integer values, making LP problems the easiest to solve among all optimization problems.
- Certainty—this assumption states that all parameters assumed in the model are known constants with certainty. This means that the unit cost c_k, the unit consumption a_{ik} and resource availability b_i are known constants with certainty. However, in the real world, these constants are not strictly constants, and they could have variability. Thus, a sensitivity analysis is usually performed to determine how the solution may change. We will be looking at reduced cost calculation for the sensitivity analysis of the unit cost c_k and shadow price calculation for the sensitivity analysis of the availability b_i.

6.1.4 Project-Manpower Example Optimal Solution

Let us formulate the LP model for the project-manpower example:

- $k =$ index for project type, $k = 1$ to 2.
- $i =$ index for manpower resources, $i = 1$ to 3.
- $x_k =$ number of projects of type $k \rightarrow x_1$ and x_2 (decision variables).
- $r_k =$ unit revenue associated with decision variable $x_k \rightarrow r_1 = 3$ and $r_2 = 5$.
- $c_{ik} =$ unit consumption of resource i by decision variable x_k.
  - $c_{11} = 1$, $c_{12} = 0$.
  - $c_{21} = 0$, $c_{22} = 2$.
  - $c_{31} = 3$, $c_{32} = 2$.

- b_i = resource availability → $b_1 = 4$, $b_2 = 12$ and $b_3 = 18$.

  Objective function

$$\text{Maximize revenue } Z = r_1x_1 + r_2x_2 = 3x_1 + 5x_2$$

Constraints

$$1x_1 + 0x_2 \leq 4 \rightarrow x_1 \leq 4 \quad (1)$$

$$0x_1 + 2x_2 \leq 12 \rightarrow x_2 \leq 6 \quad (2)$$

$$3x_1 + 2x_2 \leq 18 \quad (3)$$

Decision variables: $x_1, x_2 \geq 0$

To solve this problem, let us map the constraints on a two-dimensional chart where the horizontal axis represents x_1 and the vertical axis represents x_2. Adding the three constraints into the chart, we will be able to define the feasible region by shading out the infeasible regions as shown in Fig. 6.4. A similar example can be seen in Hillier and Lieberman (2001) in a different business context.

After the feasible region is mapped out, we will add the objective function $Z = 3x_1 + 5x_2$ into the chart. To add, we will assume a value of Z, and usually we will choose a value that is divisible by both 3 and 5. Let us assume Z = 15. With Z = 15, we can determine two points (0, 3) and (5, 0) to draw the straight-line $15 = 3x_1 + 5x_2$ as shown in Fig. 6.5. This line represents the $15 line, which means

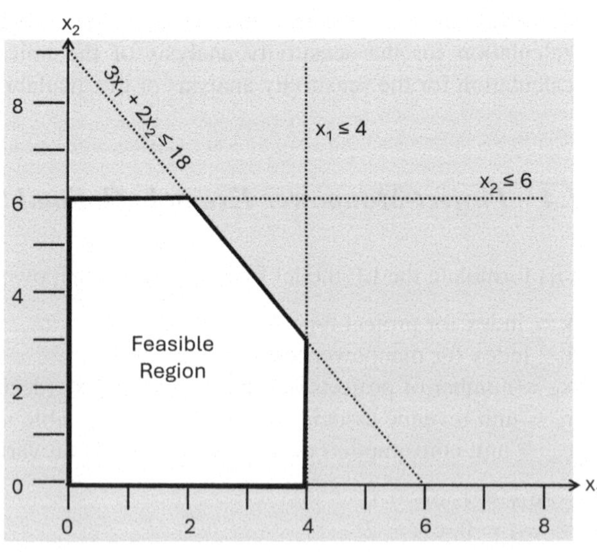

Fig. 6.4 Project-manpower example feasible region

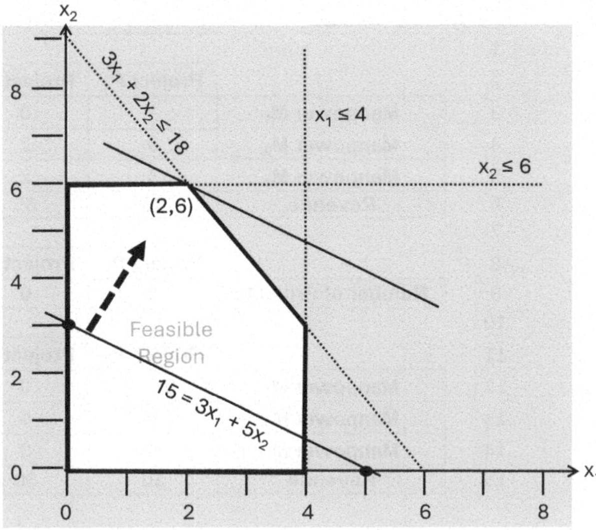

Fig. 6.5 Project-manpower example optimal solution (2, 6)

that any number of project combinations (x_1, x_2) along this line will earn the company $15.

To maximize revenue, we will move this line up until the corner point (2, 6) and stop. Moving beyond the corner point will end up in the infeasible region. Thus, the optimal solution is $x_1 = 2$ and $x_2 = 6$, which means that the firm should undertake two project P_1 and six project P_2, which will earn the maximum revenue of $Z = \$3 \times 2 + \$5 \times 6 = \$36$, and the solution satisfies all constraints.

We have seen how to obtain the optimal solution for this example by charting. This is possible when the problem has only two decision variables. When there are more decision variables, manual charting will not be possible. This is when we will need optimization engines or optimizers (e.g. Excel Solver Add-in), which can enumerate all the possible answer combinations in high-dimension space to find the optimal solution. In LP model, the most efficient optimization algorithm is the Simplex Method, which will find the optimal solution by traversing only the corner points to reach the optimal solution instead of all possible combinations (Dantzig, 1947, 1998, 2002).

Figures 6.6 and 6.7 show the layout of the problem in Excel spreadsheet and the corresponding Solver definition, respectively. In Fig. 6.6, the formula in cell C12 = C$9*C3 is used to compute the manpower consumption and should be filled up for the cells C12:D15 to compute for all the manpower consumptions and revenue earned. Cells E12:E15 will sum up the total manpower consumption and the total revenue earned.

Figure 6.7 shows the selection of the objective function cell E15 and to maximize it; the decision variables C9:D9 are the changing variable cells; and the constraint for

	A	B	C	D	E
1					
2			Project P_1	Project P_2	Total Available
3		Manpower M_1	1	0	4
4		Manpower M_2	0	2	12
5		Manpower M_3	3	2	18
6		Revenue	$3	$5	
7					
8			Project P_1	Project P_2	
9		Number of Projects	0	0	
10					
11			Project P_1	Project P_2	Total Needed
12		Manpower M_1	=C$9*C3	0	0
13		Manpower M_2	0	0	0
14		Manpower M_3	0	0	0
15		Revenue	$0	$0	$0

Fig. 6.6 Excel spreadsheet model for project-manpower example

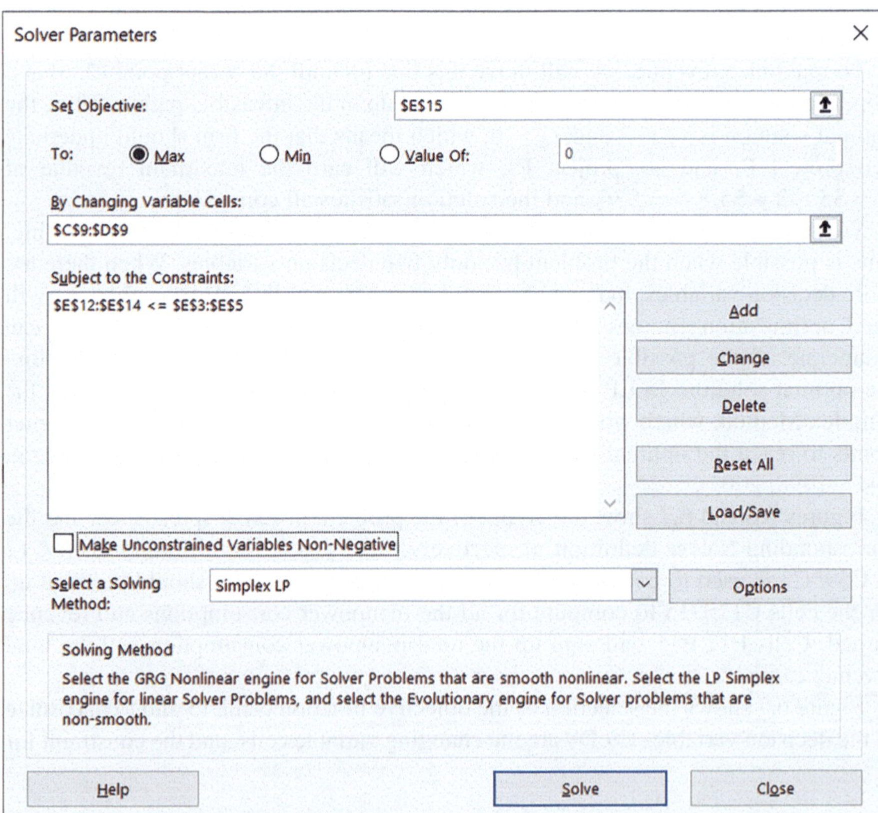

Fig. 6.7 Excel solver definition for project-manpower example

the consumption of manpower in cells E12:E14 cannot exceed the availability in cells E3:E5. Note that we did not include the constraint that the decision variables must be ≥ 0, and did not check the checkbox option "Make Unconstrained Variables Non-Negative". This is because we are maximizing the total revenue earned, and it will not make sense for the optimizer to choose negative values for the decision variables, and thus this constraint is optional.

6.1.5 Four Possible Outcomes for Optimization of LP Problems

For the project-manpower example, its optimal solution occurs at the corner point of the feasible region, which means that there is only one optimal solution. However, in the real world, there are four possible outcomes when solving optimization problems as shown in Fig. 6.8.

- Unique optimal solution—this is the case where there is only one optimal solution and the solution must be at the corner point of the feasible region.
- Multiple optimal solutions—this is the case where the objective function line lies exactly on a constraint, resulting in multiple optimal solutions. To obtain the different solutions, set different initial values for the decision variables to allow the optimizer to traverse the corner points in different directions.
- Unbounded feasible region—this is the case where the feasible region is unbounded, which will result in the optimal solution being infinity since the objective function line can keep moving up without limit.
- No solution—this is the case where all the constraints, when considered together, resulted in no feasible region and thus no solution.

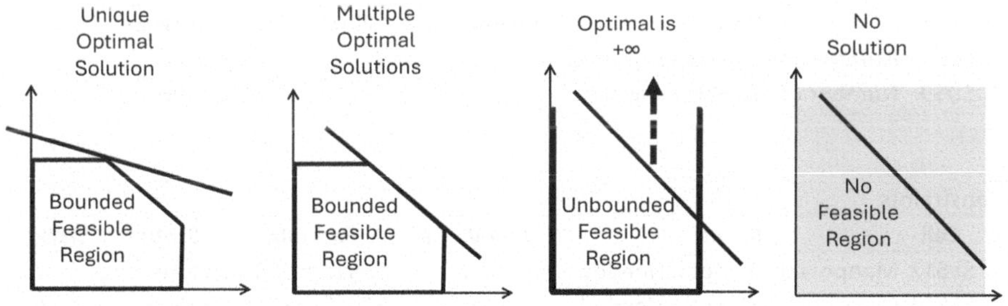

Fig. 6.8 Four possible outcomes of LP problems

6.1.6 Binding and Non-binding Constraints

After solving an optimization problem, one can typically generate an answer report from the optimization software, which will list the status of the constraints as either *binding* or *non-binding*. A constraint has the left-hand side (LHS), which computes the total consumption, and the right-hand side (RHS), which denotes the resource availability.

- Binding—a binding constraint is one where the total consumption of the resource is exactly equal to the resource availability, or LHS = RHS. This means that this resource is used to its maximum limit. When such a situation occurs, there will be zero slack, where slack is the amount of leftover resources.
- Non-binding—a non-binding constraint is one where the total consumption of the resource is less than the resource availability, or LHS < RHS. When such a situation occurs, there will be a positive slack.

Slack is the remaining unused RHS value, and since it is unused, it indicates how much we can change the RHS without changing the optimal solution. Thus, slack is also referred to as the allowable increase or decrease of the RHS values.

Let us revisit the project-manpower example. We can generate the answer report given in Fig. 6.9 when using Excel Solver to solve the problem. The report has three segments: the top segment shows the maximized objective function value of $36; the second segment shows the optimal solution, which is (2, 6) for the number of

Objective Cell (Max)

Cell	Name	Original Value	Final Value
$E$15	Revenue Total Needed	$0	$36

Variable Cells

Cell	Name	Original Value	Final Value	Integer
$C$9	Number of Projects Project P1	0	2	Contin
$D$9	Number of Projects Project P2	0	6	Contin

Constraints

Cell	Name	Cell Value	Formula	Status	Slack
$E$12	Manpower M1 Total Needed	2	$E$12<=$E$3	Not Binding	2
$E$13	Manpower M2 Total Needed	12	$E$13<=$E$4	Binding	0
$E$14	Manpower M3 Total Needed	18	$E$14<=$E$5	Binding	0

Fig. 6.9 Answer report for project-manpower example

projects; and the bottom segment shows the status of the three constraints. Constraint 1 is non-binding and has a slack of 2, while constraints 2 and 3 are both binding and do not have slack. We know that manpower type 1 has availability of four units, and only two units are consumed, leaving two units as slack. Thus, the allowable decrease for manpower type 1 will be two units, and the optimal solution will remain unchanged.

6.1.7 Reduced Cost

Reduced cost is the rate at which the objective function value will deteriorate, which means increase for minimization problem and decrease for maximization problem, for a unit change in the decision variable value. Reduced cost will be zero if the optimal decision variable value is not at the boundary values and will be non-zero otherwise.

Let us revisit the project-manpower example again. The lower bound for the decision variables is zero, as the number of projects cannot be negative, while the upper bound is infinity. Thus, the boundary values are zero and infinity. We can generate the sensitivity report given in Fig. 6.10 when using Excel Solver to solve the problem. The reduced costs for both decision variables are zeroes because the optimal values (2, 6) are not at the boundary values. If in case any of the decision variables is zero (at the lower bound), then its reduced cost will be a non-zero value, representing the amount which the objective function value will reduce.

The allowable increase and decrease refer to the allowable change to the coefficient of the decision variable for which the objective function value will remain the same (that is, decision variable values remain the same). For the decision variable x_1 (number of project P_1), its coefficient value can only be in the range between 0 (= 3 − 3) and 7.5 (= 3 + 4.5), for the objective function value to remain the same. Similarly, for the decision variable x_2 (number of project P_2), its coefficient value can only be in the range between 2 (= 5 − 3) and infinity (= 5 + 1E+30), for the objective function value to remain the same.

Let us change the coefficient value of decision variable x_1 to 7 (still below the maximum value of 7.5) and re-run the Solver. You will get the same optimal solution of (2, 6) for the number of projects. Now, change the coefficient value of decision variable x_1 to 8 (which exceeds the maximum value of 7.5), and re-run the Solver. This time, the optimal solution is changed to (4, 3) for the number of projects.

Variable Cells

Cell	Name	Final Value	Reduced Cost	Objective Coefficient	Allowable Increase	Allowable Decrease
$C$9	Number of Projects Project P1	2	0	3	4.5	3
$D$9	Number of Projects Project P2	6	0	5	1E+30	3

Fig. 6.10 Sensitivity report with reduced cost for project-manpower example

Constraints

Cell	Name	Final Value	Shadow Price	Constraint R.H. Side	Allowable Increase	Allowable Decrease
$E$12	Manpower M1 Total Needed	2	0	4	1E+30	2
$E$13	Manpower M2 Total Needed	12	1.5	12	6	6
$E$14	Manpower M3 Total Needed	18	1	18	6	6

Fig. 6.11 Sensitivity report with shadow price for project-manpower example

6.1.8 Shadow Price or Lagrange Multiplier Value

Shadow price or Lagrange multiplier value is the amount by which the objective function value will increase if the RHS value is increased by 1 unit. Since non-binding constraint has slack, there is no meaning to increase the RHS further; thus, the shadow price is zero for non-binding constraint. For binding constraint, the resource is used to its maximum limit, which implies that there is value increasing the RHS value to increase the objective function value.

For the project-manpower example, the shadow price in the sensitivity report is shown in Fig. 6.11. We know that since manpower type 1 has slack of 2 units, its Lagrange multiplier value is zero. For manpower types 2 and 3, they are binding constraints, and their Lagrange multiplier values are 1.5 and 1, respectively. This means that for 1 unit increase in manpower type 2, the objective function value will increase by 1.5, while for 1 unit increase in manpower type 3, the objective function value will increase by 1. This will provide businesses with information to decide which manpower resource to hire if there are only enough funds to hire one new headcount. In this case, hiring one more manpower type 2 will bring in more revenue.

The allowable increase and decrease refer to the allowable change to the manpower availability for which the shadow price will remain the same. For manpower 1, since it is a non-binding constraint with a slack of 2, decreasing its availability by 2 units will not change its shadow price of zero. Also, increasing its availability to a very large number (shown as 1E+30) will also not change the shadow price, as it just means that the slack becomes a very large number. For manpower types 2 and 3, they are binding constraints. For manpower type 2, its availability can only be in the range between 6 (= 12 − 6) and 18 (= 12 + 6), for its shadow price is to remain at 1.5. Similarly, for manpower type 3, its availability can only be in the range between 12 (= 18 − 6) and 24 (= 18 + 6), for its shadow price is to remain at 1. Increasing or decreasing beyond this range will cause the constraint to become non-binding.

6.1.9 Worked Example for LP Problem

The police department needs to respond quickly to calls for help while patrolling in their patrol vehicles around the neighbourhood. The neighbourhood areas are laid out in rectangular blocks, and the patrol vehicles will travel along the horizontal and vertical road segments, which form the boundaries of the neighbourhood areas. The average speeds of the vehicles are 20 km/h and 15 km/h for traveling horizontally and vertically, respectively.

At any point in time, the nearest patrol vehicle to respond to call for help needs to travel an average of one-third of the horizontal patrol distance (x) and one-third of the vertical patrol distance (y), to reach the place that called for help. Each patrol vehicle must cover a rectangular perimeter of a minimum of 10 km and maximum of 12 km. In addition, all patrol vehicles need to cover overlapping areas to ensure that all road segments are patrolled to ensure the safety of the community. To do this, the vertical patrol distance must be at least 50% more than the horizontal patrol distance. Formulate the model to determine the patrol distances to achieve the fastest response time to call for help.

In this example, we will formulate the model with the following definition:

- x = horizontal patrol distance (decision variable).
- y = vertical patrol distance (decision variable).
- T = average response time (objective).

Objective function

$$\text{Minimize average response time } T = \frac{x/3}{20} + \frac{y/3}{15}$$

Constraints

$$2(x + y) \geq 10 \quad (1)$$

$$2(x + y) \leq 12 \quad (2)$$

$$y \geq 1.5x \quad (3)$$

Decision variables: $x, y \geq 0$

The objective function calculates the total average time taken to respond to calls for help. Using the knowledge of time = distance/speed, we can compute the average time along the horizontal and vertical road segments and sum them up. Constraints (1) and (2) will compute the perimeter and ensure that they are between 10 and 12. Constraint (3) will ensure that the vertical patrol distance must be at least 50% more than the horizontal patrol distance. Using Excel spreadsheet, we can lay out the problem as shown in Fig. 6.12 and the corresponding Solver definition in Fig. 6.13.

In Fig. 6.12, the average distances on x and y in cells C4:D4 are computed as 1/3 of the patrol distances x and y in cells C3:D3. The average time taken in cells C6:D6 are computed using the average distance divided by the average speed. The total time taken will be summed up in cell E6. The perimeter is computed in cell E3, and cells F3 and G3 contain the maximum and minimum perimeter values. Cell H3 computes 1.5 times of patrol distance x meant for constraint (3).

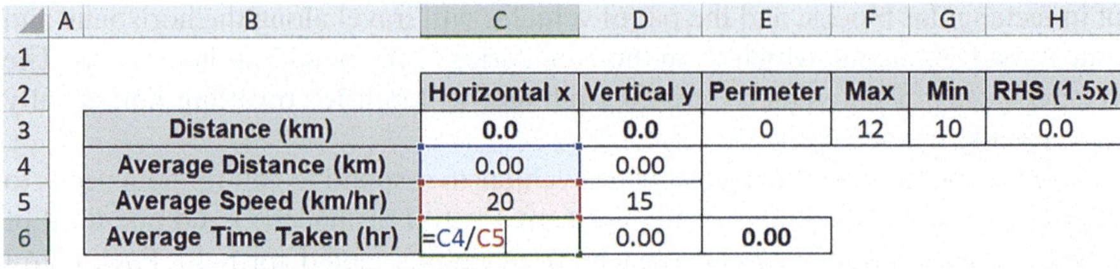

	A	B	C	D	E	F	G	H
1								
2			Horizontal x	Vertical y	Perimeter	Max	Min	RHS (1.5x)
3		Distance (km)	0.0	0.0	0	12	10	0.0
4		Average Distance (km)	0.00	0.00				
5		Average Speed (km/hr)	20	15				
6		Average Time Taken (hr)	=C4/C5	0.00	0.00			

Fig. 6.12 Excel spreadsheet model for worked example

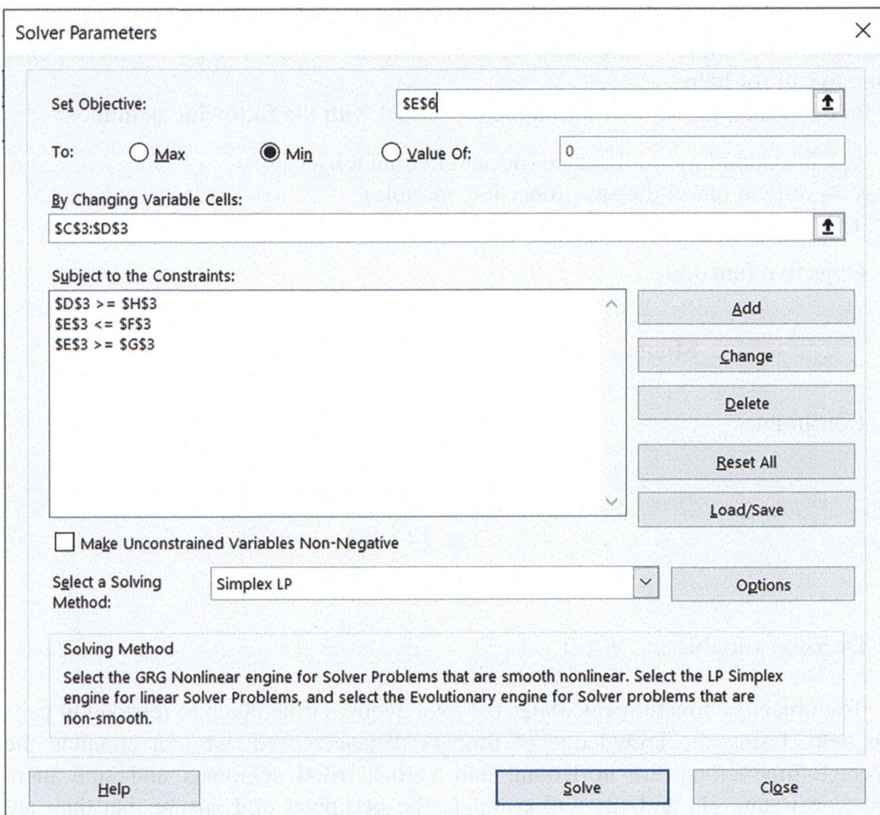

Fig. 6.13 Excel solver definition for worked example

Figure 6.13 shows the minimization of the objective function cell E6; the decision variables C3:D3 are the changing variable cells; the constraints for the perimeter in cell E3 must be between 12 and 10 given in cells F3 and G3, respectively; and a last constraint for the vertical patrol distance in cell D3 to be ≥ 1.5 times of patrol distance x given in cell H3. Note that we did not include the constraint that the

	A	B	C	D	E	F	G	H
1								
2			Horizontal x	Vertical y	Perimeter	Max	Min	RHS (1.5x)
3		Distance (km)	2.0	3.0	10	12	10	3.0
4		Average Distance (km)	0.67	1.00				
5		Average Speed (km/hr)	20	15				
6		Average Time Taken (hr)	0.03	0.07	0.10			

Fig. 6.14 Optimal solution for worked example

decision variables must be ≥ 0 and did not check the checkbox option "Make Unconstrained Variables Non-Negative". This is because the three constraints considered together will ensure that the decision variables will be positive, so this constraint is optional.

The optimal solution obtained is x = 2.0, y = 3.0, and the minimized average time to call for help is 0.1 hour (or 6 minutes) as shown in Fig. 6.14. One may notice that the perimeter covered is exactly equal to the minimum of 10. Thus, in fact, the constraint to limit the maximum perimeter to 12 is a redundant constraint since the objective is to minimize total average time taken.

6.2 Integer Programming

There are three types of integer programming models, and they include:

- Pure integer programming (IP)—this is simply a linear programming model with one additional constraint that all the decision variables must be integers.
- Mixed integer programming (MIP)—this is also a linear programming model where only some of the decision variables must be integers, while the remaining ones need not be integers.
- Binary integer programming (BIP)—this is also a linear programming model, but some or all the decision variables can only be binary, 0 or 1.

Among the three types, we will discuss BIP in detail as it offers special formulation techniques which can convert an originally intractable IP or LP problem into a tractable BIP problem, by adding auxiliary binary variables into the model.

6.2.1 Formulating BIP with Either-or Constraints

There are many instances in modeling optimization problems that may lead to the problem becoming intractable. For example, if we have resource constraints for two different resources and a solution can only use one of the two resources. In modeling such a problem, there is an either-or situation, where the optimal solution will either choose resource type 1 or choose resource type 2. How would we model it?

Let us use an example to understand how to model such an either-or situation. A factory must produce two products, A and B, using a certain raw material. This raw material comes in two different forms, Type 1 and Type 2, and the two types differ in terms of strength, and thus the amount to use in production will differ. To produce one unit of product A, it can either use three units of Type 1 or four units of Type 2. To produce one unit of product B, it can either use two units of Type 1 or three units of Type 2. The availability of the raw material is 300 units and 350 units for Type 1 and Type 2, respectively. The production quantity for each product must be at least 50 units. How many units of products A and B does the factory need to produce to maximize the total production output?

To formulate this model, we will define the decision variables:

- x_1 = number of product A to produce.
- x_2 = number of product B to produce.

Objective function

$$\text{Maximize output } Z = x_1 + x_2$$

Constraints

$$3x_1 + 2x_2 \leq 300 \quad (1)$$

$$4x_1 + 3x_2 \leq 350 \quad (2)$$

$$x_1, x_2 \geq 50 \quad (3)$$

At this point, the model does not include the consideration that only one of the two resources, Type 1 or Type 2, needs to be used when maximizing the production output. To include this consideration, we will need to add in an auxiliary binary decision variable y to be the third decision variable and a very large number represented by M. Constraints (1) and (2) will be reformulated, and we need to add a new constraint (4) to restrict y to be a binary variable.

Constraints

$$3x_1 + 2x_2 \leq 300 + yM \quad (1)$$

$$4x_1 + 3x_2 \leq 350 + (1 - y)M \quad (2)$$

$$x_1, x_2 \geq 50 \quad (3)$$

$$y \in \{0, 1\} \quad (4)$$

Let us understand the reformulated constraints (1) and (2).

- When y = 1, this means that the RHS of constraint (1) will become a very large number due to M, making constraint (1) no longer a constraint, while for constraint (2), the RHS value remains as 350.
- When y = 0, this means that the RHS of constraint (2) will become a very large number due to M, making constraint (2) no longer a constraint, while for constraint (1), the RHS value remains as 300.

Thus, the optimizer will choose the appropriate value for y, either 0 or 1, to ensure that the objective function value is maximized.

Using Excel spreadsheet, we can lay out the problem as shown in Fig. 6.15 and the corresponding Solver definition in Fig. 6.16. In Fig. 6.15, the objective function in cell D2 is the total production quantity, which is the sum of the production units for products A and B in cells B2:C2 being the decision variables. The binary decision variable y is initially set to 0 in cell B9. The total consumptions of the resources are computed in cells D12:D13 as the LHS of constraints (1) and (2), respectively. The RHS of constraints (1) and (2) are computed in cells E12:E13, taking into account the binary variable y and the very large number M, which is assumed to be 9999999 (or any large value) in cell B10. The RHS values of constraint (3) are set in cells B3:C3. Constraint (4) defines y as binary.

Figure 6.16 shows the maximization of the objective function cell D2; the decision variables B2:C2 are the changing variable cells for the production units, and cell B9 is the binary decision variable; the constraints for minimum production quantities for B2:C2 ≥ B3:C3; B9 must be binary; and the last constraint for the resource consumption LHS in cells D12:D13 must not exceed the RHS in cells E12: E13. Note that the solving method selected is GRG Nonlinear as we have a binary decision variable in the model. Note that we did not include the constraint that all the decision variables must be ≥ 0 and did not check the checkbox option "Make Unconstrained Variables Non-Negative". This is because we are maximizing total

	A	B	C	D	E
1		Product A	Product B	Total Production	
2	Production units	0.0	0.0	0.0	
3	Minimum	50	50		
4					
5	Raw Materials			Availability	
6	Type 1	3	2	300	
7	Type 2	4	3	350	
8					
9	Binary (y)	0			
10	Very large number M	9999999			
11				LHS	RHS
12	Constraint (1)	0	0	0	=D6+B9*B10
13	Constraint (2)	0	0	0	10000349

Fig. 6.15 Excel spreadsheet model for either-or constraint example

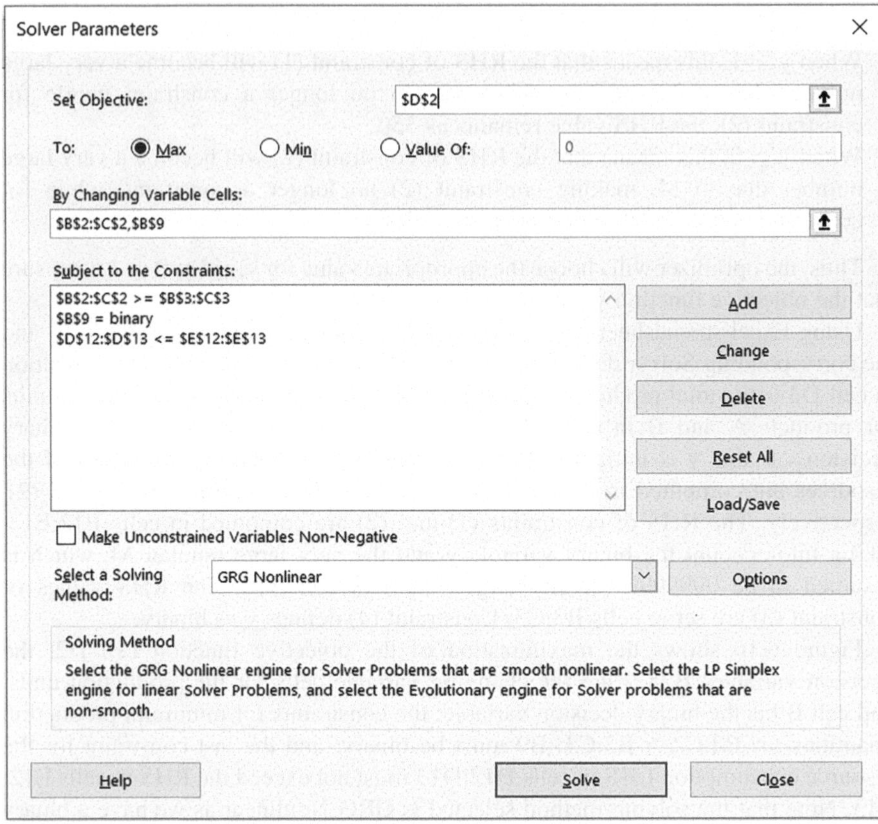

Fig. 6.16 Excel solver definition for either-or constraint example

production, which will ensure that the production units will be positive, and setting the binary constraint for B9 will naturally restrict it to a positive value. So, this constraint is optional.

The optimal solution obtained is $x_1 = 50.0$, $x_2 = 75.0$, $y = 0$, which means that resource Type 1 is used, and the maximized total production is 125.0 units as shown in Fig. 6.17.

6.2.2 *Formulating BIP with K-Out-of-N Constraints*

What if we must choose K resources out of N possible resources to use? We can generalize the either-or constraint model to include N resource constraints and structure another constraint to pick only K of them. Consider the original N resource constraints to be given below where the total consumption of resources on the LHS is

	A	B	C	D	E
1		Product A	Product B	Total Production	
2	Production units	50.0	75.0	125.0	
3	Minimum	50	50		
4					
5	Raw Materials			Availability	
6	Type 1	3	2	300	
7	Type 2	4	3	350	
8					
9	Binary (y)	0			
10	Very large number M	9999999			
11				LHS	RHS
12	Constraint (1)	150	150	300	300
13	Constraint (2)	200	225	425	10000349

Fig. 6.17 Optimal solution for either-or constraint example

computed as a function of the decision variables $x_1, x_2, \ldots, x_N$ and the RHS are the respective resource availabilities $a_1, a_2, \ldots, a_N$,

$$
\begin{aligned}
f_1(x_1, x_2, \ldots, x_N) &\le a_1 \quad (1)\\
f_2(x_1, x_2, \ldots, x_N) &\le a_2 \quad (2)\\
\ldots & \qquad (\ldots)\\
f_N(x_1, x_2, \ldots, x_N) &\le a_N \quad (N)
\end{aligned}
$$

We will reformulate the N constraints using N auxiliary binary decision variables $y_1, y_2, \ldots, y_N$ and a very large M, which means that we will introduce N more decision variables into the model. We will also need to add another constraint to ensure that the model chooses only K out of N constraints. Constraints (1) to (N) will have their RHS modified as shown below. Whenever a binary variable $y_i = 1$, this would mean that this i^{th} constraint will have a very large RHS value, making it no longer a constraint. Therefore, constraint (N + 1) is added to ensure that (N − K) of the constraints have their $y_i = 1$, leaving only K constraints with their $y_i = 0$.

$$
\begin{aligned}
f_1(x_1, x_2, \ldots, x_N) &\le a_1 + My_1 \quad (1)\\
f_2(x_1, x_2, \ldots, x_N) &\le a_2 + My_2 \quad (2)\\
\ldots & \qquad (\ldots)\\
f_N(x_1, x_2, \ldots, x_N) &\le a_N + My_N \quad (N)\\
\textstyle\sum_{i=1}^{N} y_N &= N - K \quad (N+1)
\end{aligned}
$$

We can see that the either-or constraint model is a special case of K-out-of-N constraints model, where K = 1 and N = 2.

6.2.3 *Formulating BIP with N Possible RHS Values for the Same Constraint*

In many purchasing scenarios, suppliers of materials may impose a requirement that orders placed must be in multiples of a fixed quantity (e.g. 50, 100, 150 and so on) or the materials only come in certain fixed order quantities (e.g. 50, 80, 120 and so on). This could be due to the way the materials are packaged and the supplier is not willing to break up the original packaging to sell them as loose units. In this case, an optimal solution will need to determine the correct RHS value.

Consider the original N constraints with N possible RHS values given below, where the total consumption of resources on the LHS is computed as a function of the decision variables x_1, x_2, ..., x_N and the RHS are the respective resource availabilities a_1, a_2, . . ., a_N,

$$f_1(x_1, x_2, \ldots, x_N) \le a_1 \quad (1)$$

$$f_2(x_1, x_2, \ldots, x_N) \le a_2 \quad (2)$$

$$\ldots \quad (\ldots)$$

$$f_N(x_1, x_2, \ldots, x_N) \le a_N \quad (N)$$

These constraints are the same as that for the K-out-of-N constraint model. We could re-formulate the constraints like what we did for K-out-of-N constraint model by setting $K = 1$, so that the optimal solution will choose only one constraint with the correct RHS value. Alternatively, we can re-formulate the N constraints by combining them into one *single* constraint using N auxiliary binary decision variables y_1, y_2, . . ., y_N, which means that we will introduce N more decision variables into the model. We will also add another constraint to ensure that the model chooses only one RHS value.

$$f(x_1, x_2, \ldots, x_N) \le \sum\nolimits_{i=1}^{N} a_i y_i \quad (1)$$

$$\sum\nolimits_{i=1}^{N} y_i = 1 \quad (2)$$

Let us use an example to understand how to model this situation. A factory needs 27 effective man-hours per day to fulfil a production order. The factory can choose to hire a combination of full-time (FT) or part-time (PT) workers. A FT worker is expected to work 8 hours a day and will be paid \$12 per man-hour, so the daily rate will be $\$12 \times 8 = \$96$. However, if overtime is needed, the factory will have to pay 1.5 times the hourly rate per hour, that is, $\$12 \times 1.5 = \$18$ per hour.

FT workers may lose productivity during normal working hours as they get too comfortable socializing with one another, delivering lower effective man-hour than expected. It was found that:

- When one FT worker is hired, productivity is 100%, so the effective man-hour is 8.
- When two FT workers are hired, productivity falls, and the effective man-hour drops to 15, instead of the expected 16.
- When three FT workers are hired, productivity falls further, and the effective man-hour drops to 22, instead of the expected 24.
- When four FT workers are hired, productivity falls even further, and the effective man-hour drops to 29, instead of the expected 32.

Note that the factory still needs to pay the FT worker $96 per day for normal working hours despite the productivity loss. It is assumed that there will be no productivity loss if the FT worker needs to work overtime.

On the other hand, PT workers do not have productivity loss issues, but they are more expensive to hire. A PT worker is paid $15 per hour and must be hired in 4-hour block per day. If eight effective man-hour is needed from PT workers, the factory must hire two PT workers. The factory manager would like to determine the optimal number of FT and PT workers he needs to hire. Design an optimization model to determine the solution by minimizing the total labour cost.

Let us define the parameters as follows:

- x_e = total number of FT expected man-hour.
- x_f = total number of FT effective man-hour.
- x_p = total number of PT effective man-hour.
- x_o = total number of effective overtime man-hour by FT workers.
- $y_1, y_2, \ldots, y_5$ = binary decision variables corresponding to 0, 1, 2, 3 and 4 FT workers, respectively.
- N_f = number of FT workers to hire.
- N_p = number of PT workers to hire.

Objective function

$$\text{Minimize total labor cost } Z = 12x_e + 15x_p + 18x_o$$

Constraints

$$x_e = 0y_1 + 8y_2 + 16y_3 + 24y_4 + 32y_5 \quad (1)$$

$$x_f = 0y_1 + 8y_2 + 15y_3 + 22y_4 + 29y_5 \quad (2)$$

$$x_p = 4N_p \quad (3)$$

$$x_f + x_p + x_o = 27 \quad (4)$$

$$y_1 + y_2 + y_3 + y_4 + y_5 = 1 \quad (5)$$

$$x_o, N_p \quad \text{integer} \quad (6)$$

$$y_1, y_2, y_3, y_4, y_5 \quad \text{binary} \quad (7)$$

Decision variables: $y_1, y_2, y_3, y_4, y_5, x_o, N_p \geq 0$

	A	B	C	D	E	F	G
1	Number of work-hour per FT worker per day	8					
2	Number of work-hour per PT worker per day	4					
3	Hourly rate of FT worker	$ 12.00					
4	Overtime Hourly rate of FT worker	$ 18.00					
5	Hourly rate of PT worker	$ 15.00					
6							
7		Number of FT workers					
8		0	1	2	3	4	
9	Expected man-hour	0	8	16	24	32	
10	FT worker effective man-hour	0	8	15	22	29	
11	Binary (Y1, Y2, Y3, Y4, Y5)	0	0	0	0	0	0
12	Total FT expected man-hour (Xe)	0	*Constraint(1)*				*Constraint(5)*
13	Total FT effective man-hour (Xf)	0	*Constraint(2)*				
14	Number of OT hours by FT workers (Xo)	0					
15	Number of FT workers to hire (Nf)	0					
16							
17	Number of PT workers to hire (Np)	0					
18	Total PT hours (Xp)	0	*Constraint(3)*				
19			Required				
20	Total number of effective man-hour (Xf + Xo + Xp)	0	27	*Constraint(4)*			
21	Total labour cost incurred	$ -					

Fig. 6.18 Excel spreadsheet model for N possible RHS values example

In this formulation, constraints (1), (2) and (3) need not be added into the Solver definition as they can be computed as part of the Excel spreadsheet model. Only constraints (4)–(7) need to be defined in Solver.

Using Excel spreadsheet, we can layout the problem as shown in Fig. 6.18 and the corresponding Solver definition in Fig. 6.19. In Fig. 6.18, the objective function in cell B21 is the total labour cost, which is the sum product of the work hours at the different rates for FT, PT and overtime work. The binary decision variables y_1, y_2, y_3, y_4, y_5 in cells B11:F11 are initially set to 0. The total FT expected man-hour is computed in cell B12 as constraint (1), while the total FT effective man-hour is computed in cell B13 as constraint (2). The total PT hours is computed in cell B18 as constraint (3). The total effective man-hour is computed in cell B20 as constraint (4). And finally, the sum of all binary decision variables is computed in cell G11 as constraint (5).

Figure 6.19 shows the minimization of the objective function cell B21; the decision variable in cell B14 is the number of OT hours, cell B17 is the number of PT workers and cells B11:F11 are the binary decision variables; the constraint for total effective man-hour in cell B20 must be equal to 27 in cell C20; the constraint in cell G11 for the sum of all binary decision variables must be = 1; all binary decision variables must be binary; and number of OT hours and number of PT workers must be integer. We check the checkbox option "Make Unconstrained Variables Non--Negative" to ensure that number of OT hours and number of PT workers are positive. Note that the solving method selected is GRG Nonlinear as we have integer and binary decision variables in the model.

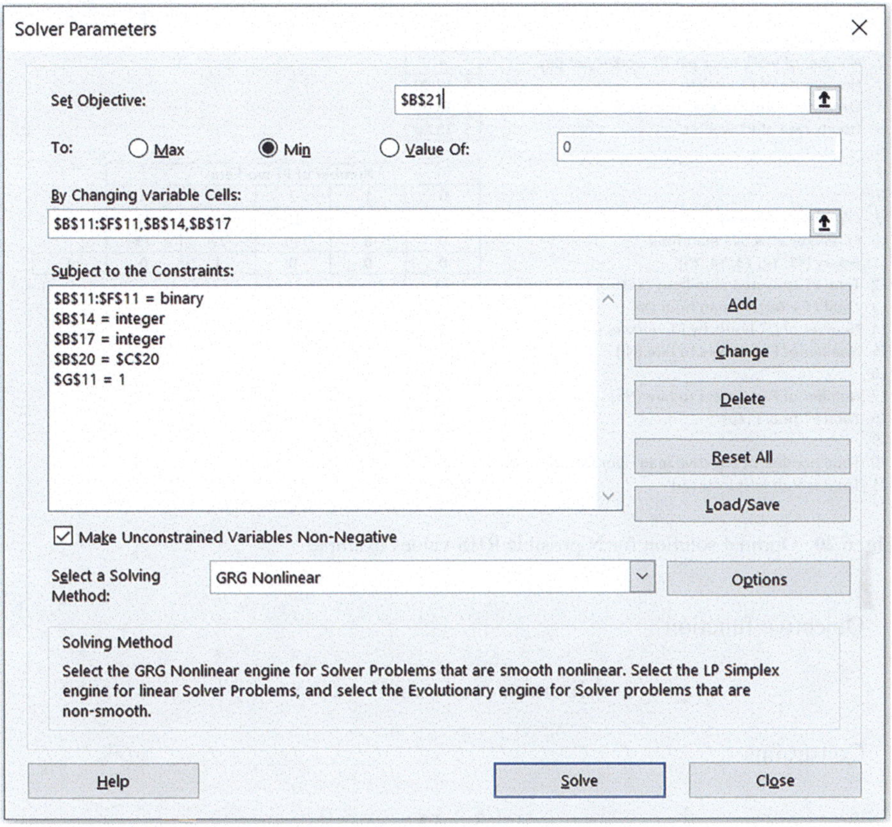

Fig. 6.19 Excel solver definition for N possible RHS values example

The optimal solution obtained is to hire three FT workers and one PT worker and to have one overtime hour to meet the 27 effective man-hours required, and the minimized total labour cost is $366 as shown in Fig. 6.20.

6.2.4 Formulating BIP for Fixed Charge Problem

A fixed charge problem occurs when there is an upfront setup cost and a unit variable cost which is dependent on the activity level. If the activity level is zero, then both costs will be zero. For example, when one buys a car, there will be an upfront cost of buying the car, and the total variable cost incurred will depend on how much distance one drives. If one does not drive at all, then there is no need to buy the car, and there will be no driving; thus, both costs will be zero.

The standard formulation for a single decision fixed charge problem where k is the setup cost, c is the unit variable cost and x is the activity level, is given as follows:

	A	B	C	D	E	F	G
1	Number of work-hour per FT worker per day	8					
2	Number of work-hour per PT worker per day	4					
3	Hourly rate of FT worker	$ 12.00					
4	Overtime Hourly rate of FT worker	$ 18.00					
5	Hourly rate of PT worker	$ 15.00					
6							
7		Number of FT workers					
8		0	1	2	3	4	
9	Expected man-hour	0	8	16	24	32	
10	FT worker effective man-hour	0	8	15	22	29	
11	Binary (Y1, Y2, Y3, Y4, Y5)	0	0	0	1	0	1
12	Total FT expected man-hour (Xe)	24	*Constraint(1)*				*Constraint(5)*
13	Total FT effective man-hour (Xf)	22	*Constraint(2)*				
14	Number of OT hours by FT workers (Xo)	1					
15	Number of FT workers to hire (Nf)	3					
16							
17	Number of PT workers to hire (Np)	1					
18	Total PT hours (Xp)	4	*Constraint(3)*				
19			Required				
20	Total number of effective man-hour (Xf + Xo + Xp)	27	27	*Constraint(4)*			
21	Total labour cost incurred	**$366.00**					

Fig. 6.20 Optimal solution for N possible RHS values example

Objective function

$$\text{Minimize total cost } Z = f(x)$$

Constraints

$$f(x) = \begin{cases} k + cx & , x > 0 \\ 0 & ; x = 0 \end{cases}$$

As the constraint is made up of two parts, which is dependent on the value of x, we need to reformulate it using a binary decision variable y and a very large M as follows:

Objective function

$$\text{Minimize total cost } Z = ky + cx$$

Constraint

$$x \leq My$$

This reformulated model implies that when $x > 0$, the constraint will make $y = 1$ due to the very large M; then the total cost will be computed as k + cx. When $x = 0$, the constraint will result in either $y = 0$ or $y = 1$. As we are minimizing total cost, this will force $y = 0$, and thus the total cost will also be 0.

Let us generalize this single-decision fixed charge problem to a N-decision fixed charge problem, where j represents the index for decisions and $j = 1$ to N.

Objective function

$$\text{Minimize total cost } Z = f_1(x_1) + f_2(x_2) + \ldots + f_N(x_N)$$

Constraints

$$f_j(x_j) = \begin{cases} k_j + c_j x_j & , x_j > 0 \\ 0 & , x_j = 0 \end{cases} \quad , j = 1, 2, \ldots, N$$

The reformulated model will have N auxiliary binary decision variables and the very large M.

Objective function

$$\text{Minimize total cost } Z = \sum_{j=1}^{N} k_j y_j + c_j x_j$$

Constraints

$$x_j \leq M y_j \quad \forall j$$

The interpretation for this reformulated model is the same as the single-decision problem. When $x_j > 0$, the constraint will make $y_j = 1$ due to the very large M. When $x_j = 0$, the constraint will result in either $y_j = 0$ or $y_j = 1$. As we are minimizing total cost, this will force $y_j = 0$. As this is a multiple-decision model, it may end up some $x_j > 0$ and some $x_j = 0$. Note the use of the symbol $\forall$j, which represents "for all j", implies that we need to repeat this constraint for all j values.

Let us use an example to understand how to model a two-decision fixed charge problem. A manufacturer can produce two products, A and B. Product A has a setup cost of \$100 and a unit variable cost of \$5. Product B has a setup cost of \$150 and a unit variable cost of \$4. The manufacturer has to produce at least 2000 units of either product A or B, or both. Determine the optimal production which will incur the lowest total cost.

Let us define the parameters as follows:

- x_1, x_2 = number of units of products A and B, respectively (decision variables).
- k_1, k_2= setup cost for products A and B, respectively.
- c_1, c_2 = unit variable cost for products A and B, respectively.
- y_1, y_2 = binary decision variables for products A and B, respectively.

Objective function

$$\text{Minimize total cost } Z = k_1 y_1 + c_1 x_1 + k_2 y_2 + c_2 y_2$$

Constraints

$$x_1 \leq My_1 \quad (1)$$

$$x_2 \leq My_2 \quad (2)$$

$$x_1 + x_2 \geq 2000 \quad (3)$$

$$y_1, y_2 \quad \text{binary} \quad (4)$$

Using Excel spreadsheet, we can lay out the problem as shown in Fig. 6.21 and the corresponding Solver definition in Fig. 6.22. In Fig. 6.21, the objective function in cell B9 is the total cost, which is the sum of the setup cost and variable cost for both decisions. The binary decision variables y_1, y_2 in cells B4:C4 and the decision variables for production in cells B6:C6 are initially set to 0. The RHS of the constraints (1) and (2) are computed in cells B5:C5. Constraint (3) is the total production in cell D6, which must be at least 2000 units in cell E6.

Figure 6.22 shows the minimization of the objective function cell B9; the decision variables in cells B6:C6 are the production units for products A and B, and cells B4:C4 are the corresponding binary decision variables; the constraint for the production units for products A and B in cells B6:C6 must be ≤ to the RHS of My_i in cells B5:C5, and the total production in cell D6 must be at least 2000 units in cell E6; all binary decision variables must be binary. We check the checkbox option "Make Unconstrained Variables Non-Negative" to ensure that production units for products A and B are positive. Note that the solving method selected is GRG Nonlinear as we have integer and binary decision variables in the model.

The optimal solution obtained is to produce 2000 units of product B, and the minimized total cost is $8150 as shown in Fig. 6.23.

	A	B	C	D	E
1		Product A	Product B		
2	Setup cost	100	150		
3	Variable cost	5	4		
4	Binary variable y	0	0		
5	M*y	0	0	Total Production	Minimum Production
6	Production units	0.0	0.0	0.0	2000.0
7					
8	Very large number M	9999999			
9	Total Cost	0.0			

Fig. 6.21 Excel spreadsheet model for fixed charge problem example

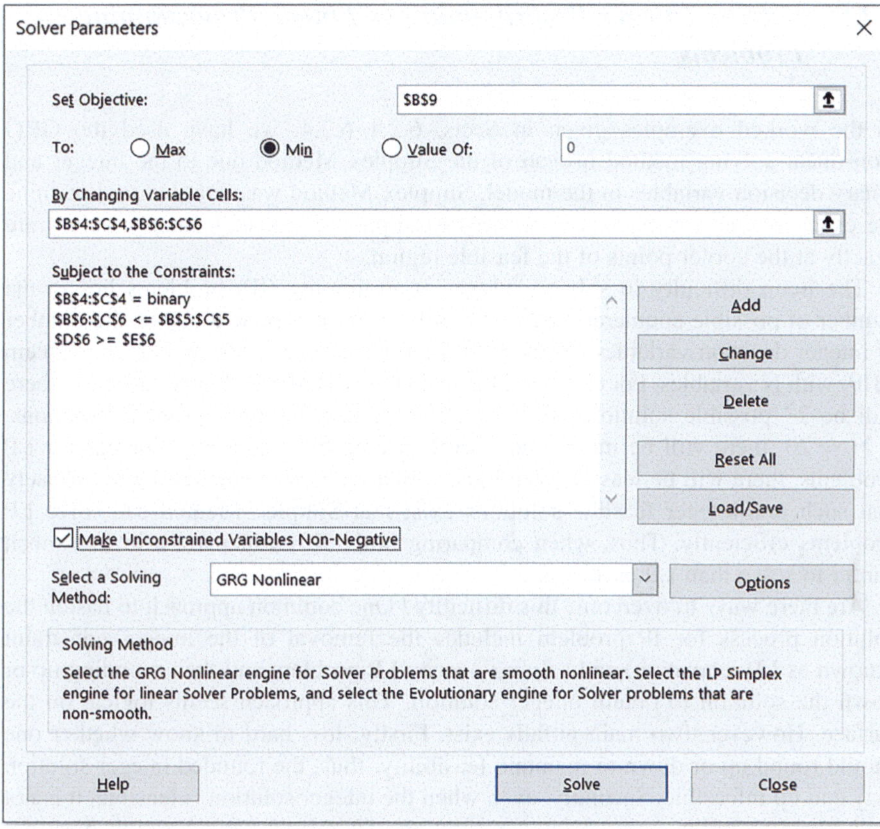

Fig. 6.22 Excel solver definition for fixed charge problem example

	A	B	C	D	E
1		Product A	Product B		
2	Setup cost	100	150		
3	Variable cost	5	4		
4	Binary variable y	0	1		
5	M*y	0	9999999	Total Production	Minimum Production
6	Production units	0.0	2000.0	2000.0	2000.0
7					
8	Very large number M	9999999			
9	Total Cost	8150.0			

Fig. 6.23 Optimal solution for fixed charge problem example

6.2.5 Solving Integer Programming vs Linear Programming Problems

In the worked examples given in Sects. 6.2.1–6.2.4, we have used the GRG Non-linear solving method instead of the Simplex Method due to the integer and binary decision variables in the model. Simplex Method was not able to determine the exact integer values for our worked examples unless such integer values are exactly at the corner points of the feasible region.

The main difficulty in solving integer programming (IP) problems lies in the number of possible enumerations, which will increase exponentially as the number of integer decision variables increases. Take for example, a binary integer problem (BIP) with N variables. For each variable, it can only be 0 or 1. For N variables, there will be 2^N possible solutions. If $N = 10$, there will be 1024 possible solutions. If $N = 20$, there will be more than 1 million possible solutions. Whereas for LP problems, there will be feasible solutions, which are non-integer, and it is precisely that such non-integer feasible solutions exist that Simplex Method can solve LP problems efficiently. Thus, when comparing both, IP problems are in fact much harder to solve than LP problems.

Are there ways to overcome this difficulty? One common approach to hasten the solution process for IP problem includes the removal of the integer constraint (known as LP relaxation) and solving it as an LP problem and then rounding up or down the solution to obtain integer solution. This approach seems logical on the surface. However, two main pitfalls exist. Firstly, it is hard to know whether one should round up or down to maintain feasibility; thus, the rounded integer solution may end up infeasible. Secondly, even when the integer solution is feasible, it is not guaranteed to be an optimal integer solution. Therefore, LP relaxation does not always work. However, there are some special cases of LP relaxation problems where the optimal solutions to the LP problems satisfy the integer constraints, meaning the solutions are integers and therefore are optimal solutions to the original IP problems. We will be discussing such special optimization problems in Chap. 7.

There are a few common solving methods to solve IP problems including branch-and-bound, cutting-plane method and branch-and-cut (combination of branch-and-bound and cutting-plane methods). Such solving methods are heuristic algorithms which are iterative in nature. In solving large-scale IP and MIP problems, heuristic algorithms can be designed and built to provide quick feasible solutions; however, optimality is not guaranteed. We will be discussing heuristic algorithms in Chap. 9.

6.3 Non-linear Programming

Non-linear programming (NLP) models have non-linear objective function and/or constraints. We can express an NLP with n decision variables and m constraints in general form as follows:

Objective function

$$\text{Minimize } Z = f(\mathbf{x}) \qquad \text{where } \mathbf{x} = (x_1, x_2, \ldots, x_n)$$

Constraints

$$g_i(\mathbf{x}) \leq b_i \qquad \text{where } i = 1, 2, \ldots, m$$

Decision variables: $\mathbf{x} \geq 0$

The general form looks very similar to that of the LP problem, but the main difference is the non-linear functions. It is important to note that there is no one single algorithm that can solve every specific problem that fits the general form of NLP, unlike in LP where Simplex Method guarantees it. However, there are some basic NLP problem types where solutions do exist and specific algorithms have been developed, and they include:

- Unconstrained Optimization
- Linearly Constrained Optimization
- Quadratic Programming
- Convex Programming
- Separable Programming
- Non-convex Programming
- Geometric Programming
- Fractional Programming

It is not the focus of this book to understand the mathematics behind each algorithm but rather to have a good understanding of the concepts and then use the appropriate tools to find solutions to problems. We will discuss some characteristics of optimal solutions of NLP problems and solve a worked example.

6.3.1 Characteristics of Optimal Solutions of NLP Problems

For LP problems, we know that the optimal solution will either be at the corner point or at the boundary for bounded feasible region. However, in NLP, both situations may not occur. Let us revisit the project-manpower example to determine the optimal number of projects x_1 and x_2 to maximize the total revenue.

Objective function

$$\text{Maximize revenue } Z = r_1 x_1 + r_2 x_2 = 3x_1 + 5x_2$$

Constraints

$$1x_1 + 0x_2 \le 4 \rightarrow x_1 \le 4 \quad (1)$$

$$0x_1 + 2x_2 \le 12 \rightarrow x_2 \le 6 \quad (2)$$

$$3x_1 + 2x_2 \le 18 \quad (3)$$

Decision variables: $x_1, x_2 \ge 0$

If we were to replace constraint (3) with a non-linear function, $9x_1^2 + 5x_2^2 \le 216$, the boundary at the top of the feasible region will now become a curve rather than a straight line as shown in Fig. 6.24. This non-linear function, $9x_1^2 + 5x_2^2 \le 216$, is the same as that used in the example found in Hillier and Lieberman (2001). Using the same objective function, maximizing the revenue will move the objective function line up until it reaches the optimal solution. In this case, the optimal solution remains as (2, 6); however, it is no longer a corner point.

Now, let us try to change the objective function to a non-linear function $Z = 54x_1 - 9x_1^2 + 78x_2 - 13x_2^2$, which will be a curve shown in Fig. 6.25. This non-linear function $Z = 54x_1 - 9x_1^2 + 78x_2 - 13x_2^2$ is the same as that used in the example found in Hillier and Lieberman (2001). The optimal solution in this case is at (3, 3), which lies inside the feasible region. Because the optimal solution is not guaranteed to be at the corner point, and also not guaranteed to be on the boundary, determining the optimal solution for NLP will be much harder.

Fig. 6.24 Optimal solution for NLP not at corner point

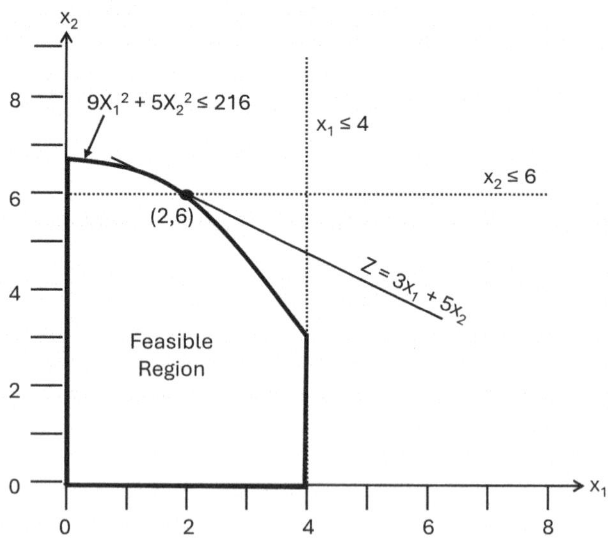

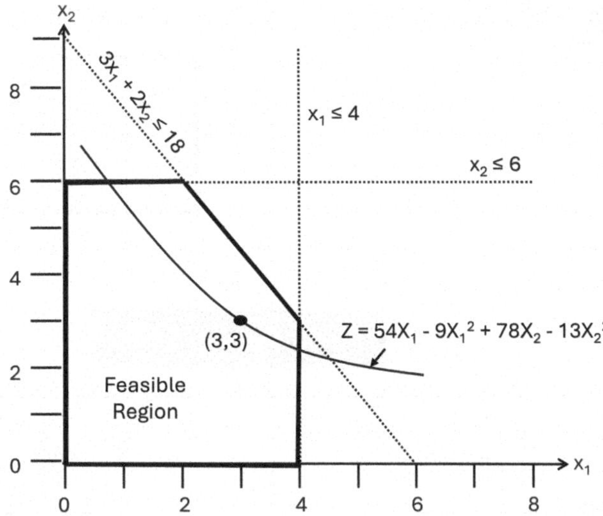

Fig. 6.25 Optimal solution for NLP not at boundary

6.3.2 Local Optimal and Global Optimal

As discussed, there are some basic NLP problem types where solutions do exist. However, one challenge faced is that NLP is unable to distinguish whether the solution obtained is a local optimal solution or a global optimal solution. Therefore, we need to know the conditions under which any local optimal solution is guaranteed to be the global optimal solution. For this, we need to explore convex and concave functions.

Recall for a single variable function f(x), we can double-differentiate the function into $d^2f(x)/dx^2$.

- If $d^2f(x)/dx^2 < 0$, then we will have a global maximum and f(x) is a concave function.
- If $d^2f(x)/dx^2 > 0$, then we will have a global minimum and f(x) is a convex function.

What about functions with multiple variables, e.g. f(**x**) and $\mathbf{x} = (x_1, x_2, \ldots, x_n)$? We can apply the concept for a single variable function accordingly.

- If each term is concave, then the function f(**x**) is a concave function.
- If each term is convex, then the function f(**x**) is a convex function.

If this non-linear problem does not have any constraints, which means that the solution space is the entire universe, then double-differentiating a concave function will guarantee a global maximum, while double-differentiating a convex function will guarantee a global minimum.

However, if there are constraints that will restrict the feasible region, then we need to know if the feasible region is a convex set. It is only when the feasible region is a convex set will a global optimal be guaranteed. What is a convex set? A convex set is a set of points where with connecting any two points in the collection with a

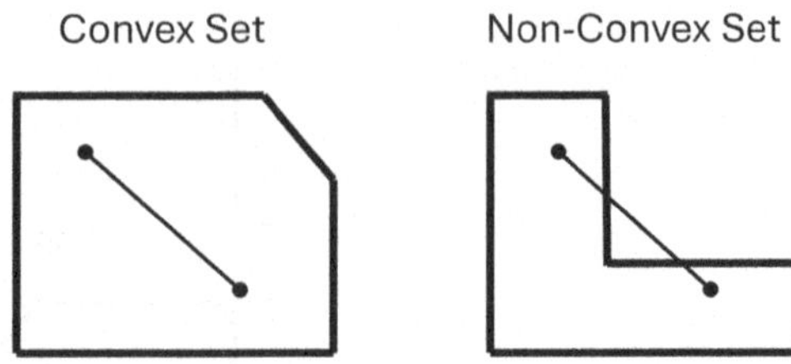

Fig. 6.26 Convex set and non-convex set

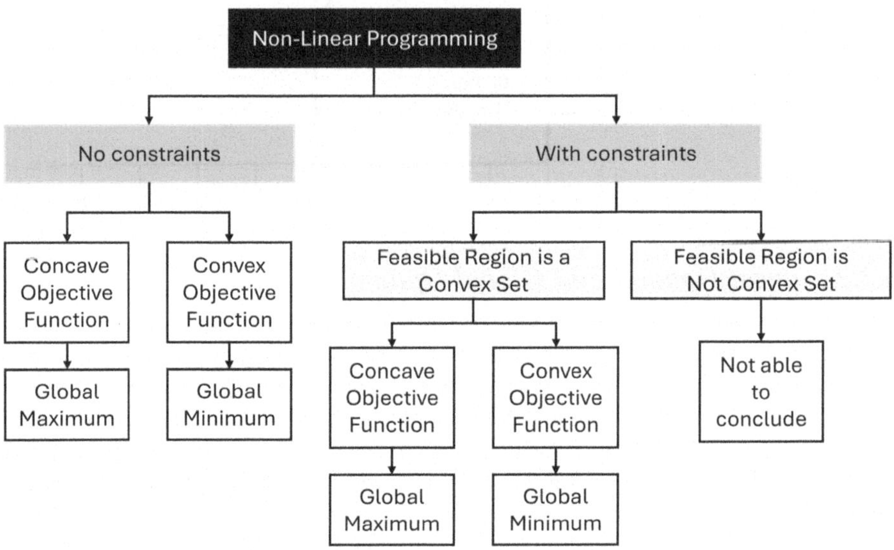

Fig. 6.27 Conditions for NLP global optimal solutions

straight line, the *entire* line segment must also be in the collection. Figure 6.26 shows the illustrations for convex set and a non-convex set.

Let us summarize the conditions for an NLP solution to be global optimal as shown in Fig. 6.27.

6.4 Case 6A: Container Optimization for Carbon Footprint Reduction

This case is modified from the paper published by Chong et al. (2014). In this case, Company CC is a manufacturer of consumer goods with several production plants at several locations in China, and the finished products are shipped to customers in the USA via ocean freight.

Table 6.2 Container volumes at 95% fill rate

	20 FT	40 FT	40 HC
Maximum container volume (cubic meters)	33.2	66.7	76.2
~95% container volume (cubic meters)	31.5	63.4	72.4

It is quite common to ship containers which are not full, known as Less-than-Container Load (LCL) from the source location to destination location. Shipping LCL will result in higher shipping costs and increased carbon footprint. We define carbon footprint for this case study to be the total carbon emission for all shipments via sea and land transportation. In the shipping industry, there are three types of container sizes, namely, 20-footer container (20FT), 40-footer container (40FT) and 40-footer high-cube (40HC) container. To estimate the carbon emission contributed by each container size, we used the ratio for 20FT, 40FT and 40HC containers to be 1:2:2.2.

In this case, the objective would be to build a Container Size Optimization (CSO) model to minimize the total carbon emission by determining the optimal container mix (number of containers of different sizes) that will satisfy the total shipment volume required. Based on Company CC's past data collected, the fill rates of the containers were relatively low, and 65% of the shipments are LCL. In the best case, the containers were usually filled up to the maximum of 95%, and we would use 95% as a capacity constraint in our optimization model. Table 6.2 shows the container volumes for different container sizes and their respective volumes at 95% fill rate.

A few assumptions were made to solve the CSO:

- Containers can only be packed up to 95% of their volume and will be considered as Full-Container-Load (FCL).
- All shipments are completed via FCL for all container types.
- There is no limit on the number of containers available for each type.
- The weight of the shipment does not impact the carbon emission of the containers.

Let us define the parameters as follows:

- i = Container type, 1 for 20FT, 2 for 40FT and 3 for 40HC, $i = 1, 2, 3$.
- j = Port of loading (source), $j = 1, 2, 3, \ldots, n$.
- k = Port of discharge (destination), $k = 1, 2, 3, \ldots, m$.
- C_i = Carbon emission per container km for each container size, such that $C_2 = 2C_1$ and $C_3 = 2.2C_1$.
- Q_{jk} = Shipping distance between port of loading and port of discharge in km.
- V_i = Volume for each size of container (based on 95% fill rate).
- S_{jk} = Volume to be shipped on each trade lane (j, k), where a trade lane is a pair of unique port of loading and port of discharge.
- E = Maximum excess volume, which was set to 10 m^3.
- X_{ijk} = Number of containers of size i for port of loading j and port of discharge k (decision variables).

Objective function: Minimize total carbon emission Z

$$Z = \sum_{i=1}^{3} C_i \sum_{j=1}^{n} \sum_{k=1}^{m} X_{ijk} Q_{jk}$$

Constraints

$$\sum_{i=1}^{3} V_i X_{ijk} \geq S_{jk} \quad \forall j, k \quad (1)$$

$$\sum_{i=1}^{3} V_i X_{ijk} - S_{jk} \leq E \quad \forall j, k \quad (2)$$

$$X_{ijk} \in \text{Positive Integer} \quad (3)$$

Constraint (1) ensures that the required volume is met by mandating that the optimized volume across the containers is equal or larger than the required volume for each trade lane represented by j and k. Constraint (2) considers minimizing excess volume of the optimized solution, by setting it to an arbitrary upper limit of 10 m^3. The reason for including such a constraint is to ensure that the model provides a feasible solution with minimal excess volume; otherwise, there could be a possibility that this constraint cannot be met and results in no solution. Finally, constraint (3) ensures that the number of each container type must be positive integer.

Let us map the problem and solution method for this case study against the *data and decision analytics framework* proposed in Chap. 1. As shown in Fig. 6.28, in this case study, the problem faced was increased carbon footprint due to excessive LCL shipments. Therefore, the right question to ask was "How to reduce carbon footprint?". Next was to collect the relevant data needed to answer the question, including shipping volumes on all trade lanes, container volumes and carbon ratios for different container types. With the historical order data collected, the analyst can perform initial analysis to determine the current fill rates of the containers. From the insights obtained, it was found that many shipments have low fill rates and the maximum fill rate was 95%. Thus, the problem objective would be to determine the best mix of container types to satisfy the shipping volumes on all trade lanes. Several assumptions were made, and the CSO model was built to determine the optimal container mix satisfying all the constraints. The company was able to reduce their carbon emission by 13.4% with 15% reduction in container requirements, as compared to their current practice.

6.5 Case 6B: Container Consolidation and Optimization for Carbon Footprint Reduction

This case is a continuation of Case 6A. Company CC was interested in increasing the container fill rates by consolidating several shipments bound for the same destination to further reduce their carbon footprint. This will require a new optimization model, called the Consolidation of Shipment within Country (CSC) model, to combine

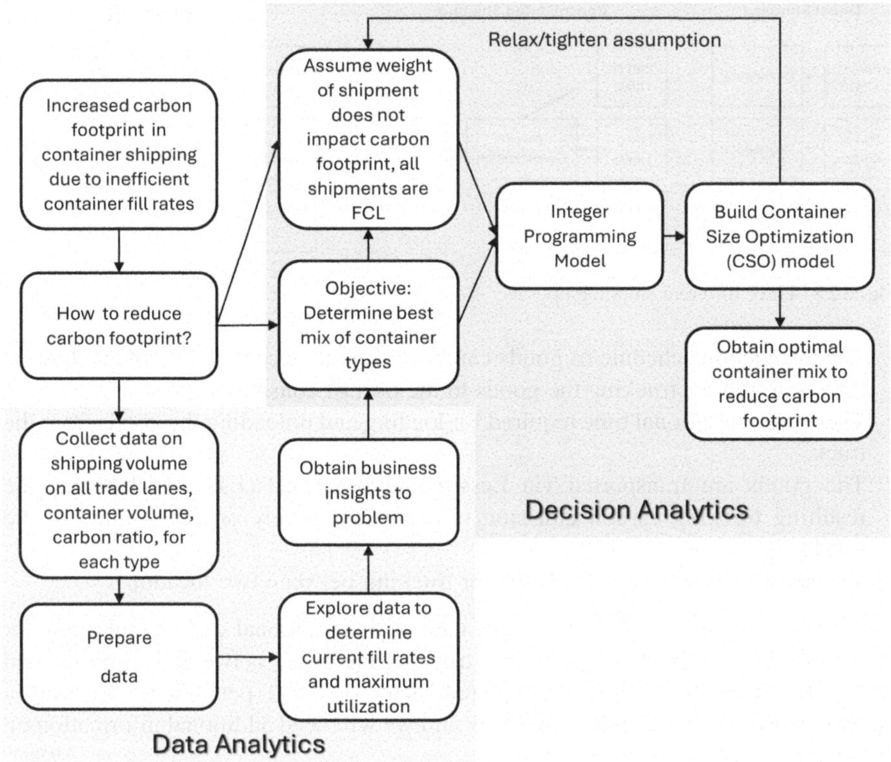

Fig. 6.28 Data and decision analytics framework map for Case 6A

shipments from different ports of origin within China to a single consolidation port before shipping. We assume that such consolidation was possible only when there was more than one shipment (from different manufacturing plants) in a single day. For each shipment, it can either be transported by truck via road to a port of consolidation or be shipped directly from its port of origin.

The CSC model takes the total volume of shipments (from various loading ports), origin and destination as inputs. The output of the model minimizes the overall carbon emission and provides three options, as shown in Fig. 6.29. The first option is direct shipment from the original port of loading to the destination; the second option is to use road freight to consolidate all shipments at a single port of consolidation in the same country before shipping to the destination; and finally, the last option is to use a combination of direct and consolidated shipment. In the case of consolidation (options 2 and 3), the model will also identify the most suitable loading port for consolidation.

There are a few assumptions made for the CSC model:

- The original trucking distance between the supplier/manufacturer and the original port of loading (before consolidation) is negligible and hence set to zero.

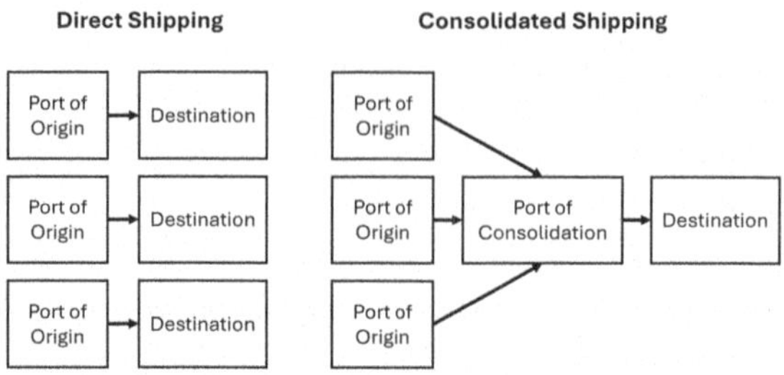

Fig. 6.29 Three different shipping options

- The production schedule of goods can be shifted to accommodate the additional time required for trucking the goods to the port of consolidation.
- There is no additional time required for loading and unloading the goods from the truck.
- The goods are transported via Less-than-Truck-Load (LTL), and hence, the resulting trucking carbon emission is dependent purely on the volume of the goods.
- Transportation is always available for trucking between two locations.

In addition, the model needs to take care of the additional carbon emissions for the consolidation model that stem from trucking the goods between the original and consolidation locations. We used a fixed factor of 0.011 per unit for trucking a volume of 1 m^3/km of distance travelled, and we will need additional information on the trucking distance between cities.

Let us define the parameters used in the CSC model:

- i = Type of container size, 1 for 20FT, 2 for 40FT and 3 for 40HC, $i = 1, 2, 3$.
- j = Port of loading, $j = 1, 2, \ldots, n$.
- $\hat{j}$ = Port of consolidation, which will be one of the ports of loading, $\hat{j} = 1, 2, 3, \ldots, n$.
- k = Port of discharge, $k = 1, 2, \ldots, m$.
- C_i = Carbon emission per container per km for each container size, such that $C_2 = 2C_1$ and $C_3 = 2.2C_1$.
- V_i = Volume for each size of container (based on 95% fill rate).
- T = Trucking carbon emission for 1 m^3 per km, assumed to be 0.011.
- $P_{j\hat{j}}$ = Trucking distance between supplier/manufacturer and port of consolidation in km.
- Q_{ik} = Shipping distance between port of loading and port of discharge in km.
- $Q_{\hat{j}k}$ = Shipping distance between port of consolidation and port of discharge in km.
- S_{jk} = Volume to be shipped directly from each port of loading to one port of discharge.

- $R_{\hat{j}jk}$ = Volume to be trucked from supplier/manufacturer to port of consolidation and consolidated volume to be shipped to port of discharge (i.e. let the volume to be the same as S_{jk}).
- D_k = Total volume expected at port of discharge.

There are two sets of decision variables. The first set involves binary decision variables to indicate whether a particular shipment should be shipped directly or consolidated, and the second set of decision variables is to determine the optimal container sizes and the number of each container size required while minimizing the overall carbon footprint.

- X_{ijk} = Number of containers of size i for port of loading j and port of discharge k.
- $Y_{i\hat{j}k}$ = Number of containers of size i for port of consolidation $\hat{j}$ and port of discharge k.
- $f_{\hat{j}jk}$ = Binary decision variable for consolidation at port $\hat{j}$.

$$f_{\hat{j}jk} = \begin{cases} 1, & \text{if consolidate} \\ 0, & \text{otherwise} \end{cases}$$

- g_{jk} = Binary decision variable for direct shipping.

$$g_{jk} = \begin{cases} 1, & \text{if direct shipping} \\ 0, & \text{otherwise} \end{cases}$$

The objective function is to minimize total carbon emission from direct shipping and consolidated shipping (ocean transport and trucking from each city to port of consolidation).

Minimize total carbon emission Z

$$Z = \sum_{i=1}^{3} C_i \sum_{j=1}^{n} \sum_{k=1}^{m} X_{ijk} Q_{jk} + \left\{ \sum_{i=1}^{3} C_i \sum_{\hat{j}=1}^{n} \sum_{k=1}^{m} Y_{i\hat{j}k} Q_{\hat{j}k} + \sum_{j=1}^{n} \sum_{\hat{j}=1}^{n} \sum_{k=1}^{m} T\,P_{\hat{j}j} R_{\hat{j}jk} f_{\hat{j}jk} \right\}$$

Subject to

$$1 - \left(\sum_{\hat{j}=1}^{n} f_{\hat{j}jk} + g_{jk} \right) = 0 \quad \forall j, k \quad (1)$$

$$S_{jk}\, g_{jk} + \sum_{\hat{j}=1}^{n} R_{\hat{j}jk} f_{\hat{j}jk} = S_{jk} \quad \forall j, k \quad (2)$$

$$\sum_{j=1}^{n} S_{jk}\, g_{jk} + \sum_{j=1}^{n} \sum_{\hat{j}=1}^{n} R_{\hat{j}jk} f_{\hat{j}jk} = D_k \quad \forall k \quad (3)$$

$$\sum_{i=1}^{3} V_i X_{ijk} + \sum_{i=1}^{3} V_i Y_{i\hat{j}k} \geq S_{jk} g_{jk} + \sum_{j=1}^{n} R_{j\hat{j}k} f_{j\hat{j}k} \quad \forall j, \hat{j}, k \quad (4)$$

$$f_{\hat{j}jk} \in \{0, 1\}$$

$$g_{jk} \in \{0, 1\}$$

$$X_{ijk} \in \text{Positive Integer}$$

$$Y_{i\hat{j}k} \in \text{Positive Integer}$$

In the objective function, the first term is the total carbon emission for direct shipping. The second term considers the carbon emission due to trucking the goods for consolidation and the ocean freight carbon emission from the port of consolidation to the port of discharge.

Constraint (1) ensures that each shipment within the consolidation problem can only be either shipped directly or consolidated at the port, and it is a mutually exclusive event (i.e. no partial shipment is allowed). Constraint (2) denotes that the total volume shipped directly and consolidated through the loading port is the same as the total supply. Constraint (3) ensures that the total volume that the discharge port receives is equal to the total volume to be sent directly and from multiple loading ports to the same port of discharge. Constraint (4) ensures that the required volume for each trade lane for direct shipping plus any consolidated volume is met by the optimal number of containers of each size required.

Let us map the problem and solution method for this case study against the *data and decision analytics framework* proposed in Chap. 1. As shown in Fig. 6.30, the data analytics portion is the same as that in Fig. 6.28. For the decision analytics portion, the problem objective is changed to determine the best mix of container types and best decisions for direct shipping and consolidation to satisfy the shipping volumes on all trade lanes. Additional assumptions related to trucking were made, and the CSC model was built to determine the optimal container mix and direct shipping and consolidation port decisions to satisfy all the constraints. Using the CSC optimization model, the company was able to further reduce their carbon emission by another 12.1%, as compared to the results from CSO model.

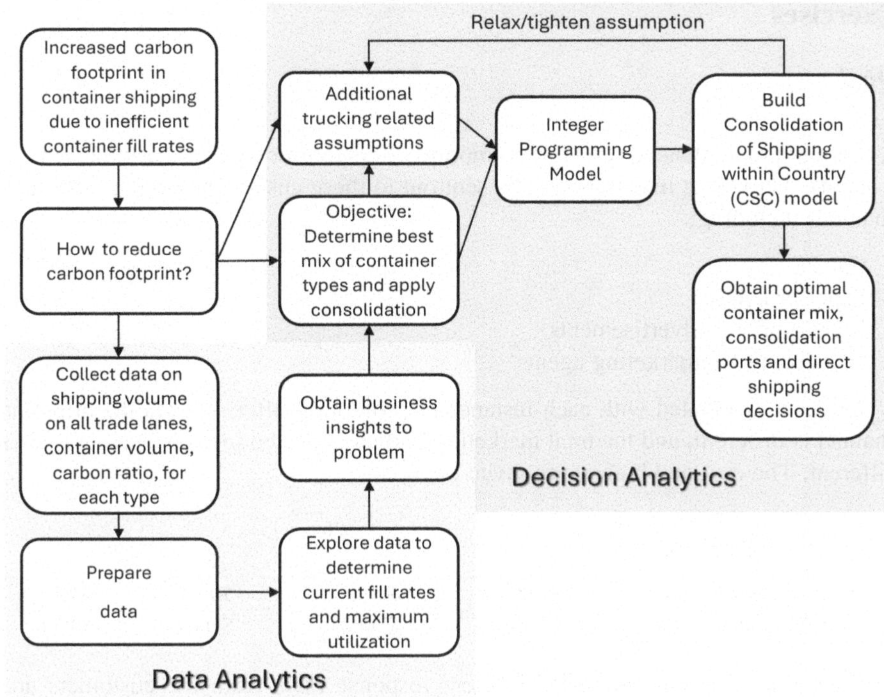

Fig. 6.30 Data and decision analytics framework map for Case 6B

6.6 Summary

This chapter covered the key concepts of optimization and the construction of LP and IP problems to obtain optimal solutions to business problems. For NLP, the characteristics of NLP solutions and conditions which allow us to determine if the solution obtained is a global optimal solution were covered. Two connected cases on optimizing container mix and container consolidation to reduce carbon footprint in the shipping industry were covered. After acquiring knowledge on constructing and solving optimization models, we will zoom into a special class of optimization problems in the next chapter. This class of problems requires the optimal solution to be integer, and yet the integer constraint is removed (known as LP relaxation), and the optimal solution to the LP is also the optimal solution to the original IP. We will cover the minimum cost flow problem and its specialized cases including the transshipment problem, the transportation problem, the assignment problem, the shortest path problem and the maximum flow problem.

Exercises

Q6.1

A shopping mall plans to send out promotion offers to four types of customers (1, 2, 3 and 4). Marketing materials will be sent out to these customers via four different channels including:

- Emails
- Paper brochures
- Mobile phone advertisements
- Calls using telemarketing agents

The cost associated with each instance of promotion offer sent via the different channel is different, and the total marketing budget allocated to each channel is also different. The cost and budget are given below.

	Channel			
	1	2	3	4
Cost per instance	\$2.00	\$1.00	\$0.50	\$1.50
Budget allocated	\$1000	\$2000	\$400	\$3000

Using the different channels, different response rates from the customers are obtained as shown in the table below.

		Channel			
		1	2	3	4
Customer type	1	0.4	0.3	0.2	0.6
	2	0.2	0.2	0.15	0.3
	3	0.15	0.1	0.15	0.2
	4	0.1	0.3	0.1	0.2

For those who responded, the amount of potential revenue from each customer that can be obtained is given in the table below.

		Channel			
		1	2	3	4
Customer type	1	\$10	\$12	\$15	\$3
	2	\$5	\$6	\$7	\$9
	3	\$20	\$8	\$9	\$2
	4	\$15	\$13	\$5	\$17

Customers do not like to be reached more than once on the same promotion offer, so the company has decided that only one channel will be selected for each customer type, and every marketing channel must be used. Determine the best allocation of the budget for this marketing effort which will maximize the total net income.

Q6.2

The coach of the national basketball team is faced with the decision of selecting 12 players from 20 players for the upcoming international tournament. The players are labelled as P_i, where i is from 1 to 20.

There are roles that each player can play in the basketball team, including play maker (PM), shooting guards (SG), forwards (FW) and centres (CT). For each player, the coach has collected data on their individual scoring average Si, the roles that they can play (PM, SG, FW and CT) as given in the table below. Notice that some players can play one role, while others can play two roles. In addition, players P4, P8, P15 and P20 play in the NCAA college-level team, while the rest play in the NBA professional-level team.

Player	Scoring average	PM	SG	FW	CT
P_1	3.76	1			
P_2	5.74	1			
P_3	4.37	1			
P_4	4.30	1	1		
P_5	4.26	1	1		
P_6	3.84		1		
P_7	4.64		1		
P_8	3.35		1		
P_9	3.96		1	1	
P_{10}	4.35		1	1	
P_{11}	3.03		1	1	
P_{12}	4.51			1	
P_{13}	2.61			1	
P_{14}	2.89			1	
P_{15}	5.12			1	
P_{16}	2.82			1	1
P_{17}	3.55				1
P_{18}	3.99				1
P_{19}	4.93				1
P_{20}	3.05				1

The dream team should consist of at least three play makers (PM), four shooting guards (SG), four forwards (FW) and three centres (CT), as well as at least two players who play for the NCAA college-level team.

The problem is further complicated by the fact that there are incompatibility problems with some players. Player P5 has declared that if player P9 is selected, then he does not want to be selected. The same sentiment is shared by player P9—that if player P5 is selected, he also does not want to be selected. Players P2 and P19 have been playing basketball together since they were young, and they have the most effective combination. Both players have declared that they should be selected together, or else, neither would play at all.

Faced with these difficulties, help the coach decide which players to choose to maximize the total scoring average while satisfying all the constraints.

Q6.3

Many countries were hard-hit by the COVID-19 pandemic, and healthcare facilities were stretched to serve patients of different levels of severity.

- Type 1: Low—patient is able to recover on his/her own with minimal care.
- Type 2: Medium—patient requires monitoring twice a day and stays in a normal hospital ward.
- Type 3: High—patient requires close monitoring and stays in the intensive care unit (ICU) (if possible).

Among these patients, most of them would fall under Type 1 and Type 2, and only a small percentage of them will be Type 3. As the number of infected patients increases, the number of beds at the normal hospital ward available can no longer house all the patients of Type 1 and Type 2. The situation is made worse when the number of Type 3 patients increases beyond the number of beds available in the ICU. In such a dire situation, Type 3 patients are moved to the normal ward bed, and the care for such patients at the normal ward is not as efficient and may cost even more.

If and when such a dire situation occurs, the care for patients will be in this priority order:

- Type 3 patients should be taken care of first, and try to put them in the ICU. Only when beds at the ICU runs out should they be moved to a normal ward.
- Then take care of Type 2 patients in the normal ward.
- And last will be Type 1 patients. Put them in the normal ward if there are beds available; otherwise, move them somewhere else. For Type 1 patients, the government has decided to use alternate facilities (e.g. exhibition halls) to house and care for them when beds in the normal hospital wards are no longer available.

Setting up a new alternate facility to house Type 1 patients requires careful planning as the addition of new beds can only be added in blocks of 100, due to economies of scale. The setting up of one such facility with 100 beds will be referred to as one setup, and we assume that the setup will be completed at the start of a specific month, ready to serve Type 1 patients in that month. Once a setup is completed, the setup will be used for 1 month only and will be torn down at the end of the month for fear of spreading the disease downstream. The cost of setting up and tearing down one setup is $100,000. The maximum number of such setups available is five, which means 100, 200, 300, 400 or 500 beds are available to serve Type 1 patients, in any month.

The pandemic is expected to last for 12 months, and the projected number of patients for each type per month is given in the table below.

Month	Type 1	Type 2	Type 3
1	50	30	15
2	60	35	25
3	120	55	30
4	150	68	35
5	320	77	38
6	440	120	42
7	380	105	36
8	280	64	26
9	160	43	22
10	70	25	18
11	10	14	9
12	5	8	2

We assume that all patients will stay for 1 month at their assigned facility, that is, patients in month 1 will stay at their assigned facility in month 1 and will be discharged, and the same applies for the remaining months. The unit cost of taking care of different types of patients at the three different facilities is given in the table below.

	Facility		
	Alternate facility	Normal ward	ICU ward
Type 1	\$300	\$3500	
Type 2		\$5000	
Type 3		\$12,000	\$8000

The number of beds available in the next 12 months is given in the table below.

Month	Normal ward	ICU ward
1	100	20
2	100	20
3	150	25
4	150	25
5	200	25
6	200	30
7	200	30
8	200	25
9	150	25
10	150	20
11	100	20
12	100	20

Determine the optimal number of setups that would be required in each month, minimizing the total cost, given the limited number of beds available in the normal wards and ICU, for the next 12 months.

Q6.4

You run a Web site that sells theme park admission tickets. There are three classes of admission tickets:

- Class 1—admits one patron only.
- Class 2—admits one patron; priority fast lane for rides.
- Class 3—admits one patron; priority fast lane for rides; and one meal at the restaurant.

You have projected the demand for each class of tickets for the next 12 months, and it is given in the table below.

Month	Class 1	Class 2	Class 3	Total
1	50	30	15	95
2	60	35	25	120
3	120	55	30	205
4	150	68	35	253
5	320	77	38	435
6	340	120	42	502
7	380	105	36	521
8	280	64	26	370
9	160	43	22	225
10	70	25	18	113
11	10	14	9	33
12	500	8	2	510

The best strategy would be to buy the exact number of tickets for each class from the theme park owner. However, the theme park owner restricts the maximum number of tickets you can buy per month so that other Web sites can also sell the theme park tickets. Once bought, the tickets can only be sold and used in the same month. That is, if the ticket is bought in January, it can be sold and used in January only. The maximum limit, ticket cost and selling price for each ticket class are given below.

	Maximum limit	Ticket cost	Selling price
Class 1	200	$50	$70
Class 2	180	$70	$100
Class 3	150	$100	$150
Total	530		

In case the demand for a certain ticket class is much higher than the number of tickets you have for that class in a particular month, you can always sell the higher-class ticket to a lower-class demand. For example, a customer wants to buy a Class 1 ticket, but you only have Class 2 tickets left. You will then sell the Class 2 ticket to the customer at the Class 1 ticket price. This is called downgrade of Class 2 ticket to

Class 1. However, it is not possible to upgrade a lower-class ticket to a higher-class ticket.

You must satisfy all the projected demand for the next 12 months, which means that there cannot be any lost sales. Determine how many tickets for each class you should buy in each month and the number of tickets you need to downgrade to maximize your net income.

References

Chong, E. L. M., Ma, N. L., & Tan, K. W. (2014). *Reducing carbon emission of ocean shipments by optimizing container size selection* (pp. 480–485). 2014 IEEE International Conference on Automation Science and Engineering (CASE), New Taipei, Taiwan. https://doi.org/10.1109/CoASE.2014.6899369.

Dantzig, G. B. (1947). Maximization of a linear function of variables subject to linear inequalities. In T. C. Koopmans (Ed.), *Activity analysis of production and allocation* (pp. 339–347). Wiley & Chapman-Hall.

Dantzig, G. B. (1998). *Linear programming and extensions*. Princeton University.

Dantzig, G. B. (2002). Linear programming. *Operations Research, 50*(1), 42–47.

Hillier, F. S., & Lieberman, G. J. (2001). *Introduction to operations research* (7th ed.). McGraw-Hill.

Chapter 7
Special Optimization Problems

There are operations problems which require the optimal solutions to be strictly integer, such as the number of containers to use to minimize carbon emission in the case study we have seen in Chap. 6. There are also problems in which the optimal decisions must be binary, usually to represent to do or not to do decision. A typical binary integer problem is resource allocation, which looks at assigning limited resources to tasks, and the decision would be which resource will be used to complete which task. A value of 1 will indicate the assignment, while 0 will indicate non-assignment. A good reference on this topic is that by Winston and Albright (2015), which focuses on the practical aspects of solving such problems.

In this chapter, we will delve into a special class of problems where the integer constraint is removed, known as LP relaxation, and the optimal solution to the LP problem is guaranteed to be integer and thus will also be the optimal solution to the original IP problem. Such a special class of problems has a distinct pattern in the resource consumption matrix, known as the **[A]** matrix, that makes such problems easier to solve than general IP problems. Finally, we will discuss how optimization concepts and models are applied in a real-world scenario to assign airlines to airport terminals to improve load balancing.

Learning Outcomes

By the end of this chapter, readers will achieve the following learning outcomes:

- Explain the distinct pattern in the [A] matrix.
- Explain that the Integer Solutions Property ensures integer solution without integer constraint.
- Formulate the Minimum Cost Flow Problem using graph.
- Apply the Minimum Cost Flow Problem model.
- Formulate the trans-shipment problem, and explain that it is a special case of the minimum cost flow problem.
- Apply the Trans-shipment Problem model.
- Formulate the transportation problem, and explain that it is a special case of the trans-shipment problem.

M. L. F. Cheong, Ma Nang Laik, *Data and Decision Analytics for Business Operations*, https://doi.org/10.1007/978-3-031-72255-4_7

- Apply the Transportation Problem model.
- Formulate the assignment problem, and explain that it is a special case of the transportation problem.
- Apply the Assignment Problem model.
- Formulate the shortest path problem, and explain that it is a special case of the minimum cost flow problem.
- Apply the Shortest Path Problem model.
- Formulate the maximum flow problem, and explain that it is a special case of the minimum cost flow problem, with a modified objective function.
- Apply the Maximum Flow Problem model.
- Discuss how optimization concepts and models are applied in a real-world scenario to assign airlines to airport terminals to improve load balancing using the *data and decision analytics framework.*

7.1 Distinct Pattern in [A] Matrix

To understand the distinct pattern in the consumption matrix **[A]**, we will first revisit the standard form of LP model introduced in Chap. 6, which is given as:

Objective function

$$\text{Minimize } Z = c_1x_1 + c_2x_2 + \ldots + c_nx_n$$

Constraints

$$a_{11}x_1 + a_{12}x_2 + \ldots + a_{1n}x_n \leq b_1$$

$$a_{21}x_1 + a_{22}x_2 + \ldots + a_{2n}x_n \leq b_2$$

$$\ldots$$

$$a_{m1}x_1 + a_{m2}x_2 + \ldots + a_{mn}x_n \leq b_m$$

Decision variables: $x_1, x_2, \ldots, x_n \geq 0$

Let us reformulate the constraints into a matrix multiplication format below.

$$[\mathbf{A}][\mathbf{X}] \leq [\mathbf{b}]$$

$$\begin{bmatrix} \mathbf{a_{11}} & \mathbf{a_{12}} & \ldots & \mathbf{a_{1n}} \\ \mathbf{a_{21}} & \mathbf{a_{22}} & \ldots & \mathbf{a_{2n}} \\ \ldots & \ldots & \ldots & \ldots \\ \mathbf{a_{m1}} & \mathbf{a_{m2}} & \ldots & \mathbf{a_{mn}} \end{bmatrix} \begin{bmatrix} \mathbf{x_1} \\ \mathbf{x_2} \\ \ldots \\ \mathbf{x_n} \end{bmatrix} \leq \begin{bmatrix} \mathbf{b_1} \\ \mathbf{b_2} \\ \ldots \\ \mathbf{b_m} \end{bmatrix}$$

The sizes of the matrices are given below, to represent the matrix multiplication with * denoting multiplication.

$$[\mathbf{m\ x\ n}] * [\mathbf{n\ x\ 1}] \quad \le \quad [\mathbf{m\ x\ 1}]$$

In these special optimization problems, the **[A]** matrix will assume a distinct pattern where:

- Most of the a_{ij} coefficients are zero.
- Non-zero a_{ij} coefficients will appear in a distinct pattern.

To appreciate the distinct pattern, let us explore the transportation problem where the objective is to transport goods from m sources to n destinations with the minimum total transportation cost. We will define the following parameters and decision variables:

- Source $i = 1, 2, \ldots, m$.
- Supply quantity from source i, s_i.
- Destination, $j = 1, 2, \ldots, n$.
- Demand quantity from destination j, d_j.
- Transportation cost between i and j, c_{ij}.
- Quantity to transport from source i to destination j, x_{ij}.

The assumptions for transportation problem are:

- Requirement assumption
  - Each source has a fixed supply s_i, and the entire supply must be distributed to the destinations.
  - Each destination has a fixed demand d_j, and the entire demand must be received from the sources.
- Cost assumption—Cost per unit c_{ij} is directly proportional to the number of units distributed, implying that the total cost is a linear multiplication $c_{ij}x_{ij}$.

Let us model the transportation problem as follows with constraints (1) and (2) satisfying the requirement assumption and the objective function satisfying the cost assumption.

$$\text{Minimize} \quad Z = \sum_{i=1}^{m} \sum_{j=1}^{n} c_{ij} x_{ij}$$

Constraints

$$\sum_{j=1}^{n} x_{ij} = s_i \quad \forall i \quad (1)$$

$$\sum\nolimits_{i=1}^{m} x_{ij} = d_j \quad \forall j \quad (2)$$

Decision variables: $x_{ij} \geq 0$

We will now convert the constraints into matrix multiplication format. The supply constraint (1) is represented as the expression below where all a_{ij} are 1.

$$\begin{bmatrix} \mathbf{a_{11}} & \mathbf{a_{12}} & \cdots & \mathbf{a_{1n}} \\ \mathbf{a_{21}} & \mathbf{a_{22}} & \cdots & \mathbf{a_{2n}} \\ \cdots & \cdots & \cdots & \cdots \\ \mathbf{a_{m1}} & \mathbf{a_{m2}} & \cdots & \mathbf{a_{mn}} \end{bmatrix} \begin{bmatrix} \mathbf{x_{11}} & \mathbf{x_{21}} & \cdots & \mathbf{x_{m1}} \\ \mathbf{x_{12}} & \mathbf{x_{21}} & \cdots & \mathbf{x_{m2}} \\ \cdots & \cdots & \cdots & \cdots \\ \mathbf{x_{1n}} & \mathbf{x_{2n}} & \cdots & \mathbf{x_{mn}} \end{bmatrix} \leq \begin{bmatrix} \mathbf{s_1} & & & \\ & \mathbf{s_2} & & \\ & & \cdots & \\ & & & \mathbf{s_m} \end{bmatrix}$$

And the sizes of the matrices are

$$[\mathbf{m\ x\ n}] * [\mathbf{n\ x\ m}] \quad = \quad [\mathbf{m\ x\ m}]$$

Similarly, the demand constraint (2) is represented as the expression below where all a_{ij} are 1.

$$\begin{bmatrix} \mathbf{x_{11}} & \mathbf{x_{21}} & \cdots & \mathbf{x_{m1}} \\ \mathbf{x_{21}} & \mathbf{x_{22}} & \cdots & \mathbf{x_{m2}} \\ \cdots & \cdots & \cdots & \cdots \\ \mathbf{x_{1n}} & \mathbf{x_{2n}} & \cdots & \mathbf{x_{mn}} \end{bmatrix} \begin{bmatrix} \mathbf{a_{11}} & \mathbf{a_{12}} & \cdots & \mathbf{a_{1n}} \\ \mathbf{a_{21}} & \mathbf{a_{22}} & \cdots & \mathbf{a_{2n}} \\ \cdots & \cdots & \cdots & \cdots \\ \mathbf{a_{m1}} & \mathbf{a_{m2}} & \cdots & \mathbf{a_{mn}} \end{bmatrix} \leq \begin{bmatrix} \mathbf{d_1} & & & \\ & \mathbf{d_2} & & \\ & & \cdots & \\ & & & \mathbf{d_n} \end{bmatrix}$$

And the sizes of the matrices are

$$[\mathbf{n\ x\ m}] * [\mathbf{m\ x\ n}] \quad = \quad [\mathbf{n\ x\ n}]$$

Combining the two groups of matrix multiplication equations will result in a large matrix multiplication equation where all the non-blank cells with $a_{ij} = 1$ are arranged in a distinct pattern where the top half represents supply constraints arranged in rows, while the bottom half represents demand constraints arranged in diagonals. All blank cells will be 0.

$$
\begin{bmatrix}
a_{11} & a_{12} & \cdots & a_{1n} & & & & & & & & & \\
& & & & a_{21} & a_{22} & \cdots & a_{2n} & & & & & \\
& & & & & & & & \cdots & & & & \\
& & & & & & & & & a_{m1} & a_{m2} & \cdots & a_{mn} \\
a_{11} & & & & a_{21} & & & & & a_{m1} & & & \\
& a_{12} & & & & a_{22} & & & & & a_{m2} & & \\
& & \cdots & & & & \cdots & & & & & \cdots & \\
& & & a_{1n} & & & & a_{2n} & \cdots & & & & a_{mn}
\end{bmatrix}
\begin{bmatrix} x_{11} \\ x_{12} \\ \cdots \\ x_{1n} \\ x_{21} \\ x_{22} \\ \cdots \\ x_{2n} \\ \cdots \\ x_{m1} \\ x_{m2} \\ \cdots \\ x_{mn} \end{bmatrix}
=
\begin{bmatrix} s_1 \\ s_2 \\ \cdots \\ s_m \\ d_1 \\ d_2 \\ \cdots \\ d_n \end{bmatrix}
$$

And the sizes of the matrices are

$$[(\mathbf{m}+\mathbf{n})\ \mathbf{x}\ (\mathbf{m}*\mathbf{n})] * [(\mathbf{m}*\mathbf{n})\ \mathbf{x}\ \mathbf{1}] \quad = \quad [(\mathbf{m}+\mathbf{n})\ \mathbf{x}\ \mathbf{1}]$$

It is this distinct pattern of the **[A]** matrix that distinguishes this problem as a transportation problem, rather than the context related to transportation. And since every s_i and d_j are integer values, then all the basic variables in every basic feasible solution also have integer values, which is called the Integer Solutions Property. This removes the need for the integer constraint, known as LP relaxation. Thus, the optimal solution to the LP problem will be the optimal solution to the IP problem, applicable to all the six different problems we will be discussing in Sects. 7.2–7.7. We will discuss more on transportation problem in Sect. 7.4.

7.2 Minimum Cost Flow Problem

After appreciating the special structure of the **[A]** matrix, we will introduce the concept of graph to learn about the minimum cost flow problem. A graph consists of nodes N and edges E where the nodes are connected using edges. If the edges have direction, for example, from A $\rightarrow$ B, then the graph is called a directed graph. If there is no direction, the edge only shows the connection between A and B (meaning A to B or B to A are both possible), then the graph is called an undirected graph.

Fig. 7.1 Directed graph

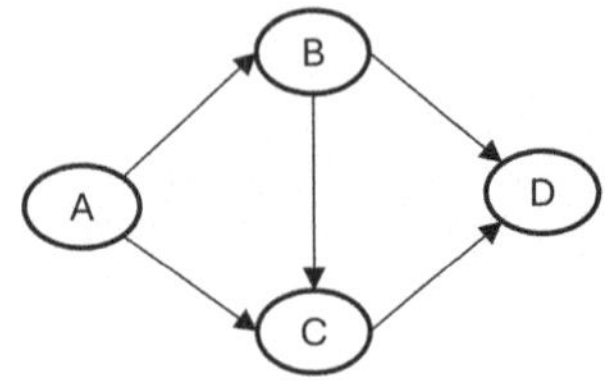

Fig. 7.2 Undirected graph

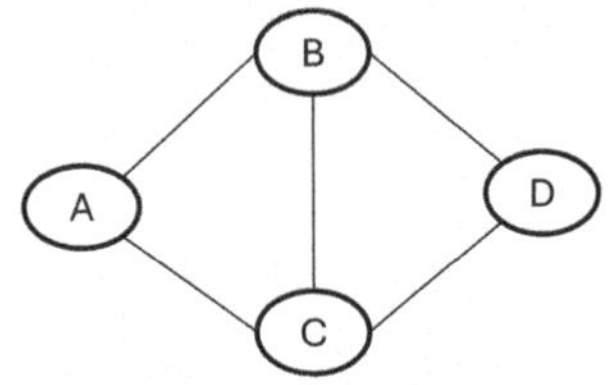

The visual representation of a directed graph is shown in Fig. 7.1. We will denote an edge connecting node A to node B by (a, b). Using this notation, the directed graph G = (N, E) can be characterized in terms of nodes N = {A, B, C, D} and a set of edges E = {(a, b), (b, c), (a, c), (b, d), (c, d)}. Furthermore, self-edges like (a, a) are not allowed. The visual representation of an undirected graph is shown in Fig. 7.2.

A network flow problem can be represented using a directed graph G = (N, E) where N denotes a set of nodes and E denotes a set of edges, with additional information b_i, which represents the external supply to each node $i \in N$. If $b_i > 0$, the node is a source; otherwise, if $b_i < 0$, the node is a sink, and if $b_i = 0$, it is a trans-shipment node.

The capacity of each edge (i, j) is denoted as u_{ij}, and the cost of transporting one unit of flow quantity along edge (i, j) is denoted as c_{ij}. We use x_{ij} to denote the flow quantity through edge (i, j). In the minimum cost flow problem, we want to determine the flow quantities that minimize the total transportation cost subject to capacity constraints and flow conservation constraints. The linear program is defined as follows:

Objective Function

$$\min \sum_{(i,\ j)\in E} c_{ij}x_{ij}$$

Constraints

$$\sum_{\substack{\text{outflow}\\ \{k|(i,k)\in E, i\neq k\}}} x_{ik} - \sum_{\substack{\text{inflow}\\ \{j|(j,i)\in E, i\neq j\}}} x_{ji} = b_i, \forall i \in N \quad (1)$$

$$0 \le x_{ij} \le u_{ij} \quad , \forall (i,j) \in E \quad (2)$$

$$x_{ij} \in \text{positive integer}$$

The objective function aims to minimize the total transportation cost computed as the sum of the product of per unit cost and flow quantity. Constraint (1) ensures flow conservation where the sum of outflow (from node i to all nodes k) minus the sum of inflow (from all nodes j into node i) must be equal to the external supply b_i to node i. Constraint (2) ensures that the flow quantity on edge (i, j) is less than or equal to the capacity constraint of edge (i, j). And finally, the flow quantity must be a positive integer value.

The assumptions for the minimum cost flow problem are:

- The graph is directed.
- Cost and capacity values are positive integer values.
- The sum of all external supply values must be zero. That is, $\sum_{i\in N} b_i = 0$.

Let us look at an application example. A factory in location A supplies goods to two warehouses located at B and C. The goods will be transported to three suppliers, D, E and F, at different locations. In each month, the factory can supply a total of 50,000 units of the goods. The capacity of warehouse B is 20,000 units, and capacity of warehouse C is 30,000 units. The transport cost to transfer the goods from A to B and from A to C is \$2 and \$3 per unit, respectively. The demand for each supplier and the transport cost from the warehouses to each supplier are given in Table 7.1, and the flow constraints on each edge are given in Table 7.2.

Table 7.1 Supplier demand, transport cost and warehouse capacity

	D	E	F	Warehouse capacity
B	\$2.5	\$3	\$0.5	20,000
C	\$1	\$2	\$2.3	30,000
Demand	5000	25,000	20,000	

Table 7.2 Flow constraints for minimum cost flow problem

Capacity of edge	B	C	D	E	F
A	25,000	40,000			
B			1000	15,000	10,000
C			5000	20,000	20,000

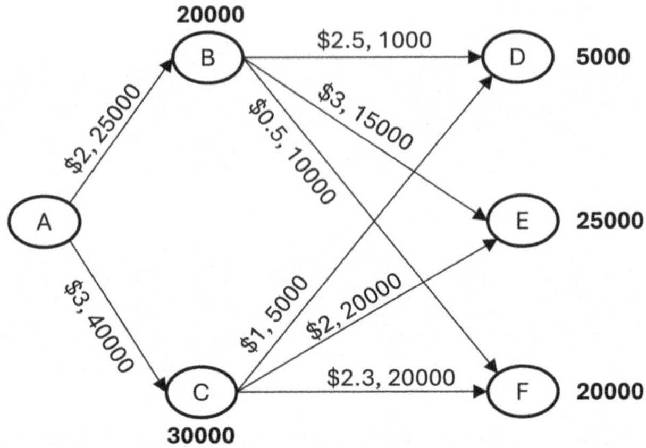

Fig. 7.3 Visual representation using directed graph

The objective is to determine how much goods to transport via each edge subjected to flow capacity on each edge, to fulfil the suppliers' demand and to conserve the flow to achieve the minimum transportation cost. Figure 7.3 shows the graphical representation of the model using a network graph where the numbers on the edges represent the unit cost and capacity of each edge and the numbers at the nodes denote the supplier demand or warehouse capacity.

We can formulate the model as follows:

Objective Function

$$\text{Min} \quad 2x_{ab} + 3x_{ac} + 2.5x_{bd} + 3x_{be} + 0.5x_{bf} + x_{cd} + 2x_{ce} + 2.3x_{cf}$$

Capacity constraints for all the edges

$$x_{ab} \leq 25{,}000 \quad (1a)$$

$$x_{ac} \leq 40{,}000 \quad (1b)$$

$$x_{bd} \leq 1000 \quad (1c)$$

$$x_{be} \leq 15{,}000 \quad (1d)$$

$$x_{bf} \leq 10{,}000 \quad (1e)$$

$$x_{cd} \leq 5000 \quad (1f)$$

$$x_{ce} \leq 20{,}000 \quad (1g)$$

$$x_{cf} \leq 20{,}000 \quad (1h)$$

Capacity constraints of the warehouses

$$x_{ab} \leq 20{,}000 \quad (2a)$$

$$x_{ac} \leq 30{,}000 \quad (2b)$$

Flow conservation constraints

$$x_{ab} + x_{ac} = 50{,}000 \quad (3a)$$

$$x_{ab} - x_{bd} - x_{be} - x_{bf} = 0 \quad (3b)$$

$$x_{ac} - x_{cd} - x_{ce} - x_{cf} = 0 \quad (3c)$$

$$x_{bd} + x_{cd} = 5000 \quad (3d)$$

$$x_{be} + x_{ce} = 25{,}000 \quad (3e)$$

$$x_{bf} + x_{cf} = 20{,}000 \quad (3f)$$

The objective function minimizes the total cost through the entire flow network. There are three groups of constraints. The first group of constraints, (1a) to (1h), represents the capacity constraints for all the edges. The second group of constraints, (2a) and (2b), represents the warehouse capacity constraints, which will make constraints (1a) and (1b) redundant since the warehouse capacities are smaller than the capacities of edges (a, b) and (a, c). The third group of constraints, (3a) to (3f), represent the flow conservation constraints.

Using Excel spreadsheet, we can lay out the problem as shown in Fig. 7.4. The objective function in cell C2 is the total network cost, which is the sum of the product

Total Cost: $0

Factory	Warehouse	Suppliers
A	B	D
	C	E
		F

⇨

Factory	Warehouse	Suppliers
50000	20000	5000
	30000	25000
		20000

Cost, c_{ij}	b	c	d	e	f
a	2	3	9999	9999	9999
b	9999	9999	2.5	3	0.5
c	9999	9999	1	2	2.3

Capacity, u_{ij}	b	c	d	e	f
a	25000	40000	0	0	0
b	0	0	1000	15000	10000
c	0	0	5000	20000	20000

Flow, x_{ij}	b	c	d	e	f	Total	Flow Conservation
a	0	0	0	0	0	0	50000
b	0	0	0	0	0	0	0
c	0	0	0	0	0	0	0
Total	0	0	0	0	0		
Demand	20000	30000	5000	25000	20000		

Fig. 7.4 Excel spreadsheet model for minimum cost flow problem example

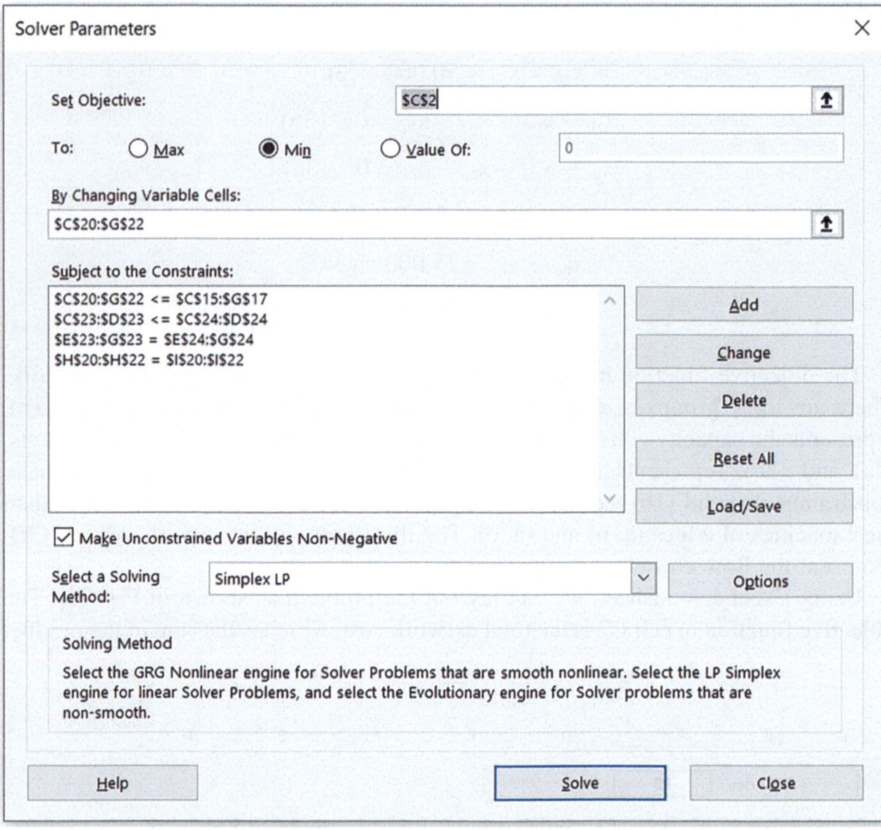

Fig. 7.5 Excel solver definition for minimum cost flow problem example

of unit cost c_{ij} in cells C10:G12 and the flow quantities x_{ij} in cells C20:G22. Note that there are cells with unit cost set as 9999 to represent infeasible connections between nodes. As such, the optimal solution should set $x_{ij} = 0$ for such connections.

We use cells H20:H22 to sum up the outflows and inflows for nodes A, B and C and set them to their respective b_i values in cells I20:I22, to ensure that flow conservation is preserved. We use cells C23:G23 to sum up the inflows into nodes B, C, D, E and F and set them to their respective demand values in cells C24:G24 to ensure that the demand for the warehouses and suppliers are met.

The corresponding Solver definition is shown in Fig. 7.5. The minimum cost flow problem is a special class of problems where the optimal solution to the LP problem will be the optimal solution to the integer problem. Thus, we did not add the integer constraints implying LP relaxation, and the Solving Method was set as Simplex LP.

As shown in Fig. 7.6, the minimum transportation cost is $223,000. Warehouse B will supply 10,000 units each to the suppliers E and F, while warehouse C will

Total Cost	$223,000

Factory	Warehouse	Suppliers
A	B	D
	C	E
		F

Factory	Warehouse	Suppliers
50000	20000	5000
	30000	25000
		20000

Cost, c_{ij}	b	c	d	e	f
a	2	3	9999	9999	9999
b	9999	9999	2.5	3	0.5
c	9999	9999	1	2	2.3

Capacity, u_{ij}	b	c	d	e	f
a	25000	40000	0	0	0
b	0	0	1000	15000	10000
c	0	0	5000	20000	20000

Flow, x_{ij}	b	c	d	e	f	Total	Flow Conservation
a	**20000**	**30000**	**0**	**0**	**0**	50000	50000
b	**0**	**0**	**0**	**10000**	**10000**	0	0
c	**0**	**0**	**5000**	**15000**	**10000**	0	0
Total	20000	30000	5000	25000	20000		
Demand	20000	30000	5000	25000	20000		

Fig. 7.6 Optimal solution for minimum cost flow problem example

supply 5000 to supplier D, 15,000 to supplier E and 10,000 to supplier F. This optimal solution satisfies all the constraints.

7.3 Trans-shipment Problem

For the trans-shipment problem, the objective is to determine the transfer quantities from each source to each destination and the route they need to follow to minimize the total shipping cost. There may also be cases where the sources or destinations act as intermediate nodes or trans-shipment points.

Assuming there are m sources and n destinations. The supply capacity at each source is denoted as s_i, and the demand at each destination is denoted as d_j. The unit cost of shipping the goods from source i to destination j is denoted as c_{ij}. We use x_{ij} to denote the number of units which are transported from source i to destination j. In the trans-shipment problem, there are trans-shipment nodes where the inflow is the same as the outflow at the node. The trans-shipment problem looks almost similar to the minimum cost flow problem, except there are no capacity constraints on the edges. Therefore, the trans-shipment problem is a special case of the minimum cost flow problem.

The model of a trans-shipment problem is given as
Objective function

$$\text{Minimize} \quad Z = \sum_{i=1}^{m} \sum_{j=1}^{n} c_{ij} x_{ij}$$

Constraints

$$\sum_{\substack{\text{outflow} \\ \{j|(i,j) \in E, i \neq j\}}} x_{ij} = s_i, \forall m \quad (1)$$

$$\sum_{\substack{\text{inflow} \\ \{i|(i,j) \in E, i \neq j\}}} x_{ij} = d_j, \forall n \quad (2)$$

$$\sum_{\substack{\text{outflow} \\ \{k|(i,k) \in E, i \neq k\}}} x_{ik} = \sum_{\substack{\text{inflow} \\ \{j|(j,i) \in E, i \neq j\}}} x_{ji}, \forall \text{transshipment node} \quad (3)$$

Decision variables: $x_{ij} \in$ Positive Integer

The objective function is to minimize the total transportation cost, which is the sum of the product of per unit cost and flow quantity transported between sources and destinations via some trans-shipment nodes. Constraint (1) ensures that the total quantity transported out from each source is the same as the supply at source i. Constraint (2) ensures that the total quantity transported into each destination is the same as the demand required at destination j. Constraint (3) ensures that the total inflow quantity is the same as the total outflow quantity at trans-shipment nodes. Finally, the quantities transported must be positive integer.

Similarly, let us look at an example. Company XYZ has two production plants, A and B, which have capacities of 500 and 700 each month, respectively. There are three customers, E, F and G, who need the goods with monthly demand of 300, 400 and 500, respectively. If the company ships the goods to the customers directly, the unit cost of transportation will be relatively high. Thus, the company plans to set up two warehouses as intermediate points C and D to consolidate all the goods and distribute the required amount to each customer. We assume that the intermediate points do not have capacity constraint. The unit cost to transport goods between nodes and the demand and supply are shown in Table 7.3. Note that the intermediate

Table 7.3 Unit transport cost, demand and supply for trans-shipment problem

Cost	C	D	E	F	G	Supply
A	8	10	30	40	50	500
B	9	9	20	25	55	700
C	999	999	5	7	8	
D	999	999	8	6	9	
Demand			300	400	500	

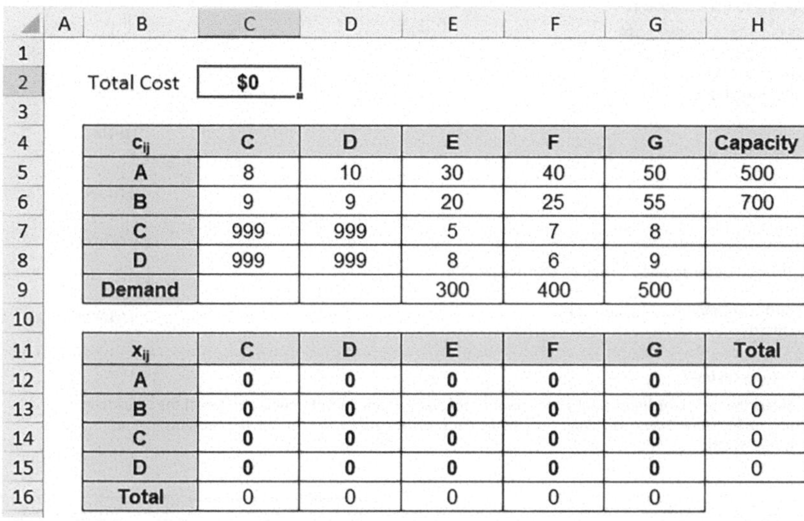

	A	B	C	D	E	F	G	H
1								
2		Total Cost	$0					
3								
4		c_{ij}	C	D	E	F	G	Capacity
5		A	8	10	30	40	50	500
6		B	9	9	20	25	55	700
7		C	999	999	5	7	8	
8		D	999	999	8	6	9	
9		Demand			300	400	500	
10								
11		x_{ij}	C	D	E	F	G	Total
12		A	0	0	0	0	0	0
13		B	0	0	0	0	0	0
14		C	0	0	0	0	0	0
15		D	0	0	0	0	0	0
16		Total	0	0	0	0	0	

Fig. 7.7 Excel spreadsheet model for trans-shipment problem example

points are not permitted to transport goods between them; thus, their unit transport costs are set as a large number 999.

The objective is to determine the number of units to transport from each plant to each customer with the minimum cost, considering the possibility of using the intermediate points, while satisfying the plants' supply capacities and the customers' demand. Using Excel spreadsheet, we can lay out the problem as shown in Fig. 7.7. The objective function in cell C2 is the transportation cost, which is the sum of the product of unit cost c_{ij} in cells C5:G8 and the transport quantities x_{ij} in cells C12:G15.

We use cells H12:H13 to sum up the transport quantities from plants A and B and set them to their respective supply values in cells H5:H6, according to constraint (1). We use cells E16:G16 to sum up the transport quantities into each customer and set them to their respective demand values in cells E9:G9, according to constraint (2). We set the total inflow quantities for intermediate points C and D computed in cells

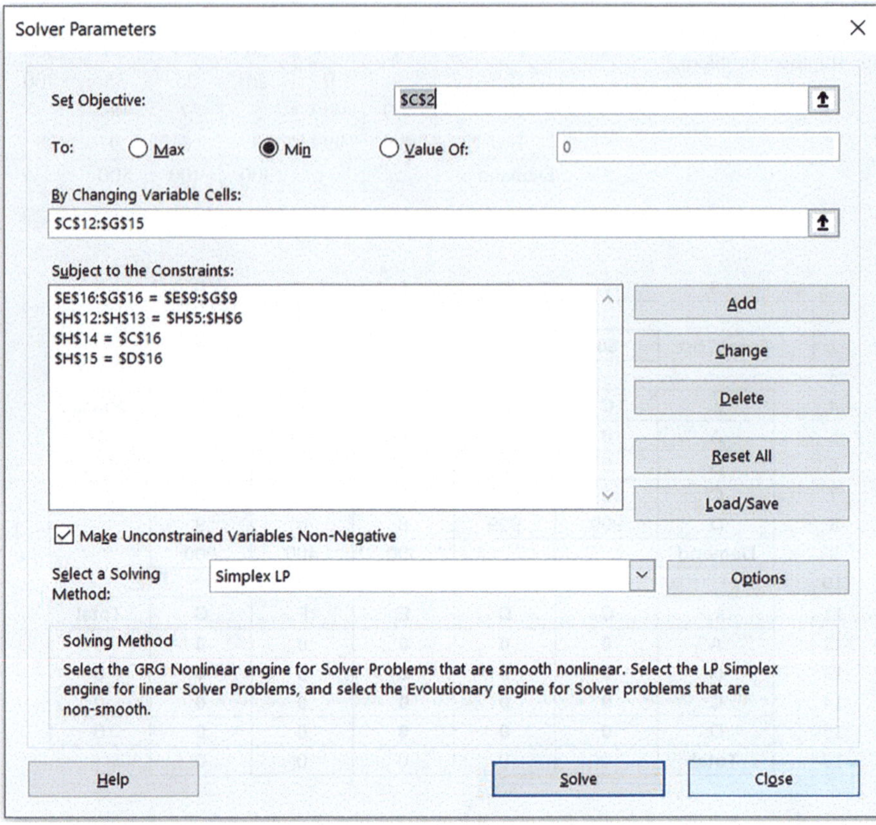

Fig. 7.8 Excel solver definition for trans-shipment problem example

C16:D16, to be equal to the outflow quantities computed in cells H14:H15, respectively, according to constraint (3).

The corresponding Solver definition is given Fig. 7.8. Again, due to the Integer Solutions Property, we do not need to add the integer constraints. The Solving Method was set as Simplex LP, and the solutions are guaranteed to be integers.

As shown in Fig. 7.9, the minimum transportation cost is $18,200, and all the transport quantities are determined, with all supplies distributed and all demand satisfied. Intermediate point C will receive 500 and 300 units from plants A and B, respectively, and supply 300 and 500 units to customers E and G, respectively. While intermediate point D will receive 400 units from plant B and supply to customer F.

Total Cost **$18,200**

c_{ij}	C	D	E	F	G	Capacity
A	8	10	30	40	50	500
B	9	9	20	25	55	700
C	999	999	5	7	8	
D	999	999	8	6	9	
Demand			300	400	500	

x_{ij}	C	D	E	F	G	Total
A	**500**	**0**	**0**	**0**	**0**	500
B	**300**	**400**	**0**	**0**	**0**	700
C	**0**	**0**	**300**	**0**	**500**	800
D	**0**	**0**	**0**	**400**	**0**	400
Total	800	400	300	400	500	

Fig. 7.9 Optimal solution for trans-shipment problem example

7.4 Transportation Problem

We have seen the transportation problem in Sect. 7.1 when we explored the distinct pattern in the **[A]** matrix. The model can be represented as follows with the following parameters and decision variables:

- Source, $i = 1, 2, \ldots, m$.
- Supply quantity from source i, s_i.
- Destination, $j = 1, 2, \ldots, n$.
- Demand quantity from destination j, d_j.
- Transportation cost between i and j, c_{ij}.
- Quantity to transport from source i to destination j, x_{ij}.

Objective function

$$\text{Minimize} \quad Z = \sum_{i=1}^{m} \sum_{j=1}^{n} c_{ij} x_{ij}$$

Constraints

$$\sum_{j=1}^{n} x_{ij} = s_i \quad \forall i \quad (1)$$

$$\sum_{i=1}^{m} x_{ij} = d_j \quad \forall j \quad (2)$$

Decision variables: $x_{ij} \in$ Positive Integer

Table 7.4 Unit transport cost, demand and supply for transportation problem

	R1	R2	R3	R4	R5	Supply
A	10	4	5	9	6	1000
B	8	6	7	4	5	1500
C	6	8	4	3	8	1200
Demand	700	800	900	800	500	3700

Compared to the trans-shipment problem, the transportation problem is simpler, as the goods are transported directly from source to destination without intermediate nodes. Therefore, the transportation problem is a special case of the trans-shipment problem. In addition to the Integer Solutions Property discussed in Sect. 7.1, the transportation problem has the Feasible Solutions Property where:

- The necessary and sufficient condition to have any feasible solution is that

$$\sum_{i=1}^{m} s_i = \sum_{j=1}^{n} d_j$$

- When $\sum s_i > \sum d_j$, introduce a dummy destination to receive the excess supply to make $\sum s_i = \sum d_j$
- Conversely, when $\sum s_i < \sum d_j$, introduce a dummy source to handle the excess demand to make $\sum s_i = \sum d_j$

Let us look at an application example. A company which sells electronic appliances has three plants (A, B, C) and ships the finished goods to five retailers (R1 to R5). The unit transport cost, demand and supply are given in Table 7.4. Since the total supply is equal to the total demand at 3700 units, there is no need to add any dummy supply or dummy demand.

The objective is to determine the number of units to transport from each plant to each retailer with the minimum cost while staying within the plants' supply capacities and meeting the retailers' demand. Using Excel spreadsheet, we can lay out the problem as shown in Fig. 7.10. The objective function in cell C2 is the transportation cost, which is the sum of the product of unit cost c_{ij} in cells C5:G7 and the transport quantities x_{ij} in cells C11:G13.

We use cells H11:H13 to sum up the transport quantities out from plants A, B and C and set them to their respective supply values in cells H5:H7, according to constraint (1). We use cells C14:G14 to sum up the transport quantities into each retailer and set them to their respective demand values in cells C8:G8, according to constraint (2).

The corresponding Solver definition is given in Fig. 7.11. Again, due to the Integer Solutions Property, we do not need to add the integer constraints. The Solving Method was set as Simplex LP, and the solutions are guaranteed to be integers.

As shown in Fig. 7.12, the minimum transportation cost is $17,300, and all the transport quantities are determined, with all supplies distributed and all demand satisfied.

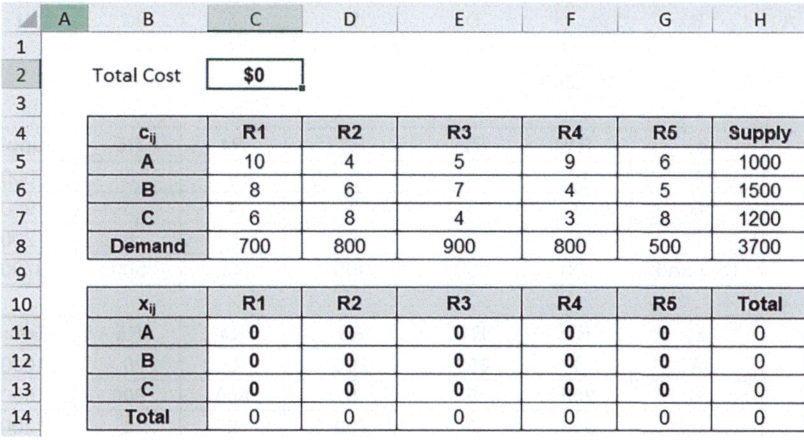

	A	B	C	D	E	F	G	H
1								
2		Total Cost	**$0**					
3								
4		**c_{ij}**	**R1**	**R2**	**R3**	**R4**	**R5**	**Supply**
5		**A**	10	4	5	9	6	1000
6		**B**	8	6	7	4	5	1500
7		**C**	6	8	4	3	8	1200
8		**Demand**	700	800	900	800	500	3700
9								
10		**x_{ij}**	**R1**	**R2**	**R3**	**R4**	**R5**	**Total**
11		**A**	**0**	**0**	**0**	**0**	**0**	0
12		**B**	**0**	**0**	**0**	**0**	**0**	0
13		**C**	**0**	**0**	**0**	**0**	**0**	0
14		**Total**	0	0	0	0	0	0

Fig. 7.10 Excel spreadsheet model for transportation problem example

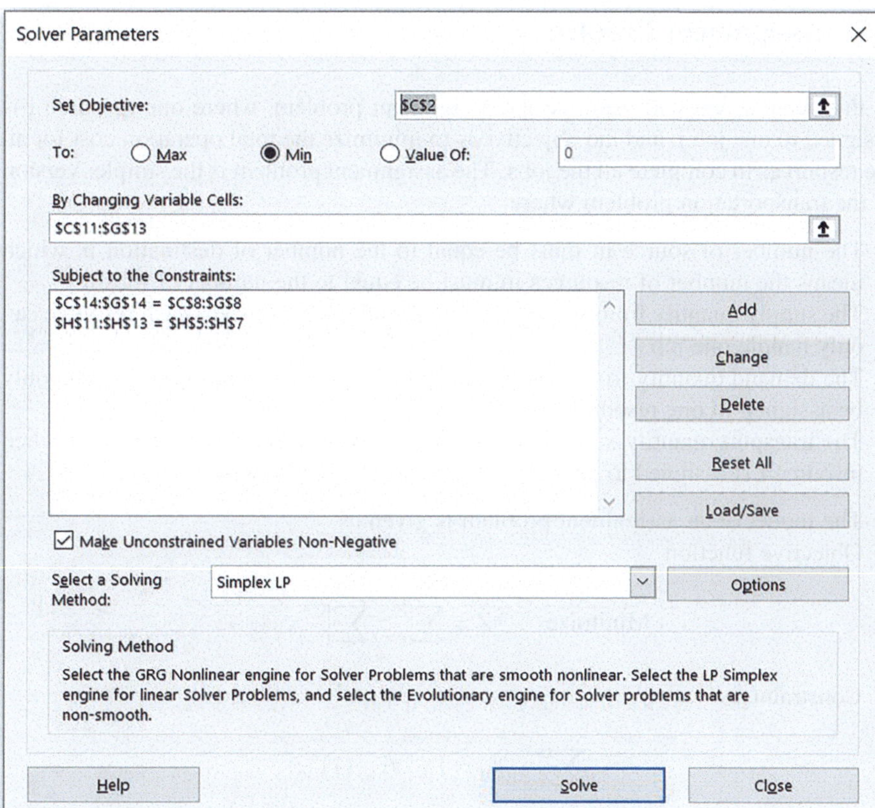

Fig. 7.11 Excel solver definition for transportation problem example

Total Cost **$17,300**

c_{ij}	R1	R2	R3	R4	R5	Supply
A	10	4	5	9	6	1000
B	8	6	7	4	5	1500
C	6	8	4	3	8	1200
Demand	700	800	900	800	500	3700

x_{ij}	R1	R2	R3	R4	R5	Total
A	**0**	**800**	**200**	**0**	**0**	1000
B	**200**	**0**	**0**	**800**	**500**	1500
C	**500**	**0**	**700**	**0**	**0**	1200
Total	700	800	900	800	500	3700

Fig. 7.12 Optimal solution for transportation problem example

7.5 Assignment Problem

In this section, we will examine the assignment problem, where one resource i is assigned to one job j, and the objective is to minimize the total operation cost for all the resources to complete all the jobs. The assignment problem is the simpler version of the transportation problem where:

- The number of source m must be equal to the number of destination n, which means the number of resources m must be equal to the number of jobs n
- The supply quantity from source i, $s_i = 1$ for all i, which means each resource can only handle one job
- The demand quantity from destination j, $d_j = 1$, which means each job can only be assigned to one resource
- The transport quantity x_{ij} will be a binary decision variable where $x_{ij} = 1$ when resource i is assigned to perform job j, and $x_{ij} = 0$ otherwise

The model of an assignment problem is given as
Objective function

$$\text{Minimize} \qquad Z = \sum_{i=1}^{m} \sum_{j=1}^{n} c_{ij} x_{ij}$$

Constraints

$$\sum_{j=1}^{n} x_{ij} = 1 \quad \forall i \quad (1)$$

$$\sum_{i=1}^{m} x_{ij} = 1 \quad \forall j \quad (2)$$

Decision variables: $x_{ij} \in \{0, 1\}$

The objective function is to minimize the total operation cost, which is the sum of the product of operation cost and the binary decision variable. Constraint (1) ensures that each resource i can only handle one job, while constraint (2) ensures that each job j is only assigned to one resource.

Similarly, let us look at an example. A consultancy company has four staff members, namely, A, B, C and D, and there are four projects, P1, P2, P3 and P4, to be assigned to the staff. The staff cost varies according to which staff handles which project, as given in Table 7.5.

The objective is to determine which staff will handle which project with the minimum cost. Using Excel spreadsheet, we can lay out the problem as shown in Fig. 7.13. The objective function in cell C2 is the total cost incurred, which is the sumproduct of the staff cost c_{ij} in cells C5:F8 and the assignment decision variables x_{ij} in cells C11:F14.

We use cells G11:G14 to sum up values of the decision variables for staff members A to D and set them to be 1, according to constraint (1). We use cells C15:F15 to sum up values of the decision variables for projects P1 to P4 and set them to be 1, according to constraint (2).

Table 7.5 Cost for assigning staff to projects

c_{ij}	P1	P2	P3	P4
A	80	60	40	50
B	100	50	80	70
C	30	80	50	60
D	120	70	90	40

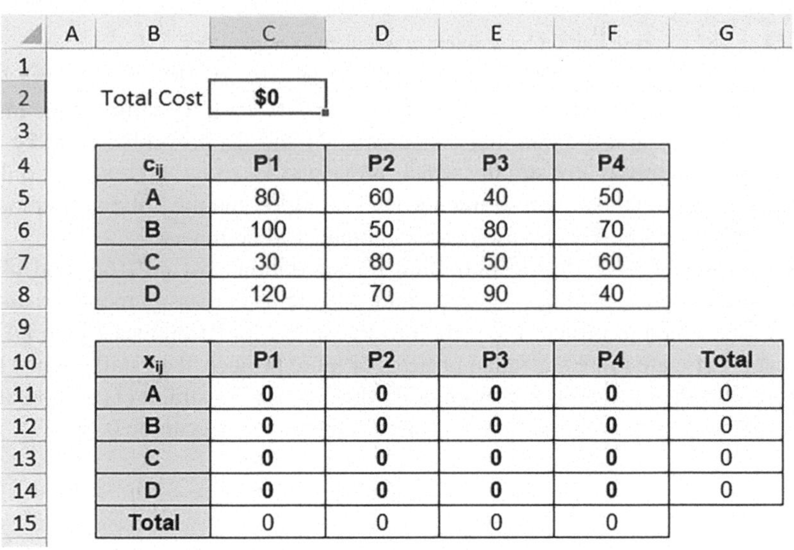

Fig. 7.13 Excel spreadsheet model for assignment problem example

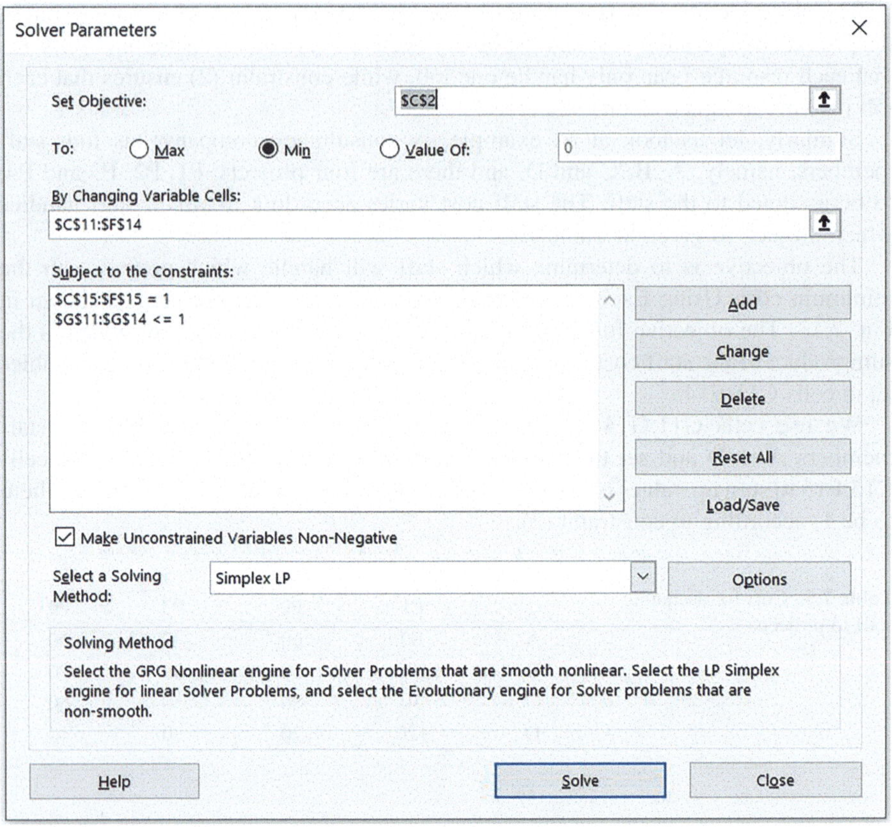

Fig. 7.14 Excel solver definition for assignment problem example

The corresponding Solver definition is given in Fig. 7.14. By virtue of the Integer Solution Property and the fact that constraints (1) and (2) prevented x_{ij} to be > 1, plus the non-negativity constraints which prevented x_{ij} to be < 0, x_{ij} can only be binary. As such, the binary constraint need not be added and the Solving Method can be set as Simplex LP. The solutions are guaranteed to be binary.

As shown in Fig. 7.15, the minimum transportation cost is $160, and all the projects are assigned to staff members, and the one-to-one assignment is satisfied. Staff A is assigned to project P3, staff B to P2, staff C to P1 and staff D to P4.

What if there are more staff than projects or more projects than staff? When there are more staff than projects, we will modify the sign for constraint (1) to ≤, to allow some staff to be not assigned to any project, so that their x_{ij} can be 0.

$$\sum_{j=1}^{n} x_{ij} \leq 1 \quad \forall i \quad (1)$$

Total Cost **$160**

c_{ij}	P1	P2	P3	P4
A	80	60	40	50
B	100	50	80	70
C	30	80	50	60
D	120	70	90	40

x_{ij}	P1	P2	P3	P4	Total
A	0	0	1	0	1
B	0	1	0	0	1
C	1	0	0	0	1
D	0	0	0	1	1
Total	1	1	1	1	

Fig. 7.15 Optimal solution for assignment problem example

Conversely, when there are more projects than staff, we will modify the sign for constraint (2) to ≤, to allow some projects to be not assigned to any staff, so that their x_{ij} can be 0.

$$\sum_{i=1}^{m} x_{ij} \leq 1 \quad \forall j \quad (2)$$

7.6 Shortest Path Problem

The shortest path problem aims to find the path between the source and destination nodes such that the sum of distance (usually represented by cost) which constitutes the path is minimized.

Let G = (N, E) be a directed graph, where N is a set of nodes which include source s and sink t such that there exists a path s → t and E is a set of edges. We define the following parameters and decision variables:

- Cost function between i and j, c_{ij}
- Binary decision variable if the edge between i and j is used, x_{ij}
- Index value to indicate if the node is a source, sink or an intermediate node, b_i

Objective function

$$\text{Minimize} \quad Z = \sum_{i=1}^{I} \sum_{j=1}^{J} c_{ij} x_{ij}$$

Subject to constraints where for each node $j \in N$, the net sum of flow is the sum of outflow minus the sum of inflow represented by b_i.

$$\sum_{\substack{\text{outflow} \\ \{k|(i,k) \in E,\ i \neq k\}}} x_{ik} - \sum_{\substack{\text{inflow} \\ \{j|(i,j) \in E, i \neq j\}}} x_{ji} = b_i, \forall i \in N$$

$$b_i = \begin{cases} 1, & \text{if } i = s \\ 0, & \text{if } i \neq s, i \neq t \\ -1, & \text{if } i = t \end{cases}$$

Decision variables: $x_{ij} \in \{0, 1\}$

The objective is to minimize the total net sum of cost for all the edges that are used. For conservation of flow:

- For the source node s, the sum of outflow is 1, and there is no inflow; thus, the net sum of flow $b_i = 1$.
- For the sink node t, the sum of inflow is 1, and there is no outflow; thus, the net sum of flow $b_i = -1$.
- For other nodes, the sum of inflow is the same as the sum of outflow; thus, the net sum of flow $b_i = 0$.

Thus, the shortest path problem is again a special case of the minimum cost flow problem where there are no capacity constraints on the edges and the net flow b_i can only be 1, 0 or −1 instead of the net quantity flow values.

Let us consider an example of a directed graph shown in Fig. 7.16. Costs of transport are given on the edges. We will develop a spreadsheet model to find the shortest path from node A to node F.

We first translate the graph to a cost matrix table describing the connections between two nodes (from, to) and the cost c_{ij} associated with the edge joining them, as shown in Table 7.6.

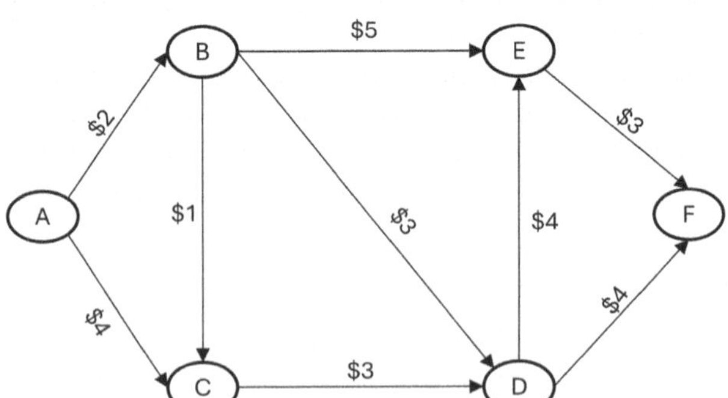

Fig. 7.16 Directed graph of shortest path problem example

Table 7.6 Cost matrix for shortest path problem example

From	To	c_{ij}
A	B	2
A	C	4
B	C	1
B	D	3
B	E	5
C	D	3
D	E	4
D	F	4
E	F	3

	A	B	C	D	E	F	G
1							
2		Total Cost	0				
3							
4		From	To	c_{ij}	x_{ij}		
5		A	B	2			
6		A	C	4			
7		B	C	1			
8		B	D	3			
9		B	E	5			
10		C	D	3			
11		D	E	4			
12		D	F	4			
13		E	F	3			
14							
15		Constraints					
16		Node	Source or Sink	RHS (b_i)	Total Out Flow	Total In Flow	LHS
17		A	Source	1	0	0	0
18		B	Other	0	0	0	0
19		C	Other	0	0	0	0
20		D	Other	0	0	0	0
21		E	Other	0	0	0	0
22		F	Sink	-1	0	0	0

Fig. 7.17 Excel spreadsheet model for shortest path problem example

The objective is to minimize the total net sum of cost for all the edges from node A to F, considering the costs at the edges. Using Excel spreadsheet, we can lay out the problem as shown in Fig. 7.17. The objective function in cell C2 is the sumproduct of the product of unit cost c_{ij} in cells D5:D13 and the binary decision variables x_{ij} in cells E5:E13.

We use the second table to indicate whether the nodes are source, sink or other in cells C17:C22 and their respective b_i values in cells D17:D22, where source will be 1, sink −1 and other 0. In cells E17:E22, we compute the total outflow from each node by using SUMIF function to sum x_{ij} for that node in the From column. For example,

$$E17 = SUMIF(\$B\$5 : \$B\$13, \$B17, \$E\$5 : \$E\$13)$$

will compute the total outflow from node A by summing x_{ij} where the From node is node A.

In cells F17:F22, we compute the total inflow into each node by using SUMIF function to sum x_{ij} for that node in the To column. For example,

$$F17 = SUMIF(\$C\$5 : \$C\$13, \$B17, \$E\$5 : \$E\$13)$$

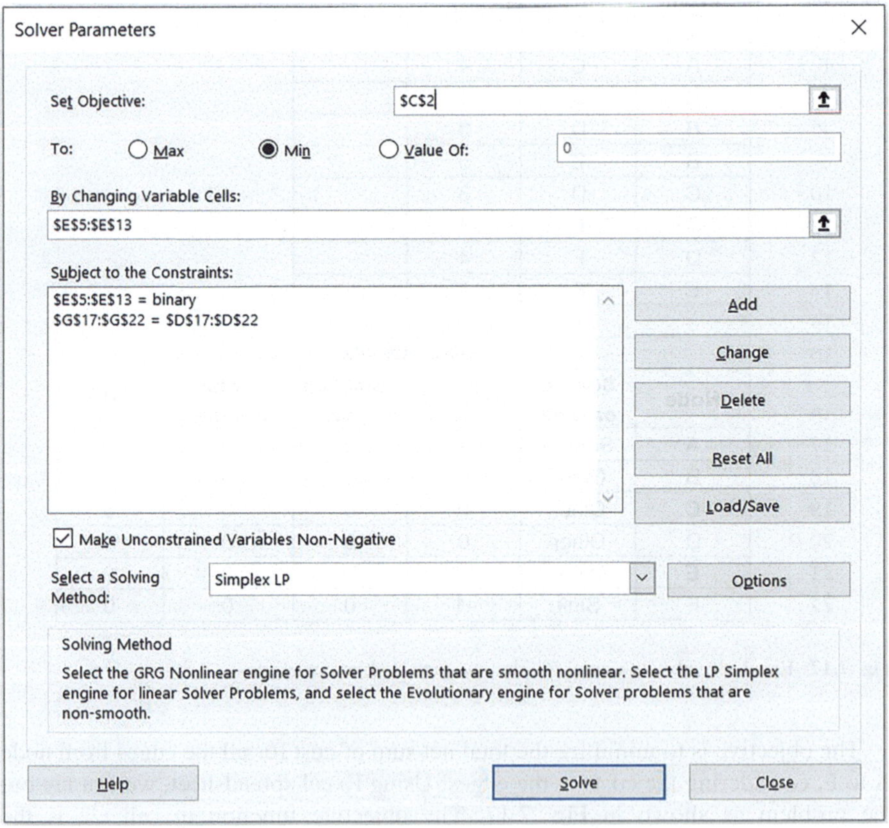

Fig. 7.18 Excel solver definition for shortest path problem example

Total Cost | 9

From	To	c_{ij}	x_{ij}
A	B	2	1
A	C	4	0
B	C	1	0
B	D	3	1
B	E	5	0
C	D	3	0
D	E	4	0
D	F	4	1
E	F	3	0

Constraints					
Node	Source or Sink	RHS (b_i)	Total Out Flow	Total In Flow	LHS
A	Source	1	1	0	1
B	Other	0	1	1	0
C	Other	0	0	0	0
D	Other	0	1	1	0
E	Other	0	0	0	0
F	Sink	-1	0	1	-1

Fig. 7.19 Optimal solution for shortest path problem example

will compute the total inflow to node A by summing x_{ij} where the To node is node A.

In cells G17:G22, we compute the net sum of flow for each node by using the total outflow minus the total inflow for each node. They form the LHS of the constraints, which must be set equal to the RHS values in cells D17:D22.

The corresponding Solver definition is given Fig. 7.18. We define the decision variables x_{ij} in cells E5:E13 to binary, and by virtue of the Integer Solutions Property, the Solving Method can be set as Simplex LP.

As shown in Fig. 7.19, the minimum transportation cost is $9, and the shortest path will be from A → B → D → F.

7.7 Maximum Flow Problem

The maximum flow problem aims to find a maximum feasible flow from the source to the sink subjected to the capacity constraints on various edges and flow conservation constraints. To solve, we need to artificially connect the sink t to source s by setting the total outflow from the source s to be equal to the total inflow into the sink t. The objective function would be to maximize the total inflow into the sink t, so that the maximum flow can be achieved through the network.

The general mathematical formulation for the maximum flow problem is given as Objective function

$$\text{Maximize} \quad \underset{\{i|(i,t) \in E, i \neq t\}}{\underset{\text{inflow}}{\sum}} x_{it}$$

Constraints

$$\underset{\{k|(i,k) \in E, i \neq k\}}{\underset{\text{outflow}}{\sum}} x_{ik} = \underset{\{j|(j,i) \in E, i \neq j\}}{\underset{\text{inflow}}{\sum}} x_{ji}, \forall i \in N, i \neq s, i \neq t \quad (1)$$

$$\underset{\{i|(s,i) \in E, i \neq s\}}{\underset{\text{outflow}}{\sum}} x_{si} = \underset{\{i|(i,t) \in E, i \neq t\}}{\underset{\text{inflow}}{\sum}} x_{it} \quad (2)$$

$$0 \leq x_{ij} \leq u_{ij} \quad , \forall (i,j) \in E \quad (3)$$

$$x_{ij} \in \text{positive integer}$$

From the formulation, we can see that the maximum flow problem is a special case of the minimum cost flow problem with the objective function modified to maximizing the inflow into the sink node. Constraint (1) shows that there is conservation of flow for all the nodes other than the source s and sink t. Constraint (2) ensures that the total outflow from the source must be equal to the total inflow into the sink. Constraint (3) ensures that the flow along each edge does not exceed the capacity. All the flows are positive integers.

Let us consider an example of a directed graph shown in Fig. 7.20. Capacities are given on the edges. We will develop a spreadsheet model to find the maximum flow path(s) from node A to node E.

The objective is to maximize the total inflow into the sink node E, considering the capacities at the edges. Using Excel spreadsheet, we can lay out the problem as shown in Fig. 7.21. The objective function in cell C2 is the total inflow into the sink node E computed in cell G17. The capacities u_{ij} of the edges are in cells C5:G9, and

Fig. 7.20 Graphical representation of maximum flow problem example

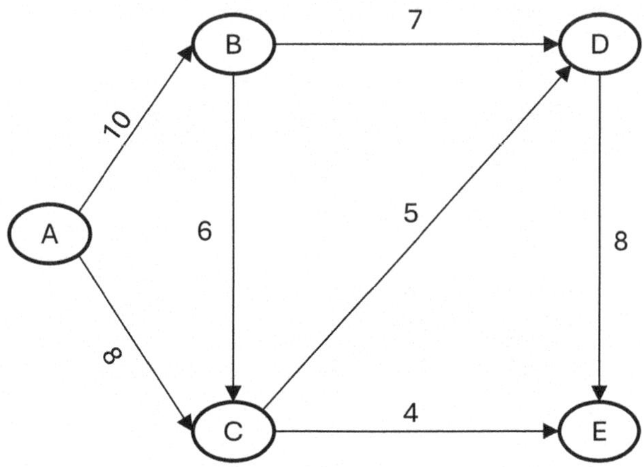

	A	B	C	D	E	F	G	H	I
1									
2		Maximize	0						
3									
4		u_{ij}	A	B	C	D	E		
5		A	0	10	8	0	0		
6		B	0	0	6	7	0		
7		C	0	0	0	5	4		
8		D	0	0	0	0	8		
9		E	0	0	0	0	0		
10									
11		x_{ij}	A	B	C	D	E	Total	RHS
12		A	0	0	0	0	0	0	
13		B	0	0	0	0	0	0	0
14		C	0	0	0	0	0	0	0
15		D	0	0	0	0	0	0	0
16		E	0	0	0	0	0		
17		Total		0	0	0	0		

Fig. 7.21 Excel spreadsheet model for maximum flow problem example

the decision variables x_{ij} are in cells C12:G16. When there are no links between two nodes, we will put the value of u_{ij} as zero.

The total outflow of the source node A is computed in cell H12, and the total outflows of the other nodes B, C and D are computed in cells H13:H15. The total inflows of the other nodes B, C and D are computed in cells D17:F17. The RHS of the flow conservation constraints for nodes B, C and D in cells I13:I15 are set equal to the respective inflows in cells D17:F17.

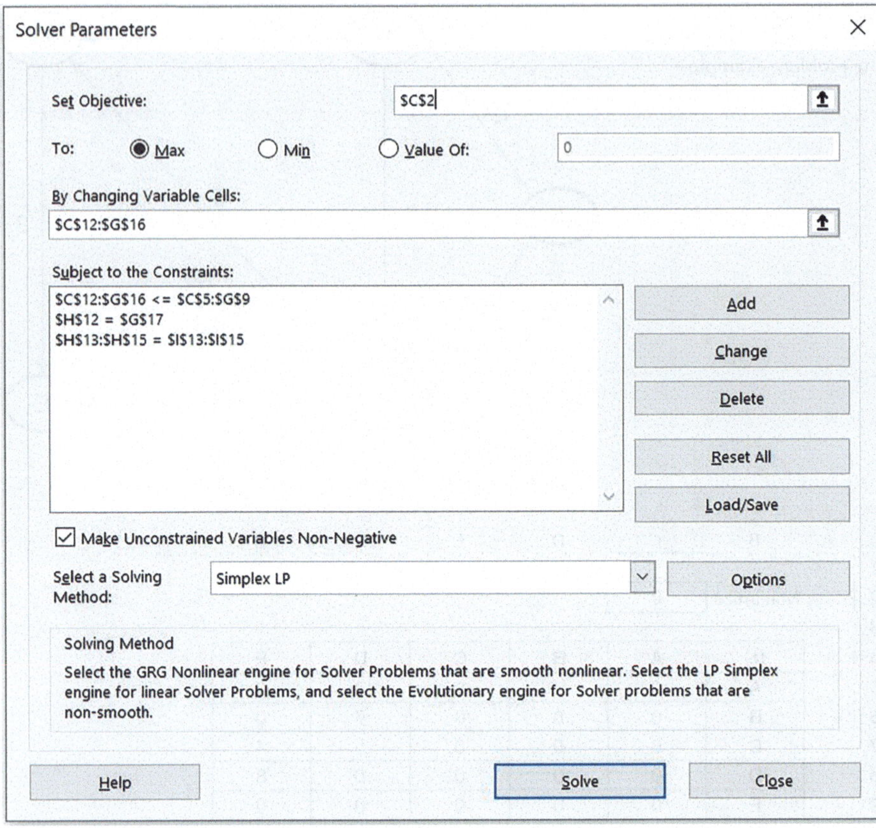

Fig. 7.22 Excel solver definition for maximum flow problem example

The corresponding Solver definition is given in Fig. 7.22. By virtue of the Integer Solutions Property, the Solving Method can be set as Simplex LP.

As shown in Fig. 7.23, the maximized flow into the sink node E is 12, and there are three flow paths including from A → B → D → E, from A → C → D → E and from A → C → E. Figure 7.24 depicts the graphical representation of the three flow paths to achieve maximum flow, where the values on the edges denote the flow quantities and the values in parenthesis are the respective capacities of the edge. For example, from A → B, the flow quantity is 7, while the capacity of this edge is (10). The dotted line joining node E to node A is the artificially added link.

	Maximize	12

u_{ij}	A	B	C	D	E
A	0	10	8	0	0
B	0	0	6	7	0
C	0	0	0	5	4
D	0	0	0	0	8
E	0	0	0	0	0

x_{ij}	A	B	C	D	E	Total	RHS
A	**0**	**7**	**5**	**0**	**0**	12	
B	**0**	**0**	**0**	**7**	**0**	7	7
C	**0**	**0**	**0**	**1**	**4**	5	5
D	**0**	**0**	**0**	**0**	**8**	8	8
E	**0**	**0**	**0**	**0**	**0**		
Total		7	5	8	12		

Fig. 7.23 Optimal solution for maximum flow problem example

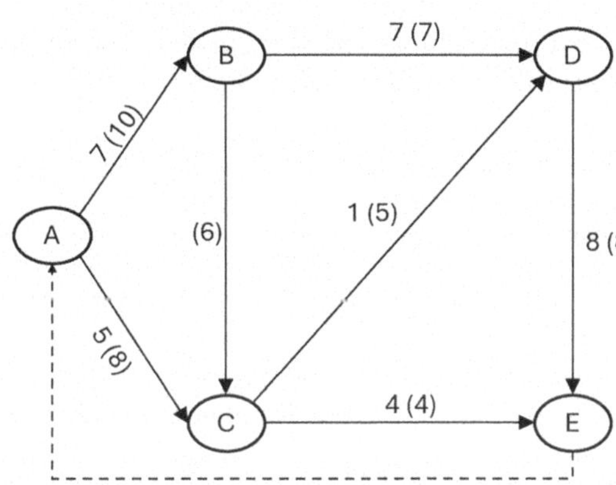

Fig. 7.24 Graphical representation of optimal solution for maximum flow problem example

7.8 Case 7: Load Balancing at Airport Terminals

This case is modified from the paper published by Ma et al. (2012). In this case study, we explored the assignment of airlines to different terminals based on passenger and flight loads at one of the busiest airports in Asia. The airport has three terminals that serve the major airlines in the world. The airport also has a large transit area where spaces are rented to retailers to sell goods to passengers as duty-free shopping. One-third of the airport's revenue comes from the rental income and the sale of goods at these retailers. Thus, the objective of the airport is to check in the passengers quickly so that they have sufficient time to shop at the transit areas, which will boost the revenues for the retail shops as well as for the airport.

However, due to the imbalance load at different terminals caused by inefficient assignment of airlines to the terminals, problems such as long waiting time at check-in counters at busier terminals have caused dissatisfaction among passengers. Thus, the airport management was keen to harness the power of data and decision analytics to improve load balancing by efficiently assigning airlines to terminals.

The following data are given in Table 7.7 for the three terminals:

- Passenger capacity of each terminal
- Flight capacity of each terminal

From Table 7.7, we observe that Terminal 2 has the largest capacity, followed by Terminal 1 and Terminal 3. Therefore, to achieve comparable service level at the three terminals, one would expect that Terminal 2 will handle the most flights and passengers, followed by Terminal 1 and lastly Terminal 3. However, using the historical data for a specific year on the number of passengers and flights served at each terminal, it was found that Terminal 1 handled the highest load for the different days of the week, followed by Terminal 2, and Terminal 3 handled the lowest load, as shown in Figs. 7.25 and 7.26.

To achieve a more balanced load for all three terminals, the problem was modeled as an assignment problem with a huge twist formulated as a Binary Integer-Non-linear Programming (BINLP) model. The twist comes from the requirement that some airlines are code share airlines and they would prefer to be assigned to the same

Table 7.7 Passenger and flight capacities at the terminals

Terminal	Passenger capacity	Flight capacity
1	22,000,000	105,850
2	27,000,000	127,750
3	21,000,000	102,200

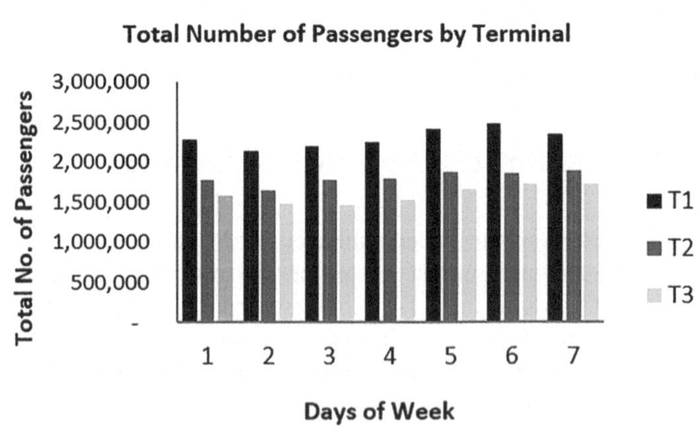

Fig. 7.25 Total passengers by days of week at different terminals

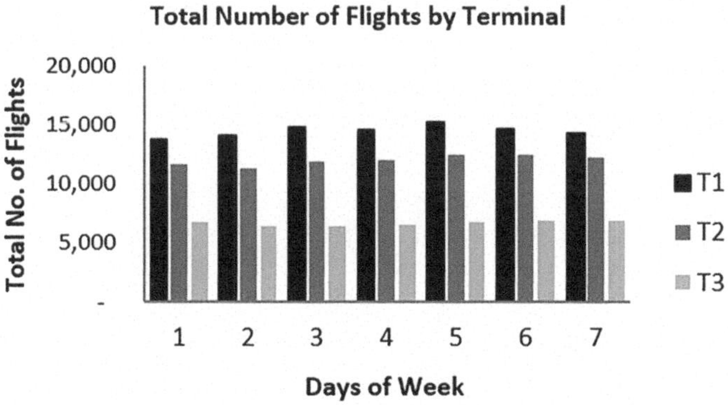

Fig. 7.26 Total flight load by days of week at different terminals

terminal for business operation purpose, while some airlines do not prefer to be assigned to the same terminal.

We will define the following parameters and decision variables:

- $i =$ index for airlines, $i = 1$ to N.
- $j =$ index for terminals, $j = 1$ to 3.
- $A_i =$ total number of passengers handled by airline i in a year.
- $K_i =$ total number of flights by airline i in a year.
- $Z_j =$ total number of passengers handled by terminal j in a year.
- $F_j =$ total number of flights handled by terminal j in a year.
- $P_j =$ passenger capacity of terminal j.
- $G_j =$ flight capacity of terminal j.
- B = group of airlines that need to be assigned to the same terminal.
- C = group of airlines that need to be assigned to different terminals.
- $x_{ij} =$ binary decision variable to indicate if airline i is assigned to terminal j.

Objective function

$$\min_j \left(\max\left\{\mathrm{Var}\left(Z_j\right), \mathrm{Var}\left(F_j\right)\right\}\right)$$

Constraints

$$\sum_j x_{ij} = 1 \quad , \forall i \quad (1)$$

$$\sum_i x_{ij} * A_i = Z_j \quad , \forall j \quad (2)$$

$$\sum_i x_{ij} * K_i = F_j \quad , \forall j \quad (3)$$

$$Z_j \leq P_j \quad , \forall j \quad (4)$$

$$F_j \leq G_j \quad , \forall j \quad (5)$$

$$x_{ij} \leq M * x_{i'j} \quad , \forall j, \{(i, i') \in B \quad (6)$$

$$x_{ij} + x_{i'j} \leq 1 \quad , \forall j, \{(i, i') \in C \quad (7)$$

The objective function is to minimize the maximum variance among the passengers and flight loads assigned to each terminal. Constraint (1) ensures that each airline is assigned to only one terminal to avoid any confusion for the passengers. Constraint (2) computes the total number of passengers handled by terminal j in a year, while constraint (3) computes the total number of flights handled by terminal j in a year. Constraints (4) and (5) ensure that the total number of passengers and flights assigned to the terminal i is less than the capacities for the passengers and flights for that terminal, respectively. Lastly, constraint (6) ensures that code-share airlines in group B will be assigned to the same terminal, while constraint (7) ensures that airlines which belong to group C will be assigned to different terminals.

Using the above model formulation, we used a commercial software tool SAS/OR to solve the problem with 1 year of historical data consisting of 87 airlines. Figures 7.27 and 7.28 show the percentage load as compared to the terminal capacities, before and after the assignment. The flight and passenger loads are more evenly distributed among the three terminals with Terminal 2 handling the highest passenger load.

Let us map the problem and solution method for this case study against the *data and decision analytics framework* proposed in Chap. 1. As shown in Fig. 7.29, in this case study, the problem faced was long-wait time leading to customer dissatisfaction. Therefore, the right question to ask was "How to reduce long wait time?".

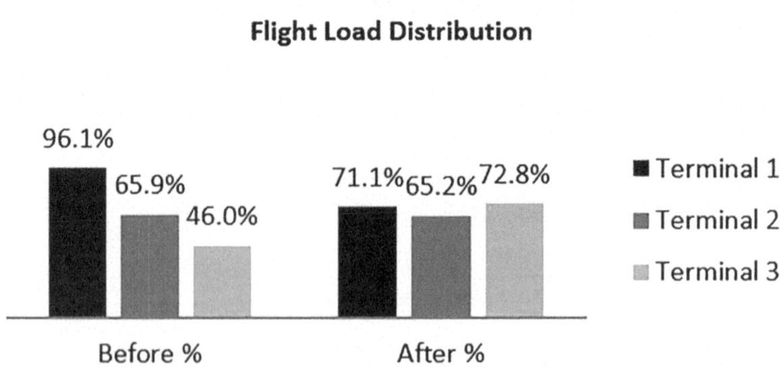

Fig. 7.27 Flight load distribution before and after assignment

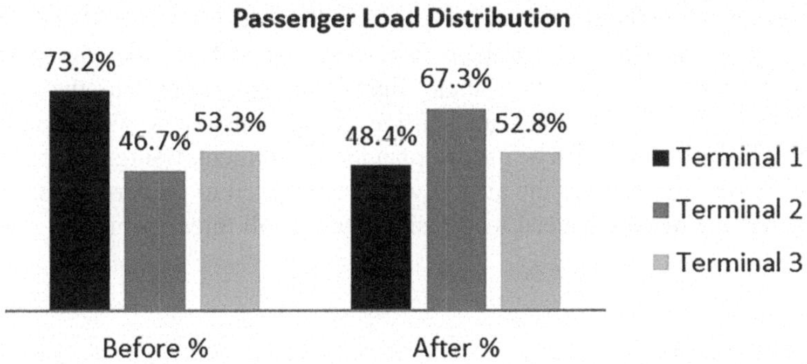

Fig. 7.28 Passenger load distribution before and after assignment

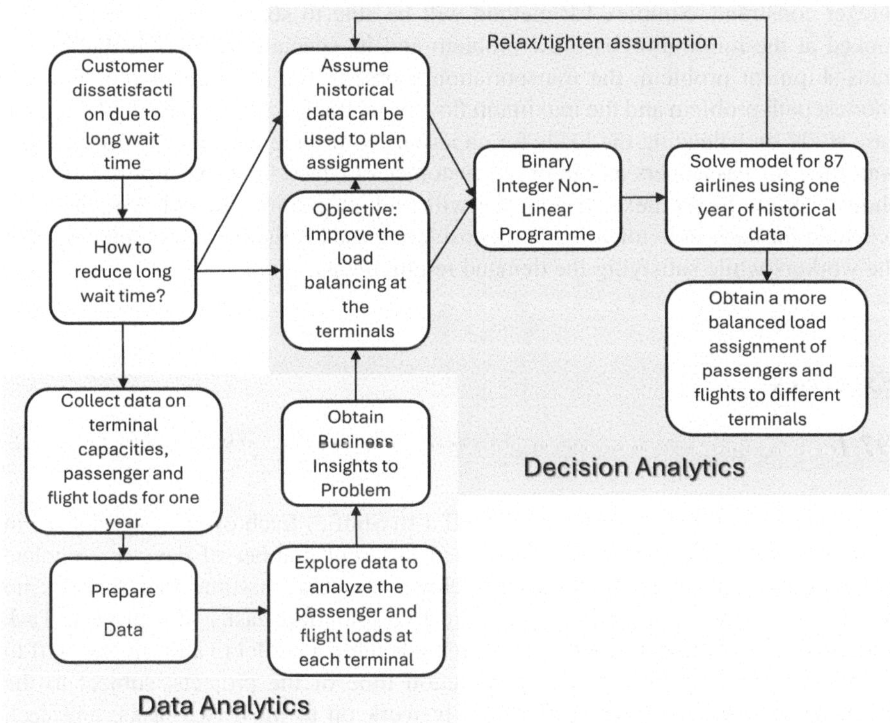

Fig. 7.29 Data and decision analytics framework map for Case 7

Next was to collect the relevant data needed to answer the question, including the terminal capacities for passengers and flights and 1-year historical data on the number of passengers and flights served by each terminal. With the data collected, the analyst can perform initial analysis to determine the current load distribution. From the insights obtained, it was found that there was unbalanced load distribution where Terminal 2, being the largest, was not handling the highest load and Terminal 1 was overloaded. Thus, the problem objective would be to determine the best assignment of airlines (and thus their flights and passengers) to the terminals, considering capacity constraints and airline group constraints. We assumed that one year of historical data can be used to plan the assignment. Using the optimization model, 87 airlines served by the airport were re-assigned to the terminals that were able to achieve a more balanced load assignment for all three terminals.

7.9 Summary

This chapter covered the special class of optimization problems where the optimal solution to the LP is also the optimal solution to the original IP, without the need for integer constraint. Simplex LP method will be able to solve them efficiently. We looked at the minimum cost flow problem and its specialized cases including the trans-shipment problem, the transportation problem, the assignment problem, the shortest path problem and the maximum flow problem. Finally, we also looked into a case study on balancing the loads for an airport with three terminals to reduce long wait time for passengers and improve customer satisfaction at the airport and retail shop revenue. In the next chapter, we will look at planning workforce and work schedule for each individual worker, considering the availability and preferences of the workers while satisfying the demand requirements.

Exercises

Q7.1

A company has three staff members, Staff 1 to Staff 3. Each of them specializes in their own field of expertise and may need different number of days to complete different tasks as given in the table below. You may assume that there is no dependency between the tasks. There are five important tasks in a project, Task 1 to Task 5. As a project manager, you are to develop a model to allocate the staff to the task to minimize the overall completion time of the projects, subject to the following constraints: Each staff can only work on at most two tasks, and each staff has 12 days available. What is the minimum completion time for all the tasks?

	Staff 1	Staff 2	Staff 3
Task 1	4	5	8
Task 2	6	5	5
Task 3	8	10	9
Task 4	9	7	8
Task 5	3	5	4

Q7.2

A factory in node A wants to send the maximum number of products to its retailer at location F. The graph below shows the capacity of the flow on each edge. What is the maximum number of products that can be transported via the network from A to F?

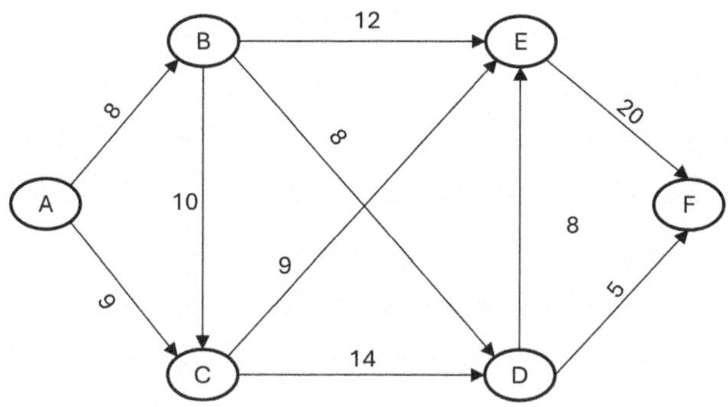

Q7.3

Find the shortest path from A to F in the following diagram shown.

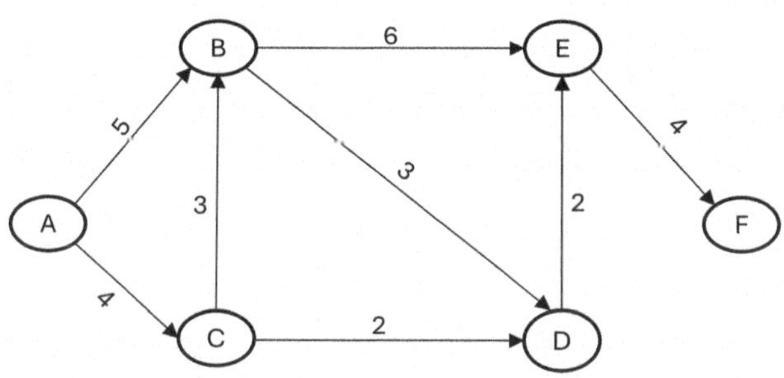

References

Ma, N. L., Cheong, M. L. F., & Choy, J. (2012), *Uncovering insights through data analytics for an airport operation to improve profitability* (pp. 803–810). SRII 2012 Service Research and Innovation Institute, 24–27 July, San Jose, CA.

Winston, W. L., & Albright, S. C. (2015). *Practical management science* (5th ed.). Cengage Learning.

Chapter 8
Workforce Planning and Scheduling

In Chap. 5, we learned about capacity planning for resources and looked into the case of planning hospital beds for the next 7 years. In this chapter, we will be planning workforce and scheduling the work schedule for each individual worker. Considerations are very different than planning resources such as machines, warehouse space, spare parts and hospital beds, purely because human workforce has personal preferences, can fall sick on certain days, and have different productivity rates.

In many business operations, labour constitutes a large portion of the total cost of running the business. Thus, controlling labour cost through effective planning and scheduling is important, as we know that every worker is different in terms of skill sets, availability and preferences. Why is it important to satisfy the workers' preferences? Preferences are usually complementary, for example, some workers may prefer to work on day shifts, while others may prefer to work on night shifts. A schedule that matches workers' preferences is less likely to change and translate to better workforce performance and in turn higher customer satisfaction. In addition, there could be job roles which are subjected to strict rules and regulations which cannot be violated (e.g. nursing), thus adding to the complexity of planning and scheduling such workforce. Thompson (2004) provides a guide on how to plan capacity in the hospitality industry, which can be applicable to any industry.

In this chapter, we will first learn about planning the workforce in terms of the number of workers needed at different time periods to meet demand requirements and then match the availability and preferences of each worker to the number of workers needed. The overall objective is to put the right worker to work at the right job at the right time, maximizing or minimizing a certain objective while satisfying the constraints. We will discuss how optimization concepts and models are applied in a real-world scenario to plan and schedule ambulance drivers.

M. L. F. Cheong, Ma Nang Laik, *Data and Decision Analytics for Business Operations*, https://doi.org/10.1007/978-3-031-72255-4_8

Learning Outcomes
By the end of this chapter, readers will achieve the following learning outcomes:

- Identify and forecast labour drivers.
- Convert forecast into number of workers required.
- Formulate an optimization model to determine the demand for workers that minimizes total cost.
- Formulate an optimization model to minimize the total number of full-time workers needed to fulfil shift schedule.
- Formulate an optimization model to maximize the total preference scores of all full-time workers needed to fulfil shift schedule.
- Discuss how optimization concepts and models are applied in real-world scenarios to plan and schedule ambulance drivers and faculty teaching schedule using the *data and decision analytics framework.*

8.1 Identifying and Forecasting Labor Drivers

In satisfying customer demand, some work processes must be executed by workers, be it operating machines to churn out products or providing services to satisfy customers' requests. For example, running a hotel business will require two types of work processes to be executed: one is guest check-in process, and the other is housekeeping of hotel rooms. These two types of work process have labour drivers that will affect the number of workers needed.

For guest check-in process, the labour driver will be the number of guest arrivals. The larger this number, the more check-in workers will be needed. For housekeeping, the labour driver will be the number of rooms and the types of room to be cleaned. The larger the number of rooms, the more workers will be needed, and a suite room will need more workers to clean than a normal deluxe room.

In this section, we need to first identify the correct labour driver for a work process and then apply the most suitable forecasting model (covered in Chap. 1) to forecast the labour driver, which will then be converted to the number of workers needed based on a selected labour standard, for planning and scheduling purposes, as depicted in Fig. 8.1.

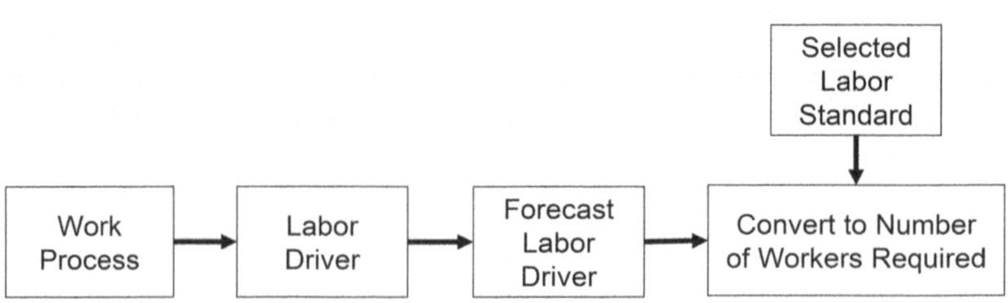

Fig. 8.1 Identify and forecast labour driver

8.2 Convert Forecast into Number of Workers Required

The conversion of labour driver to the number of workers needed is assumed to be linear and will be based on a selected labour standard. We consider three different types of labour drivers:

- Productivity standard—this standard is chosen when we assume that every worker has the same productivity. For example, if one worker can produce 10 pieces of products in 1 hour, then two workers will be needed to produce 20 pieces of products in 1 hour.
- Economic standard—this standard is chosen when we assume that every worker can bring in the same financial performance. For example, if one worker can bring in \$500 of contract value, then we will need four workers to bring in \$2000 of contract value.
- Service standard—this standard is chosen when we assume that every worker can provide the same service standard expected. For example, if one worker can provide guest check-in service in 5 min, three workers will be needed to provide guest check-in service for three guests in 5 min.

Apart from assuming a linear relationship, two additional assumptions were made when using a labour standard to perform the conversion. One is that the forecast is accurate, but we know that forecast is always wrong from Chap. 1. Two is that there will be no absenteeism among the workers, and again, we know that this is not true. As such, the number of workers required will need to be adjusted accordingly.

For forecast accuracy, if the mean squared error (MSE) is large, then an adjustment will be needed. As a rule of thumb, if MSE/Mean >20%, then the MSE is considered large. For large MSE, if the forecasting method tends to underestimate when there is an increasing trend, we will increase the number of workers required. Conversely, if the forecasting method tends to overestimate when there is a decreasing trend, then we will decrease the number of workers required. The number to increase or decrease will be based on business estimation. For absenteeism, we can use past data to determine the availability of the workers similar to availability A of machines, which we have discussed in Chap. 5, so that the number of workers can be increased when there is high absenteeism.

8.3 Workforce Planning and Scheduling

We will discuss a basic framework where we first determine the number of workers needed to meet the demand of the labour driver, then determine the supply of workers considering pre-defined shift schedule and then finally assign each named worker to a specific shift schedule, taking into account their preferences.

8.3.1 Demand for Number of Workers

In this step, we aim to minimize the total cost of providing service using different types of workers with different unit costs and different unit supply of labour driver. Let us define the following parameters:

- i = index for workers of type i where $i = 1$ to n.
- x_i = demand for workers of type i.
- c_i = unit cost of engaging worker of type i.
- a_i = unit supply of labor driver from worker of type i.
- D = demand for labour driver.

The optimization model minimizes the total cost to determine the demand for workers x_i, and can be represented as

Objective function

$$\text{Minimize Total Cost}, Z = \sum_{i=1}^{n} c_i x_i$$

Constraints

$$\sum_{i=1}^{n} a_i x_i \geq D$$

Decision variables: $x_i \geq 0$, integer

The constraint ensures that the total supply of labour driver is sufficient to meet the demand for labour driver.

8.3.2 Shift Schedules

After the demand for workers x_i to satisfy the labor driver is determined, we need to determine the actual number of full-time (FT) workers to supply in each shift on each day, based on shift schedule (SS) pre-defined by the business. Here, we consider only FT workers because only FT workers can be assigned to shift schedules, as part-time (PT) workers are meant to fill any supply gaps.

A business pre-defined shift schedule (SS) is a schedule that follows certain business rules or regulations. For example, for a 7-day plan, the business may have a regulation that each FT worker should work only 6 days and rest 1 day. Therefore, a total of seven possible shift schedules can be created as shown in Table 8.1, where "1" denotes a working day and 0 denotes a rest day. With shift schedules, the allocation of work will be fair among the FT workers since all workers work the same number of days and rest the same number of days, in a 7-day schedule. However, the actual number of FT workers to supply will tend to be higher than the demand for FT workers due to the rigidness introduced by the shift schedule.

Table 8.1 Seven shift schedules example

Shift schedule	Day 1	Day 2	Day 3	Day 4	Day 5	Day 6	Day 7
SS1	0	1	1	1	1	1	1
SS2	1	0	1	1	1	1	1
SS3	1	1	0	1	1	1	1
SS4	1	1	1	0	1	1	1
SS5	1	1	1	1	0	1	1
SS6	1	1	1	1	1	0	1
SS7	1	1	1	1	1	1	0

To determine the number of FT workers to assign to each shift schedule, we need an optimization model to ensure that the supply of FT workers can meet the demand in each shift on each day. Let us define the following parameters:

- s = index for shift schedule, where $s = 1$ to S.
- d = index for day.
- c_{ds} indicates if this day d for shift schedule s is a working day or not, 1 for working day, and 0 for rest day.
- W_d = demand for FT worker on day d.
- $\widehat{x}_s$ = number of FT workers assigned to shift schedule s.

The optimization model minimizes the number of FT workers assigned to all the shift schedules and can be presented as

Objective function

$$\text{Minimize Total Number of FT Workers Assigned, } Z = \sum\nolimits_{s=1}^{S} \widehat{x}_s$$

Constraints

$$\sum\nolimits_{s=1}^{S} c_{ds}\widehat{x}_s \geq W_d \quad , \forall d$$

Decision variables: $\widehat{x}_s \geq 0$, integer

The constraint ensures that the supply of FT workers can meet the demand in each shift on each day d.

8.3.3 *Schedule Named Workers Based on Preferences*

After the number of FT workers assigned to each shift schedule (SS) is determined, the next task is to allocate the named worker to each SS based on each worker's preference. Every worker is a unique individual with his/her own preference. Some may prefer to work consecutive days before a rest day, while others may prefer to have their rest days in the middle of the week. There are other forms of preferences, for example, preference for day shift versus night shift.

To take into account preferences, a preference score can be assigned by named worker for each shift schedule. A high score can denote preferred option, while a low score can denote non-preferred option. Let us define the following parameters:

- s = index for shift schedule, where $s = 1$ to S.
- j = index for named worker, where $j = 1$ to J.
- p_{js} = preference score of named worker j for shift schedule s.
- $\hat{x}_s$ = number of FT workers required for each shift schedule s.
- b_{js} = binary variable to indicate if this named worker j is allocated to shift schedule s, 1 for yes and 0 for no.

The optimization model maximizes the total preference scores can be presented as Objective function

$$\text{Maximize Total Preference Score, } Z = \sum_{j=1}^{J} \sum_{s=1}^{S} b_{js} p_{js}$$

Constraints

$$\sum_{j=1}^{J} b_{js} = \hat{x}_s \quad , \forall s$$

$$\sum_{s=1}^{S} b_{js} = 1 \quad , \forall j$$

Decision variables: $b_{js} = \{0, 1\}$

The constraints ensure that the total number of named worker allocated is the same as the number of workers required, and each named worker is only allocated one shift schedule.

8.4 Case 8A: Planning and Scheduling for Ambulance Drivers

In this case, we will plan and schedule ambulance drivers for 7 days, and for each day, there will be morning (AM) and night (PM) shifts, assuming 12-hour per shift. The labour driver will be the number of calls for ambulance received in each shift for each day. We will assume that the forecasted number of calls for ambulance received in each shift for each day is available. We will approach this problem following the *data and decision analytics framework* proposed in Chap. 1, and the planning and scheduling calculations and optimization will be discussed.

We consider two types of ambulance drivers, full-time (FT) and part-time (PT). An FT driver is assumed to handle a maximum of 12 ambulance calls per shift and will cost \$180 per driver per shift to hire. A PT driver will be paid by the number of

Table 8.2 Plan for ambulance drivers

Day (shift)	# Calls	# FT drivers	# PT drivers	FT calls capacity	PT calls capacity	Total capacity
e.g. Sun (AM)	D	x_1	x_2	$y_1 = x_1*12$	$y_2 = \text{Max}(D - y_1, 0)$	$y_1 + y_2$

calls attended to at \$25 per call, which is higher than the per call rate for full-time driver at \$15 (= \$180/12). For simplicity, we will equate one PT driver to one ambulance call assigned. Thus, a PT driver will be useful to fill supply gaps when it does not make economic sense to hire an FT driver. Additionally, if we compute the ratio of \$180/\$25, we obtain 7.2, which means that it will be more economical to engage an FT driver when the number of calls to attend to is at least eight (> 7.2).

The forecasted number of ambulance calls received for the next 7 days for each AM and PM shift is given as D in Table 8.2. We will determine the number of FT drivers (x_1) and PT drivers (x_2) needed to minimize the total cost and compute the calls capacity provided by both FT drivers (y_1) and PT drivers (y_2) to meet the number of calls received. As it is not possible to carry over unattended calls to the next day, any calls which cannot be attended to by the FT drivers will be taken care of by the PT drivers. Therefore, we can optimize the number of drivers needed, x_1 and x_2, for each shift on each day separately.

Applying the optimization model provided in Sect. 8.3.1, we define the following parameters:

- i = index for workers of type i, where i = 1 for FT drivers and i = 2 for PT drivers.
- x_i = number of workers of type i, where x_1 for FT drivers and x_2 for PT drivers.
- c_i = unit cost of engaging worker of type i, where $c_1 = \$180$ and $c_2 = \$25$.
- a_i = unit supply of labor driver from worker of type i, where $a_1 = 12$ and $a_2 = 1$.
- D = number of ambulances calls at each shift for each day.

Objective function

$$\text{Minimize Total Cost}, Z = \sum_{i=1}^{n} c_i x_i = 180x_1 + 25x_2$$

Constraints

$$\sum_{i=1}^{n} a_i x_i \geq D \rightarrow 12x_1 + x_2 \geq D$$

Decision variables: $x_1, x_2 \geq 0$, integer

The optimal solution for x_1 and x_2 (in cells B7:O7 and B9:O9) and the total cost for 7 days for both AM and PM shifts, which works out to be \$11,840 (in cell P11), are shown in Fig. 8.2.

	A	B	C	D	E	F	G	H	I	J	K	L	M	N	O	P
1		Sun (AM)	Sun (PM)	Mon (AM)	Mon (PM)	Tue (AM)	Tue (PM)	Wed (AM)	Wed (PM)	Thu (AM)	Thu (PM)	Fri (AM)	Fri (PM)	Sat (AM)	Sat (PM)	
2	#-Calls (d)	60	55	65	49	57	50	61	47	63	45	59	49	60	44	
3	FT Calls Capacity (y1)	60	48	60	48	60	48	60	48	60	48	60	48	60	48	
4	PT Calls Capacity (y2)	0	7	5	1	0	2	1	0	3	0	0	1	0	0	
5	Total Capacity (y1 + y2)	60	55	65	49	60	50	61	48	63	48	60	49	60	48	
6																
7	# of FT drivers (x1)	5	4	5	4	5	4	5	4	5	4	5	4	5	4	
8	Total Cost (FT)	$900	$720	$900	$720	$900	$720	$900	$720	$900	$720	$900	$720	$900	$720	$11,340
9	# of PT drivers (x2)	0	7	5	1	0	2	1	0	3	0	0	1	0	0	
10	Total Cost (PT)	$0	$175	$125	$25	$0	$50	$25	$0	$75	$0	$0	$25	$0	$0	$500
11															Total Cost	$11,840

Fig. 8.2 Optimal number of drivers needed

Table 8.3 Seven shift schedules each for day and night shifts

Shift schedule	Day 1	Day 2	Day 3	Day 4	Day 5	Day 6	Day 7
AM1	0	1	1	1	1	1	1
AM2	1	0	1	1	1	1	1
AM3	1	1	0	1	1	1	1
AM4	1	1	1	0	1	1	1
AM5	1	1	1	1	0	1	1
AM6	1	1	1	1	1	0	1
AM7	1	1	1	1	1	1	0
PM1	0	0	1	1	1	1	1
PM2	1	0	0	1	1	1	1
PM3	1	1	0	0	1	1	1
PM4	1	1	1	0	0	1	1
PM5	1	1	1	1	0	0	1
PM6	1	1	1	1	1	0	0
PM7	0	1	1	1	1	1	0

After figuring out the number of FT and PT drivers demanded in each shift on each day, we will proceed to determine the actual number of FT drivers assigned to each shift schedule and then adjust the actual number of PT drivers needed. In this case, we pre-define seven shift schedules for day shift (AM1 to AM7), and seven shift schedules for night shift (PM1 to PM7), for a 7-day plan. We assume that there will be one rest day for the day shift schedule and two consecutive rest days for the night shift schedules as given in Table 8.3.

Applying the optimization model provided in Sect. 8.3.2, we define the following parameters:

- $s =$ index for shift schedule, where $s = 1$ to 7 for AM shift and 8 to 14 for PM shift.
- $d =$ index for day, where $d = 1$ to 7.
- c_{ds} indicates if this day d for shift schedule s is a working day or not, 1 for working day and 0 for rest day.
- $A_d =$ demand for FT drivers on day d for AM shift, where $d = 1$ to 7.

- P_d = demand for FT drivers on day d for PM shift, where d = 1 to 7.
- $\widehat{x}_s$ = actual number of FT drivers assigned to shift schedule s.

The optimization model that minimizes the actual number of FT drivers assigned to each shift schedule $\widehat{x}_s$ can be presented as

Objective function

$$\text{Minimize Total Number of Actual FT Workers Assigned, } Z = \sum_{s=1}^{14} \widehat{x}_s$$

Constraints

$$\sum_{s=1}^{7} c_{ds}\widehat{x}_s \geq A_d \quad , d = 1 \text{ to } 7$$

$$\sum_{s=8}^{14} c_{ds}\widehat{x}_s \geq P_d \quad , d = 1 \text{ to } 7$$

Decision variables: $\widehat{x}_s \geq 0$, integer

The optimal solution for $\widehat{x}_s$ for s = 1 to 14 is given in Fig. 8.3 in column I, where a total of 12 FT drivers will be supplied. Using the values of $\widehat{x}_s$, we can compute the actual supply of FT drivers in row 13 (for AM) and row 14 (for PM). Comparing the actual supply to the demand of FT drivers (in rows 4 and 5) obtained in the earlier optimization model, we note that the actual supply > demand for some days/shifts. For example, the demand of FT driver for Sun PM shift is 4, but the supply is 5. With the actual supply of FT drivers, we can now adjust the actual supply of PT drivers by using the formula

$$\text{Supply of PT drivers} = \text{MAX}\left[0, \text{Demand for PT Drivers} - (\text{Actual Supply of FT Drivers–Demand for FT Drivers}) \times 12\right]$$

This formula ensures that supply of PT drivers can be reduced accordingly when the actual supply of FT drivers increases due to pre-defined shift schedules. The final total cost is increased to $12,080 in cell K5.

The next task is to assign named driver to each shift schedule according to the number required. Since a total of 12 FT drivers are needed, we will obtain the shift schedule preference scores of 12 named drivers as shown in Fig. 8.4.

Applying the optimization model provided in Sect. 8.3.3, we define the following parameters:

- s = index for shift schedule, where s = 1 to 14.
- j = index for named driver, where j = 1 to 12.
- p_{js} = preference score of named driver j for shift schedule s.
- $\widehat{x}_s$ = number of FT workers required for each shift schedule s.
- b_{js} = binary variable to indicate if this named driver j is allocated to shift schedule s, 1 for yes and 0 for no.

Demand for FT Drivers

	Sun	Mon	Tue	Wed	Thu	Fri	Sat
AM	5	5	5	5	5	5	5
PM	4	4	4	4	4	4	4

Total Cost

FT Drivers	$11,880
PT Drivers	$200
Total	$12,080

Demand for PT Drivers

	Sun	Mon	Tue	Wed	Thu	Fri	Sat
AM	0	5	0	1	3	0	0
PM	7	1	2	0	0	1	0

Actual Supply of FT Drivers

AM Supply	5	6	5	5	5	5	5
PM Supply	5	4	4	4	5	4	4

Adjusted Supply of PT Drivers

	Sun	Mon	Tue	Wed	Thu	Fri	Sat
AM	0	0	0	1	3	0	0
PM	0	1	2	0	0	1	0

Shift Schedule for FT Drivers

Shift	Sun	Mon	Tue	Wed	Thu	Fri	Sat	# FT
AM1	0	1	1	1	1	1	1	1
AM2	1	0	1	1	1	1	1	0
AM3	1	1	0	1	1	1	1	1
AM4	1	1	1	0	1	1	1	1
AM5	1	1	1	1	0	1	1	1
AM6	1	1	1	1	1	0	1	1
AM7	1	1	1	1	1	1	0	1
PM1	0	0	1	1	1	1	1	1
PM2	1	0	0	1	1	1	1	1
PM3	1	1	0	0	1	1	1	1
PM4	1	1	1	0	0	1	1	1
PM5	1	1	1	1	0	0	1	0
PM6	1	1	1	1	1	0	0	2
PM7	0	1	1	1	1	1	0	0
							Total	12

Fig. 8.3 Optimal number FT drivers assigned to each shift schedule

Worker Preference Table

Driver	AM1	AM2	AM3	AM4	AM5	AM6	AM7	PM1	PM2	PM3	PM4	PM5	PM6	PM7
Alan	14	7	6	9	13	12	2	11	10	3	1	8	4	5
Bryan	11	2	3	1	8	13	10	4	6	14	9	7	12	5
Charles	12	5	8	7	2	1	9	3	4	10	6	13	11	14
Dan	12	14	13	10	9	7	3	6	8	5	11	1	2	4
Eric	11	10	3	14	6	2	4	13	5	8	7	12	1	9
Foster	2	12	11	8	4	10	1	9	6	14	13	7	5	3
Gabriel	7	5	14	10	8	2	11	1	13	12	3	4	9	6
Hugh	6	12	9	4	13	11	3	10	1	5	2	7	14	8
Ian	7	3	8	13	12	14	2	9	1	6	5	11	10	4
Jack	12	8	14	9	1	13	2	4	10	3	7	11	6	5
Keith	9	7	1	8	12	14	13	2	6	10	3	5	4	11
Larry	1	2	9	10	3	4	11	12	5	6	13	7	8	14

Fig. 8.4 Preference scores (p_{js}) of 12 named drivers for each shift schedule

	A	B	C	D	E	F	G	H	I	J	K	L	M	N	O	P	Q
55							**FT Driver Allocation Table**										
56	**Driver**	**AM1**	**AM2**	**AM3**	**AM4**	**AM5**	**AM6**	**AM7**	**PM1**	**PM2**	**PM3**	**PM4**	**PM5**	**PM6**	**PM7**	**Total**	**Preference**
57	**Alan**	0	0	0	0	0	0	0	0	0	0	0	0	1	0	1	4
58	**Bryan**	0	0	0	0	0	0	0	0	0	1	0	0	0	0	1	14
59	**Charles**	0	0	0	0	0	0	0	0	1	0	0	0	0	0	1	4
60	**Dan**	0	0	0	0	0	0	0	1	0	0	0	0	0	0	1	6
61	**Eric**	0	0	0	0	0	0	1	0	0	0	0	0	0	0	1	4
62	**Foster**	0	0	0	0	0	1	0	0	0	0	0	0	0	0	1	10
63	**Gabriel**	0	0	0	0	1	0	0	0	0	0	0	0	0	0	1	8
64	**Hugh**	0	0	0	1	0	0	0	0	0	0	0	0	0	0	1	4
65	**Ian**	0	0	1	0	0	0	0	0	0	0	0	0	0	0	1	8
66	**Jack**	1	0	0	0	0	0	0	0	0	0	0	0	0	0	1	12
67	**Keith**	0	0	0	0	0	0	0	0	0	0	1	0	0	0	1	3
68	**Larry**	0	0	0	0	0	0	0	0	0	0	0	0	1	0	1	8
69																12	**85**
70	**Allocated**	1	0	1	1	1	1	1	1	1	1	1	0	2	0		
71	**Required**	1	0	1	1	1	1	1	1	1	1	1	0	2	0		

Fig. 8.5 Optimal allocation of named drivers to each shift schedule

Objective function

$$\text{Maximize Total Preference Score, } Z = \sum_{j=1}^{12} \sum_{s=1}^{14} b_{js} p_{js}$$

Constraints

$$\sum_{j=1}^{12} b_{js} = \widehat{x}_s \quad , \forall s$$

$$\sum_{s=1}^{14} b_{js} = 1 \quad , \forall j$$

Decision variables: $b_{js} = \{0, 1\}$

The optimal solution is shown in Fig. 8.5, where b_{js} are indicated in cells B57:O68 and the maximized total preference score is 85 in cell Q69.

Let us map the problem and solution method for this case study against *the data and decision analytics framework* proposed in Chap. 1. As shown in Fig. 8.6, in this case study, the problem faced was to efficiently allocate named FT drivers and at the same time determine the number of PT drivers needed. Therefore, the right question to ask was “How to efficiently allocate full-time named drivers while minimizing cost and maximizing preference score?”. Next was to collect the relevant data needed to answer the question, which includes the forecasted number of calls per shift per day for the next 7 days (which are the labour drivers), the unit cost of engaging a FT and PT driver, unit supply of labour driver by each FT and PT driver, shift schedules for AM and PM shifts and the preference scores of each named driver for each shift schedule. With the data collected and forecasted values, the analyst can perform initial analysis to determine the cost ratio which makes economic sense to engage FT drivers. From the insights obtained, it was found that since unmet calls cannot be carried over to the next day, all unmet calls by FT drivers will be allocated to PT drivers, and also, due to pre-defined shift schedule, the supply of FT drivers

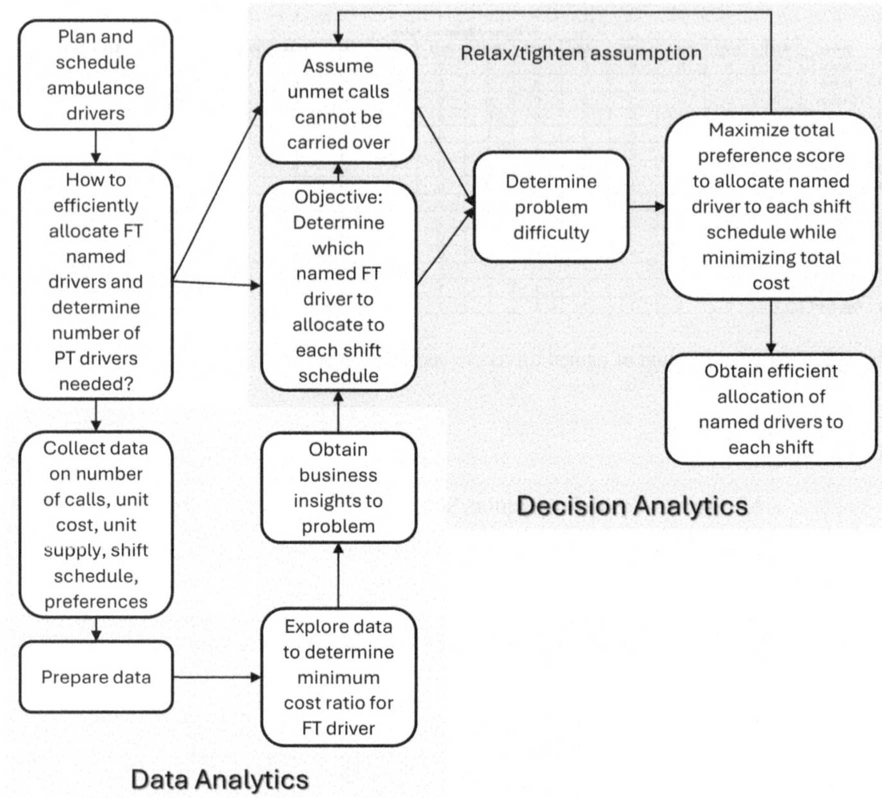

Fig. 8.6 Data and decision analytics framework map for Case 8A

will increase, thereby reducing the number of PT drivers needed. Thus, the problem objective would be to determine the best allocation of named FT drivers to each shift schedule which will maximize the total preference score and at the same time minimize total cost. This problem is solved by optimization, and the optimal allocation solution can be obtained.

8.5 Case 8B: Faculty Members' Teaching Schedule

In this case, we will plan and schedule faculty members to teach two courses in a business school. In this school, there are five full-time faculty members who are able to teach two courses, namely, Course 1 and Course 2. Each course will be taken by more than 500 undergraduate students in a term, requiring 13 class sections to be offered for each course, totalling 26 class sections, which is the labour driver.

To convert the labour driver into the number of workers needed, we look at the supply of faculty members to teach the 26 class sections. With only five full-time faculty members and each member able to only teach 3 class sections in a term, the shortfall of 11 class sections must be fulfilled by part-time faculty members. The cost of hiring a part-time faculty member to teach one class section is \$8500, while the cost of full-time faculty member teaching one class section is \$7500. It is a norm to pay part-time faculty members more per class section because they do not enjoy other employment benefits. Each part-time faculty member can teach 1 to 2 class sections only per term. To fulfil the 11 class sections, the school will need to hire a minimum of 6 to a maximum of 11 part-time faculty members.

In this case, we will consider five full-time faculty members (FT1 to FT5) and ten part-time faculty members (PT1 to PT10). This is different than the ambulance driver case where the optimal number of full-time and part-time drivers is not known and must be determined by the optimization model provided in Sect. 8.3.1. In this case, since the number of faculty members is already known, our problem is to figure out which faculty member will be allocated to teach which course. The optimization model will be modified as follows with the following parameters:

- i = index for full-time faculty members, where $i = 1$ to 5.
- j = index for part-time faculty members, where $j = 1$ to 10.
- k = index for course, $k = 1, 2$.
- x_{ik} = number of class sections of course k allocated to full-time faculty i.
- x_{jk} = number of class sections of course k allocated to part-time faculty j.
- c_i = cost of allocating one class section to full-time faculty i = \$7500.
- c_j = cost of allocating one class section to part-time faculty j = \$8500.
- D = number of class sections required for each course = 13.

Objective function

$$\text{Minimize Total Cost, } Z = \sum_i \sum_k c_i x_{ik} + \sum_j \sum_k c_j x_{jk}$$

Constraints

$$\sum_i x_{ik} + \sum_j x_{jk} \geq D \quad , \forall k \quad (1)$$

$$\sum_k x_{ik} = 3 \quad , \forall i \quad (2)$$

$$1 \leq \sum_k x_{jk} \leq 2 \quad , \forall j \quad (3)$$

Decision variables: $x_{ik}, x_{jk} \geq 0$, integer

Constraint (1) states that the total number of class sections allocated to both full-time and part-time faculty members must meet the number of class sections required.

	Number of classes needed
Course 1	13
Course 2	13
Total	26

	Cost per class	Max number	Min number
Full-time faculty	$7,500	3	3
Part-time faculty	$8,500	2	1

Objective	$206,000

	Course 1	Course 2	Total
FT1	3	0	3
FT2	2	1	3
FT3	0	3	3
FT4	3	0	3
FT5	0	3	3
PT1	1	0	1
PT2	0	2	2
PT3	0	1	1
PT4	0	1	1
PT5	0	1	1
PT6	0	1	1
PT7	1	0	1
PT8	1	0	1
PT9	1	0	1
PT10	1	0	1
Total	13	13	26

Fig. 8.7 Optimal allocation of faculty members to teach courses

Constraint (2) states that the total number of class sections allocated to full-time faculty must be three, while constraint (3) states that the total number of class sections allocated to part-time faculty must be between one and two. The optimal solution for x_{ik} (in cells H3:I7) and x_{jk} (in cells H8:I17) incurring the minimum cost of $206,800 (cell C11) is shown in Fig. 8.7. Note that this is a combinatorial problem with multiple optimal solutions for x_{ik} and x_{jk}, but all optimal solutions will incur the same minimum cost of $206,800.

After knowing which faculty member will teach which course and the number of class sections, we need to allocate them to the class time slots from Monday to Friday. On each day, there are three class time slots, 8:30 a.m. to 12:00 p.m., 12:00 p.m. to 3:30 p.m. and 3:30 p.m. to 7:00 p.m. On some days, some time slots are not used as they are reserved for students' extracurricular activities. In total, there are 11 time slots available for classes (T1 to T11) over 5 weekdays. To cater for the possibility of a certain time slot having more than one class section, there are three classrooms available at each time slot.

This is again different than the ambulance driver case where there are pre-defined shift schedules, and there is no preference score to maximize. In this case, the 11 class time slots are fixed, and each class section will be scheduled in each time slot. Therefore, there is no need to apply the optimization models in Sects. 8.3.2 and 8.3.3. In fact, this is an assignment problem discussed in Chap. 7, Sect. 7.5. In the assignment problem, one resource i is only assigned to one job j. However, in this case, one faculty member i can be assigned one or more time slots j as he/she needs to teach one or more class sections. In addition, each time slot j can have more than one faculty member teaching at the same time because there are three classrooms available.

Therefore, we will modify the assignment problem optimization model to allocate faculty members to each time slot with the following parameters:

	Course 1	Course 2	Total
FT1	3	0	3
FT2	2	1	3
FT3	0	3	3
FT4	3	0	3
FT5	0	3	3
PT1	1	0	1
PT2	0	2	2
PT3	0	1	1
PT4	0	1	1
PT5	0	1	1
PT6	0	1	1
PT7	1	0	1
PT8	1	0	1
PT9	1	0	1
PT10	1	0	1
Total	13	13	26

Objective 26

	T1	T2	T3	T4	T5	T6	T7	T8	T9	T10	T11	T12	T13	Total
FT1	1	0	0	0	0	0	0	0	0	0	0	1	1	3
FT2	0	1	1	1	0	0	0	0	0	0	0	0	0	3
FT3	0	0	0	0	1	1	1	0	0	0	0	0	0	3
FT4	0	0	0	0	0	0	0	1	1	1	0	0	0	3
FT5	0	0	0	0	0	0	0	0	0	1	1	1	0	3
PT1	0	0	0	0	0	0	0	0	0	0	0	1	0	1
PT2	0	0	0	0	0	0	0	0	0	1	1	0	0	2
PT3	0	0	0	0	0	0	0	0	0	0	1	0	0	1
PT4	0	0	0	0	0	0	0	0	1	0	0	0	0	1
PT5	0	0	0	0	0	0	0	0	1	0	0	0	0	1
PT6	0	0	0	0	0	0	0	1	0	0	0	0	0	1
PT7	0	0	0	0	0	0	1	0	0	0	0	0	0	1
PT8	0	0	0	0	0	0	1	0	0	0	0	0	0	1
PT9	0	0	0	0	0	0	0	0	0	0	0	0	1	1
PT10	0	0	0	0	0	0	0	0	0	0	0	0	1	1
Total	1	1	1	1	1	1	3	2	3	3	3	3	3	26
Max	3	3	3	3	3	3	3	3	3	3	3	3	3	

Fig. 8.8 Optimal allocation of faculty members to on different time slots

- i = index for faculty members (both full and part time), where $i = 1$ to 15.
- j = index for time slot, where $j = 1$ to 11.
- $x_{ij} = 1$ when faculty i is allocated to teach in time slot j.
- s_i = number of class sections to be taught by faculty i (solution from earlier).
- d_j = maximum number of class sections at time slot j.

Objective function

$$\text{Minimize or Maximize } Z = \sum_i \sum_j x_{ij}$$

Constraints

$$\sum_j x_{ij} = s_i \quad , \forall i \quad (1)$$

$$\sum_i x_{ij} \leq 3 \quad , \forall j \quad (2)$$

Decision variables: $x_{ij} \in \{0, 1\}$

Note that the objective function is simply minimizing or maximizing the total allocation. The choice of minimizing or maximizing is immaterial as the objective is to ensure that all required numbers of class sections are assigned. Constraint (1) states that the total number of time slots allocated to the faculty member must meet the number of class sections to be taught by faculty. Constraint (2) states that the total number of faculty members (or class sections) allocated to teach in a time slot cannot exceed the number of classrooms available. The optimal solutions for x_{ij} (in cells H3: T17) are the binary decision variables, where 1 indicates the allocation, and the objective function value must be the total number of class sections allocated (cell

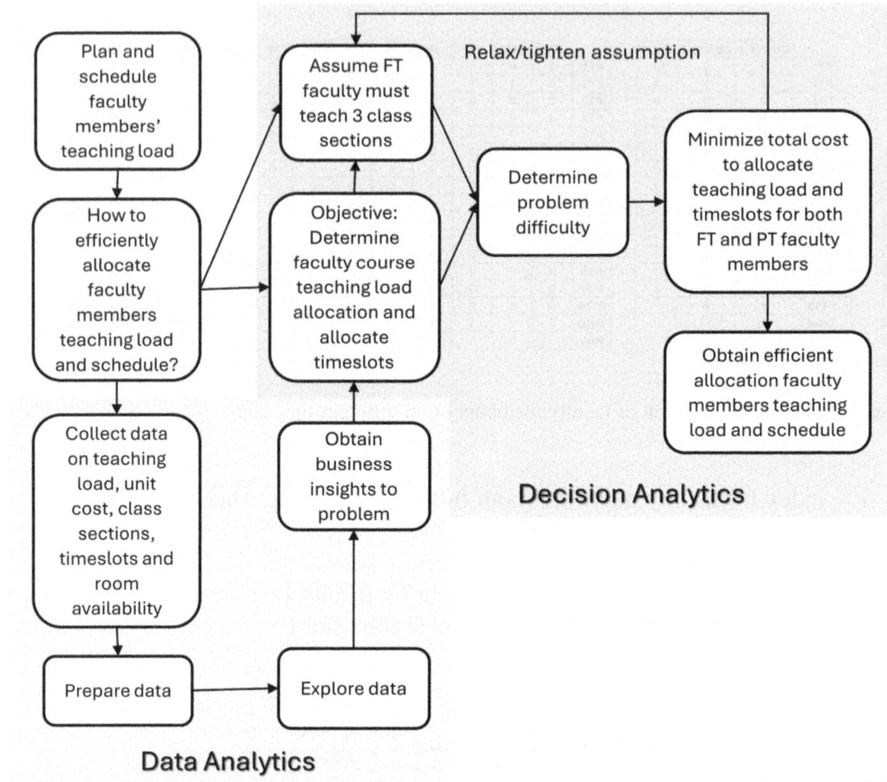

Fig. 8.9 Data and decision analytics framework map for Case 8B

C20), shown in Fig. 8.8. Similar to the first model, this is also a combinatorial problem with multiple optimal solutions for x_{ij}, and all optimal solutions will have the same objective function value of 26.

Let us map the problem and solution method for this case study against the *data and decision analytics framework* proposed in Chap. 1. As shown in Fig. 8.9, in this case study, the problem faced was to plan and schedule the faculty members' teaching load. Therefore, the right question to ask was "How to efficiently allocate faculty members teaching load and schedule?". Next was to collect the relevant data needed to answer the question, which includes teaching load requirements, unit cost, number of class sections required, time slots and room availability. With the data collected, the analyst can perform initial analysis to explore the data if needed. The problem objective would be to determine the best faculty course teaching load and allocation and allocate the time slots to obtain the teaching schedule while minimizing total cost. The assumption is that all full-time faculty members must teach three class sections each. This problem is solved by two optimization models, and the optimal allocation solution can be obtained.

8.6 Summary

This chapter covered the steps to identify and forecast labour drivers and then convert the forecasted labour drivers into the number of workers needed. Three sequential optimization models are formulated to determine the optimal number of workers needed, then adjusted according to a given shift schedule and then finally adjusted according to each worker's preference. Finally, two case studies were discussed, including planning and scheduling of ambulance drivers, and planning and scheduling of faculty members' teaching load, applying the concepts and models learned. So far, all the problems we have discussed can be solved using optimization models. However, in businesses, there are many NP-hard problems which cannot be solved to optimality using optimization models. In the next chapter, we will look at three different heuristic algorithms which are commonly used to solve NP-hard problems. They include depth-first search, breath-first search and Dijkstra's algorithm.

Exercises

Q8.1

A small hospital would like to schedule its nurse schedule on a 5-day basis. For every ward, there will be six nurses taking care of the ward. Formulate an optimization model to obtain the best 5-day schedule for six nurses based on the two sets of constraints below.

Nurse requirement constraint: the number of nurses required for the 5-day schedule

	Day of the week				
	1	2	3	4	5
AM shift	1	1	2	1	2
PM shift	2	2	1	2	1
Midnight shift	1	2	2	2	2

Nurse shift constraint: the required number of AM shift, PM shift, midnight shift and rest day for the 5-day schedule for each nurse

	AM shift	PM shift	Midnight shift	Rest day
Nurse 1	1	1	2	1
Nurse 2	1	2	1	1
Nurse 3	2	1	1	1
Nurse 4	1	1	2	1
Nurse 5	2	1	1	1
Nurse 6	1	2	1	1

Hint: You should set the decision variable as integer and use 0 to indicate rest day, 1 to indicate AM shift, 2 to indicate PM shift and 3 to indicate midnight shift. Note that the problem size is large = 4 ^ (5*6) = 1.15×10^{18}. Therefore, Excel Solver will require many iterations to solve to optimality. Thus, it is suggested to set the number of iterations to 100k under Solver option, to allow Solver to reach the optimal solution.

Q8.2

A tuition centre enrols the following number of students at each level. The number of classes for each level per week is based on the enrolment number subjected to a maximum of ten students per class.

Level	Student enrolment
P1	26
P2	28
P3	30
P4	28
P5	36
P6	46

For weekdays (i.e. Monday to Friday), only one time slot is available from 7:00 p.m. to 8:00 p.m. for all levels. At each time slot, there are three classrooms available. For example, at time slot T1 (Monday 7:00 p.m. to 8:00 p.m.), the centre can only conduct three classes. This applies to time slots T2 to T5 as well. There should be at least one class for both P5 and P6 levels on weekdays.

During weekends (i.e. Saturday and Sunday), the centre runs from 10:00 a.m. to 1:00 p.m. (i.e. four time slots on Saturday and Sunday). Since weekends are very popular for the students, at least one class for each level should be scheduled on Saturday or Sunday. You should also balance the number of classes scheduled on both Saturday and Sunday. In total, there are 13 time slots available for the entire week, five on weekdays and eight on weekends, denoted as T1 to T13.

Based on the scenario, develop a model to generate a feasible weekly timetable to assist the tuition centre. You may refer to the template below for a feasible timetable layout. The number in the cell represents the number of classes to be scheduled for each time slot. Describe the objective and constraints, and obtain a feasible schedule for a week.

	Start time	Time slot	P1	P2	P3	P4	P5	P6
Mon	7:00 p.m.	T1						
Tue	7:00 p.m.	T2						
Wed	7:00 p.m.	T3						
Thu	7:00 p.m.	T4						

(continued)

	Start time	Time slot	P1	P2	P3	P4	P5	P6
Fri	7:00 p.m.	T5						
Sat	10:00 a.m.	T6						
Sat	11:00 a.m.	T7						
Sat	12 noon	T8						
Sat	1:00 p.m.	T9						
Sun	10:00 a.m.	T10						
Sun	11:00 a.m.	T11						
Sun	12 noon	T12						
Sun	1:00 p.m.	T13						

Q8.3

Jim's restaurant operates one shift daily and is open 7 days a week. The operation hours are from 11:00 to 15:00 and from 18:00 to 22:00. The restaurant has five full-time and six part-time staff. Full-time staff are paid $2400 monthly, working 5 days a week and a maximum of 8 hour daily. The part-time staff are paid $18 per hour and will be paid based on 8-hour shifts. According to the past demand, the number of staff required for each day of the week is given below. You may assume that there are 4 weeks in a month.

Day of week	# of staff required
Mon	6
Tue	7
Wed	7
Thu	8
Fri	9
Sat	10
Sun	10

On any one shift, you should have at least two full-time staff. The number of shifts assigned to each part-time staff member must be equal and fair. Each part-time staff should rest at least 1 day a week. Based on the required resources, obtain a feasible schedule for all the full-time and part-time staff in a week that minimizes the staff costs.

Reference

Thompson, G. M. (2004). Workforce scheduling: A guide for the hospitality industry. *CHR Reports, 4*(6).

Chapter 9
Heuristic Algorithms

Most real-world problems are complex and sophisticated, and optimal solutions are hard to achieve. In Chap. 4, we have looked at the traveling salesman problem (TSP), which is NP-hard, and we have explored using the nearest neighbour procedure (NNP) and Clarke and Wright (C&W) savings heuristic to obtain good feasible solutions.

The process of searching for an answer in a state space often begins with an initial state selected as a starting point, and there will be a rule to guide how one moves from one state to the next. The rule will be applied recursively until some goal condition is satisfied, for example, the maximum number of iterations is reached, the solution converges to 0.000001, or no further improvement in the solution can be found.

In this chapter, we will explore three commonly used heuristic algorithms including the Depth-First Search (DFS), Breath-First Search (BFS) and Dijkstra's Algorithm (DA) to solve the Shortest Path Problem (refer to Chap. 7 for the discussion on Shortest Path Problem). We will look at two case studies, nurse scheduling problem and beer distribution problem, to understand how each case study applied heuristic algorithms to obtain good feasible solutions for their respective problems.

Learning Outcomes

By the end of this chapter, readers will achieve the following learning outcomes:

- Explain Depth-First Search (DFS) algorithm.
- Apply Depth-First Search (DFS) algorithm to solve an example problem.
- Explain Breadth-First Search (BFS) algorithm.
- Apply Breadth-First Search (DFS) algorithm to solve an example problem.
- Compare the advantages and disadvantages between DFS and BFS
- Explain the Dijkstra's Algorithm (DA).
- Apply the Dijkstra's Algorithm (DA) to solve an example problem.
- Discuss how heuristic algorithms are applied in real-world scenarios to plan and schedule nurses in the nurse scheduling problem (NSP) and beer distribution problem, using the *data and decision analytics framework*.

M. L. F. Cheong, Ma Nang Laik, *Data and Decision Analytics for Business Operations*, https://doi.org/10.1007/978-3-031-72255-4_9

9.1 Depth-First Search

Depth-First Search (DFS) is a recursive algorithm which will conduct an exhaustive search for all the nodes in the graph by going forward if possible, otherwise backtrack. There are two lists, "Visited" and "Not visited". Nodes which are visited will be put in the "Visited" list, and those which are not visited will be in the "Not visited" list. The purpose of the algorithm is to ensure that all the nodes are visited while avoiding cycles (meaning that nodes are not visited more than once).

Nodes in the "Not visited" list will be implemented as a stack based on last-in-first-out (LIFO) principle. To insert a node into the stack is a *push* operation to add the node to the top of the stack. To select a node from the stack is a *pop* operation where the node at the top of the stack is selected.

Algorithms are usually described using pseudo-codes, so we will describe the DFS algorithm as follows:

1. Initialize by adding all nodes into the "Not visited" list. The "Visited" list and the stack are both empty.
2. Start by selecting any node from the "Not visited" list. Usually, the root node of a graph will be selected. Add it to the top of the stack using the push operation.
3. Pop the top item of the stack, and add it to the "Visited" list.
4. Create a list of adjacent or successor node(s). Add the ones that are not already in the "Visited" list to the top of the stack.
5. Repeat steps 3 and 4 until the stack is empty.

The time complexity of DFS using an adjacency list is $O(|N|+|E|)$, where $|N|$ is the number of nodes and $|E|$ is the number of edges. DFS visits every node once and every edge once, making it an efficient algorithm.

Due to the nature of the algorithm, DFS is often used for topological sorting, where the linear order of nodes can be determined. That is, if there exists a directed edge from node u to node v, then node u must come before node v in the linear order. There are many applications which can apply the linear order determined by topological sorting, for example, to plan a sequence of tasks in a project which have dependencies and to recommend courses for learners to read based on what the learner have already learnt in terms of course pre-requisites.

DFS can also be used to determine if a graph is bipartite or not. A bipartite graph is a graph where nodes can be distinctly divided into two disjoint sets U and V, where all edges either connect a node from U to a node from V or vice versa. There are no edges that connect nodes within the same set. The process to identify bipartite graph is to start with assigning a first colour (e.g. black) to the first node and assign a second colour (e.g. white) to the adjacent node(s), following the algorithm. A bipartite graph is one where all nodes are coloured using two different colours (e.g. black and white) and no two adjacent nodes will have the same colour. Figure 9.1 shows a bipartite graph, while Fig. 9.2 shows a non-bipartite graph.

A bipartite graph is useful for modeling relationships as illustrated in Fig. 9.3 with two distinct sets of nodes. For example, when allocating tasks to workers in a

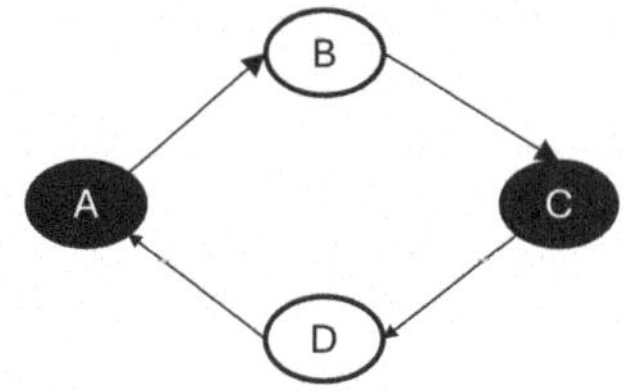

Fig. 9.1 A bipartite graph

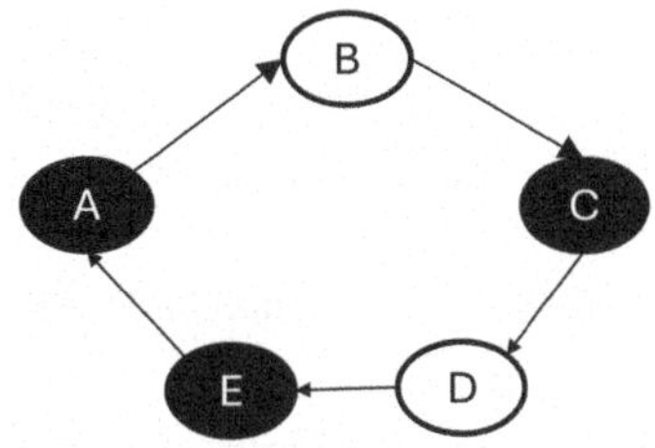

Fig. 9.2 A non-bipartite graph

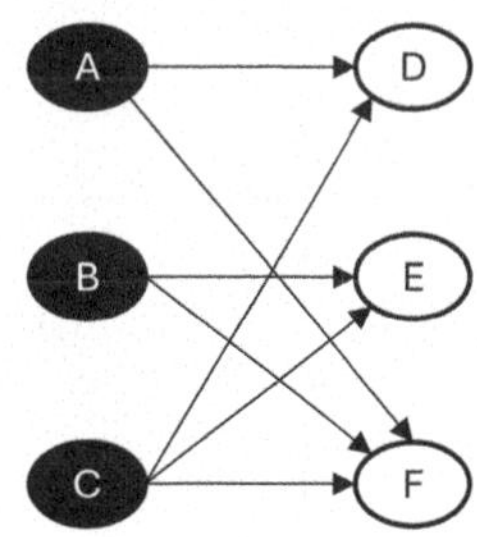

Fig. 9.3 A bipartite graph modelling relationships

resource allocation problem, the left-hand side nodes can represent workers, while the right-hand side nodes can represent tasks. Worker A can handle tasks D and F, worker B can handle tasks E and F and worker C can handle all tasks. Using the bipartite graph, an efficient allocation can be achieved, which minimizes cost or maximizes revenue. In a recommender system commonly found in e-commerce platforms, the left-hand side nodes can represent customers, while the right-hand side nodes can represent products. In the bipartite graph, customers A and C share the same preference for product D, while customers B and C prefer product E. Using the graph, the system can recommend products to customers based on their similarities with other customers.

Let us consider an example of a graph shown in Fig. 9.4. The objective is to search for the shortest path from the root node A to the goal node G (coloured black for easy identification). There are a few duplicated nodes in the graph (nodes C, D, E and F), and we shall see how DFS manages de-duplication to ensure that every node is only visited once.

Following the DFS algorithm, the path {A, B, E, F, C, D, G} is obtained as explained in Table 9.1 and illustrated in Fig. 9.5. In Fig. 9.5, the nodes visited are coloured grey following the edges marked with numbers 4 to 9 aligned with the steps

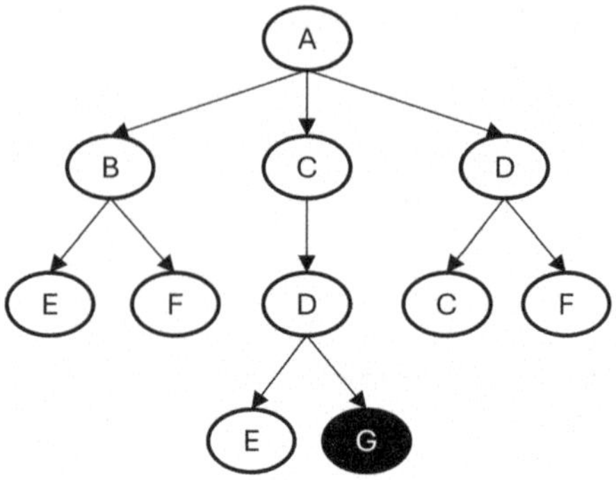

Fig. 9.4 Graph for Depth-First Search (DFS) example

Table 9.1 Path solution for Depth-First Search (DFS) example

	Not visited	Stack	Visited	Remarks
1	{A, B, C, D, E, F, G}	{}	{}	
2	{B, C, D, E, F, G}	{A}	{}	Root node A selected and added to the Stack
3	{E, F, G}	{B, C, D}	{A}	A is popped and added to Visited list. B, C and D are adjacent nodes of A and are added to the top of the Stack
4	{G}	{E, F, C, D}	{A, B}	B is popped and added to Visited list. E and F are adjacent nodes of B and are added to the top of the Stack
5	{G}	{F, C, D}	{A, B, E}	E is popped and added to Visited list. E does not have any adjacent nodes
6	{G}	{C, D}	{A, B, E, F}	F is popped and added to Visited list. F does not have any adjacent nodes
7	{G}	{D}	{A, B, E, F, C}	C is popped and added to Visited list. D is the adjacent node of C, but it is duplicated, so it is not added to the Stack (de-duplication)
8	{}	{G}	{A, B, E, F, C, D}	D is popped and added to Visited list. E and G are the adjacent nodes of D, but node E is duplicated, so it is not added to the Stack. Only node G is added to the top of the Stack
9	{}	{}	{A, B, E, F, C, D, G}	G is popped and added to Visited list, and as it is the goal node, the algorithm ends

in Table 9.1. Nodes which are not visited are not coloured, and edges which are not used are replaced with dashed arrows. As illustrated in this example, DFS did not find the shortest path, which should be {A, C, D, G}. The other disadvantage is that DFS may not find the solution even if the solution exists if the graph has cycles and the algorithm loops forever.

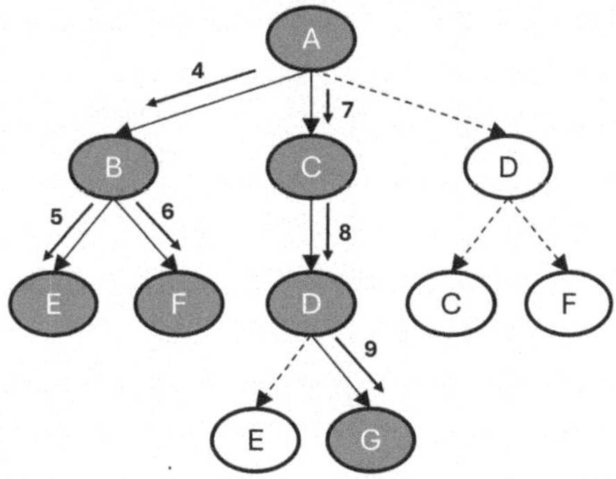

Fig. 9.5 Path solution for Depth-First Search (DFS) example

9.2 Breath-First Search

Breath-First Search (BFS) traverses or searches a graphs breath wise or horizontally, thus exploring the neighbouring nodes which are directly connected to the source node before moving to the next level. Similar to DFS, there will be the "Visited" and "Not visited" lists. Nodes in the "Not Visited" list will be implemented as a queue based on first-in-first-out (FIFO) principle. To insert a node into the queue is called *enqueue* that adds the node to the end of the queue. To select a node from the queue is called *dequeue* where the node at the start of the queue is selected.

The BFS algorithm is as follows:

1. Initialize by adding all nodes into the "Not visited" list. The "Visited" list and the queue are both empty.
2. Start by selecting any node from the "Not visited" list. Usually, the root node of a graph will be selected. Add it to the end of the queue using the enqueue operation.
3. Dequeue the top item of the queue and add it to the "Visited" list.
4. Create a list of adjacent or successor node(s). Add the ones which are not already in the "Visited" list to the end of the queue.
5. Repeat steps 3 and 4 until the queue is empty.

So, which is better? BFS or DFS? Let's compare them. The advantages of BFS are:

1. BFS can traverse through the graph in the smallest number of steps. That is, the first solution path found is the shortest possible one, since the nodes are generated level by level as the deeper nodes will not be expanded once the goal is reached.
2. It is guaranteed that BFS iterations will find a solution in a finite number of steps if the solution exists.
3. BFS can be parallelized for parallel computing to speed up the search.

The disadvantages of BFS are:

1. It can be more memory intensive than DFS as it needs to keep track of all the nodes with depth smaller than the shortest possible solution length.

Table 9.2 Path solution for Breadth-First Search (BFS) example

	Not visited	Queue	Visited	Remarks
1	{A, B, C, D, E, F, G}	{}	{}	
2	{B, C, D, E, F, G}	{A}	{}	Root node A selected and enqueued to the Queue
3	{E, F, G}	{B, C, D}	{A}	A is dequeued and added to Visited list. B, C and D are adjacent nodes of A and are enqueued to the end of the Queue
4	{G}	{C, D, E, F}	{A, B}	B is dequeued and added to Visited list. E and F are adjacent nodes of B and are added to the end of the Queue
5	{G}	{D, E, F}	{A, B, C}	C is dequeued and added to Visited list. D is the adjacent node of C, but it is duplicated, so it is not added to the Queue
6	{}	{E, F, G}	{A, B, C, D}	D is dequeued and added to Visited list. C and F are adjacent nodes of D, but they are duplicated and so are not added to the Queue
7	{}	{F, G}	{A, B, C, D, E}	E is dequeued and added to Visited list. E does not have any adjacent nodes
8	{}	{G}	{A, B, C, D, E, F}	F is dequeued and added to Visited list. F does not have any adjacent nodes
9	{}	{}	{A, B, C, D, E, F, G}	As D and E are both duplicates and are already in the Visited list, G is dequeued and added to Visited list. As G is the goal node, the algorithm ends

2. It may only find sub-optimal solutions unless the edges have uniform weights (e.g. same distance or cost), which will guarantee optimal solution.
3. It may be slower as it needs to search all the nodes at each level before moving to the next level.

Time complexity of BFS using an adjacency list is $O(|N|+|E|)$, where $|N|$ is the number of nodes and $|E|$ is the number of edges, which is the same as DFS. Just like DFS, BFS can be used to determine if a graph is bipartite or not. In addition, because BFS traverses all the nodes at the same level first before going to the next level, it is useful for finding neighbouring nodes with applications in finding neighbouring locations in GPS system and indexing Web pages for search engines.

Let us consider the same example as shown in Fig. 9.4 to search for the shortest path from the root node A to the goal node G. Following the BFS algorithm, the path {A, B, C, D, E, F, G} is obtained as explained in Table 9.2 and illustrated in Fig. 9.6. In Fig. 9.6, the nodes visited are coloured grey following the edges marked with numbers 4 to 9 aligned with the steps in Table 9.2. Nodes which are not visited are not coloured, and edges which are not used are replaced with dashed arrows.

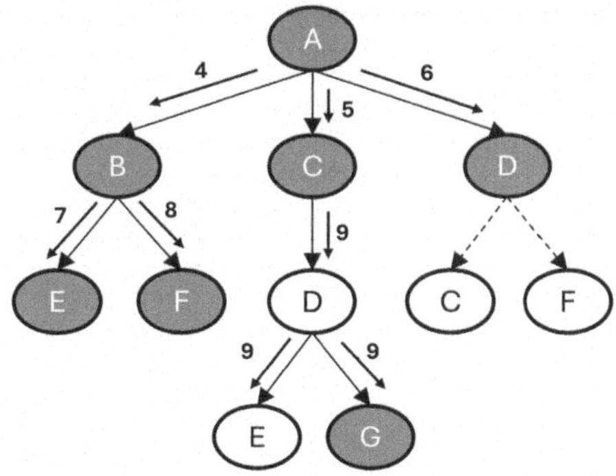

Fig. 9.6 Path solution for Breadth-First Search (BFS) example

9.3 Dijkstra's Algorithm

Dijkstra's Algorithm (DA) finds the shortest path between the two given nodes in a weighted network graph, normally from the source node to all the other nodes in the graph. A weighted graph is a graph whose edges have a distance or cost, which connects the nodes in the graph. To find the optimal solution, DA proposed a greedy search strategy where it states that any sub-path of an optimal path must be optimal itself. For example, for the optimal path from nodes s to v, the minimum distance from s to v is equal to the minimum distance from nodes s to u, where u is the predecessor node of v, plus the edge weight between nodes u and v.

Similar to DFS and BFS, there will be the "Visited" and "Not visited" lists to manage the nodes in the algorithm. In addition, there will be a table to keep track for each node, the predecessor node and the current distance from the source node. The algorithm starts from the source node and analyses the graph to find the shortest path between the source and the other nodes in a graph. Once the shortest path between the source and another node is found, the node will be added into the "Visited" list and added to the path. The process stops when all the other nodes have been visited.

The Dijkstra's Algorithm is described as follows:

1. Initialize by adding all nodes into the "Not visited" list. The "Visited" list is empty.
2. For each node in the table, initialize the current distance from the source as zero for the source node and as infinity for the other nodes.
3. Start with the source node, and set it as the current node.
4. For the current node, determine the adjacent node(s) which are not in the "Visited" list:

   - Add the distance of the edge from the current node to the adjacent node to the current distance to get the total distance.
   - If the total distance is smaller than the current distance of the adjacent node from the source, set it as the current distance of the adjacent node.
   - Once all the adjacent nodes are visited, add the current node into the "Visited" list, and remove it from the "Not Visited" list.

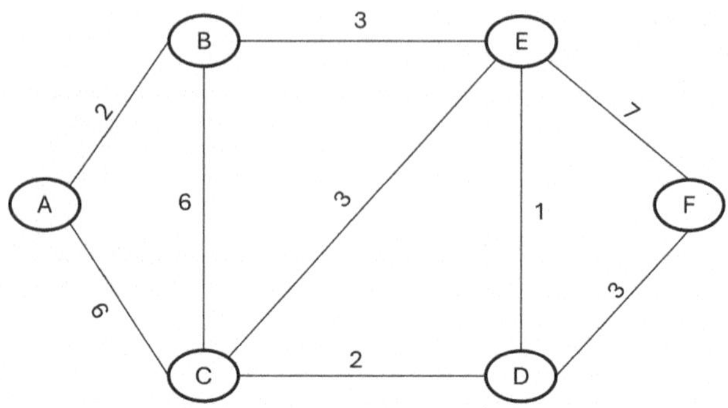

Fig. 9.7 Weighted graph for Dijkstra's Algorithm (DA) example

5. Select the next current node from the "Not Visited" list with the smallest current distance, and repeat step 4 until the "Not Visited" list is empty.

In the worst case, the time complexity of DA is $O((|N|^2) \log|N|)$ where $|N|$ is the number of nodes in the graph. This occurs when the graph is very dense with many edges and the priority queue operations to select the node with the smallest distance is not optimized. In the best case, the time complexity can be reduced to $O((|N|+|E|) \log|N|)$ using optimized data structure to implement the priority queue operation. For DA to work effectively, the graph should have positive weights to avoid getting trapped in infinite loops. Due to its ability to find the shortest path, it has applications in transportation and logistics to find the most efficient routes, in games development to enable game characters to navigate through obstacles towards their goals.

Let us consider an example of a graph shown in Fig. 9.7. The objective is to search for the shortest path from source node A to all the other nodes, with the weights at each edge indicated.

Step 1: Initialize by adding all nodes into the "Not visited" list. The "Visited" list is empty. Node A is the source node.

- Not Visited = {A, B, C, D, E, F}.
- Visited = {}.

Step 2: For each node in the table, initialize the current distance from the source node A. It will be zero for node A and infinity for the other nodes.

Node	Distance from source node A	Predecessor node
A	0	
B	∞	
C	∞	
D	∞	
E	∞	
F	∞	

Step 3: Start with the source node A, and set it as current node.

Step 4: For the current node, determine the adjacent node(s) which are not in the "Visited" list. For node A, the non-visited adjacent nodes are B and C.

- Compute distance from A to B as min (0 + 2, ∞) = 2. Update the distance table for node B as 2, and add A as the predecessor node.
- Compute distance from A to C as min (0 + 6, ∞) = 6. Update the distance table for node C as 6, and add A as the predecessor node.
- Once all the adjacent nodes are visited, add the current node A into the "Visited" list, and remove it from the "Not Visited" list.
  - Not Visited = {B, C, D, E, F}.
  - Visited = {A}.

Node	Distance from source node A	Predecessor node
A	0	
B	2	A
C	6	A
D	∞	
E	∞	
F	∞	

Step 5: Select the next current node from the "Not Visited" list with the smallest current weight, and repeat Step 4. It will be node B. For node B, the non-visited adjacent nodes are C and E.

- Compute distance from A to C as min (2 + 6, 6) = 6. 2 + 6 represents the total distance from A to B to C, while 6 is the current distance of node C from source A. Since the minimum is still 6, we do not update the current distance for node C.
- Compute distance from A to E as min (2 + 3, ∞) = 5. Update the distance table for node E as 5, and add B as the predecessor node.
- Once all the adjacent nodes are visited, add the current node B into the "Visited" list, and remove it from the "Not Visited" list.
  - Not Visited = {C, D, E, F}.
  - Visited = {A, B}.

Node	Distance from source node A	Predecessor node
A	0	
B	2	A
C	6	A
D	∞	
E	5	B
F	∞	

Step 5 (repeat): Select the next current node from the "Not Visited" list with the smallest current weight, and repeat Step 4. It will be node E. For node E, the non-visited adjacent nodes are C, D and F.

- Compute distance from A to C as min (5 + 3, 6) = 6. 5 + 3 represents the total distance from A to B to E to C, while 6 is the current distance of node C from the source A. Since the minimum is still 6, we do not update the current distance for node C.
- Compute distance from A to D as min (5 + 1, ∞) = 6. Update the distance table for node D as 6, and add E as the predecessor node.
- Compute distance from A to F as min (5 + 7, ∞) = 12. Update the distance table for node F as 12, and add E as the predecessor node.
- Once all the adjacent nodes are visited, add the current node E into the "Visited" list, and remove it from the "Not Visited" list.

  – Not Visited = {C, D, F}.
  – Visited = {A, B, E}.

Node	Distance from source node A	Predecessor node
A	0	
B	2	A
C	6	A
D	6	E
E	5	B
F	12	E

Step 5 (repeat): Select the next current node from the "Not Visited" list with the smallest current weight, and repeat Step 4. It will be node C. For node C, the non-visited adjacent node is only node D.

- Compute distance from A to D as min (6 + 2, 6) = 6. 6 + 2 represents the total distance from A to C to D, while 6 is the current distance of node D from A to E to D. Since the minimum is still 6, we do not update the current distance for node D.
- Once all the adjacent nodes are visited, add the current node C into the "Visited" list, and remove it from the "Not Visited" list.

  – Not Visited = {D, F}.
  – Visited = {A, B, E, C}.

Node	Distance from source node A	Predecessor node
A	0	
B	2	A
C	6	A
D	6	E
E	5	B
F	12	E

Step 5 (repeat): Select the next current node from the "Not Visited" list with the smallest current weight, and repeat Step 4. It will be node D. For node D, the non-visited adjacent node is only node F.

Table 9.3 Path solution for Dijkstra's Algorithm example

Path	Distance
A → B	2
A → C	6
A → B → E → D	6
A → B → E	5
A → B → E → D → F	9

- Compute distance from A to F as min (6 + 3, 12) = 9. 6 + 3 represents the total distance from A to E to D to F, while 12 is the current distance of node F from A to E to F. Since the minimum is 9, we will update the current distance for node F as 9 and update D as the predecessor node.
- Once all the adjacent nodes are visited, add the current node D into the "Visited" list, and remove it from the "Not Visited" list.
  - Not Visited = {F}.
  - Visited = {A, B, E, C, D}.

Node	Distance from source node A	Predecessor node
A	0	
B	2	A
C	6	A
D	6	E
E	5	B
F	9	D

Step 5 (repeat): Select the next current node from the "Not Visited" list with the smallest current weight, and repeat Step 4. It will be node F. Since node F does not have any non-visited adjacent node, we will add node F into the "Visited" list and remove it from the "Not Visited" list.

- Not Visited = {}.
- Visited = {A, B, E, C, D, F}.

In the end, we can get the shortest distance from A to all the nodes using the table by tracing back the predecessor nodes, as shown in Table 9.3.

9.4 Case 9A: Nurse Scheduling for 14 Days and 15 Nurses

This case is modified from the paper published by Choy and Cheong (2012). In this case study, we explored the scheduling of a 14-day nurse schedule for a hospital ward for 15 nurses. There are three shifts in a day, morning AM shift (denoted as 1), afternoon PM shift (denoted as 2) and midnight MN shift (denoted as 3). On days where the nurses rest or go on leave, it will be denoted as 0. In this case study, we considered regulatory requirements known as hard constraints which must be satisfied in the schedule, as well as soft constraints which represent nurses' preferences. While soft constraints can be violated when planning the schedule, a schedule which does not take care of nurse preferences will lead to unhappiness among the nurses.

The hard constraints to be satisfied for every nurse include:

- Minimum rest day constraint: For a 14-day schedule, there must be at least 3 rest days.
- Maximum consecutive workdays constraint: For every five consecutive workdays, there must be at least one rest day.
- Maximum consecutive night shifts constraint: After three consecutive night shifts, there must be one sleep day and one rest day. After four consecutive night shifts, there must be one sleep day and two rest days.
- Nurse requirement constraint: A minimum number of nurses is required for each day for each shift.
- Leave constraint: Leave applied by the nurses must be fulfilled.
- No consecutive shift constraint: consecutive shifts including AM–PM, PM–MN, MN–AM (next day) are not permitted.

The soft constraints or preferences to be satisfied whenever possible for every nurse include:

- Well-spaced shift: PM shift should not be followed by AM shift the next day.
- Continuous rest days: Continuous rest days are not preferred unless it is meant to follow four consecutive night shifts.
- More than one workday: A rest day should be followed by more than one workday.
- Consecutive night shifts: Consecutive three or four night shifts are not preferred.

Nurse scheduling problem (NSP) is a well-known NP-hard problem. In our case, we have to consider four possible settings (0, 1, 2, 3) for each nurse on each day. With 15 nurses and 14 days, the number of possible combinations is 4^(15×14) $= 2.70768525 \times 10^{126}$, which is clearly impossible to solve to optimality. In addition, to ensure that the schedule satisfies all the hard constraints and at the same time satisfy as many soft constraints as possible is no doubt a mammoth task.

Therefore, we designed and implemented the Greedy Double Swap Heuristic (GDSH) algorithm to determine a good feasible schedule. In this algorithm, we set two measures to guide the algorithm to reach a better solution in each iteration. The first measure is the hard constraint condition, which is a measure of the number of hard constraints satisfied divided by the number of hard constraints. When the hard constraint condition reaches 100%, it represents that all the hard constraints are satisfied. The second measure is the total penalty score. For each soft constraint, we will set a penalty cost if the constraint is not satisfied. For a schedule that satisfies all the hard constraints, there will be some soft constraints which are not satisfied, and thus a total penalty score will be incurred. The overall objective will be to achieve 100% for the hard constraint condition and the lowest possible total penalty score.

The pseudo code for GDSH algorithm is described as follows, and the flowchart of the algorithm is shown in Fig. 9.8.

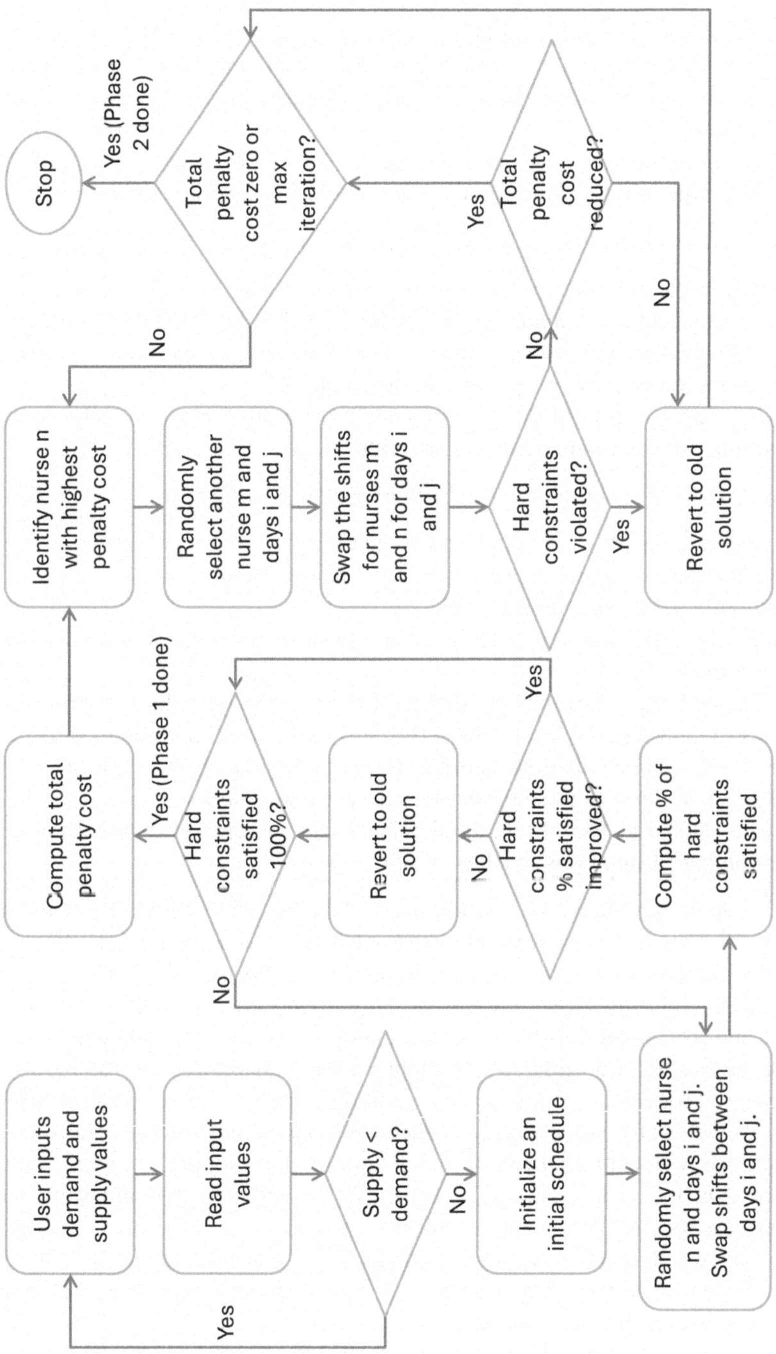

Fig. 9.8 Greedy Double Swap Heuristic (GDSH) algorithm flowchart

Initialization

1. Read in the input values including the number of nurses required for each day for each shift, nurses' supply for each day for each shift, and nurses' leave days.
2. Calculate the nurses' supply and demand. If demand exceeds supply, terminate, else continue.
3. Initialize an initial schedule based on the nurses' supply for each day for each shift only. This initial solution may violate the hard constraints.

Phase 1: First swap between shifts for the same nurse

4. Randomly select a nurse n.
5. Randomly select day i and day j. Swap the shifts for day i and day j for nurse n.
6. Check for hard constraints condition. If the percentage improves, then use the new solution; else, revert by undoing the swap.
7. Repeat steps 4 to 6 until the hard constraints condition reaches 100% or when the number of iterations reaches 1,000,000.

Phase 2: Double swap with minimization of total penalty cost

8. Calculate the penalty cost incurred by each nurse.
9. Select the nurse n which incurred the most penalty cost.
10. Randomly select another nurse m.
11. Randomly select day i and day j. Swap the shifts for nurse n and nurse m for days i and j.
12. Check for hard constraints condition. If the percentage reduces below 100%, revert by undoing the swap, and return to step 8; else, continue to step 13.
13. Check for total penalty cost incurred. If there is no reduction, revert by undoing the swap, and return to step 10; else, use the new solution.
14. Repeat steps 8 to 13 until the total penalty cost incurred goes to zero or when the number of iterations reaches 10,000.

Let us map the problem and solution method for this case study against the *data and decision analytics framework* proposed in Chap. 1. As shown in Fig. 9.9, in this case study, the problem faced was to prepare a 14-day schedule for 15 nurses. Therefore, the right question to ask was "How to obtain a schedule that satisfies both hard and soft constraints?". Next, was to collect the relevant data which will be needed to answer the question, which includes the demand data on the number of nurses required for each shift on each day, and the supply of nurses for each shift on each day, as well as the penalty cost for each soft constraint. With the data collected, the analyst can perform initial analysis to determine if the supply can meet demand, and if not met, the supply should be increased for affected day and shift before scheduling can begin. The problem objective would be to determine a good and feasible schedule that satisfies all hard constraints while minimizing penalty cost. The assumption made here is that while soft constraints are important, they can be violated, and some penalty cost will be incurred. The problem is known to be NP-hard, and thus the GDSH was used to obtain a good and feasible solution that can satisfy all hard constraints and at the same time satisfy as many soft constraints as possible while incurring the minimum penalty cost.

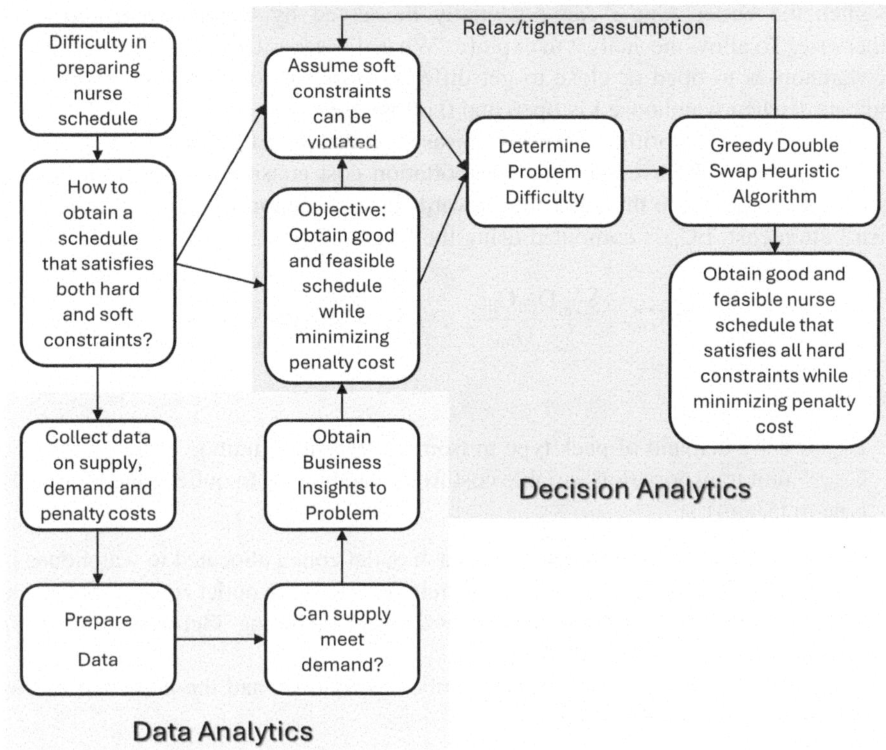

Fig. 9.9 Data and decision analytics framework map for Case 9A

9.5 Case 9B: Beer Distribution

This case is modified from the paper published by Cheong (2014). In this case study, the objective is to allocate 81 retail outlet zones to a maximum of eight warehouses to distribute different pack types of beer from the warehouses to the retail outlet zones, minimizing the total logistics cost.

In practice, many distribution costs are concave cost functions, which will make the problem NP-Complete. In addition, there are practical business considerations in distribution such as truck drivers' familiarity with the outlet zones, restriction of certain vehicle types in the central business district, restriction of certain vehicle types on some roads, and some loading and unloading bays that can only allow certain vehicle types. Including all these considerations into a mathematical model would likely lead to an intractable problem.

To solve the problem, we proposed to use a heuristic algorithm with the candidate choice approach, where the candidate warehouses are pre-selected from among all the warehouses. These candidate warehouses are pre-selected as they have the right vehicle types and truck drivers, which have the capability to perform the distribution task satisfying all the business considerations. We used a parameter Z_{ij} to indicate

1 when the outlet zone i can potentially be served by warehouse j, and zero otherwise. To allow the analyst to explore "What-if" scenarios with different subsets of warehouses to open or close to get different possible solutions, we used Y_j to indicate 1 when warehouse j is open and 0 otherwise.

In the heuristic algorithm, we used a measure called the Effective Unit Cost, EC_{ij}, which represents the average unit transportation cost considering all the different pack types m, to guide the algorithm towards better solutions which will minimize distribution cost. EC_{ij} is computed using the formula below:

$$EC_{ij} = \frac{\sum_m D_{im} C_{ijm}}{\sum_m D_{im}} \quad , \forall i, j \quad \text{where } Z_{ij} = 1$$

where:

- D_{im} = daily demand of pack type m from outlet zone i (units).
- C_{ijm} = unit transportation variable cost from warehouse j to outlet zone i for pack type m ($/unit).

Using the value of EC_{ij} computed for each outlet zone i allocated to warehouse j, the algorithm will select the lowest cost warehouse j to serve outlet zone i for all pack types m. There are six different pack types for beer including 33cl cans, 50cl cans, pints, quarts, 20L kegs and 30L kegs.

The pseudo code for algorithm is described as follows, and the flowchart of the algorithm is shown in Fig. 9.10.

Initialization

1. Read in the input values including the daily demand of pack type m from outlet zone D_{im}, unit transportation variable cost from warehouse j to outlet zone i for pack type m C_{ijm}, warehouse capacity W_j and warehouse fixed cost F_j.
2. Set $Y_j = 1$ for warehouses which are open and 0 otherwise. For warehouses which are open, the corresponding warehouse fixed cost F_j will be incurred.
3. Set $Z_{ij} = 1$ for candidate warehouse when outlet zone i can potentially be served by warehouse j and 0 otherwise.
4. Compute EC_{ij} for all outlet zones i with candidate warehouses j which are set as open ($Z_{ij} = 1$).
5. Rank EC_{ij} in ascending order for each outlet zone i.
6. Establish warehouse j ranking corresponding to the ranked EC_{ij} for each outlet zone i.

Allocation

7. For each unassigned outlet zone i, identify the smallest EC_{ij} and the corresponding warehouse j.
8. For all the smallest EC_{ij} identified in step 7, determine the smallest among them, and let it be SBest _ EC_{ij}, and identify that particular outlet zone i as SBest _ i and its corresponding warehouse j as SBest _ j.
9. Sum D_{im} for all outlet zones i already assigned to warehouse SBest _ j, plus the D_{im} for this SBest _ i allocation, and check if it exceeds the warehouse capacity W_j of SBest _ j.

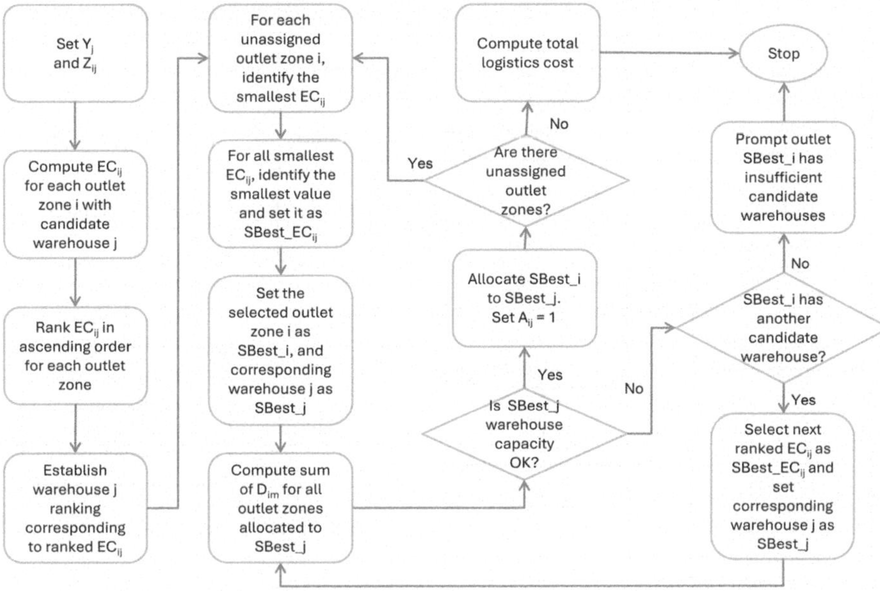

Fig. 9.10 Heuristic algorithm flowchart for beer distribution

(a) If capacity is not violated, set $A_{ij} = 1$ to indicate that outlet zone i is allocated to warehouse j. Continue to step 7 if there are still unassigned outlet zones.
(b) If capacity is violated, check if outlet zone SBest _ i has another candidate warehouse.

   (i) If yes, set the next ranked EC_{ij} of SBest _ i as SBest _ EC_{ij}, and identify the corresponding warehouse j as SBest_j. Continue to step 9.
   (ii) If no, prompt the message that SBest _ i has insufficient candidate warehouses, and exit the algorithm.

Heuristic Solution

10. The allocation of outlet zones i to warehouse j will be given by A_{ij}.
11. The corresponding total logistics cost incurred will be the total transportation variable cost and total fixed cost given as

$$TC = \sum_{i,j,m} A_{ij} D_{im} C_{ijm} + \sum_j Y_j F_j$$

Let us map the problem and solution method for this case study against the *data and decision analytics framework* proposed in Chap. 1. As shown in Fig. 9.11, in

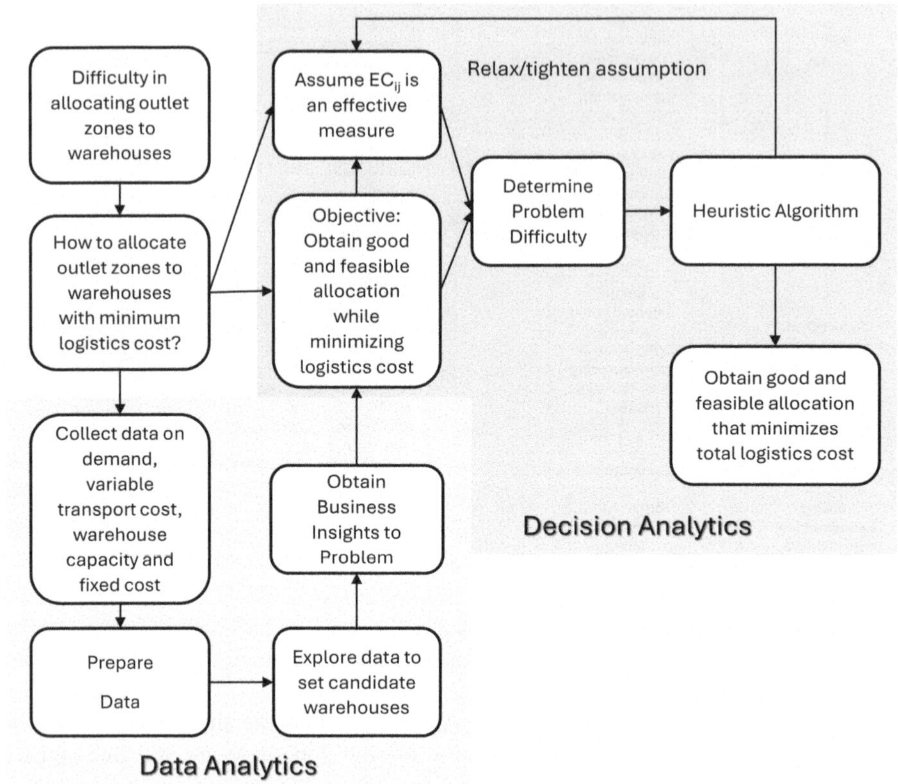

Fig. 9.11 Data and decision analytics framework map for Case 9B

this case study, the problem faced was to allocate 81 outlet zones to a maximum of eight warehouses. Therefore, the right question to ask was "How to allocate the outlet zones to warehouses with minimum logistics cost?". Next was to collect the relevant data which will be needed to answer the question, which includes the demand data on the different pack types of beer from each outlet, the unit transportation cost between warehouse j to outlet i for different pack types, the warehouse capacity and fixed cost. With the data collected, the analyst can perform initial analysis to determine the candidate warehouses for each outlet zone. The problem objective would be to determine a good and feasible allocation to minimize total logistic cost. The assumption made here is that EC_{ij} is an effective measure to guide the heuristic algorithm to reach better solutions. A heuristic algorithm is used to obtain a good and feasible solution that can minimize the total logistics cost.

9.6 Summary

This chapter covered three different heuristic algorithms, which are commonly used to solve problems which are NP-hard. They include Depth-First Search (DFS), Breath-First Search (BFS) and Dijkstra's Algorithm (DA), and worked examples are used to illustrate how to apply them. Finally, we looked at two case studies, nurse scheduling problem and beer distribution problem, to show how we can use heuristic algorithms to solve real-world problems. In the next chapter, we will cover one of the most important problems in management science—queueing theory, where we will look at the different types of queues, understand the Kendall's notation to represent queues, learn how to compute queue performance measures and cover a case study on how to use queue buster to improve queue performance in a grocery store.

Exercises

Q9.1

Refer to the undirected weighted graph below, and apply the Dijkstra's Algorithm to find the shortest path between nodes A and E.

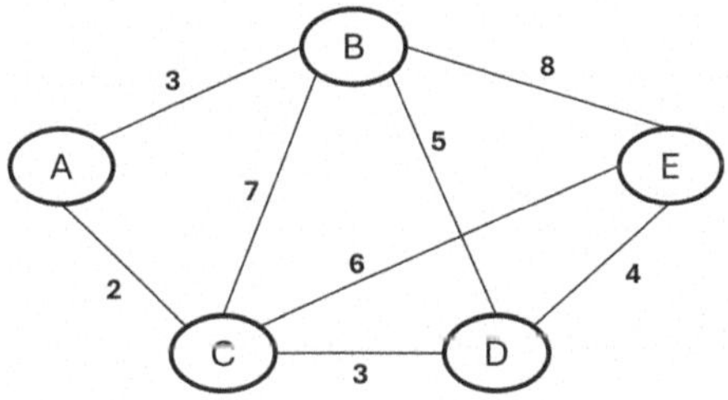

Q9.2

Refer to the graph in Q9.1, and apply the Dijkstra's Algorithm to find the shortest path between node C and all other nodes, and fill up the answer according to the table format given below.

From C to	Shortest path	Distance
A		
B		
D		
E		

Q9.3

The table below shows the shipping cost between cities A to E. Assuming undirected weighted graph, a dash in the table represents that there is no shipping route available between the two cities. Use the Dijkstra's Algorithm to find the minimum shipping cost to ship a parcel from city A to E.

	A	B	C	D	E
A	–	13	15	14	45
B		–	8	12	–
C			–	6	10
D				–	14
E					–

Q9.4

Use the table in Q9.3, and this time, the values in the table represent distance between cities instead of shipping cost. Use the Dijkstra's Algorithm to find the shortest path between city C and all other cities, and fill up the answer according to the table format given below.

From C to	Shortest path	Distance
A		
B		
D		
E		

References

Cheong, M. L. F. (2014). *Strategic decision support system using heuristic algorithm for practical outlet zones allocation to dealers in a beer supply distribution network* (pp. 1720–1731). Proceedings of the 2014 International Conference on Industrial Engineering and Operations Management (IEOM), Indonesia. http://iieom.org/ieom2014/pdfs/386.pdf

Choy, J., & Cheong, M. L. F. (2012). A greedy double swap heuristic for nurse scheduling. *Management Science Letters, 2*(6), 2001–2010. https://doi.org/10.5267/j.msl.2012.06.021

Chapter 10
Queuing Theory

Every business has some form of queue system within their daily operations. It could be patients queuing at the emergency department of a hospital, calls waiting to be answered at a call centre, customers queuing to pay for their purchases at a retail store, or passengers queuing to check in at the airport.

Queues can either be visible or invisible. Invisible queues include calls waiting to be answered at a call centre or concert goers waiting to make an online purchase of concert tickets. Such invisible queues improve their "visibility" by letting customers know their positions in the queue using a queue numbering system or provide customers the estimated waiting time. One would expect all queues, visible or invisible, to be neatly arranged in lines. However, there are queues which are not neatly arranged in lines, such as cars on ride-hailing apps waiting to serve the next customer booking are dispatched all over the city.

The purpose of having a queue system is to enable the processing of demand for services to serve customers or customer groups one at a time at the servers. There are many known problems associated with queue systems, including long wait times and long queue lengths, leading to customer dissatisfaction. It is thus important to study how to measure and improve queue performance.

In this chapter, we will first understand queue system terminology used to describe the different parts of the queue and then discuss six different types of queue systems. Following that, we will discuss queue performance and the Kendall's Notation to represent queue. The Universal Relationships which include Little's Law are discussed and applied into four queue systems, M/M/1, M/M/m, G/G/1 and G/G/m. Finally, a case study on determining the optimal system length to trigger queue busting in a grocery store will be discussed.

Learning Outcomes

By the end of this chapter, readers will achieve the following learning outcomes:

- Explain the queue system terminology.
- Describe six different types of queue systems.
- Understand the Kendall's Notation.

M. L. F. Cheong, Ma Nang Laik, *Data and Decision Analytics for Business Operations*, https://doi.org/10.1007/978-3-031-72255-4_10

- Explain the Universal Relationships.
- Derive the formulas for average system length, average system time, average queue time and average queue length for M/M/1 queue.
- Explain the average queue time formula for M/M/m queue.
- Explain the average queue time formula for G/G/1 queue.
- Explain the average queue time formula for G/G/m queue.
- Break down queues into single-stage systems.
- Apply the correct formulas to compute performance for M/M/1, M/M/m, G/G/1 and G/G/m queues.
- Discuss how queue performance formulas can be applied in a real-world case to determine the optimal system length to trigger queue busting in a grocery store using the *data and decision analytics framework.*

10.1 Queue System Terminology

To understand the terminology used in queue management, let us look at a typical queue system as shown in Fig. 10.1.

- A single server queue system will have a *server* that provides the service demanded by the customers.
- Customers or customer groups will arrive at the queue line one at a time and wait for their turn to be served. The *arrival time* will be the clock time that the customer arrives and joins the queue system.
- When the customer starts service with the server, we termed this clock time as the *service start time.*
- When the customer ends service with the server, we termed it as the *service end time*, and this is the clock time that the customer leaves the queue system.
- The duration from arrival time to service start time is termed as the *wait time* or *queue time*. This represents the time the customer must wait or queue in line before being served.

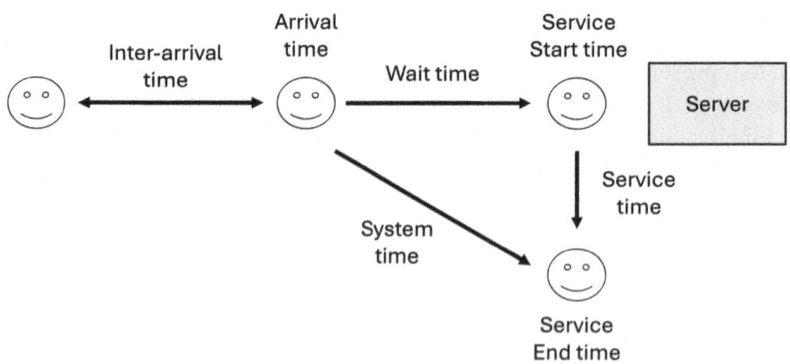

Fig. 10.1 Typical queue system

- The duration from service start time to service end time is termed as the *service time*. This represents the time the customer spends at the server.
- The total duration from arrival time to service end time is termed as the *system time*. This represents the total time the customer spends in the queue system, and it is the sum of wait time and service time.
- The time between two consecutive customer arrivals is termed as the *inter-arrival time*.
- *Queue length* will denote the number of customers in the queue waiting to be served by the server.
- *System length* will denote the number of customers waiting in the queue plus customers who are currently being served by the server.

The usual assumptions made about queue system are:

- Customer who needs the service will join the queue regardless of the queue length. This implies that the customer will not balk. We can relax this assumption and set a *balk limit*, for example, 12 persons, which means that if the queue length is more than 12 persons, the customer will not join the queue upon arrival and balked.
- Customer who needs the service and decides to join the queue will stay in the queue system until he or she receives the service and leaves the queue system. This implies that the customer will not renege. We can relax this assumption and set a *renege time limit*, for example, 30 minutes, which means that if the wait time exceeds 30 minutes, the customer will leave the queue system before being served and reneged.
- Customer will not engage in *queue jockeying*. Jockeying refers to the behaviour of a customer who is already waiting in one queue and decides to leave the original queue and join a different queue, which could be shorter in queue length or appears to move faster. Again, this assumption can be relaxed to take care of jockeying.
- Customers will not queue out of turn or *queue jumping*. This refers to the behaviour of a customer who decides to cut in front of other customers who joined the queue before him or her to obtain an advantage or priority. Queue jumping is usually not tolerated in the real world; thus, this assumption will not be relaxed.

10.2 Types of Queues

We will be discussing six different types of queue systems:

- Single-stage system (SSS)
- Multiple-stage system (MSS)
- Parallel single-stage system (PSSS)
- Multi-channel single-stage system (MCSSS)

- Multi-line system (MLS)
- Customer discrimination system (CDS)

10.2.1 Single-Stage System

In a single-stage system (SSS), customers arrive at rate λ and join a single queue and wait to be served by a single server. This single server takes care of all the services demanded by the customers at service rate μ, and customers will leave the queue system after being served. A good example of an SSS is an ATM queue, where the ATM is the server which can provide all the services demanded, as depicted in Fig. 10.2.

10.2.2 Multiple-Stage System

In a multiple-stage system (MSS), customers join a single queue and must be served by more than one server, one after another sequentially. Each server will take care of some of the services demanded by the customers and may operate at different service rates. As depicted in Fig. 10.3, the customer arrives at arrival rate λ_1 and is served by server 1 at service rate μ_1. After that, the customer will join the end of the second queue at arrival rate λ_2 and served by server 2 at service rate μ_2. A good example of an MSS is the queue at the emergency department of a hospital, where the patients have to go through several stages of triage and served by different departments.

Fig. 10.2 Single-stage system (SSS)

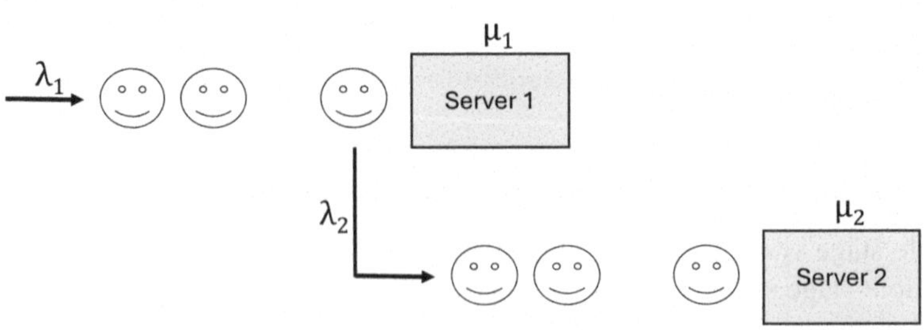

Fig. 10.3 Multiple-stage system (MSS)

10.2.3 Parallel Single-Stage System

In a parallel single-stage system (PSSS), there will be multiple queues with multiple servers providing similar service, and each queue has a single server. Customers can choose to join any queue (thus different arrival rates), and the single server will take care of all the services demanded by the customers. As depicted in Fig. 10.4, when customers choose to join any queue, each queue may have its respective arrival rate λ_1 and λ_2. Since the servers provide similar services, they are assumed to have the same service rate μ. A good example of a PSSS is the queue at a typical fast-food restaurant, where patrons can choose to join any queue and get served by the server of the queue they joined. Such a queue system tends to encourage queue jockeying.

10.2.4 Multi-channel Single-Stage System

In multi-channel single-stage system (MCSSS), there are multiple servers and customers join a single queue and wait to be served by one of the servers based on a selected queue discipline, for example, first-come-first served, shortest processing time, or priority system.

As depicted in Fig. 10.5, customers arrive at rate λ and join a single queue and wait to be served by a single server. The servers provide similar services and are assumed to have the same service rate μ. The next free server, Server 1, will then

Fig. 10.4 Parallel single-stage system (PSSS)

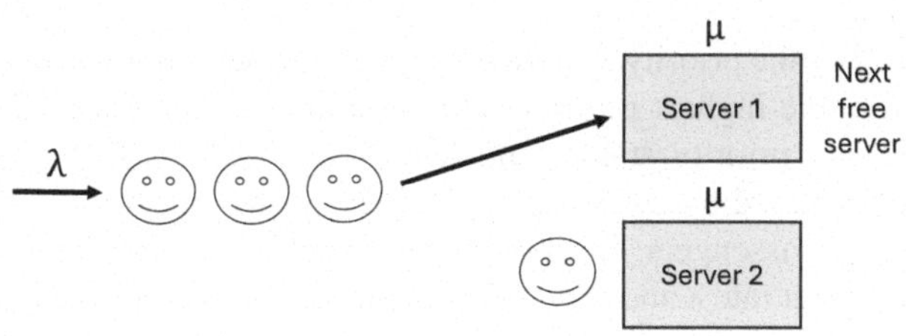

Fig. 10.5 Multi-channel single-stage system (MCSSS) with first-come-first-served discipline

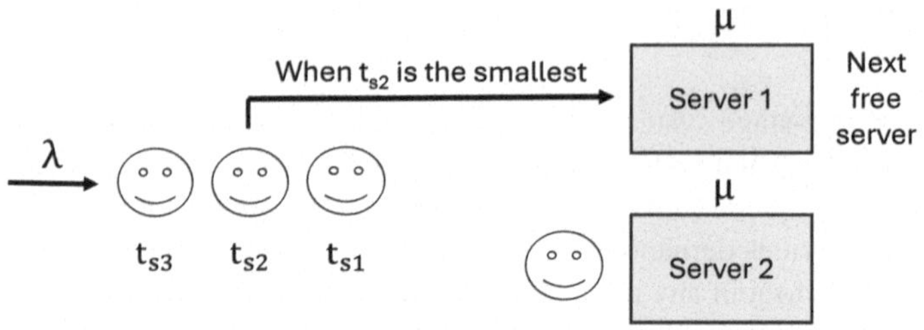

Fig. 10.6 Multi-channel single-stage system (MCSSS) with shortest processing time discipline

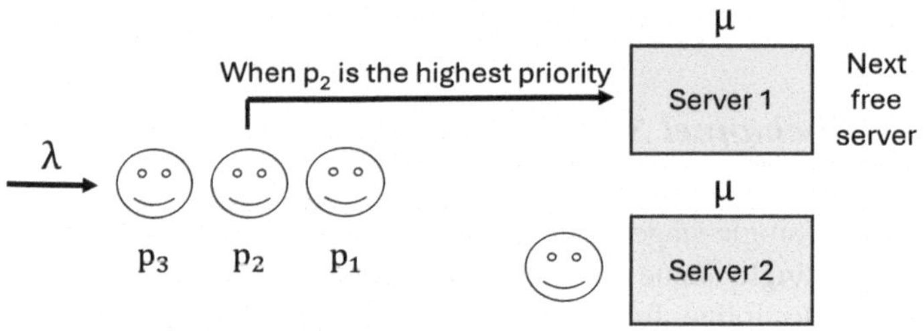

Fig. 10.7 Multi-channel single-stage system (MCSSS) with priority system discipline

serve the next customer at the front of the queue without bias and based on the first-come-first served discipline. A good example is the queue at a bank branch, where bank customers will get served by the next free server.

For the shortest processing time discipline, the next free server will serve the next customer with the shortest processing time. Such a queue system is used when the services demanded by each individual customer are different with different average service time. As depicted in Fig. 10.6, customers arrive at rate λ and join a single queue. If the second customer in the queue has the shortest processing time t_{s2}, he/she will be served first by the next free server. A good example would be the queue at the pharmacy dispensing department. Due to different ailments, different patients will be prescribed different drugs, and thus each prescription will require different processing time. Patients with the shortest processing time could be served first.

For the priority system discipline, the next free server will serve the next customer with the highest priority. This is somewhat similar to the shortest processing time, except priority status will determine who gets to be served first. Priority can be determined by age to serve the elderly customers first or by status to serve business class passengers first before the coach class. As depicted in Fig. 10.7, customers arrive at rate λ and join a single queue. The second customer in the queue has highest priority p_2 and will be served first by the next free server.

10.2.5 Multi-line System

In a multi-line system (MLS), the server is available at the intersection of multiple queues. Customers will get served based on a selected queue discipline, which could be first-come-first-served, shortest processing time, or priority system. Such a queue system is usually employed when the server is a limited resource and multiple queues of customers are demanding service from this server. As depicted in Fig. 10.8, the first set of customers arrive at the left-side queue at rate λ_1, while a second set of customers arrive at the right-side queue at rate λ_2. Assume that the first customer on the left-side queue arrived at time t_1 while the first customer on the right-side queue arrived at time t_4. If $t_4 < t_1$, then the first customer on the right-side queue will be served first based on a first-come-first-served discipline. A good example is the airport runway where many queues of departing and arriving flights are waiting to be served by the runway for take-off and landing.

10.2.6 Customer Discrimination System

In a customer discrimination system (CDS), servers are not the same, and they are differentiated according to the service provided or the types of customers they serve. In such a queue system, customers will join the appropriate queue accordingly. As depicted in Fig. 10.9, there are two types of customers, and their arrival rates are λ_1 and λ_2, respectively. Servers will have their own service rates μ_1 and μ_2, respectively. One good example will be airport check-in counters, which are differentiated into business class and coach class, and customers will join the appropriate queue according to their ticket class. Another example will be call centre queues where

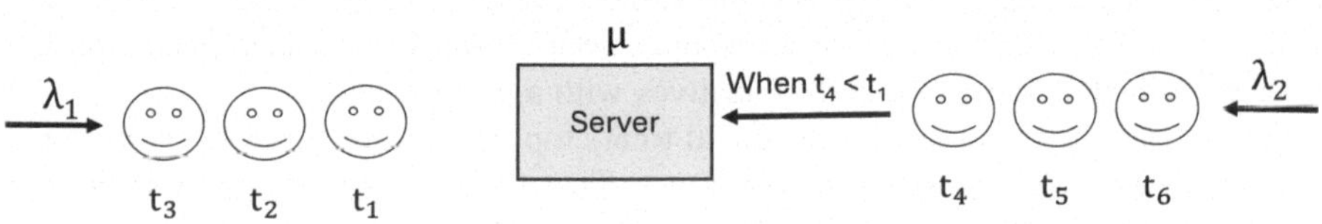

Fig. 10.8 Multi-line system (MLS)

Fig. 10.9 Customer discrimination system (CDS)

customers will be directed to the appropriate channels by choosing the service options available.

10.3 Queue Performance

There are two main groups of queue performance measurements, time-based and length-based performance. In terms of time, we are mostly interested in the average wait time and average system time. There are other forms of time-based performance such as the probability that customers have to wait for more than 15 minutes before being served, and the percentage of customers having to spend no more than 10 minutes in the queue system. In terms of length, we are mostly interested in average queue length and average system length. Similarly, there are other forms of length-based performance such as the probability of having a queue length of more than 10 people, number of customers being served in a given time, number of customers who balked and number of customers who reneged.

From the customer's perspective, system time (= wait time + service time) is important. Businesses will try to manage their system time by reducing the wait time or service time. Some businesses can have longer wait times but shorter service times, while others will have shorter wait times but longer service times. For example, when seeing a specialist doctor at a clinic, one would experience a long wait time and short consultation time. When dining at an expensive restaurant, one may experience very short or no wait time and long dining duration.

On the other hand, from the business' perspective, the utilization of the server is usually more important. Utilization is referred to as the percentage of time the server is busy, computed as the average service time divided by the average inter-arrival time. Increasing server utilization will inevitably increase the wait time and system time. Therefore, the objectives of the customers and the businesses are in fact conflicting. Thus, it is important to design queue systems to manage queue performance optimally, satisfying both objectives with a good balance.

It will be costly and even impractical to attempt to achieve the shortest possible wait times or shortest possible service times. To satisfy real-world requirements, we will determine the optimal queue setting in terms of the number of servers to achieve queue performance that is acceptable to the customers at feasible business implementation cost.

10.4 Kendall's Notation

To compute queue performance measures, we will adopt a standard notation known as Kendall's Notation to represent different types of queues. The notation is

$$A/B/m/b$$

where:

- A = distribution of inter-arrival time.
- B = distribution of service time.
- m = number of servers.
- b = maximum queue length.

Typical values for A and B include:

- D = deterministic value.
- M = exponential distribution, also known as Markovian thus the letter M.
- G = general distribution which can be uniform, normal or others.

In addition, we need to denote some of the key parameters including:

- λ = arrival rate = $1/t_a$ where t_a = average inter-arrival time.
- μ = service rate = $1/t_s$ where t_s = average service time.
- L_q = average queue length.
- L = average system length.
- W_q = average queue time.
- W = average system time = $W_q + t_s$.

We will be studying four different queue systems and determine the formulas to compute the four key queue performance measures, namely, L, L_q, W and W_q. The four queue systems are:

- M/M/1
- M/M/m
- G/G/1
- G/G/m

10.5 Universal Relationships

Using Kendall's Notation, we will proceed to determine the formulas to compute the four key queue performance measures. Queue systems often experience the cold-start situation where the queue has just started to form and the queue system has not reached its steady state. The formulas we will be exploring next should only be applied to steady-state queues where the cold-start situation does not exist.

The following are the universal relationships that can be applied to *any single-stage system* regardless of the distributions of the arrival and service processes A and B, respectively, and the number of servers m. According to Little's Law,

Average system length, $L = \lambda W$

Average queue length, $L_q = \lambda W_q$

Together with the formula for average system time, $W = W_q + t_s$, we will be able to compute three of the four performance measures if we know one of them, for a given queue system with known arrival rate λ and service rate μ. To extend the relationships to other types of queues as described in Sect. 10.2, one only needs to break down the queue into several single-stage systems (with one or m servers) and solve each system independently with its own arrival rate and service rate.

10.5.1 M/M/1 Queue

To solve for an M/M/1 queue, we need to consider its state transition diagram with n arrivals. Figure 10.10 illustrates the birth-death process of the queue where each birth represents a customer arrival with rate λ and each death represents the customer leaving the queue system after receiving the service of rate μ.

At the start, we begin with state 0. A customer arrival (birth) will bring the state to 1, the next arrival will bring the state to 2 and so on, until the state reaches n. Similarly, any customer departure (death) will bring the state down from state n to n−1, from n−1 to n−2 and so on, until state 0. Obviously, both birth and death processes can occur concurrently. If the birth process is occurring at a faster rate than the death process, that is, $\lambda > \mu$, then the state will increase towards n. Conversely, if the death process is occurring at a faster rate than the birth process, that is, $\mu > \lambda$, then the state will decrease towards 0.

After a queue system runs for some time, it will reach a steady state. At steady state, we define the following:

- p_n = steady-state probability that the system is in state n.
- p_{n-1} = steady-state probability that the system is in state n−1.

Therefore, the birth rate at which the system moves from state n−1 to state n will be given as λp_{n-1}. Similarly, the death rate at which the system moves from state n to state n−1 will be given as μp_n. For the queue system to be stable, the birth rate

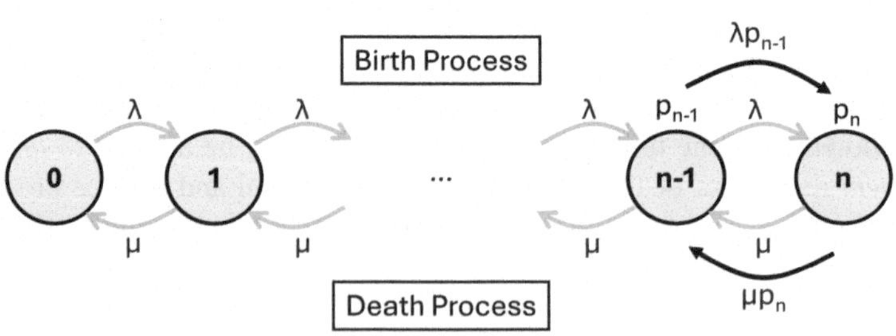

Fig. 10.10 State transition diagram for an M/M/1 queue system

must be equal to the death rate, or else, the state will move towards one of the two ends of the state transition diagram. Thus, for a stable queue system, $\lambda p_{n-1} = \mu p_n$.

Let us define the server utilization to be $\rho = \frac{\lambda}{m\mu}$. For a single server queue system, the utilization $\rho = \frac{\lambda}{\mu}$ since $m = 1$. We can further define that for a stable queue system, $p_n = \frac{\lambda}{\mu} p_{n-1}$ or $p_n = \rho p_{n-1}$.

What does it mean for a queue system to be stable? Since ρ is the server utilization, then $(1 - \rho)$ must represent the long-term fraction of time that server is idle. This means that $p_0 = (1 - \rho)$. We can then compute the steady-state probabilities of all the states from 1 to n as follows:

$$p_1 = \rho p_0 = \rho(1 - \rho)$$

$$p_2 = \rho p_1 = \rho^2(1 - \rho)$$

$$\ldots$$

$$p_n = \rho p_{n-1} = \rho^n(1 - \rho)$$

In general, $p_n = \rho p_{n-1} = \rho^n(1 - \rho)$, where $n = 1, 2, \ldots, n$. In addition, since sum of all the steady-state probabilities must be 1, we can express

$$p_0 + p_1 + p_2 + \ldots + p_n = 1$$

$$p_0(1 + \rho + \rho^2 + \ldots + \rho^n) = 1$$

Inferring from the equation above, since $(1 + \rho + \rho^2 + \ldots + \rho^n) > 1$, then $p_0 < 1$. This means that $(1 - \rho) < 1$, since $p_0 = (1 - \rho)$. In order for $(1 - \rho) < 1$, then $\rho < 1$. This concludes that for a queue system to be stable, $\rho < 1$, which means that $\lambda < \mu$.

Now, let's move on to derive the expected system length L formula using the state transition diagram. Since p_n = steady-state probability that the system is in state n,

$$L = \sum_n n p_n = p_1 + 2p_2 + 3p_3 + \ldots + np_n$$

$$= \rho(1 - \rho) + 2\rho^2(1 - \rho) + 3\rho^3(1 - \rho) + \ldots + n\rho^n(1 - \rho)$$

$$= (1-\rho)\left[\rho + 2\rho^2 + 3\rho^3 + \ldots + n\rho^n\right]$$

$$= (1-\rho)\left[\sum\nolimits_n n\rho^n\right]$$

$$= \rho(1-\rho)\left[\sum\nolimits_n n\rho^{n-1}\right]$$

$$= \rho(1-\rho)(1-\rho)^{-2}$$

$$= \frac{\rho}{(1-\rho)}$$

Now that we have derived the average system length $L = \frac{\rho}{(1-\rho)}$, we can apply the universal relationships to derive the formulas for the other three performance measures.

- Average system time

$$W = \frac{L}{\lambda} = \frac{\rho}{\lambda(1-\rho)} = \frac{t_s}{(1-\rho)}$$

- Average queue time

$$W_q = W - t_s = \frac{t_s}{(1-\rho)} - t_s = \frac{\rho}{(1-\rho)} t_s$$

- Average queue length

$$L_q = \lambda W_q = \frac{\lambda\rho}{(1-\rho)} t_s = \frac{\rho^2}{(1-\rho)}$$

Side-box: To understand how did $\sum_n n\rho^{n-1} = (1-\rho)^{-2}$ in the derivation of L, let us look at the derivation below.

$$\text{Let } U = \sum\nolimits_n \rho^n = \rho^0 + \rho^1 + \rho^2 + \ldots = 1 + \rho^1 + \rho^2 + \ldots \quad (1)$$

Multiply both sides by ρ:

$$\rho U = \rho + \rho^2 + \rho^3 + \ldots \quad (2)$$

Let (1) − (2):

$$U - \rho U \approx 1$$

$$U(1 - \rho) = 1$$

$$U = \frac{1}{(1 - \rho)} \quad (3)$$

Set (1) = (3):

$$U = \sum_n \rho^n = \frac{1}{(1 - \rho)} \quad (4)$$

Differentiate LHS of (4):

$$\frac{dU}{d\rho} = \sum_n n\rho^{n-1} \quad (5)$$

Differentiate RHS of (4):

$$\frac{dU}{d\rho} = (-1)(1 - \rho)^{-2}.(-1) = \frac{1}{(1 - \rho)^2} \quad (6)$$

We can see that (5) = (6), which answers $\sum_n n\rho^{n-1} = (1 - \rho)^{-2}$.

10.5.2 M/M/m Queue

To obtain the formulas for the four key queue performance measures for M/M/m queue, we begin with a closed-form approximation for the average queue time W_q given by Sakasegawal (1977).

$$W_q = \frac{\rho^{\sqrt{2(m+1)}-1}}{m(1 - \rho)} t_s$$

Using the formula for W_q, we can apply the universal relationships to derive the formulas for the other three performance measures.

- Average system time

$$W = W_q + t_s$$

- Average queue length

$$L_q = \lambda W_q$$

- Average system length

$$L = \lambda W$$

10.5.3 G/G/1 Queue

We cannot compute the exact performance measures for G/G/1 queue, but we can estimate using the two-moment approximation where we use only the mean and the standard deviation of the distributions of the arrival and service processes A and B, respectively. Let C_a and C_s be the coefficient of variation (CV) of the arrival and service distributions, respectively, where CV = SD/mean.

For M/M/1 queue, the average queue time W_q is given by

$$W_q = \frac{\rho}{(1 - \rho)} t_s$$

Using the two-moment approximation, we add the factor $\left(\frac{C_a^2 + C_s^2}{2}\right)$ to approximate average queue time W_q for a G/G/1 queue as

$$W_q = \left(\frac{C_a^2 + C_s^2}{2}\right) \frac{\rho}{(1 - \rho)} t_s$$

Note that the W_q formula for a G/G/1 queue is a generalized form of W_q formula for M/M/1 queue. For M/M/1 queue, both C_a and C_s will be equal to 1, since SD = mean for an exponential distribution, and this will make the first term = 1.

Similarly, we can apply the universal relationships to derive the formulas for the other three performance measures.

- Average system time

$$W = W_q + t_s$$

- Average queue length

$$L_q = \lambda W_q$$

- Average system length

$$L = \lambda W$$

10.5.4 G/G/m Queue

Using the closed-form approximation for average queue time W_q for a M/M/m queue and the two-moment approximation, we can get the average queue time W_q for a G/G/m queue as

$$W_q = \left(\frac{C_a^2 + C_s^2}{2}\right)\frac{\rho^{\sqrt{2(m+1)}-1}}{m(1-\rho)}t_s$$

Once again, we can apply the universal relationships to derive the formulas for the other three performance measures.

- Average system time

$$W = W_q + t_s$$

- Average queue length

$$L_q = \lambda W_q$$

- Average system length

$$L = \lambda W$$

10.5.5 Breaking Down Queues into Single-Stage Systems

With the formulas derived for M/M/1, M/M/m, G/G/1 and G/G/m, we can apply them to any types of queues once we are able to break the queue down into several single-stage systems (SSS) and solve each one independently.

For a multi-stage system (MSS), each stage can be broken down into independent single-stage system (SSS) as shown in Fig. 10.11, where SSS-1 has arrival rate λ_1 and service rate μ_1, while SSS-2 has arrival rate λ_2 and service rate μ_2. The performance of each SSS can be computed using M/M/1 or G/G/1 formulas depending on the distributions of the arrival and service processes.

For a parallel single-stage system (PSSS), each queue is essentially an independent single-stage system (SSS) as shown in Fig. 10.12, where SSS-1 has arrival rate λ_1 and service rate μ, while SSS-2 has arrival rate λ_2 and service rate μ. The performance of each SSS can be computed using M/M/1 or G/G/1 formulas depending on the distributions of the arrival and service processes.

For a multi-channel single-stage system (MCSSS) as shown in Fig. 10.13, it is equivalent to a single-stage system (SSS) with multiple servers. The servers provide similar services and are assumed to have the same service rate μ. The performance

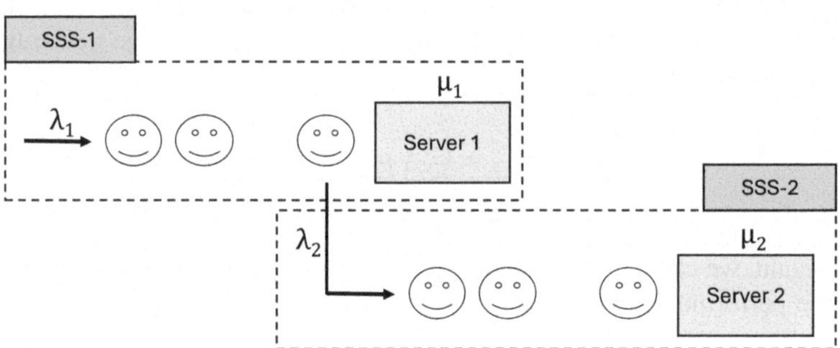

Fig. 10.11 Multiple-stage system (MSS) broken down into two single-stage systems

Fig. 10.12 Parallel single-stage system (PSSS) broken down into two single-stage systems

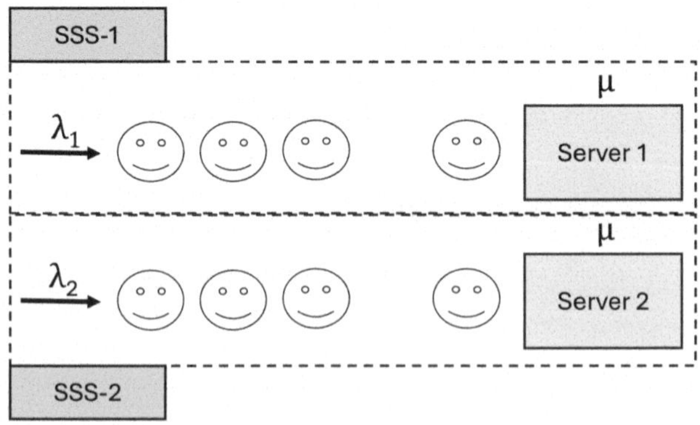

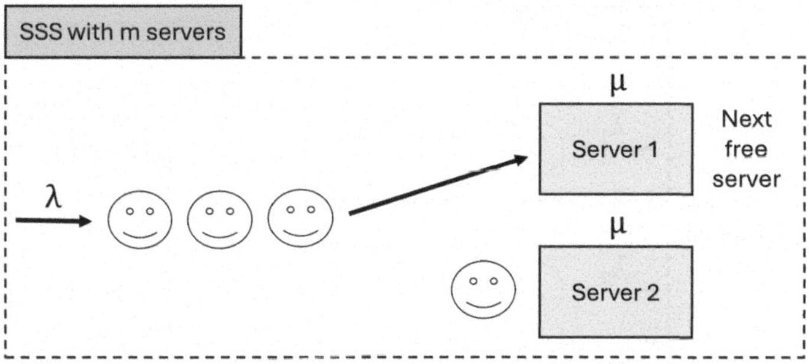

Fig. 10.13 Multi-channel single-stage system (MCSSS) as a single-stage system with m servers

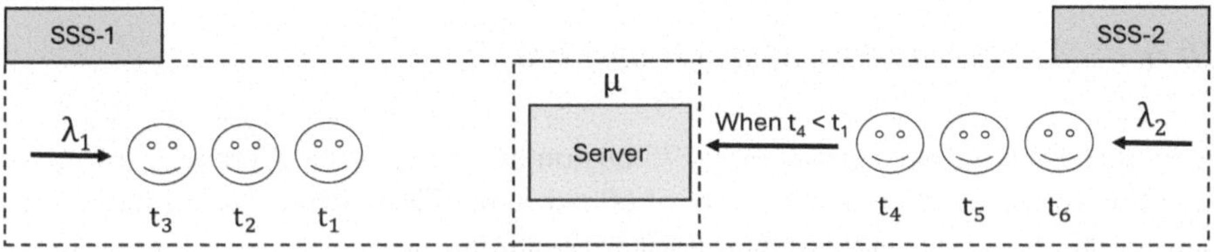

Fig. 10.14 Multi-line system broken down into two single-stage systems

can be computed using M/M/m or G/G/m formulas depending on the distributions of the arrival and service processes.

For a multi-line system (MLS) as shown in Fig. 10.14, each line is an independent single-stage system (SSS) with the same single server, where SSS-1 has arrival rate λ_1 and service rate $\mu/2$, while SSS-2 has arrival rate λ_2 and service rate $\mu/2$ (assuming the server serves each SSS evenly). The performance of each SSS can be computed using M/M/1 or G/G/1 formulas depending on the distributions of the arrival and service processes.

Finally, for a customer discrimination system (CDS) as shown in Fig. 10.15, each queue is an independent single-stage system (SSS), where SSS-1 has arrival rate λ_1 and service rate μ_1, while SSS-2 has arrival rate λ_2 and service rate μ_2. The performance of each SSS can be computed using M/M/1 or G/G/1 formulas depending on the distributions of the arrival and service processes.

10.6 Worked Examples

After understanding and obtaining the formulas for computing the four key performance measures for the different queue systems, we will apply them into two examples to study queue performance and behaviour.

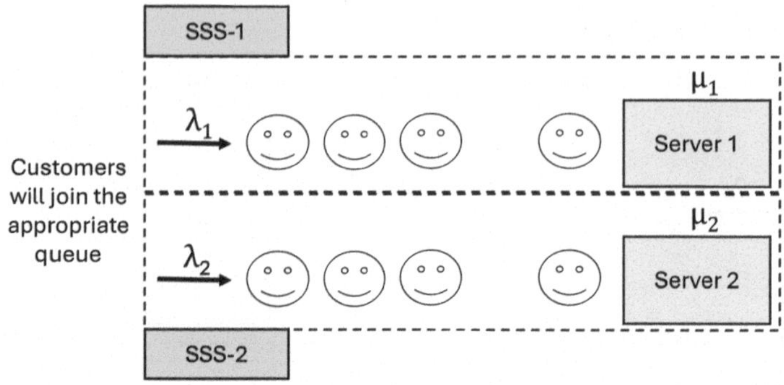

Fig. 10.15 Customer discrimination system (CDS) broken down into two single-stage systems

10.6.1 M/M/1 and M/M/m Queue Example

A food stand with one server serves 75 customers per hour on average. Customers arrive at the queue at an average rate of 60 per hour. The distributions of the arrival and service processes are assumed to be exponential.

1. Determine L_q, W_q, L and W.
2. Due to complaints that the waiting time is too long, the food stand owner hopes to improve the performance of the queue by considering a few possible strategies:
   (a) Adding one more server, that is, m = 2.
   (b) Invest in automation equipment to reduce the service time by half, that is, service rate is doubled to 150 customers per hour.
   (c) Open a second food stand, and shift half the customers to the new food stand, that is, arrival rate is now 30 per hour.

Determine the new L_q, W_q, L and W for each strategy, and comment on the improvements that can be achieved as compared to the base case.

This is an M/M/1 queue with $\mu = 75$ per hour and $\lambda = 60$ per hour. Therefore, $\rho = \frac{\lambda}{\mu} = \frac{60}{75} = 0.8$. Applying the M/M/1 queue performance measure formulas, we will compute the following:

- Average system length

$$L = \frac{\rho}{(1-\rho)} = \frac{0.8}{(1-0.8)} = 4.0$$

- Average system time

$$W = \frac{L}{\lambda} = \frac{4}{60} * 60 = 4.0 \text{ min}$$

- Average queue length

$$L_q = \frac{\rho^2}{(1-\rho)} = \frac{0.8^2}{(1-0.8)} = 3.2$$

- Average queue time

$$W_q = \frac{L_q}{\lambda} = \frac{3.2}{60} * 60 = 3.2 \text{ min}$$

For Strategy 1, adding one more server will modify the queue into an M/M/m queue system and utilization $\rho = \frac{\lambda}{m\mu} = \frac{60}{2 * 75} = 0.4$. The queue performance measures are:

- Average queue time

$$W_q = \frac{\rho^{\sqrt{2(m+1)}-1}}{m(1-\rho)} t_s = \frac{\rho^{\sqrt{2(m+1)}-1}}{m(1-\rho)} \left(\frac{1}{\mu}\right) = \frac{0.4^{\sqrt{2(2+1)}-1}}{2(1-0.4)} \left(\frac{60}{75}\right) = 0.18 \text{ min}$$

- Average system time

$$W = W_q + t_s = W_q + \left(\frac{1}{\mu}\right) = 0.18 + \left(\frac{60}{75}\right) = 0.98 \text{ min}$$

- Average queue length

$$L_q = \lambda W_q = 60 * \frac{0.18}{60} = 0.18$$

- Average system length

$$L = \lambda W = 60 * \frac{0.98}{60} = 0.98$$

For Strategy 2, reducing the service time by half will increase the service rate μ to 150 customers per hour. Thus, utilization $\rho = \frac{\lambda}{\mu} = \frac{60}{150} = 0.4$. The queue performance measures following M/M/1 queue are:

- Average system length

$$L = \frac{\rho}{(1-\rho)} = \frac{0.4}{(1-0.4)} = 0.67$$

- Average system time

$$W = \frac{L}{\lambda} = \frac{0.67}{60} * 60 = 0.67 \text{ min}$$

- Average queue length

$$L_q = \frac{\rho^2}{(1-\rho)} = \frac{0.4^2}{(1-0.4)} = 0.27$$

- Average queue time

$$W_q = \frac{L_q}{\lambda} = \frac{0.27}{60} * 60 = 0.27 \text{ min}$$

For Strategy 3, shifting half the customers to the new food stand, the arrival rate λ is now 30 per hour. Thus, utilization $\rho = \frac{\lambda}{\mu} = \frac{30}{75} = 0.4$. The queue performance measures following M/M/1 queue are:

- Average system length

$$L = \frac{\rho}{(1-\rho)} = \frac{0.4}{(1-0.4)} = 0.67$$

- Average system time

$$W = \frac{L}{\lambda} = \frac{0.67}{30} * 60 = 1.33 \text{ min}$$

- Average queue length

$$L_q = \frac{\rho^2}{(1-\rho)} = \frac{0.4^2}{(1-0.4)} = 0.27$$

- Average queue time

$$W_q = \frac{L_q}{\lambda} = \frac{0.27}{30} * 60 = 0.53 \text{ min}$$

With the computed results, we will tabulate the values in Table 10.1 to compare the improvements that can be achieved for each strategy as compared to the base case.

- Strategy 1—Adding one server will improve all performance measures, with L_q and W_q improving most significantly (almost 95% improvement)
- Strategy 2—Doubling the service rate will improve all performance measures. When compared to Strategy 1, L_q and W_q are longer, but L and W are shorter.
- Strategy 3—Halving the arrival rate will improve all performance measures. When compared to Strategy 1, L_q, W_q and W are longer, but L is shorter.

Depending on the trade-off between the cost of investment and the improvements that can be achieved for each strategy, the food stand will decide which strategy to proceed with. For example, if the investment cost for Strategy 2 to reduce the service time by half is too costly or it is very difficult to reduce the service time, then Strategy 1 or Strategy 3 may be more suitable. Strategy 1 represents one queue with two servers, while Strategy 3 represents two independent queues with two independent servers. Strategy 1 has an overall better performance than Strategy 3 and will likely incur a lower overall cost and thus could be the preferred option.

Table 10.1 Comparison of queue performance for M/M/1 and M/M/m example

	L_q	W_q (min)	L	W (min)
Base case	3.2	3.2	4.0	4.0
Strategy 1—add one server	0.18	0.18	0.98	0.98
Strategy 2—double service rate	0.27	0.27	0.67	0.67
Strategy 3—half arrival rate	0.27	0.53	0.67	1.33

10.6.2 G/G/1 and G/G/m Queue Example

A canned food factory produces canned food using an automated production line. Each empty can will arrive at the server who will scoop the food into the can. Due to automation, the arrival of the empty cans follows a fixed 10-second interval. The server takes about 7 to 9 seconds to fill up each can, following a uniform distribution.

1. Determine L_q, W_q, L and W.
2. The factory receives a large order for their canned food and the factory manager hopes to improve the queue performance considering a few strategies:

   (a) Adding one more server, that is, m = 2.
   (b) Reduce the time interval between arrivals of empty cans to 9 seconds.
   (c) Use a bigger ladle to scoop food into the can, thus reducing the time taken to fill up each can to between 5 and 7 seconds, following a uniform distribution.

Determine the new L_q, W_q, L and W for each strategy, and comment on the improvements that can be achieved as compared to the base case.

For the service rate following a uniform distribution:

- Average service time is computed as (max + min)/2 = (9+7)/2 = 8.
- Standard deviation is computed as $\frac{(\max - \min)}{\sqrt{12}} = \frac{(9-7)}{\sqrt{12}} = 0.577$.

This is a G/G/1 queue with $\lambda = 60/10 = 6$ per minute, and the service rate $\mu = 60/8 = 7.5$ per minute. The server utilization $\rho = \frac{\lambda}{\mu} = \frac{6}{7.5} = 0.8$. Applying the G/G/1 queue performance measure formulas, we will compute the following:

- Coefficient of variation of arrival process with a fixed time interval, $C_a = 0$ since SD = 0.

- Coefficient of variation of service process following a uniform distribution, $C_s = \frac{SD}{mean} = \frac{0.577}{8} = 0.072$.

- Average queue time

$$W_q = \left(\frac{C_a^2 + C_s^2}{2}\right)\frac{\rho}{(1-\rho)}t_s = \left(\frac{0^2 + 0.072^2}{2}\right)\frac{0.8}{(1-0.8)}8 = 0.083 \text{ seconds}$$

- Average queue length

$$L_q = \lambda W_q = 6 * 0.083/60 = 0.008$$

- Average system time

$$W = W_q + t_s = 0.083 + 8 = 8.083 \text{ seconds}$$

- Average system length

$$L = \lambda W = 6 * 8.083/60 = 0.808$$

For Strategy 1, adding one more server will modify the queue into a G/G/m queue system and utilization $\rho = \frac{\lambda}{m\mu} = \frac{6}{2 * 7.5} = 0.4$. The queue performance measures are:

- Average queue time

$$W_q = \left(\frac{C_a^2 + C_s^2}{2}\right) \frac{\rho^{\sqrt{2(m+1)}-1}}{m(1-\rho)} t_s = \left(\frac{0^2 + 0.072^2}{2}\right) \frac{0.4^{\sqrt{2(2+1)}-1}}{2(1-0.4)} 8 = 0.005 \text{ seconds}$$

- Average queue length

$$L_q = \lambda W_q = 6 * \frac{0.005}{60} = 0.0005$$

- Average system time

$$W = W_q + t_s = 0.005 + 8 = 8.005 \text{ seconds}$$

- Average system length

$$L = \lambda W = 6 * \frac{8.005}{60} = 0.8005$$

For Strategy 2, reducing the time interval between arrivals of empty cans to 9 seconds will increase the arrival rate λ to 6.7 per minute. Thus, utilization $\rho = \frac{\lambda}{\mu} = \frac{6.7}{7.5} = 0.89$. The queue performance measures following G/G/1 queue are:

- Average queue time

$$W_q = \left(\frac{C_a^2 + C_s^2}{2}\right) \frac{\rho}{(1-\rho)} t_s = \left(\frac{0^2 + 0.072^2}{2}\right) \frac{0.89}{(1-0.89)} 8 = 0.167 \text{ seconds}$$

- Average queue length

$$L_q = \lambda W_q = 6.7 * 0.167/60 = 0.019$$

- Average system time

$$W = W_q + t_s = 0.167 + 8 = 8.167 \text{ seconds}$$

- Average system length

$$L = \lambda W = 6 * 8.167/60 = 0.907$$

For Strategy 3, reducing the time taken to fill up each can to between 5 and 7 seconds, following a uniform distribution, will change the mean and standard deviation to:

- Average service time is computed as (max + min)/2 = (7+5)/2 = 6.
- Standard deviation is computed as $\frac{(\max - \min)}{\sqrt{12}} = \frac{(7-5)}{\sqrt{12}} = 0.577$.

The new service rate μ = 60/[(5+7)/2] = 10 per minute. Thus, utilization $\rho = \frac{\lambda}{\mu} = \frac{6}{10} = 0.6$. The queue performance measures following G/G/1 queue are:

- Coefficient of variation of service process following a uniform distribution, $C_s = \frac{SD}{mean} = \frac{0.577}{6} = 0.096$.
- Average queue time

$$W_q = \left(\frac{C_a^2 + C_s^2}{2}\right)\frac{\rho}{(1-\rho)}t_s = \left(\frac{0^2 + 0.096^2}{2}\right)\frac{0.6}{(1-0.6)}6 = 0.042 \text{ seconds}$$

- Average queue length

$$L_q = \lambda W_q = 6 * 0.042/60 = 0.004$$

- Average system time

$$W = W_q + t_s = 0.042 + 6 = 6.042 \text{ seconds}$$

- Average system length

Table 10.2 Comparison of queue performance for G/G/1 and G/G/m example

	L_q	W_q (s)	L	W (s)
Base case	0.008	0.083	0.808	8.083
Strategy 1—add one server	0.0005	0.005	0.8005	8.005
Strategy 2—reduce inter-arrival time to 9 s	0.019	0.167	0.907	8.167
Strategy 3—reduce service time to between 5 and 7 s	0.004	0.042	0.604	6.042

$$L = \lambda W = 6 * 6.042/60 = 0.604$$

With the computed results, we will tabulate the values in Table 10.2 to compare the improvements that can be achieved for each strategy as compared to the base case.

- Strategy 1—Adding one server will improve L_q and W_q significantly, but L and W remain almost the same.
- Strategy 2—Reducing the inter-arrival time of the empty cans to 9 seconds would worsen all the performance measures.
- Strategy 3—Reducing the service time to between 5 and 7 seconds improves all performance measures.

Among all the strategies, Strategy 3 seems to be the best strategy if using a bigger ladle to scoop food into the can cuts the average service time by 2 seconds, and the performance of the queue outperforms base case and the other two strategies. Sometimes, a simple solution like changing to a bigger ladle can create such a big improvement in the real world!

10.7 Case 10: Queue Buster at a Grocery Store

This case is modified from the paper published by Cheong and Chia (2019). In this case, we will determine the effectiveness of a queue buster tool to better manage the queue performance for a grocery store. Queue busting is a form of intervention action to reduce customer's wait time and system time and also system length, by pre-processing some steps in the queue system. Specifically, customers will be attended to by service staff who will scan the items using a handheld device and pack their items into bags while customers are waiting in the queue. This will remove the time needed for scanning and packing at the cashier counter, and the only remaining step is payment, reducing the service time. To facilitate payment, the cashier will scan a paper with a payment QR code generated by the handheld device.

Queue busting should only be implemented when the system length is of substantial length. Implementing it when system length is short will be premature and incur unnecessary manpower cost, while implementing when system length is too long will not enjoy significant improvements. The challenge is to determine the

Table 10.3 Mean, SD, Cs, μ and ρ for different queue situations

	Mean (m:ss)	SD (m:ss)	$C_s = \frac{SD}{Mean}$	μ	Utilization $\rho = \frac{\lambda}{\mu}$
No QB	1:12	1:36	1.345	50.3	1.15
QB Trigger 3	0:51	1:15	1.462	70.0	0.83
QB Trigger 4	0:53	1:16	1.426	67.7	0.86
QB Trigger 5	0:54	1:18	1.423	66.1	0.88
QB Trigger 6	0:56	1:22	1.451	63.9	0.91
QB Trigger 7	0:57	1:20	1.419	63.5	0.91
QB Trigger 8	0:57	1:22	1.432	62.7	0.93
QB Trigger 9	0:58	1:23	1.430	61.9	0.94
QB Trigger 10	0:59	1:25	1.458	61.4	0.95

optimal system length to trigger queue busting (termed as the trigger point) to derive a reasonable improvement in queue performance while considering the manpower time and cost to perform queue busting. We will look at how to apply the formulas for G/G/1 queue to solve this case.

First, let us understand the data collected and the related computations given in Table 10.3:

- The average inter-arrival time (t_a) of customers to the store was found to follow a distribution with mean 1:02 and standard deviation of 0:59.
- The arrival process will have an average rate $\lambda = 60$ min/1:02 = 58 per hour.
- CV of arrival process, $C_a = \frac{SD}{mean} = \frac{0:59}{1:02} = 0.949$.
- Without queue busting (denoted as No QB), the average service time (t_s) at the cashier counter will include the time taken to scan and pack the items and the payment time. The mean and standard deviation are shown in Table 10.3.
- With queue busting, only customers who are facing system length >= trigger point will be queue busted. For such customers, their service time at the cashier counter is only the payment time, while the other customers will still have to go through the scanning, packing and payment process. The average service times (t_s) for different trigger points are obtained, and the mean and standard deviation are given in Table 10.3, denoted as QB Trigger x where x is the system length.
- CV of service process, $C_s = \frac{SD}{mean}$ are also computed for all cases.
- The service rate μ for each situation, without and with queue busting, is computed and given in Table 10.3.
- Finally, using the arrival rate and service rate for each situation, the utilization $\rho = \frac{\lambda}{\mu}$ can be computed and given in Table 10.3.

Applying the G/G/1 formulas below, we will tabulate the four performance measures for all the situations in Table 10.4. Note that for No QB situation, there will be no answer for all the performance measures because $\rho = 1.15 > 1$, which will result in W_q having a negative number. This implies that the queue is unstable with

Table 10.4 Grocery store queue performance

	W_q (m:ss)	L_q	W (m:ss)	L
No QB	No answer	No answer	No answer	No answer
QB Trigger 3	6:18	6.1	7:10	6.9
QB Trigger 4	7:52	7.6	8:45	8.5
QB Trigger 5	9:39	9.3	10:34	10.2
QB Trigger 6	13:59	13.5	14:55	14.4
QB Trigger 7	14:35	14.1	15:32	15.0
QB Trigger 8	17:30	16.9	18:28	17.9
QB Trigger 9	21:19	20.6	22:18	21.6
QB Trigger 10	25:52	25.0	26:51	26.0

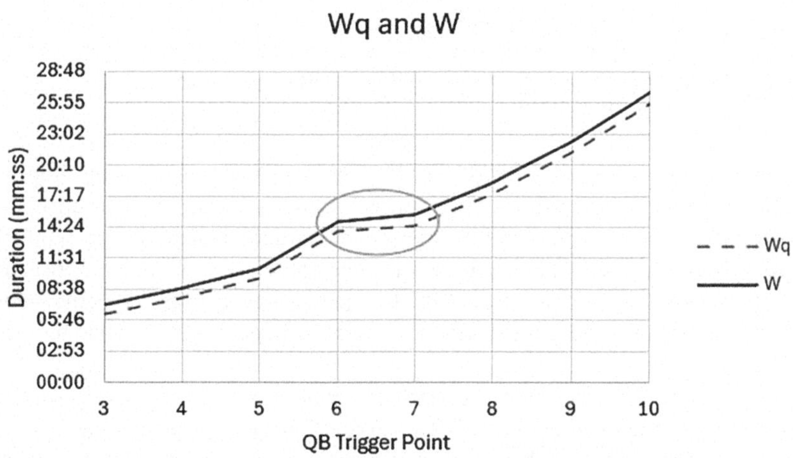

Fig. 10.16 Performance measures W_q and W at different QB trigger points

an exploding queue length, while G/G/1 formulas are for steady-state queue system computations.

- Average queue time, $W_q = \left(\frac{C_a^2 + C_s^2}{2}\right) \frac{\rho}{(1-\rho)} t_s.$
- Average queue length, $L_q = \lambda W_q.$
- Average system time, $W = W_q + t_s.$
- Average system length, $L = \lambda W.$

We can visualize the performance measures W_q and W in Fig. 10.16 and L_q and L in Fig. 10.17. All four performance measure values increase as the QB trigger point increases from 3 to 10. At low trigger points 3, 4 and 5, we can achieve larger

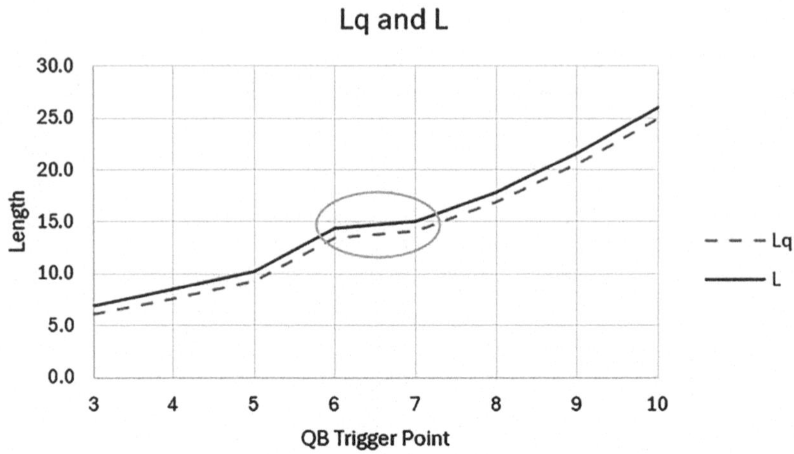

Fig. 10.17 Performance measures L_q and L at different QB trigger points

improvements in performance measures but may incur manpower cost to implement queue buster prematurely. While at high trigger points 8, 9 and 10, the improvements in performance measures may not be significant enough. Trigger points 6 and 7 are ideal to achieve a good balance between acceptable performance improvements versus the cost of manpower incurred. The performance improvements between trigger points 6 and 7 are almost identical; thus, trigger point 7 would be a better choice.

In the paper by Cheong and Chia (2019), they have used Monte Carlo simulation to simulate the queue system for 50 customer arrivals to determine the queue performance. The values of the queue performance measures W_q, W, L_q and L are different than those computed in Table 10.4, and the recommended trigger points were between 4 and 6. The difference between the answers can be attributed to the fact that formulas for G/G/1 queue are approximations based on steady-state queue, as compared to running the queue simulation from cold start.

Let us map the problem and solution method for this case study against the *data and decision analytics framework* proposed in Chap. 1. As shown in Fig. 10.18, in this case study, the problem faced was long queue at the check-out counters at the grocery store. Therefore, the right question to ask was "How to improve queue performance using queue buster?". Next, was to collect the relevant data, which will be needed to answer the question which includes the distribution of the inter-arrival time of customers and the distributions of service times for situations when there is no queue busting and when there is queue busting at different trigger points. With the data collected, the initial data exploration highlighted that the queue system will be unstable without queue busting. From this insight, it was proposed that queue busting will be needed to ensure stable queue system to achieve acceptable queue performance. Thus, the problem objective would be to determine the best trigger point to implement queue buster to balance the cost of implementation and, at the

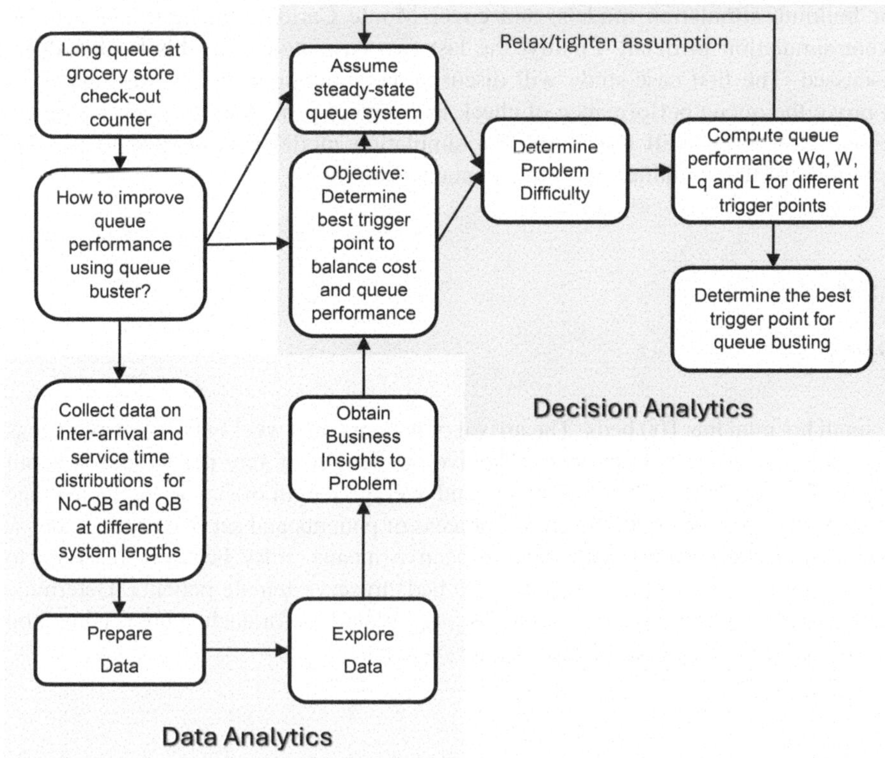

Fig. 10.18 Data and decision analytics framework map for Case 10

same time, achieve significant queue performance improvements. Using the universal formulas for G/G/1 queue system, the performance measures can be computed to obtain the solution to the problem.

10.8 Summary

This chapter began by covering the queue system terminology before discussing the six different types of queues. Next, two groups of queue performance measures, namely, time-based and length-based were discussed. Kendall's Notation was introduced to represent different types of queues, followed by universal relationships and Little's Law, which were used to compute queue performance for M/M/1, M/M/m, G/G/1 and G/G/m queues. Finally, a case study on how to use queue buster to improve queue performance at a grocery store was discussed. In the next chapter, we will cover the topic on simulation, where we will first learn about the different types of simulation models, and a few common probability distribution functions useful for building simulation models, and cover Monte Carlo Simulation and discrete event simulation in detail. Finally, the last two case studies in this book will be discussed. The first case study will discuss how simulation model was applied to improve the queue performance of check-in counters at an Asian airport, while the second case study will discuss how a simulation model was applied to test the feasibility of the container flows at a container terminal.

Exercises

Q10.1

A small hospital has 100 beds. The arrival of patients on a weekly basis on average is 120 male and 80 female patients. The average length of stay per patient is about 5 days. Consider the beds to be servers and average length of stay to be the average service time. Assume both the arrival process of patients and service process follow exponential distributions with their respective means. Fifty beds are reserved to serve male patients and the remaining 50 beds to serve female patients. Determine the performance of the queue system (W_q, L_q, W and L) for each gender. Hint: You are to model two separate M/M/m queue systems.

Q10.2

A small hospital has 100 beds. The arrival of patients on a weekly basis on average is 120 male and 80 female patients. For male patients, the average length of stay follows a uniform distribution of a minimum of 2 days to a maximum of 4 days. For female patients, the average length of stay follows a uniform distribution of a minimum of 3 days to a maximum of 5 days. Consider the beds to be servers and average length of stay to be the average service time. Assume the arrival process of patients to follow an exponential distribution with their respective means. Fifty beds are reserved to serve the male patients and the remaining 50 beds to serve the female patients. Determine the performance of the queue system (W_q, L_q, W and L) for each gender. Hint: You are to model two separate G/G/m queue systems.

Q10.3

A small hospital has 100 beds. The arrival of patients on a weekly basis on average is 120 male and 80 female patients. The average length of stay per patient follows a uniform distribution of a minimum of 3 days to a maximum of 5 days. Consider the beds to be servers and average length of stay to be the average service time. Assume the arrival process of patients to follow exponential distributions with their respective means. Thirty beds are reserved to serve male patients, 30 beds to serve female patients and the remaining 40 beds are shared between both genders. To simplify the problem, the hospital will direct 60 male patients to the 30 beds reserved for male patients and the remaining 60 male patients to the 40 shared beds. For female patients, 60 will be directed to the 30 beds reserved for female patients and the remaining 20 to the 40 shared beds. Determine the performance of the queue system (W_q, L_q, W and L) for each gender. Hint: You are to model three separate G/G/m queue systems.

References

Cheong, M. L. F., & Chia, Y. Q. (2019). *Simulation model to evaluate effectiveness of queue management tool in supermarket retail chain* (pp. 606–610). 2019 International Conference on Industrial Engineering and Engineering Management (IEEM), Macao, Proceedings. IEEE. https://doi.org/10.1109/IEEM44572.2019.8978794

Sakasegawa, H. (1977). An approximation formula $L_q \simeq \alpha \cdot \rho^{\beta}/(1-\rho)$. *Annals of the Institute of Statistical Mathematics, 29*, 67–75. https://doi.org/10.1007/BF02532775

Chapter 11
Simulation

Simulation models are commonly used to simulate environments in different business operations covering different industries. Simulation models will duplicate the characteristics of a real-world system using mathematical and statistical models to mimic the actual operations as closely as possible to represent the reality.

In the military, simulation models are used to mimic the battlefield to analyse attack and defend strategies, and to test out the new weapons of destruction within the simulated environment. In the airline industry, flight simulators are used to train pilots in the skills required to fly the plane before they get on to the actual plane for real flights. In the shipping container terminal, yard crane operators are trained using simulators in the training labs before they can operate the cranes to load and unload huge containers at the ports. In the financial world, simulation models are also vastly used to test various trading strategies to minimize investment risk or optimize the return of investment. In Chap. 10, we have discussed queuing theory and queue systems, as well as the formulas to compute the performance of different queue systems. Simulation models can also be used to represent queue systems to estimate queue performance.

In this chapter, we will first examine different types of simulation models and discuss a framework to guide the building of simulation models. Next, we will describe some commonly used probability distributions, including uniform, exponential and normal distributions, used for generating random input values to run simulation models to obtain output results. We will then focus on Monte Carlo simulation and discrete-event simulation models and illustrate their applications using worked examples and case studies.

Learning Outcomes

By the end of this chapter, readers will achieve the following learning outcomes:

- Discuss the purpose, advantages and disadvantages of simulation models.
- Identify the types of simulation models.
- Classify simulation models.
- Describe discrete-, continuous- and discrete-continuous event simulations.

M. L. F. Cheong, Ma Nang Laik, *Data and Decision Analytics for Business Operations*, https://doi.org/10.1007/978-3-031-72255-4_11

- Explain the guiding steps to build simulation models.
- Describe the commonly used probability distribution functions.
- Explain how to use the probability distribution functions for random generation of input values.
- Describe Monte Carlo simulation.
- Build Monte Carlo simulation model and obtain results.
- Describe discrete-event simulation key components.
- Discuss how discrete-event simulation was applied in real-world scenarios to determine the optimal number of check-in counters at the airport and to simulate container flows at the container port terminal, using the *data and decision analytics framework.*

11.1 Purposes, Advantages and Disadvantages

Simulated environment can help businesses save multi-million dollars in providing training without the use of actual equipment and tools, avoid creating undesirable outcomes in the real world, avoid any fatal or major accidents from happening before the actual operation, and allow testing and validating complex and stochastic systems without having to build the actual environment.

The purposes of using simulation are numerous and are not limited to the list below:

- To develop a model in a risk-free environment which can imitate the real-world system
- To achieve a better understanding of the behaviours of the system
- To test out new policies before implementation to minimize the risk
- To understand the impact of changes on system performance
- To test "what-if" scenarios that may occur in the real world
- To capture the system dynamics, which we are unable to do so in the analytical model

Simulation models are widely accepted by operations managers in the real-world due to various reasons. Some of the main advantages are listed below:

- Simulation is flexible, and input parameters can be changed easily.
- Simulation can be used to analyse large and complex real-world situations where empirical results or exact solutions cannot be solved by the conventional methods.
- Simulation allows "what-if" scenarios and questions. Users can use simulation to know in advance if a new strategy works before the actual implementation.
- Simulation also helps us identify the bottleneck in a business process by collecting system performance indicators.

The main disadvantages of simulation are as follows:

- Simulation models are time-consuming and expensive to build. It may take several months and sometimes even years to develop. So, it should not be used if analytical methods can produce the solution faster.
- Simulation model may not produce "good" or "accurate" answers if the input is not realistic and the conditions are not correctly modelled.
- Simulation result may vary each time, and it does not generate the optimal solution like linear programming model.

11.2 Types of Simulation Models

There are two main types of models: physical (replica) models and abstract (mathematical) models. In the case of building a rocket, a robot or a new airplane, due to the high investment cost involved, part of the design process is to build a physical replica model. However, there is a limit to what a physical model can provide in terms of output information, which might be of interest to the engineer or designer. A good mathematical simulation model, which can capture and represent real system behaviours, the relationships and interactions between processes, can produce more meaningful outputs and insights.

To better understand the different types of mathematical simulation models, we will introduce some terminologies based on Banks et al. (1995):

- An *entity* is a tangible object found in the real-world application. For example, a truck is an entity in a simulation model representing a road network.
- Entities have distinct *attributes*. For example, the attributes of the truck can be the truck type and the driving speed.
- A *system* is a collection of entities like trucks, traffic lights and people, which will interact together towards the accomplishment of some logical end.
- The *state* of the system is a collection of variables that describe the system at a particular time. For example, the state of a road network can be the number of vehicles waiting at a junction.
- An *event* is an instantaneous occurrence that something has happened and will change the state of the system. For example, the traffic light turns green, and the number of vehicles waiting at a junction reduces.
- An *activity* is a task that occurs at a certain time. For example, the trucks are traveling at 20 miles per hour towards the north-east direction at 9:00 a.m.

We can broadly classify simulation models according to two dimensions: static vs dynamic, and deterministic vs stochastic, as described below:

1. *Static vs dynamic simulation models*

A *static* simulation, often known as Monte Carlo simulation, represents the system at a certain point in time; therefore, time is not a factor for consideration when running the model. The model is run repeatedly over many trials by simulating different input values using probability functions and obtaining the corresponding output values. The outcome of interest from the model is computed from the output values. For example, the winning odds for the game of poker can be estimated by repeatedly playing the game with different hands of cards (as input) and obtaining the wins vs losses to compute the odds.

On the other hand, a *dynamic* simulation model simulates the *time-varying* behaviour of a dynamical system to determine the state variables over a specified duration. For example, we can simulate the migration of a virus in a neighbourhood over a period of 3 days to determine how contagious this virus can be.

2. *Deterministic vs stochastic simulation models*

A *deterministic* model does not contain any probabilistic behaviour where the input values are known and fixed values, and therefore the output values are also determined. For example, if it is known with certainty that there is a 90% chance of surviving an earthquake, then 900 people will survive the earthquake out of 1000. However, it is rare to find deterministic situations in the real world as many systems have at least some components, which are random and unpredictable. Thus, for a *stochastic* model, the input values are random, and therefore the output values will vary depending on the input values.

For dynamic (time-varying) and stochastic (probabilistic) simulation models, the three types covered in this chapter are defined below:

1. *Discrete-event simulation*

The simulation system is a collection of sequence of events for each entity's behaviour. Each event happens at an instant in time and changes the state of the system. For example, a bank customer arrives at the bank teller (an arrival event), gets served by the teller (a service event) and then leaves the bank after getting served (a departure event). In this example, the discrete-event simulation model models the sequence of events which occur at discrete time instant. The simulation clock time moves from one event to the next with random or irregular time intervals.

2. *Continuous-event simulation*

In continuous-event simulation models, the state variables in the system change continuously with respect to time. The model uses differential equations to represent the relationship between the rate of change of state variables with time. Common use of continuous-event simulation models includes engineering systems such as flight simulators, advanced engineering design tools and computer games.

3. *Combined discrete-continuous-event simulation*

It is sometimes difficult to differentiate systems as pure discrete or pure continuous systems. In such cases, we will use the combined discrete-continuous-event simulation models. For example, in a steel mill, the production process of steel can follow a discrete-event simulation, while the temperature of the steel is controlled by known physics using differential equations.

11.3 Guide to Building Simulation Models

Regardless of whether one builds a static or dynamic model, we recommend the following guiding steps to build a successful simulation model:

Step 1—problem formulation

The first step is to identify the problem statement, record the valid assumptions in the system and determine the possible inputs of the system. It is important to understand the problem clearly and define the objective of the simulation study and expected outputs. We can collect data from the real-world situation and approximate the parameters to be used for the input values; otherwise the input values will be estimated based on experience and domain knowledge.

For example, a popular burger stand is facing a long queue situation, and we are interested in determining the optimal number of servers the burger stand should have to ensure that the system time will not exceed 10 minutes. We can assume that customers arrive one at a time and there is no balking (customers decided not to join the queue when the queue length is too long) or reneging (customers leave the queue after joining the queue when the queue time is too long) phenomena. The inputs to the queue system will be the arrival process and service process parameters. By collecting data of the arrival time, service start time and service end time of the actual queue in operation, we can approximate the input parameters to the simulation model.

Step 2—conceptual model formulation

Once the objective of the system is identified, a conceptual model which captures the important essence and elements of the real-world situation will be built. The model-building process is one of the most important parts of system building, which requires full understanding and experiences with the real system. For example, the burger stand queue system can be modeled as an M/M/m or G/G/m model (see Chap. 10 on Queuing Theory) so that different sets of simulation results can be obtained by varying the number of servers.

Step 3—design and develop the simulation model

At this stage, the modeler will translate the conceptual model into a computer program, which is the simulation model. There are a few options available to build the simulation model. One can either use a third-party commercial simulation software tool like FlexSim, Arena, AutoMod or Simul8, or use simulation languages such as GPSS or Sim++, or use general-purpose programming languages like C++, C#, Java, or even use the Excel Spreadsheet tool. For example, the burger stand queue system can be built using an Excel tool to run multiple simulation trials to get the desired outcome.

Step 4—model verification and validation

After the simulation model has been developed, the final step is to verify and validate the program. Verification is the process of determining whether the problem statement has been accurately transformed to build the model right. Validation concerns whether the simulation model accurately represents the real-world system and whether the model output performs accurately according to the system objectives.

At this stage, the modeler will conduct many experimental runs, analyse the output and check if the simulation program requires modification. Finally, the output results will be presented to the intended users, who are interested in the outcome of this study. For the burger stand example, the modeler can set different number of servers and, for each setting, run multiple simulation trials to get the output results. The optimal number of servers will be the one that can achieve the desired system time of less than 10 minutes.

Step 1 to Step 4 described above are high-level guiding steps. To further break down Steps 3 and 4 into the next-level tasks, the sub-steps to develop, verify and validate the simulation model are described below:

(a) Set up probability distribution function for the input variables using historical data. If an input variable follows a known distribution such as uniform, exponential or normal, compute the parameters for the distribution accordingly.
(b) Compute the cumulative probability distribution for each input variable. If the input variable follows the known distribution, this step is not needed.
(c) Randomly generate input values using random generators for each input variable, and run the simulation. For known distributions such as uniform, exponential or normal, apply the formulas discussed in Sect. 11.4. Readers are encouraged to explore other distribution functions on their own.
(d) Obtain the output results.
(e) Repeat steps (c) and (d) many times to obtain many output results. Smaller variances are preferred by increasing the number of trials.
(f) Compute the outcome of interest, which could be the summary statistics, the distribution of the output results, or the probability of a certain desired outcome (e.g. probability that 90% of the customers at the burger stand need not wait for more than 10 minutes in the queue).

With a good understanding of the guiding steps, we will now delve into a few probability distribution functions, which are commonly used for the random generation of input values as highlighted in step (c) above.

11.4 Probability Distributions for Simulation

In this section, we will discuss a few probability distribution functions that are commonly used for the random generation of input values to the simulation models. We will provide a brief description and review of the key characteristics of each probability distribution function.

11.4.1 Continuous Uniform Distribution

The continuous uniform distribution is defined by the parameters, minimum a and maximum b values. The distribution is written as U (a, b), and it is represented as a rectangle with the horizontal axis representing the x values, which can only be between a and b, and the vertical axis is the probability density function (pdf) given as

$$f(x) = \frac{1}{(b-a)}, a \leq x \leq b$$

As seen from Fig. 11.1, the distribution has a constant f(x) for all the x values between a and b, and there are infinite number of such x values. As such, continuous uniform distribution is useful for simulating input values, which are continuous in nature, for example, the weight or height of students.

In Excel, the RAND() function is a random generator that can randomly generate a value between [0,1). We can use the formula below to randomly generate a new x' value from a continuous uniform distribution

$$x' = (b-a)^* \text{ RAND}() + a$$

In Excel, pressing the Enter key or F9 key will cause the RAND() function to recalculate and generate a new random number. This is how we can simulate different random input values to run multiple simulation trials. If we want to freeze and retain the generated values, we will Copy and Paste by Value.

11.4.2 Discrete Uniform Distribution

Similar to continuous uniform distribution, the shape for discrete uniform distribution is also rectangular, except there are finite number of x values. For example, when tossing an unbiased six-sided die, the possible x values are 1, 2, 3, 4, 5 and 6, which represent the face that turns up, as shown in Fig. 11.2. The uniform

Fig. 11.1 Continuous uniform distribution

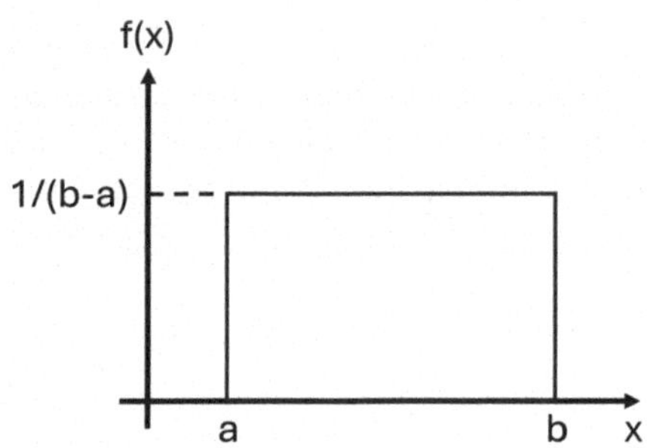

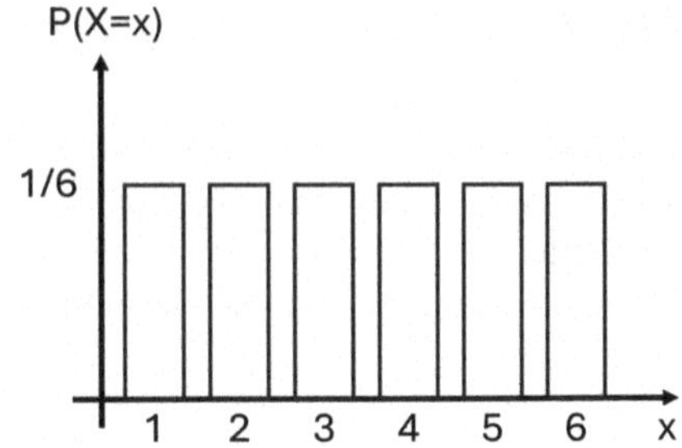

Fig. 11.2 Discrete uniform distribution

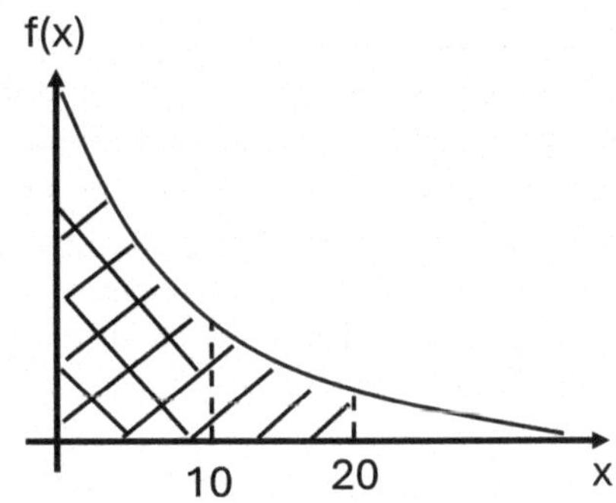

Fig. 11.3 Exponential distribution

distribution gives the same probability of 1/6, known as the probability mass function $P(X = x)$ for all the possible x values between 1 and 6, where the minimum value a is 1 and the maximum value b is 6.

In Excel, to randomly generate a new discrete x' value, we can use the Excel function RANDBETWEEN(min, max). For a tossed unbiased six-sided die, the new x' will be generated using RANDBETWEEN(1, 6) where each number between 1 and 6 will have the same probability of 1/6 of turning up. As such, discrete uniform distribution is useful for simulating input values, which are discrete in nature, for example, the number of customers turning up at the burger stand per day can follow a discrete uniform distribution of a minimum of 50 to a maximum of 100.

11.4.3 Exponential Distribution

The inter-arrival time x of an arrival process is usually described by an exponential distribution. The probability density function f(x) of the exponential distribution is shown in Fig. 11.3. An exponential distribution is defined by the parameter arrival rate λ, and $1/\lambda$ will be the average inter-arrival time. The f(x) function is given as

$$f(x) = \begin{cases} \lambda e^{-\lambda x} & , x \geq 0 \\ 0 & , x < 0 \end{cases}$$

To understand the exponential distribution curve, we use the curve to represent time to failure of a light bulb. Referring to Fig. 11.3, by integrating the f(x) function from 0 to x, the area under the curve to the left of x will be the probability. The probability that the light bulb will fail in 10 months will be the area under the curve to the left of x = 10, while the probability that the light bulb will fail in 20 months will be the area under the curve to the left of x = 20. We can see that the area for 20 months is larger than that for 10 months, which implies that the longer we use the bulb, the higher the probability that the light bulb will fail. This makes perfect sense!

To simulate the random inter-arrival time for an event with an average inter-arrival time 1/λ, we can use the following formula:

$$x' = -(1/\lambda)^{*}\ \mathrm{LN}\ (\mathrm{RAND}())$$

11.4.4 Normal Distribution

One of the most common distributions is the normal distribution. It is often called the bell-shaped curve and is symmetric about the mean μ with standard deviation σ as shown in Fig. 11.4. According to the empirical rule, about 68% of the area under the normal curve is with $\mu \pm \sigma$, and about 95% of the area under the normal curve is within two standard deviations from the mean, $\mu \pm 2\sigma$. Almost all the data under the normal curve are within three standard deviations of the mean, $\mu \pm 3\sigma$.

According to the central limit theorem, if a sample of a specific size ($n \geq 30$) is selected from a population, the sampling distribution can be approximated to a normal distribution. If the sample size is increased further ($n \gg 30$), then the sample distribution will draw closer to a normal distribution. This is why the normal distribution is widely used in many real-world situations where we have little or no information about the sample mean and its distribution. For example, normal distribution can be used to describe the salary of a graduate from a business school.

Fig. 11.4 Normal distribution

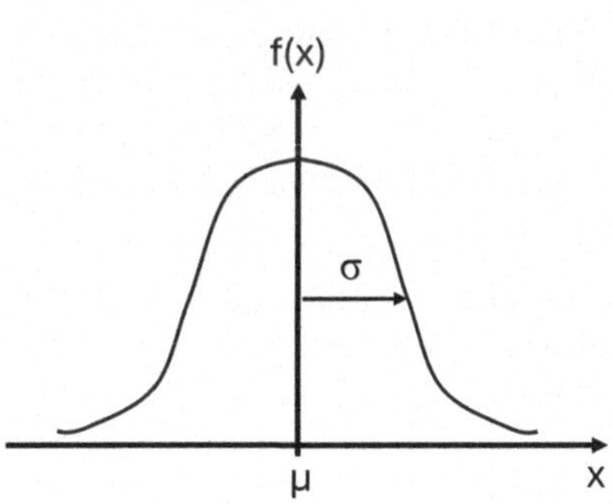

The normal distribution with parameters mean μ and variance σ^2 is written as $X \sim N(\mu,\sigma^2)$. The probability density function is given as

$$f(x) = \frac{1}{\sigma\sqrt{2\pi}} e^{-\frac{1}{2}\left(\frac{x-\mu}{\sigma}\right)^2}$$

To simulate a random value of x' following a normal distribution using Excel, we can use the NORMINV() function according to the formula

$$x' = \text{NORMINV}\ (\text{RAND}(), \mu, \sigma)$$

11.5 Monte Carlo Simulation

In this section, we will explore the Monte Carlo simulation, which is a static simulation model, and apply the steps described in Sect. 11.3 to build the Monte Carlo simulation model to obtain the desired outcome for a worked example.

Monte Carlo simulation was invented by John von Neumann and Stanislaw Ulam during WWII to improve decision-making under uncertainty (Los Alamos National Lab, n.d.). It was named after the random behaviour of a roulette wheel. The main idea is to compute the probability of different outcomes by means of repeated random sampling of input values to facilitate better decision-making from the insights obtained. In real-world systems, many variables are probabilistic in nature, for example, the chances of having a rain shower today, the likelihood of share price going up for a particular stock, the chances that the train will breakdown, the time between the machine breakdowns, and the number of customers arriving at a burger stand. Let us use an example to illustrate how to conduct Monte Carlo simulation using the Excel tool, following the steps described in Sect. 11.3.

Amy operates an online store selling tee shirts. Based on the historical data on daily demand, the probability table is given in Table 11.1. For example, the probability that the demand is 50 units is 0.05, the probability that demand is 75 units is 0.15 and so on. The unit selling price of a tee shirt is \$10, and the cost price is \$7. Due to supply issues, her supplier requires her to order exactly 100 tee shirts per day, regardless of the daily demand she faces. Using Monte Carlo simulation, determine the average profit for a year. Run the simulation for 100 trials.

Table 11.1 Probability distribution of daily demand for tee shirts

Daily demand for tee shirts	Probability
50	0.05
75	0.15
100	0.30
120	0.35
150	0.15

Table 11.2 Cumulative probability distribution of daily demand for tee shirts

Daily demand for tee shirts	Probability	Cumulative probability
50	0.05	0.0
75	0.15	0.05
100	0.30	0.20
120	0.35	0.50
150	0.15	0.85

Table A		
Unit price	$	10.00
Unit Cost	$	7.00
Order quantity	100	

Table B		
Daily demand	Probability	Cumulative Probability
50	0.05	0.00
75	0.15	0.05
100	0.30	0.20
120	0.35	0.50
150	0.15	0.85

Table C				
Day	Daily Demand	Revenue		Profit
1	120	$1,000	$	300.00
2	150	$1,000	$	300.00
3	100	$1,000	$	300.00
4	120	$1,000	$	300.00
5	100	$1,000	$	300.00
96	75	$750	$	50.00
97	100	$1,000	$	300.00
98	100	$1,000	$	300.00
99	100	$1,000	$	300.00
100	75	$750	$	50.00
101	50	$500	$	(200.00)
102	75	$750	$	50.00
103	100	$1,000	$	300.00
104	100	$1,000	$	300.00
105	120	$1,000	$	300.00
360	120	$1,000	$	300.00
361	120	$1,000	$	300.00
362	100	$1,000	$	300.00
363	75	$750	$	50.00
364	100	$1,000	$	300.00
365	100	$1,000	$	300.00
		Total annual profit	$	85,750

Table D		
Trial #	$	85,750
1	$	88,000
2	$	90,250
3	$	86,250
4	$	87,750
5	$	88,000
96	$	85,000
97	$	91,250
98	$	84,750
99	$	87,750
100	$	86,250

Table E		
Average	$	86,930
Min	$	81,500
Max	$	92,500
Standard Deviation	$	2,468

Fig. 11.5 Monte Carlo simulation model for tee shirts example

Step (a): The input variable is the daily demand for tee shirts, and the distribution is given in Table 11.1.

Step (b): Since the daily demand for tee shirts does not follow any known distribution, the cumulative probability is computed in Table 11.2. Note that we always start with cumulative probability of 0.0 to correspond to the first x value. This is to facilitate the random generation of x using Excel LOOKUP() function.

Step (c): Randomly generate the daily demand for tee shirts for 365 days using random generators, and run the simulation. Figure 11.5 shows the Monte Carlo simulation model setup.

- The unit price, unit cost and order quantity are set up in Table A.
- The probability and cumulative probability tables are set up in Table B.

- In Table C (some rows are hidden):
  - Day 1 to Day 365 is labeled in column B.
  - The daily demand is randomly generated using the formula C12 = LOOKUP (RAND(),$G$4:$G$8,$E$4:$E$8) and filled for all cells in column C.

Step (d): With the randomly generated demand in column C, we can compute the revenue per day in cells D12:D376 in Table C using the formula D12 = MIN(C12,$ C$6)*$C$4. Since the daily order quantity is 100 (in cell C6), the formula will compare the daily demand with the daily order quantity of 100 and pick the smaller value to compute the revenue. For example, if the demand is 80, then only 80 tee shirts are sold, and the revenue will be $80 \times 10 = 800$. However, if the demand is 120, only 100 tee shirts can be sold, and the revenue will be $10 \times 100 = 1000$.

Since the daily order quantity is fixed at 100, the daily cost will be $= 100 * 7 = 700$. Then, profit can be calculated as revenue − cost. In cells E12:E376 in Table C, the formula to compute the profit in Cell E12 = D12-($C$6*$C$5). A negative profit will mean that Amy is making a loss that day. The total profit for the whole year in cell E377 is computed by summing all the profit in cells E12:E376.

Step (e): The total profit for the whole year in cell E377 represents only one simulation trial. For simulation results to be reliable and useful, we will need to run the simulation for at least 100 trials or more. One-dimension Data Table function in Excel is used to automatically repeat the simulation trials and tabulate the annual profit accordingly as given in Table D, where the row input cell is left empty and column input cell can be referenced to any empty cell (e.g. A1) in the worksheet. Set the formula for the Data Table in cell H11 = E377. With the results from 100 trials, we can compute the summary statistics including average, minimum, maximum and standard deviation of annual profit in Table E.

11.6 Discrete-Event Simulation

In the previous section, we explored the Monte Carlo simulation (static model) and applied it to a worked example. In this section, we will explore discrete-event simulation, which is a dynamic simulation model. A good reference for discrete event simulation is Banks et al. (1995). The main components, which are essential to build a discrete event simulation model, are explained below.

1. *Simulation Clock*

The important component is the simulation clock which gives the current value of the simulated time as opposed to the real time. There is no relationship between the simulated time, real time and running time of the simulation. The unit of time in the simulation model varies according to the system which is modeled and is normally the same unit as the input parameter. For example, if we want to run the simulation for 24 hours in the A&E department for a hospital, we can model discrete time buckets of 1 hour interval.

In a discrete event simulation, time advances from one event to another. There are two triggers available to control the time advance. One is the *fixed-increment* trigger, and the other is the *next-event* trigger. For the fixed-increment trigger, the simulation clock is advanced after a fixed time interval, for example, after every 5 min. After each update of clock, a system check is done to identify whether any event should have happened during the time interval, say from time t to t+1. For the next-event trigger, the simulation clock is first initialized to zero at the beginning of the simulation, and it is advanced to the time of the most immediate (imminent) future event in the *event list*. The process of time advancement continues until some stopping condition has been satisfied.

2. *Event List*

Since discrete event simulation models a sequence of events for each entity in the system, we need to maintain the *event list* to keep track of the system behaviour. An event consists of the *event time* (when it happens), the *performance* of the event (what happens when the event happens) and a possible *end time* of the event (when it finishes).

Let us discuss how an event list is created for the departure process of passengers at the airport. A passenger arrives at the airport and joins the queue at the check-in counter queue at event time t_1. When the check-in counter is free to serve, the simulation program will generate the next event called the "check-in service" at a new event time t_2. This event is created and inserted into the event list. The sequences of events are stored and sorted in ascending order of event start time.

Since all new events are created and inserted into the event list, it is important to maintain a manageable size of event list; otherwise, it will grow exponentially. One common trick is to delete all the past events from the events list to improve the performance of the simulation program. Thus, the event list will only include events which are slated to happen in the future (*future events list*). It is important to keep in mind that before any event in the event list is deleted, event information such as event time and event end time must be stored in the system for statistical analysis purposes.

3. *Random Number Generator*

The simulation program needs a random number generator to generate random values for the input variables. Using the random number generator, we can generate different arrival pattern, which may follow distribution functions like Poisson process with mean arrival rate λ.

4. *Initial and Terminating Conditions*

The initial condition of the simulation program starts at time 0. Prior to initiating the simulation process, a list of random arrival times is generated based on given historical data relating to the arrival process. The stopping criteria or terminating condition of the simulation depends on the modeler. The simulation can stop after a certain time duration, when the system has reached a steady state or when the number of simulation tokens has been completed. For the passenger departure process at the airport, the simulation stops when all passengers (the simulation tokens) have completed the check-in process and boarded the plane.

5. *Collection of Statistical Results*

The simulation program keeps track of all the events which have happened during the simulation, and the results of interest can be collected for analysis. For example, the wait time, service time and system time for each passenger at the check-in counter at the airport can be collected to determine the performance of the queue system.

With a good understanding of the main components of discrete-event simulation, let us look at two case studies in the next two sections which applied discrete-event simulation to solve the congestion problem at the check-in counters at an airport and to assess yard cranes deployment policies at a container terminal.

11.7 Case 11A: Simulation to Optimize Number of Check-In Counters at an Airport

This case study is modified from the paper published by Ma et al. (2012), where the authors worked on the congestion problem at the check-in counters with a large Asian airport. The objective was to determine the optimal number of check-in counters to open, based on the predicted number of passengers, to ensure that 90% of the passengers do not need to wait more than 10 minutes at the check-in counters to meet the service-level agreements (SLA). The SLA was set up to provide good customer service and allow passengers to have sufficient time to do duty-free shopping, which will bring in more revenue for the airport.

Typically, passengers will arrive at the airport at about 2½ hours before the scheduled departure time (STD). Most airlines today will urge customers to check in online before STD to minimize waiting time at the airport. The check-in counters will close 30 minutes before STD to ensure that all the baggage will be loaded on the aircraft and the passengers can board the plane on time.

Before this study, the airport will assign the number of counters based on the airline's request. However, due to increased air traffic volume, the limited number of check-in counters will need to be optimally utilized. Following the steps described in Sect. 11.3, we set up the discrete-event simulation model to determine the optimal number of check-in counters to assign based on the flight's passenger capacity.

Step (a): Passenger arrival data was collected on the ground for 135 passengers for a particular flight over 2 hours, 3 minutes and 40 seconds (2:03:40). Based on the data, most passengers traveled alone, while some passengers traveled in groups of 2 to 5 with friends and family. The frequency count of the inter-arrival time with time bucket of 60 seconds is shown in Table 11.3 and plotted in Fig. 11.6. From Fig. 11.6, it was observed that the curve could approximate well to an exponential distribution.

Table 11.3 Frequency count for different inter-arrival times

Inter-arrival time $1/\lambda$ (s)	Frequency count	Relative frequency (RF)	Cumulative relative frequency (CRF)
$1/\lambda \leq 60$	92	0.6815	0.6815
$60 < 1/\lambda \leq 120$	28	0.2074	0.8889
$120 < 1/\lambda \leq 180$	8	0.05925	0.9481
$180 < 1/\lambda \leq 240$	4	0.02963	0.9778
$240 < 1/\lambda \leq 300$	1	0.007407	0.9852
$300 < 1/\lambda \leq 360$	1	0.007407	0.9926
$360 < 1/\lambda \leq 420$	0	0	0.9926
$420 < 1/\lambda \leq 480$	0	0	0.9926
$480 < 1/\lambda \leq 540$	0	0	0.9926
$540 < 1/\lambda \leq 600$	1	0.007407	1.0
Total	135		

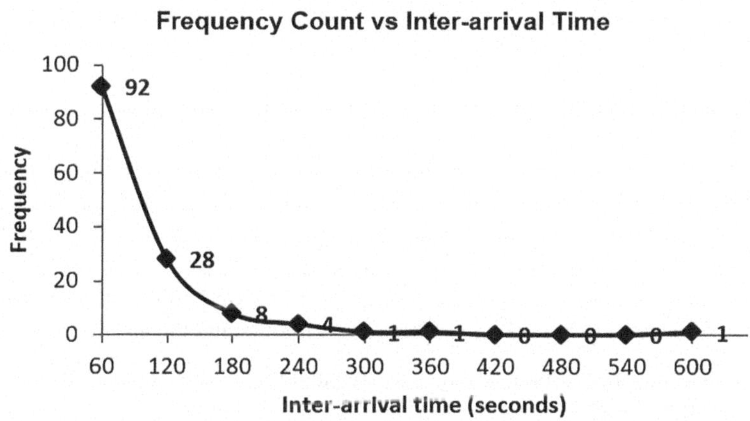

Fig. 11.6 Total frequency of inter-arrival time for sample data

Step (b): To validate if an exponential distribution with an inter-arrival time of 55 seconds (= 2:03:40 divided by 135 passengers) can represent the actual data collected on the ground, we simulated 500 passengers' arrivals using an exponential distribution with $1/\lambda = 55$ seconds. The cumulative distribution function (CDF) of the simulated data was compared with the cumulative relative frequency (CRF) of the actual data in Fig. 11.7. In addition to visual comparison, the goodness of fit using maximum absolute deviation (MAD), which is defined as the maximum difference between the CRF and CDF, was also computed using the formula

$$\text{MAD} = \max(\text{abs}(\text{CRF} - \text{CDF})).$$

Using the results of ten trials of simulation, the average MAD was found to be 0.02, which is very small. Thus, we can use an exponential distribution with $1/\lambda$

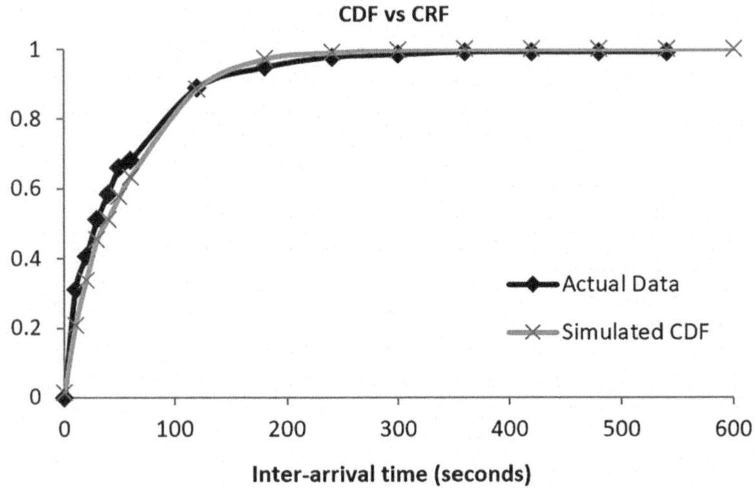

Fig. 11.7 CDF of simulated data vs CRF of actual data for passenger inter-arrival time

= 55 seconds to generate the inter-arrival time of the passengers for the check-in counters.

Step (c): To run the simulation for many passenger arrivals, the exponential distribution with $1/\lambda = 55$ seconds was used to randomly generate the inter-arrival times of passengers. Using an estimated average service time of 1 minute and 30 seconds, the service time for each passenger was also randomly generated. Based on these randomly generated values, we can determine the following for each passenger (refer to Sect. 10.1 in Chap. 10 to understand the terminologies used):

- Arrival Time = Previous Passenger's Arrival Time + Inter-arrival Time.
- Service Start Time:
  - If the system length < number of counters, then Service Start Time = Arrival Time.
  - Else, Service Start Time is the earliest Service End Time of all the counters.
- Service End Time = Service Start Time + Simulated Service Time.

Step (d): The output results will include the following:

- Wait Time = Service Start Time − Arrival Time.
- System Time = Service End Time − Arrival Time = Wait Time + Service Time.
- System Length = The number of people in front of the passenger upon his arrival at the queue.

Step (e): Using the simulation model, we varied the number of counters from one to six for 200 passenger arrivals. The outcomes of interest include performance

Table 11.4 Performance measures of check-in counters

Number of check-in counters	Average wait time (hh:mm:ss)	Average system time (hh:mm:ss)	Average system length	90th percentile of system time (hh:mm:ss)
1	01:19:48	01:21:13	52.51	02:25:15
2	00:18:33	00:20:12	23.65	00:40:01
3	00:02:49	00:04:30	6.96	00:06:16
4	00:00:10	00:01:35	2.65	00:04:05
5	00:00:02	00:01:22	2.15	00:03:44
6	00:00:00	00:01:19	2.12	00:03:23

measures such as average wait time, average system time, average system length and 90th percentile of the system time, which are tabulated in Table 11.4.

Step (f): The SLA set by the airport was that 90% of the passengers are served within 10 minutes of arrival, which implied that the 90th percentile of the system time must be $\leq$ 10 minutes. From Table 11.4, we can conclude that the optimal number of check-in counters required to meet the SLA for 200 passengers is three and the 90th percentile of system time is 6 minutes and 16 seconds. Increasing the number of counters to four or more will not improve the performance measures significantly. Repeating steps (e) and (f) with different numbers of passengers will allow the airport to determine the optimal number of counters to open for flights of different passenger capacities.

Let us map the problem and solution method for this case study against the *data and decision analytics framework* proposed in Chap. 1. As shown in Fig. 11.8, in this case study, the problem faced was the congestion problem at airport check-in counters leading to inability to meet the SLA. Therefore, the right question to ask was "What would be the optimal number of counters to open to meet the SLA?" Next was to collect the relevant data which will be needed to answer the question, which includes the distribution of the inter-arrival time of passengers and the distribution of service time. With the data collected, the initial data exploration highlighted that the queue system will be unable to satisfy the SLA with insufficient check-in counters. From this insight, the problem objective would be to determine the optimal number of check-in counters to open to satisfy SLA. The assumption is that the queue performance indicators are based on steady-state queue system. After running the simulation models for different numbers of check-in counters, we are able to determine the optimal number of check-in counters to satisfy the SLA.

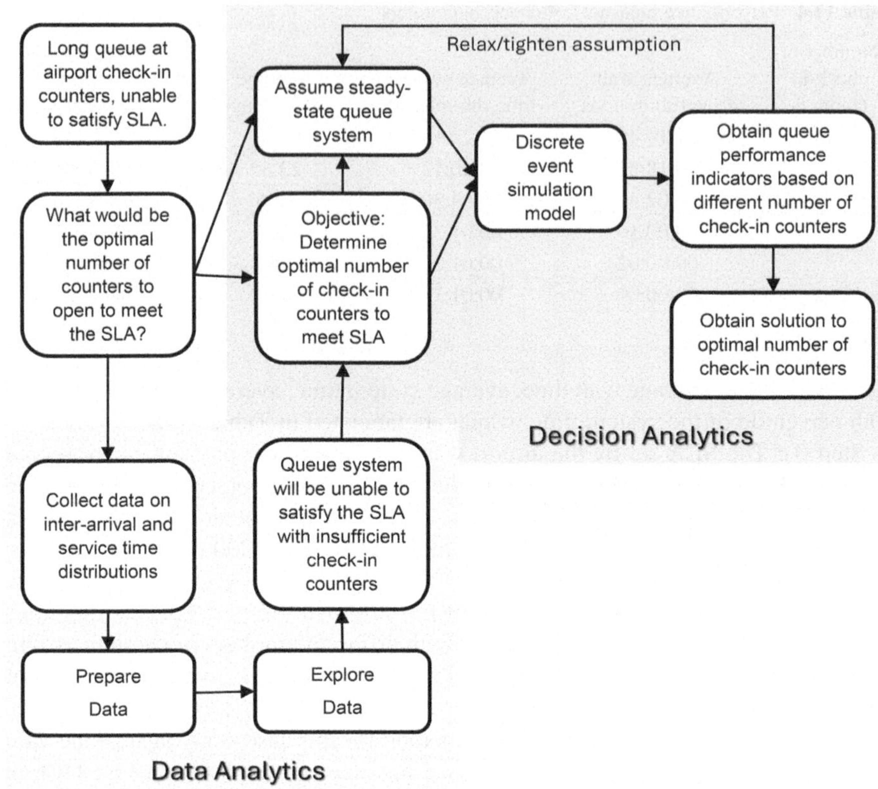

Fig. 11.8 Data and decision analytics framework map for Case 11A

11.8 Case 11B: Simulation of Container Flows at a Container Terminal

Container terminals are essential in today's world economy as border trades are prevailing due to the rise in e-commerce. The container terminal has three areas: the side near to the sea is called a quay, a yard area to store the containers and a gate where the containers will be transported in or out of the terminals. The flow of the containers within a container terminal is shown in Fig. 11.9. There are three container types in terms of the process: import container, export container and transshipment container.

This case study is modified from the papers published by Ma and Hadjiconstantinou (2008) and Hadjiconstantinou and Ma (2009). The objective of the study was to use discrete-event simulation to validate the goodness of two yard deployment policies using the optimal number of yard cranes (YC) required based on an earlier work by Ma (2008). In Ma (2008), an optimization model was designed

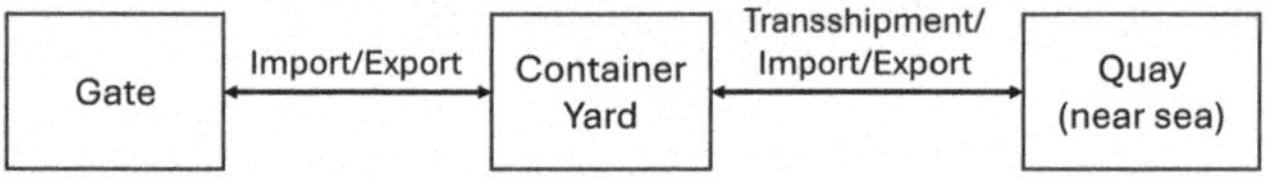

Fig. 11.9 Container flow within a container terminal

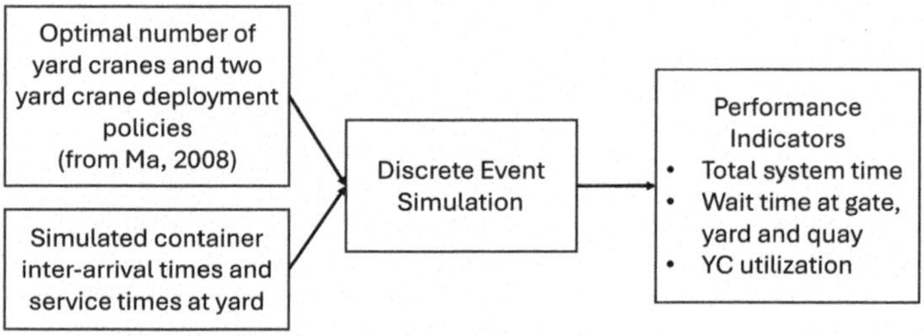

Fig. 11.10 Discrete-event simulation for optimal yard plan

to plan the container assignment and determine the optimal number of yard cranes (YC) required in the yard to load and discharge the containers within a specific time horizon. Two YC deployment policies were considered:

- Policy I—"No sharing of YC" policy. During an 8-hour work shift, there should be at most one YC deployed at a particular yard block. The YC will not be shared with neighbouring yard blocks, there should be sufficient containers in the yard to fully utilize the YC, and the queuing time in the yard will still be within the acceptable range.
- Policy II—"Sharing of YC" policy. In this case, the YC can move to another block under the following conditions:
  - Firstly, the YC still has the capacity to move the container to another block.
  - The YC can move to another neighbouring block without any operational constraints, such as the direction of the road, and the traveling distance for the YC is minimized.

Figure 11.10 depicts how the optimized yard plan from Ma (2008) serves as an input into the simulation model proposed in this case study. The simulation model can aptly capture the dynamic activities taking place in the container terminal, such as the arrival of containers through the gate; the arrival of the vessel; the traveling time of trucks from the quay to the yard, the gate to the yard and the yard to the quay; as well as the routing of the YCs.

The simulation model was developed using C# programming as commercially available simulation packages were rigid and less customizable to suit the requirements for this case. The assumptions of the model are as follows:

Table 11.5 Sequence of events for different container types

Container type	Sequence of events
Export/import (between gate and yard)	1. External truck arrives/queues at the gate 2. External truck leaves gate for yard (traveling time) 3. External truck arrives/queues at yard 4. YC serves the truck 5.External truck leaves yard and exits
Import/trans-shipment (from quay to yard)	1. Internal truck arrives/queues at quay 2. Quay crane (QC) serves the truck 3. Internal truck leaves quay for yard (traveling time) 4. Internal truck arrives/queues at yard 5. YC serves the truck 6. Internal truck leaves yard and exits
Trans-shipment/export (from yard to quay)	1. Internal truck arrives/queues at yard 2. YC serves the truck 3. Internal truck leaves yard for quay (traveling time) 4. Internal truck arrives/queues at quay 5. QC serves the truck 6. Internal truck leaves quay and exits

- The containers will arrive within the planned time.
- The queuing principle is based on a first-come-first-served principle at the gate, yard and quay.
- The truck at the gate will join the shorter queue.

As an initial setup, the simulation clock was set to 0. Using the vessel scheduled arrival time and customer booking time for export containers, the container arrival times were randomly generated using an exponential distribution function. Table 11.5 shows the sequence of events for import, export and trans-shipment containers.

The execution of the two YC deployment policies are described as follows:

- Policy I—"No Sharing of YC"

When the truck arrives at the yard and if the YC is free, then the YC will serve the truck immediately upon the truck's arrival at the yard block as we assume that there is always a YC in the yard and there is no YC traveling time involved. However, if the YC is busy when the truck arrives, the truck will join the queue in the yard, and a new job will be inserted into the YC job queue.

- Policy II—"Sharing of YC"

In this case, there is sharing of YC between yard blocks. If there is already a YC in the yard, then the truck will be served immediately. However, if there is no YC in the yard, jobs assigned to the YC will be selected according to the following rules to minimize the waiting time of the truck in the yard:

- Select the YC which is currently free.
- Select the YC which has the shortest job queue.

Table 11.6 Port configuration and input parameters for Port of Felixstowe

Port configuration and input parameters	
Area of container terminal	100 ha
Number of gate lanes	15
Number of yard blocks	96
% of yard blocks reserved for import containers	50%
% of yard blocks reserved for export/transshipment containers	50%
Number of containers in 24 hours	7841 TEUs
Number of YC deployed from optimization model as input dependent on yard activity	Between 100 and 159
Number of quay cranes (QC)	25
Speed of truck	15 km/h
Speed of YC	10 km/h
Fixed service time at gate	2 minutes
Fixed service time of QC	2 minutes
Average container inter-arrival time (exponential distribution)	6 minutes
Average YC service time (exponential distribution)	6 minutes

Table 11.7 Simulation results for Port of Felixstowe using Policies I and II

Results	Policy I—"No sharing of YC"	Policy II—"Sharing of YC"
Average total time spent in the system (minutes)	19.71	41.11
Average wait time at the gate (minutes)	0.39	0.39
Average wait time at the yard (minutes)	8.40	29.6
Average wait time at the quay (minutes)	0.02	0.08
Average YC utilization rate	61.64%	97.9%

- Select the YC so that the workload is distributed evenly across different YCs.
- Select the YC which is at the closest proximity which will require the shortest traveling time.

We used a daily 24-hour vessel schedule and container throughput from one of the largest ports in the UK, the Port of Felixstowe. Table 11.6 shows the port configuration and input parameters used in the simulation model.

The simulation results are shown in Table 11.7. Let us compare the performance of the two policies:

- Policy I—"No sharing of YC". The average system time (19.71 minutes) and wait time (8.40 minutes) at the yard are acceptable, but the YC is only about 61% utilized.
- Policy II—"Sharing of YC". While the YC is almost 100% utilized, the wait time at the yard is about 30 minutes, which is not acceptable. Thus, we proposed to limit the YC to one or two moves to different yard blocks or only share YC with neighbouring yard blocks to minimize the traveling distance.

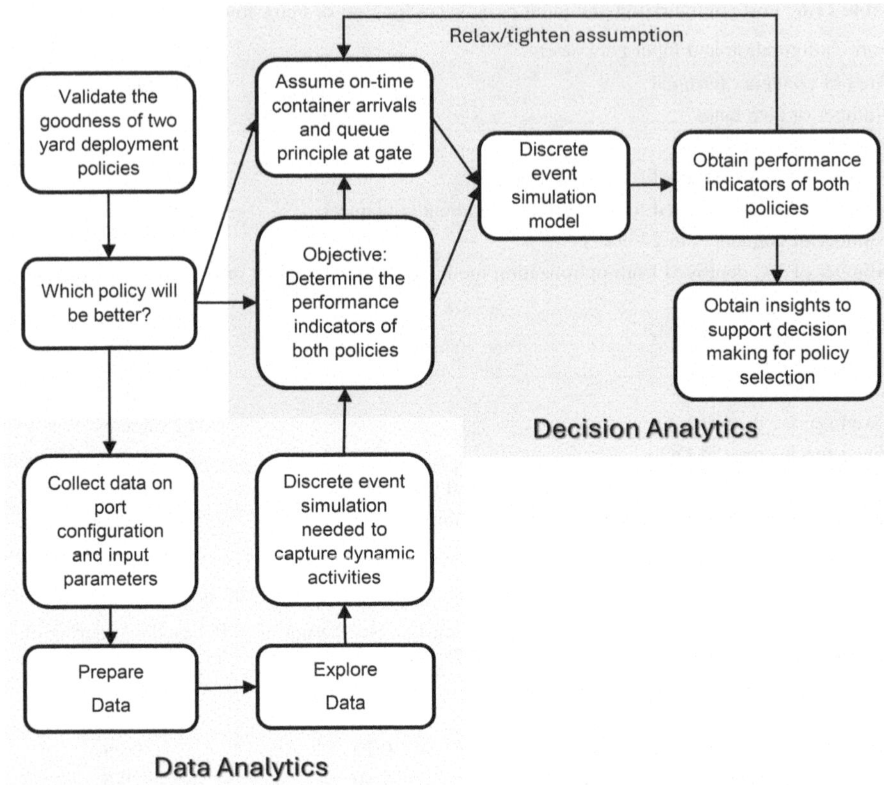

Fig. 11.11 Data and decision analytics framework map for Case 11B

Let us map the problem and solution method for this case study against the *data and decision analytics framework* proposed in Chap. 1. As shown in Fig. 11.11, in this case study, the problem faced was to validate the goodness of two different yard deployment policies using the optimal number of yard cranes (YC) required. Therefore, the right question to ask was "Which policy will be better?" Next was to collect the relevant data which will be needed to answer the question which includes the port configuration and input parameters. With the data collected, the initial data exploration highlighted that a discrete-event simulation model will be needed to capture the dynamic activities taking place in the container terminal. From this insight, the problem objective would be to use discrete-event simulation to determine the performance indicators of the two different yard deployment policies to support decision-making. Apart from the assumed input parameters, other assumptions include on-time container arrivals and the queuing principle at the gate. With the performance indicators for the two policies obtained through the simulation model, the insights will help to support decision-making for policy selection.

11.9 Summary

In this chapter, we introduced the different types of simulation models. We discussed a framework to guide the building of simulation models and the commonly used probability distributions for generating random input values. Next, we delved into Monte Carlo simulation and discrete-event simulation models and illustrated their applications using work examples and case studies. The two case studies determined the optimal number of check-in counters at the airport to support the passenger departure process and the selection of yard crane deployment policies.

This being the last chapter of the book, we encourage readers to access our Excel workbooks provided to get hands-on experience in solving the problems discussed. In addition, for details on the case studies, readers can refer to the published papers listed in the references section at the end of each chapter.

Exercises

Q11.1

A production plant incurs a fixed cost of $3000 per month. The plant produces a product with unit fixed cost of $8 and unit variable cost which is uniformly distributed between $3 and $5. The monthly demand for the product is uniformly distributed between 600 and 1000. The unit selling price for the product is $16.

(a) Develop a simulation model to analyse the plant's monthly profit. Prepare the model to simulate for 10 years, where each row represents 1 month to compute the monthly profit. What is the average monthly profit?
(b) What is the probability that the plant will incur a loss based on the 10-year simulation?

Q11.2

Jimmy has $250,000 in the bank's fixed deposit account, which will earn him an interest rate of 2.5% to 4.5% uniformly. He wants to start investing in stocks. Thus, he plans to save $50,000 each year for the next 15 years, and the savings will grow at 5% annually. The average return follows a normal distribution with mean of 8% and standard deviation of 20%.

(a) Develop a simulation model to determine his total savings at the end of 15 years.
(b) What is the probability that he can retire at 65 if he needs $500,000 to retire? Run 100 trials to obtain the probability.

Q11.3

ATM machines are busy during lunch hours, from 11:00 a.m. to 1:00 p.m. Customers' inter-arrival time follows an exponential distribution with an average inter-arrival time of 2 minutes. Customers spend an average of 3 to 5 minutes (following uniform distribution) at the ATM machines. Develop a simulation model for a typical day during lunch hours. Each row represents a single customer's arrival from 11:00 a.m. to 1:00 p.m. You may assume that no customer leaves prematurely and will stay in the queue until they are served (i.e. no reneging). You may assume there are 60 customers in 2 hours. You will need to run the simulation for 100 trials to obtain the results.

(a) What is the average queue length during lunch hours?
(b) What is the average waiting time for customers at the ATM?

Q11.4

A slot machine in the casino has four wheels. When the handle is pulled, the wheels spin independently of each other. For each wheel, the probabilities are 10% of the time, an APPLE picture will appear; 15% of the time, an ORANGE picture will appear; 20% of the time, a MELON picture will appear; 25% of the time, a BANANA picture will appear; and 30% of the time, a PINEAPPLE picture will appear. There are no other pictures on the wheels, and the probabilities are deliberately tuned this way.

For each pull of the handle (called a spin), you will place a bet of \$5. If you get three or more APPLE pictures, you will get \$50 back. The winning amount will be \$50 − \$5 = \$45. If you get any two APPLE pictures, you will get \$20 back. If you get only one APPLE picture, you will get \$10. Otherwise, you will lose your bet of \$5.

Assume that you have a stake of \$100 to start the game. Create a well-labeled spreadsheet model to simulate a session of 100 spins. You should have 100 rows, one for each spin. Prepare the model with one column for the spin number (1 through 100), one column for each of the four wheels, one column for the amount you win or lose on the spin, and one column for the amount of money you will have left at the end of the spin. Once your balance is zero, you should stop the game. You should simulate the model for 50 trials to obtain the results.

(a) What would be the total winnings?
(b) What is the balance left at the end of a session of 100 spins?
(c) Would you recommend playing the game? Justify your answer quantitatively.

References

Banks, J., Carson, J. S., Nelson, B. L., & Nicol, D. M. (1995). *Discrete-event system simulation* (5th ed.). Prentice Hall.

Hadjiconstantinou, E., & Ma, N. L. (2009). Evaluating straddle carrier deployment policies: A simulation study for the Piraeus container terminal. *Maritime Policy & Management, 36*(4), 353–366. https://doi.org/10.1080/03088830903056991

Los Alamos National Lab. (n.d.). Accessed August 1, 2024, from https://discover.lanl.gov/publications/actinide-research-quarterly/first-quarter-2023/hitting-the-jackpot-the-birth-of-the-monte-carlo-method/

Ma, N. L. (2008). *Optimal planning of container terminal operations*. Doctoral Thesis, Imperial College London.

Ma, N. L., Cheong, M. L. F., & Choy, J. (2012). *Uncovering insights through data analytics for an airport operation to improve profitability*. SRII – Service Research and Innovation Institute.

Ma, N. L., & Hadjiconstantinou, E. (2008). Evaluation of operational plans in container terminal yards using Discrete-Event Simulation. *OR Insight, 21*, 10–18. https://doi.org/10.1057/ori.2008.16

The manufacturer's authorised representative in the EU is Springer Nature Customer Service Centre GmbH, Europaplatz 3, 69115 Heidelberg, Germany. If you have any concerns regarding our products, please contact ProductSafety@springernature.com

Printed and bound by CPI Group (UK) Ltd, Croydon, CR0 4YY
30/09/2026
02225434-0014